STUDY GUIDE

to accompany

Krugman/Wells/Myatt
microeconomics
CANADIAN EDITION

Rashid Khan
McMaster University

WORTH PUBLISHERS

Study Guide
by Rashid Khan
to accompany
Krugman/Wells/Myatt: Microeconomics, Canadian Edition

Printed in the United States of America

Text design: Lee Ann Mahler/S. B. Alexander

ISBN: 0-7167-6155-6 (EAN: 9780716761556)

Second printing

Worth Publishers
41 Madison Avenue
New York, NY 10010
www.worthpublishers.com

Contents

Preface

This Study Guide is designed for use with *Microeconomics* by Paul Krugman, Robin Wells, and Anthony Myatt. It is intended to help evaluate your understanding of the material covered in the textbook and thereby reinforce the key concepts you need to learn. For each chapter of the textbook, the Study Guide provides an introduction, fill-in-the-blank chapter review, learning tips, and a set of multiple-choice questions as well as more comprehensive problems and exercises. Answers along with helpful explanations can be found at the end of each chapter.

Students often use an answer section to simply check if they have gotten the "right" answer. We caution you to use the answer section accompanying each chapter to really evaluate your comprehension of the material. In economics, the reasoning used in coming to the conclusions and correctly modeling the problems are as important as coming to an accurate answer. We have provided explanations for each problem in order for you to check that your understanding of the concepts has been appropriately applied. The understanding of economics can be accomplished through study of concepts, graphs, and equations.

Throughout this Study Guide you will find activities that test your knowledge of the material through each of these methods. In some cases, the material may go beyond what has been covered in your class. We have used an * to denote questions that can be considered *optional*. These questions may contain more mathematical material than is required in your course.

The study of economics has the potential of altering the way you evaluate and understand the world. We feel that your use of this guide will help you in your study of basic microeconomics principles and will provide a jumping-off point for further study in the economics field.

Acknowledgments

Thanks are due to a number of people for helping to create this Study Guide. Rashid Khan (McMaster University) was aided by the work of Rosemary Cunningham (Agnes Scott College), Elizabeth Sawyer Kelly (University of Wisconsin-Madison), and Martha Olney (University of California-Berkeley). Susan Kamp (University of Alberta) provided a further economic review of the material. Editorial and production guidance were provided by the supplements team at Worth Publishers: Marie McHale, Eve Conte, and Stacey Alexander.

chapter **1**

First Principles

The core of economic analysis involves four principles.

- *Scarcity of resources*

- *Opportunity costs*

- *Marginal analysis*

- *Gains from choices*

In reading this chapter, we will learn about why and how we make choices. We will see the gains from trade and the efficiency of a market system.

How Well Do You Understand the Chapter?

Use the following list of words to complete the blanks in the review of the chapter. The words may be used more than once or not at all. If you find yourself having difficulties, please refer back to the appropriate section in the text.

better off	free	margin	opportunity
choices	gains	marginal	natural
efficiency	governmental	market failure	scarce
efficiently	human	maximum	specialization
either-or	incentives	many	specializes
equilibrium	income	natural	standard
equity	interactions	produce	trade-off
exploit	inefficient	opportunities	unlimited
forego			

1. Since wants are _____ and resources are _____, individuals have to make _____ as to which wants are to be fulfilled by which resources. Because of scarcity of resources, a selection of one choice means that we _____ another choice. A resource is anything that can be used to _____ something else.

2. We distinguish between _____ resources, which include labour, skill, and intelligence, and _____ resources, which include resources from the physical environment, such as minerals and natural gas. When individuals decide what they should buy, they are constrained by _____ and time, but this merely reflects an economy that is constrained in what it can produce by _____ resources.

3. When we choose between two choices, we make a(n) _____ choice based on the real cost of the choices. The real cost of any item is its _____ cost: what you must give up in order to get the item. Every choice we make has a(n) _____ cost: choosing an item or activity implies not choosing some other item or activity.

4. Some choices we make are not either–or issues but are matters of how much. These decisions are made at the _____ by comparing the costs and additional benefits of doing a little bit more of an activity versus doing a little bit less. The study of these kinds of trade-offs at the margin is called _____ analysis.

5. Individuals make decisions guided by the principle that they should _____ opportunities to make themselves better off. In fact, this principle of people taking advantage of all _____ to make themselves better off is the basis of all predictions by economists about economic behaviour. People respond to _____; a change in incentives will alter people's behaviour.

6. An economy is a system for coordinating the productive activities of many people. In a market economy, there are _____ participants. Each participant's opportunities, and hence choices, depend to a large extent on the _____ made by other people. For us to understand a market economy, we must understand the _____ of many individuals.

7. We enjoy a higher _____ of living when we interact with one another through trade. There are _____ from trade that arise from _____, when different individuals engage in different tasks. It is critical for us to understand that the economy as a whole can produce more when each person _____ and then trades with other people.

8. All markets move toward equilibrium. An economic situation is in equilibrium when no individual would be _____ doing something different. The fact that markets move in a predictable way toward _____ allows us to understand economic interactions.

9. We can apply the principle that resources should be used as _____ as possible to achieve society's goals as a standard for evaluating an economy's performance. An economy's resources are used efficiently when they are used in a way that fully exploits all _____ to make everyone better off. A(n) _____ outcome has occurred if it is now possible to make someone better off without making someone else worse off. An efficient economy produces the _____ gains from trade that are possible from the available resources.

10. Efficiency is not the only criterion for evaluating an economy. People also care about issues of fairness, or _____. Usually there is a(n) _____ between equity and efficiency; policies that promote _____ usually entail a cost of decreased efficiency, while policies that promote _____ usually entail a cost of decreased equity.

11. Perfectly competitive markets achieve _____. In a market economy, where individuals are _____ to choose what they want to consume and what they want to produce, people will choose to take advantage of all _____ to make themselves better off.

12. It is possible for the market outcome to be inefficient and for _____ to occur. When markets fail to achieve efficiency, _____ intervention can improve society's welfare. Government policies can provide incentives to change how society's resources are used to move society closer to a(n) _____ outcome.

Learning Tips

TIP #1: Resources are scarce.

"Scarcity" of "resources" means a limited supply of resources, which are used to satisfy competing needs and uses. Examples of resources are: land, labour, entrepreneur skills, and so forth.

Question: Which of the following statements is true?

A) Technological progress will solve the problem of scarcity of resources.
B) Money is classified as a resource.
C) Clean air and water are considered to be scarce resources.
D) Machinery and equipment are considered to be non-resource items.

Answer: C

TIP #2: Every activity has an opportunity cost; opportunity cost is what you give up in order to get something else (the next best alternative).

There is no such thing as a "free lunch." Because resources are limited, it is always necessary to give up something to get something else.

Question: Which of the following statements is **false?**

A) The opportunity cost of going to university is the foregone income that you could have earned elsewhere.
B) Standing in line for six hours at the Air Canada Center to buy U2 concert tickets is not an opportunity cost.
C) The opportunity cost can be zero if unemployed people can be put to work.
D) If resources were not scarce, opportunity costs can be zero.

Answer: B

TIP #3: Incremental or marginal costs and benefits are core topics in marginal analysis. Decisions like what to do with your next hour, or next dollar, are marginal decisions. Consider an activity and see its incremental (marginal) benefit and incremental (marginal) cost.

Question: Suppose you are considering renting a movie for $5 or going to a movie theater, which will cost you $10. Which of the following statements is **false?**

A) The marginal cost of an extra movie rental is $5.
B) The marginal cost of going to a movie theater is $10.
C) The marginal cost of a movie rental is cheaper than the marginal cost of going to a movie theater.
D) The marginal cost of renting a movie is higher than the marginal cost of going to a movie theater.

Answer: D

TIP #4: When we consider all available opportunities, our choices reflect maximum benefits.

People exploit opportunities to make themselves better off.

Question: Which of the following statements is **false?**

A) If you have two choices, and the first will improve your health while the second will harm your health, you will choose the first.
B) If the price of parking at your university increases, more students will use the public transit system to go to your university.
C) A higher price of gasoline will not affect consumers' choices regarding fuel-efficient cars.
D) If earnings of economics graduates increases relatively more than earnings of graduates in other areas, there will be a greater demand for enrollment in the economics department.

Answer: C

TIP #5: There are gains from trade.

When we compare autarky (no-trade) with trade, we see mutual gains from trade. A country can specialize in a good in which that country is relatively more efficient (due to lower opportunity costs). That country can thus receive gains from trade by exchanging its goods for more of another good from another country than what it will get within the domestic economy.

TIP #6: Markets move toward equilibrium.

Question: Consider a situation of shortages, where the quantity of goods supplied is less than the quantity of goods demanded. Which of the following statements is correct?

A) This is an equilibrium situation in the market.
B) For the given quantity of goods supplied, the price that the buyers are willing to pay is greater than the supply price.
C) For the given quantity of goods supplied, the price that the buyers are willing to pay is lower than the supply price.
D) The marginal net benefit in the given situation is negative.

Answer: B

TIP #7: In general, market equilibrium leads to efficiency.

The fact that markets move toward equilibrium is why we can predict market outcomes. The perfectly competitive market equilibrium is an efficient outcome, because it means that economy's resources are used efficiently and that all opportunities are exploited to make everyone better off.

TIP #8: There exists a conflict between efficiency and equity. When there is a market failure, government intervention can improve society's welfare.

People care about issues of fairness and equity. There is a trade-off between equity and efficiency. Policies that promote equity (for example, transfer payments to individuals) often come at a cost of decreased efficiency, and vice versa.

Multiple-Choice Questions

1. The real cost of going to a movie on Saturday night includes
 a. the cost of the movie ticket.
 b. the cost of the popcorn and soda you buy at the movie theater.
 c. the value to you of whatever activity you would have done had you chosen not to go to the movie.
 d. all of the above.

2. When Ross decides whether he should eat another dessert, economics says he
 a. only considers the price of the dessert.
 b. compares the benefits and costs of eating another dessert.
 c. considers how much additional exercise he will need to do to avoid gaining weight from eating the dessert.
 d. considers whether he can do so without anyone else noticing.

3. In making choices people find that
 a. resources are scarce and that they cannot do everything or have everything that they would like.
 b. the real cost of a choice is what you must give up in order to enjoy that choice.
 c. people make choices that will make them better off.
 d. all of the above are true.

4. Which of the following statements is true?
 a. If people were less wasteful we could eliminate problems due to scarcity of resources.
 b. People usually make choices without regard to the additional benefits and costs of those choices.
 c. People consider the opportunity costs of choices.
 d. The incentives, or the rewards for certain types of behaviour, rarely influence people's decisions at the margin.

5. Specialization in production and trade
 a. increases the amount of goods and services available to an economy.
 b. benefits only the economically stronger nation.
 c. reduces opportunity costs of production to zero.
 d. may eliminate any problems posed by scarce resources.

6. Which of the following statements is true?
   a. Resources should be used as equitably as possible in order to achieve society's goals for efficiency.
   b. There is a tendency for markets to move toward equilibrium.
   c. Government intervention in markets never improves society's welfare.
   d. Trade may make one nation worse off.

7. When a market is not in equilibrium
   a. there will be a tendency for the market to continue to not be in equilibrium unless there is government intervention.
   b. there are opportunities available to people to make themselves better off.
   c. it must be because the government has intervened in the market, resulting in the market's failure to reach equilibrium.
   d. no individual would be better off doing something different.

8. We know that resources are being used efficiently when
   a. scarcity is no longer an issue.
   b. an economy utilizes every opportunity to make people better off.
   c. there are still gains from trade available.
   d. we achieve equity.

9. The concept of equity focuses on
   a. how to produce the maximum possible output from a given amount of resources.
   b. how governments can intervene to make markets work better.
   c. the issue of fairness.
   d. the amount of physical plant and equipment an employer owns.

10. Government intervention in a market can improve society's welfare when
   a. the market outcome is equitable.
   b. the market fails to provide certain goods.
   c. the market outcome is efficient.
   d. we have exploited all opportunities to make people better off.

11. When people interact in markets we know that
   a. we may move further from equilibrium.
   b. some participants will be worse off.
   c. this interaction must increase economic efficiency.
   d. this interaction must achieve equity.

12. People respond to incentives because
   a. markets move toward equilibrium.
   b. incentives act as rewards that encourage people to behave in certain ways.
   c. incentives exploit opportunities to make people better off.
   d. incentives exploit opportunities to make people worse off.

13. When individuals decide how much of an activity they should do,
   a. this is an example of marginal analysis.
   b. this involves a comparison of the trade-off between the marginal costs and marginal benefits of doing more of the activity.
   c. they are making a decision at the margin.
   d. all of the above.

   c. Land developers refuse to set aside land for parks and nature trails, so the new developments in a community do not offer these amenities.

4. Describe the opportunity costs when you decide to rent a DVD movie instead of going to a movie theater.

*5. Consider the following demand-supply equations.

$$Q^D = 200 - 2P \quad \text{(demand equation)}$$
$$Q^S = 2P \qquad\quad \text{(supply equation)}$$

where Q^D is quantity demanded, Q^S is quantity supplied and P is price
   a. Find the predicted price and quantity in a market-equilibrium situation.

   b. Why will $Q = 80$ not be an efficient output?

Answers to How Well Do You Understand the Chapter

1. unlimited, scarce, choices, forego, produce

2. human, natural, income, scarce

3. either-or, opportunity, opportunity

4. margin, marginal

5. exploit, opportunities, incentives

6. many, choices, interactions

7. standard, gains, specialization, specializes

8. better off, equilibrium

9. efficiently, opportunities, inefficient, maximum

10. equity, trade-off, equity, efficiency

11. efficiency, free, opportunities

12. market failure, governmental, efficient

Answers to Multiple-Choice Questions

1. The real cost of going to a movie on Saturday night is what you must give up in order to go out. This opportunity cost includes the price of the movie ticket, the cost of the soda and popcorn that one gets to nibble on while watching the movie, and the forgone chance to do something else that evening. **Answer: D.**

2. In this case, the best answer is the one that captures the essence of the economic approach to making decisions. Answer B focuses on the comparison of benefits to costs. We can see that the other answers only consider some aspect of the benefit or cost. **Answer: B.**

3. All of the statements are true: since resources are scarce, people must choose among alternative uses of those resources; opportunity cost measures the real cost of choosing something; and people do opt to do those things that make them better off. **Answer: D.**

4. Resources are not scarce because of wastefulness but because they are limited in quantity. People do consider the additional benefits and additional costs when making choices, and these decisions at the margin are influenced by incentives. The only statement that is true is that people do consider opportunity costs when making choices. **Answer: C.**

5. Specialization in production and trade increases total production and allows for greater levels of consumption in all countries, not just the economically stronger nation. However, it does not eliminate opportunity costs or the scarcity of resources. **Answer: A.**

6. Markets tend toward equilibrium. Resources should be used as efficiently as possible, rather than as equitably as possible, to achieve society's goals for efficiency. Government can improve society's welfare, and trade never makes any nation worse off. **Answer: B.**

7. When markets are not in equilibrium, there are unexploited opportunities to make at least one person better off while making no one else worse off. Given that people always act to make themselves better off, the market will move toward equilibrium. **Answer: B.**

8. Resources are efficiently used when every opportunity to make people better off has been exploited. At that point, there are no longer any gains from trade. Resources are still scarce but are used efficiently. **Answer: B.**

9. Equity focuses on fairness. **Answer: C.**

10. When markets fail, government intervention can increase welfare. A good may not be produced by an individual firm because the marginal costs exceed the marginal benefits; yet, if side effects were considered, the good should be produced. When this happens, the government can provide the good. **Answer: B.**

11. The only statement that is true about interaction in markets is that it must increase efficiency. **Answer: C.**

12. Incentives are the rewards that people receive when they engage in certain activities. Answers C and D seem attractive as potential answers but are nonsensical: an incentive cannot exploit, or take advantage of, an opportunity. **Answer: B.**

13. All of the statements are true: individuals when deciding how much of an activity to do should compare the costs and benefits of doing just a little bit more of the activity. This comparison of "just a little bit more" is what is meant by making a decision at the margin; it is an example of marginal analysis. **Answer: D.**

14. All choices, except A, deal with efficiency issues. **Answer: A.**

15. Free-market equilibrium for goods that produce pollution is not an efficient outcome. **Answer: D.**

Answers to Problems and Exercises

1. a. This statement illustrates principles (i) and (ii). Since resources—in this case, time—are scarce, it is impossible to do everything: you can either eat breakfast or attend class (i). The real cost of something is what you must give up to get it; in this case, the real cost of attending the lecture is the breakfast you could have eaten (ii).

   b. This statement illustrates principles (i), (ii), and (iii). Resources are scarce; therefore, choices must be made as to how to use those scarce resources (i). The real cost of working is measured by what is given up: in this case, exercise (ii). "How much?" is a decision at the margin: you decide how much work you should do each week by comparing the benefit of an additional hour of work to the cost (the lost exercise) of an additional hour of work (iii).

   c. This statement illustrates principles (i), (ii), and (iii). Resources are scarce; you must choose between sleep and attending the lecture (i). The real cost of the lecture is measured by what you must give up in order to get the lecture; you give up sleep (ii). "How much?" is a decision at the margin: you decide whether you should sleep an extra hour or attend the lecture by comparing the benefit of an extra hour of sleep to the cost (the lecture you must give up) of attending the lecture (iii).

   d. This statement illustrates principles (iii) and (iv). "How much?" is a decision at the margin: students electing to do the extra credit consider the marginal benefit of doing the work to the marginal cost and conclude that the marginal benefit is greater than the marginal cost (iii). People usually take advantage of opportunities to make themselves better off; many students perceive that doing the extra credit will help their grade and that failure to do the extra credit will hurt their grade (iv).

   e. This statement illustrates principles (i) and (iv). Resources are scarce, and our choices reflect our valuation of how best to use those scarce resources; people choose to tune up their bikes since they view it as a good use of their scarce resources (i). People usually take advantage of opportunities to make themselves better off; since this is a bargain for those who can get appointments, people will try to take advantage of the offer (iv).

2. a. This statement illustrates principles (i), (ii), (iii), and (iv). Since both the shop owner and the landlord agree to this new rental agreement, it must be the case that the new lease is beneficial to both parties. The landlord gets the certainty of an occupied building for a longer period of time, while the shop owner gets the certainty of a business address and a reduced rent. This illustrates that there are gains from trade (i), that markets lead to efficiency (iv) and tend toward equilibrium (ii), and that resources should be used as efficiently as possible (iii).

   b. This statement illustrates principles (iii) and (iv). The Ricardos recognize that the cost of eating out exceeds the cost of eating at home. Since these costs reflect the opportunity costs of eating, this family chooses to eat at home since this choice leaves them better off (they have $6.50 they can spend on other goods and services each time they forgo eating out). This illustrates that the real cost of something is what you must give up to get it and that resources should be used as efficiently as possible. The family can clearly compare the costs of eating at home to the costs of eating out due to the existence of markets; this enables them to decide on the most efficient use of their resources (iii) due to a market outcome that is efficient (iv).

   c. This statement illustrates principles (ii), (iii), and (iv). Markets move toward equilibrium; since it is not an equilibrium for some checkout lines to have shorter waits than other checkout lines, we can anticipate that people will distribute themselves across the various checkout lines until the wait is approximately equal in all checkout lines (ii). In addition, checkout lines with equal waiting time imply an efficient use of resources since no reallocation of waiting shoppers will result in a reduction in waiting time for shoppers (iii). Lastly, this efficient use of resources occurs through the natural market mechanism: markets tend toward efficiency (iv).

    d. This statement illustrates principles (ii), (iii), and (iv). The decision to use the automated scanner or the librarian takes into account the kind of transaction the individual must do (e.g., if an individual owes fines to the library, they will want to see the librarian to settle those fines since they cannot do that with the automated scanner), as well as the relative checkout speeds of the two choices. Individuals recognize that the automated scanner is quicker than waiting in line once there are at least five people in line. This illustrates the concept that markets move toward equilibrium (ii). It also illustrates the efficient use of resources, since people choose their line based on their perception of the optimal strategy for reducing their waiting time (iii and iv).

3. a. The firm fails to take into account the side effects of their production on the community. Government intervention in the form of establishing fines for pollution or enacting laws to curb certain undesirable behavior could help the market achieve a more efficient outcome.

    b. Market failure occurs because beneficial research is not undertaken, since the firm considers only *their* costs of this research and *their* benefits from the research and ignores the health benefits to others. The market does not take into account the side effects (the benefits received or costs incurred by those outside the firm) of their decisions. Government intervention to subsidize the research expenditures could alter the incentives firms face with regard to undertaking research.

    c. Developers will not provide parks and nature trails because they do not directly benefit from them. Since parks and nature trails benefit everyone, they need to be provided by the government. The government could establish laws or provisions to ensure that certain amounts of natural resources are considered off-limits for development.

4. The opportunity costs of going to a movie theater can be higher than those for a DVD rental. The opportunity costs of going to a movie theater include travel costs, parking costs, costs for waiting in line for tickets, over-priced refreshment costs, and so forth. The opportunity costs for DVD rental can be less.

5. a. Using market equilibrium condition, set $Q^D = Q^S$ and find $P = 50$ and $Q = 100$.

    b. When $Q = 100$, the total net benefit is 5,000. When $Q = 80$, the total net benefit is 4,800.

chapter 2

Economic Models: Trade-offs and Trade

Economic models are simplified representations of the real world. They deal with a set of variables, describe how these variables, given some assumptions, are related and provide some economic outcomes. After reading this chapter, we will understand the production possibility frontier (PPF) and the meaning of the opportunity cost. We will be able to comprehend the gains from trade after we analyze the theory of comparative advantage. The circular-flow diagram will allow us to see how the economy works through income-spending flows.

How Well Do You Understand the Chapter?

Fill in the blanks using the following terms to complete the following statements. Terms may be used more than once. If you find yourself having difficulties, please refer back to the appropriate section in the text.

absolute advantage	flow	less	points
change	flows	lower	positive economics
circular-flow	forecasts	models	production
comparative	gain	money	possibility
advantage	gains from trade	normative economics	frontier (PPF)
constant	goods and services	non feasible	simplified
economy	households	opportunities	specialization
efficiency	income	opportunity cost(s)	specialized
efficient	increase	outward	straight
expenditures	input-output	payment(s)	trade-offs
factor markets	labour	physical	transactions
feasible			two

1. A model is a(n) _____ description of the real world. In our economic models, we will focus on how, other things remaining constant, a change in just one factor affect an economic outcome.

2. The three _____ developed in this chapter are the production possibility frontier (PPF) model, a model that helps economists think about the _____ every economy faces; the comparative advantage model, which illustrates the _____; and the circular-flow diagram, which helps economists analyze the monetary _____ that occur in the economy as a whole.

3. The production possibility frontier (PPF) considers a simplified economy that produces only _____ goods. Points that lie inside the curve or on the curve represent _____ points of production for the economy. Points lying beyond the curve represent production choices that are not feasible for this economy given its level of resources and its technology. This model illustrates the economic concept of _____, since it is impossible to increase the production of one good without decreasing the production of the other good if an economy is producing at a point on its PPF.

4. The _____ is a good way to illustrate the general economic concept of efficiency. Points on the production possibility frontier are _____; there is no way to produce more of one good without producing _____ of the other good.

5. The _____ of producing one good is not just the amount of money it costs but also everything else that must be given up to get that good.

6. The shape of the PPF curve is usually bowed out from the origin; the _____ of producing more of one good increases as more of that good is produced.

7. The PPF also helps us to understand the meaning of economic growth. Economic growth is illustrated as a(n) _____ shift of the production possibility frontier, indicating that it is now possible to produce more of both goods. A(n) _____ shift of the production possibility frontier implies an expansion of the economy's ability to produce _____.

8. The _____ model uses the production possibility frontier concept to illustrate the gains from specialization and _____. Individuals or countries have a comparative advantage in producing a good when they can produce that good with a relatively lower opportunity cost. By specializing, according to their _____ and then engaging in trade, individuals and countries are better off. One of the most important insights for economies is that there are _____ even if one of the trading parties isn't especially good at anything.

9. We can use the _____ model to explore the gains from trade. To do this, we simplify by replacing the curved PPF line with a(n) _____ line PPF. This simplifies the model by making the opportunity cost of production _____ for any given production possibility frontier.

10. If one individual or nation can produce 1 more unit of a good with relatively lower opportunity costs, we say that they have a(n)_____ in the production of that good. However, trade can take place even when one individual or nation has a(n) _____ in producing all goods. Trade is based on _____ and not absolute advantage. The comparative advantage model clearly illustrates that _____ and trade result in a higher level of production.

11. The circular-flow diagram of an economy is a simplified model of the relationship between _____ and firms. It helps economists analyze the _____ that takes place in a market economy. The simplest of economic transactions is barter, in which an individual directly _____ a good or service he or she has for a good or service he or she wants.

12. The _____ diagram represents two kinds of flows around a circle: flows of _____, such as goods, labour, or raw materials in one direction; and flows of _____.

13. The _____ diagram consists of two kinds of markets: the markets for _____, in which households buy the goods and services they want from firms; and _____, the markets where firms hire factors of production from households. The factor market we know best is the _____ market, where workers are paid for their time. Households earn _____ in factor markets and then spend that _____ in the markets for goods and services. In the circular-flow diagram, income equals _____.

14. Economic analysis is useful in both positive and normative economics. _____ economics uses analysis to answer questions about the way the world works; this type of analysis has right and wrong answers. _____ economics employs analysis to answer questions about how the world should work. Positive economics analysis can be used to make predictions, or _____ about the future.

Learning Tips

TIP #1: The production possibility frontier provides a simple model to illustrate scarcity, opportunity cost, trade-offs, economic growth, and the distinction between efficient and inefficient points.

A production possibility frontier for a person or an economy illustrates the maximum amount of two goods that can be produced in a given amount of time given a fixed level of resources and technology. The production possibility frontier is a boundary between points that are feasible but inefficient (points inside the production possibility frontier) and points that are infeasible (points outside the production possibility frontier); thus, all points on the production possibility frontier are both feasible and efficient. Moving along the production possibility frontier, we can produce more of one good only by producing less of the other good. The opportunity cost of producing more of one good is measured as the number of units of the other good that must be forgone. Economic growth occurs when the production possibility frontier shifts out from the origin: an increase in resources or an improvement in technology will shift the production possibility frontier out, indicating an expansion in the productive capacity of the economy, as shown in Figure 2.1.

Figure 2.1

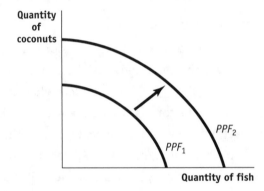

TIP #2: The model of comparative advantage illustrates why specialization and trade is advantageous to people and countries even if a person or a country does not have the absolute advantage in producing any good.

It is possible for individuals or countries to be better off if they specialize according to their comparative advantage and then trade with one another. A country has a comparative advantage in producing a good if it can produce the good at lower opportunity cost than can another country. For example, if country A's opportunity cost of producing one more unit of fish is two units of coconuts, while country B's opportunity cost of producing one more unit of fish is three units of coconuts, then country A should produce fish and trade with country B, which should produce coconuts. For example, even though the United States can absolutely produce more cars and textiles than a smaller country like Malaysia, there are still gains to be had from specialization according to one's comparative advantage and then trading. In this case, Malaysia has a comparative advantage in the production of textiles while the United States has a comparative advantage in the production of cars.

TIP #3: The circular-flow diagram of the economy illustrates the relationship between households and firms as they interact in both the product and the factor markets.

Households provide factors of production, while firms produce goods and services using those factors. Households use the income they earn from selling their factors of production to purchase the goods and services produced by the firms. In the circular-flow diagram (see p. 20), income equals expenditures. The circular-flow diagram depicts two flows: the flows of factors of production and goods and services, and the flows of income and expenditures.

TIP #4: The distinction between positive and normative economics is that the former is about how things are, while the latter is about how things should be.

Positive economics is concerned with descriptive, and hence objective, statements. Normative economics is concerned with prescriptive, and hence subjective, statements. Positive economics describes how the economy works, while normative economics focuses on how the economy should work. The statement "an increase in tax rates will result in a decrease in the amount of labor that will be provided in the market" is an example of a positive statement since it is a statement that can be proven true or false (it is an objective statement). While the statement "Canada should increase tax rates in order to generate higher levels of revenue for school funding" is a normative opinion that expresses what should be done from the speaker's point of view (it is a subjective statement). We can contrast the distinction between positive and normative statements by realizing that, once we agree on the facts, a positive statement will be either true or false; while, with a normative statement, the debate is not over the facts, but over the values and opinions held by different indivduals.

Multiple-Choice Questions

Use the following information to answer the next four questions.

Funland produces two goods, bicycles and yo-yos. In the following table, different feasible production combinations are given for Funland. Assume that Funland's production possibility frontier is linear between combinations A to B, B to C, C to D, etc.

Combination	Bicycles per year	Yo-Yos per year
A	1,000	0
B	800	8,000
C	600	12,000
D	400	15,000
E	200	17,000
F	0	18,000

1. If Funland is currently producing at combination B, the opportunity cost of producing 1,000 more yo-yos is
a. 200 bicycles.
b. 50 bicycles.
c. 750 bicycles.
d. 4,000 yo-yos.

2. If Funland is currently producing at point E, the opportunity cost of producing 10 more bicycles is
a. 1 yo-yo.
b. 10 yo-yos.
c. 100 yo-yos.
d. 1,000 yo-yos.

3. Funland's production possibility frontier exhibits
   a. constant opportunity cost.
   b. increasing opportunity cost.
   c. decreasing opportunity cost.
   d. both increasing and decreasing opportunity cost.

4. If Funland is currently producing 400 bicycles per year and 12,000 yo-yos per year, we know
   a. Funland is not at an efficient level of production.
   b. Funland is producing at a point inside its production possibility frontier.
   c. Funland could increase production of yo-yos without decreasing its production of bicycles.
   d. all of the above are true.

5. A straight-line production possibility frontier differs from a bowed-out production possibility frontier because the opportunity cost of producing one more unit of the good on the horizontal axis
   a. decreases as you move down the curve.
   b. increases as you move down the curve.
   c. is constant as you move down the curve.
   d. varies as you move down the curve.

6. Economic models
   a. should accurately represent the real world.
   b. are always complicated mathematical models.
   c. do not provide insight into economic outcomes since they do not accurately reflect the real world.
   d. are a simplified representation of reality.

7. The other things equal assumption means that
   a. all variables are equally important and that any change in one variable will result in the same outcome as an equivalently sized change in any other variable.
   b. all economic models share the same set of assumptions.
   c. the economic effect of a change in a single variable will be analyzed while holding all other variables constant.
   d. it does not matter what assumptions we make when building economic models.

8. Points that lie outside a country's production possibility frontier are
   a. efficient but not feasible.
   b. efficient and feasible.
   c. feasible.
   d. not feasible.

9. The shape of the production possibility frontier is bowed out from the origin due to
   a. scarcity of resources.
   b. specialization of resources.
   c. comparative advantage.
   d. absolute advantage.

10. If a country discovers new resources, this will, other things equal, result in the country's production possibility frontier
   a. shifting out from the origin.
   b. shifting in toward the origin.
   c. remaining the same as it was.
   d. either shifting in or out depending upon the type of resources.

Use the following information to answer the next two questions.

Two countries, Small Land and Big Land, have exactly the same amount of resources to use in the production of milk and bread. Their production possibility frontiers are given in the following graphs.

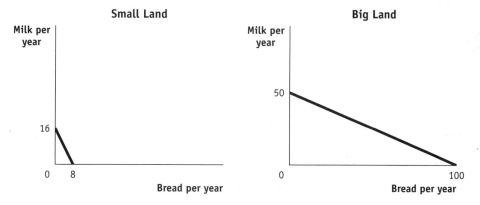

11. Which of the following statements is true?
   a. Small Land does not have a comparative advantage in the production of bread or milk.
   b. Big Land has a comparative advantage in the production of bread.
   c. Big Land has a comparative advantage in the production of milk.
   d. Small Land has a comparative advantage in the production of bread.

12. If Small Land and Big Land both specialize and then trade, then we know
   a. that both countries will benefit from this trade.
   b. that only Big Land will benefit from this trade.
   c. that only Small Land will benefit from this trade.
   d. it is impossible to know with certainty whether there are benefits from trade without further information.

13. Specialization and trade are beneficial to two countries
   a. provided their opportunity costs of production are not the same for all goods that they produce.
   b. when each country specializes in producing the good that it can produce at the lowest opportunity cost.
   c. even when one country can absolutely produce more than the other country.
   d. all of the above.

14. The circular-flow diagram of the economy illustrates
   a. the economic relationship between households and firms.
   b. the relationship between the markets for goods and services and the markets for factors of production.
   c. the equality between expenditure on goods and services and income received by factors of production.
   d. all of the above.

15. Suppose a business has two employees, Ellen and Ruth. The owner of the business wants Ellen and Ruth to take 12 orders and wrap 24 packages. Ellen and Ruth estimate their output as shown in the following table.

	Orders taken per hour	Packages wrapped per hour
Ellen	4	6
Ruth	1	5

Which of the following is true?
  a. Since Ruth has an absolute disadvantage in the production of both types of goods, Ellen has a comparative advantage in the production of both types of goods.
  b. If Ellen and Ruth do not cooperate and each takes half of the orders and wraps half of the packages, Ellen will work 3.5 hours, while Ruth will work approximately 14.5 hours.
  c. Since Ellen has an absolute advantage in both types of goods, there are no gains from specialization.
  d. If Ellen and Ruth both specialize according to their comparative advantage and produce only one type of good, Ellen will need to work only 3 hours.

16. Which of the following is a normative statement?
  a. Due to advances in health care, people live longer and therefore Social Security expenses have increased.
  b. Unemployment increased last year, even though the government sector followed an expansionary economic policy.
  c. A 5% decrease in people's income will lead to a 3% decrease in people's consumption of mild cheese.
  d. The main goal of the government should be to achieve an annual growth rate for the economy of 7%.

17. Which of the following statements is true about the circular-flow diagram shown here?

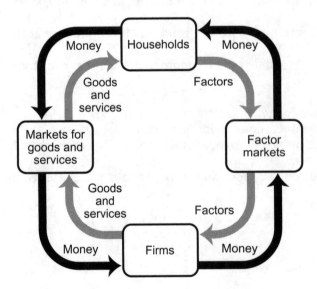

  a. The circular-flow diagram allows businesses to make transactions between each other.

b. The circular-flow diagram models government interactions with firms and households.

c. The circular-flow diagram illustrates the economic relationship between households and firms.

d. The circular flow diagram helps us understand both saving and investment behavior in the economy.

18. When economists engage in forecasting, this is an example of
   a. normative economics.
   b. positive economics.
   c. the absolute advantage economists have in this area of expertise.
   d. providing a prescription for the economy.

Answer questions 19–22 on the basis of the following table of the production possibility frontier of a given economy, which produces only two goods with given resources and a given technology.

Quantity of coconuts	Quantity of fish
20	0
18	1
16	2
14	3
12	4
10	5
8	6
6	7
4	8
2	9
0	10

19. The opportunity costs of
   a. 10 units of fish is zero quantity of coconuts.
   b. 20 units of coconut is zero quantity of fish.
   c. 1 unit of fish is 2 units of coconuts.
   d. an extra unit of fish increases.

20. The opportunity cost of 1 extra unit of fish is
   a. –2 units of coconut.
   b. –0.5 unit of coconut.
   c. +2 units of coconut.
   d. +0.5 units of coconut.

21. Suppose, due to the current unemployment situation, the economy is producing 5 units of fish and 6 units of coconuts. The opportunity cost of adding 2 more units of fish is
   a. 4 units of coconuts.
   b. 2 units of coconuts.
   c. 1 unit of coconut.
   d. zero unit of coconut.

Answer questions 22–30 on the basis of the following table. Assume that there are two countries: country A and country B, with identical resources. The production functions are given in the accompanying table.
Quantities are litre bottles.

Country A		Country B	
Wine	Beer	Wine	Beer
100	0	50	0
80	10	40	10
60	20	30	20
40	30	20	30
20	40	10	40
0	50	0	50

22. Which of the following statements is true?
   a. Country A has a comparative advantage in both wine and beer.
   b. Country B has a comparative disadvantage in both wine and beer.
   c. Country A has an absolute advantage in wine.
   d. Country B has an absolute advantage in beer.

23. The opportunity cost of an additional unit of beer in Country A is
   a. 100 bottles of wine.
   b. 20 bottles of wine.
   c. 10 bottles of wine.
   d. 2 bottles of wine.

24. The opportunity cost of an additional unit of beer in country B is
   a. 1 bottle of wine.
   b. 10 bottles of wine.
   c. 20 bottles of wine.
   d. 50 bottles of wine.

25. The opportunity cost of an additional unit of beer is
   a. less in country A.
   b. less in country B.
   c. higher in country B.
   d. impossible to determine.

26. Which of the following statements is true?
   a. Country A has a comparative advantage in beer production.
   b. Country B has a comparative advantage in beer production.
   c. Country A has a comparative advantage in both beer and wine production.
   d. Country B has a comparative advantage in both beer and wine production.

27. The opportunity cost of an additional unit of wine in country A is
   a. 50 bottles of beer.
   b. 20 bottles of beer.
   c. 1 bottle of beer.
   d. 0.5 bottle of beer.

28. The opportunity cost of an additional unit of wine in country B is
   a. 1 bottle of beer.
   b. 10 bottles of beer.
   c. 20 bottles of beer.
   d. 50 bottles of beer.

29. Which of the following statements is true?
   a. Country A has a comparative advantage in wine production.
   b. Country B has a comparative advantage in wine production.
   c. Country A has a comparative advantage in wine production, because it has an absolute advantage in wine production.
   d. Country B has a comparative advantage in beer production, because it has an absolute advantage in beer production.

30. The table indicates that
   a. country A should specialize in wine production, export wine to country B, and import beer from country B.
   b. country B should specialize in wine production, export wine to country A, and import beer from country A.
   c. country A should not trade with country B, because it has nothing to gain.
   d. country B should produce wine only.

Problems and Exercises

1. Pacifica is an isolated country producing rice and coconuts. The following table shows different combinations of rice and coconuts that Pacifica can produce in a year. Due to limited resources and technology, as Pacifica increases production of one good it must decrease production of the other good.

Maximum annual output options	Rice (bushels)	Coconuts (pounds)
A	2,000	0
B	1,600	250
C	1,200	450
D	800	600
E	400	700
F	0	800

a. Graph combinations A–F on the following graph and then connect these combinations to create Pacifica's production possibility frontier.

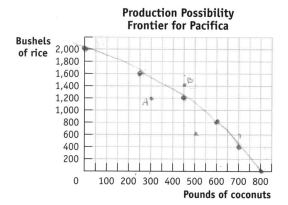

Production Possibility Frontier for Pacifica

b. Consider the following production combinations for Pacifica. For each combination determine which of the following classifications best describes the combination:
   I. The combination is feasible and efficient: the combination is on the production possibility frontier.

II. The combination is feasible but inefficient: the combination is inside the production possibility frontier.

III. The combination is not feasible: the combination is outside the production possibility frontier.

i. 300 pounds of coconuts, 1,200 bushels of rice

ii. 450 pounds of coconuts, 1,400 bushels of rice

iii. 500 pounds of coconuts, 600 bushels of rice

iv. 725 pounds of coconuts, 600 bushels of rice

v. 250 pounds of coconuts, 1,600 bushels of rice

c. What is the opportunity cost of producing:

i. 600 pounds of coconuts instead of zero pounds of coconuts?

ii. 1,600 bushels of rice instead of 800 bushels of rice?

iii. 700 pounds of coconuts instead of 250 pounds of coconuts?

2. Suppose an economy produces only two goods, oats and cotton, using only labor and land. This country's production possibility frontier for this year is given in the following graph.

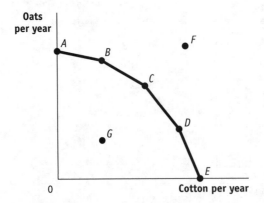

a. Which point on the graph will this economy produce at if it devotes all of its resources to oat production? Explain your answer.

b. Which point on the graph represents a feasible but inefficient point for this economy? Explain your answer.

c. Which point on the graph may become feasible if this economy experiences economic growth? Explain your answer.

d. Explain how you would measure the opportunity cost of moving from point C to point B.

3. Joe and Betty both produce butter and cheese. The following table provides information about some of the combinations of butter and cheese Joe and Betty can produce from their given resources and technology. Assume that both Joe and Betty have linear production possibility frontiers and that they each have the same amount of resources.

Joe's production		Betty's production	
Pounds of butter	**Pounds of cheese**	**Pounds of butter**	**Pounds of cheese**
100	0	120	0
80	30	90	40
60	60	60	80
40	90	30	120
20	120	0	160

a. Draw Joe's and Betty's production possibility frontiers on the following graphs.

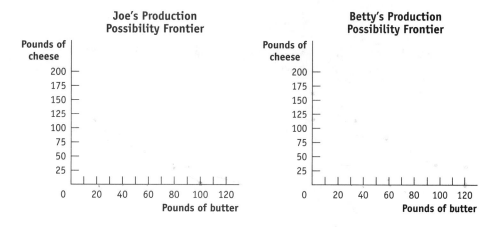

b. Which individual has the absolute advantage in the production of butter?

    c. Which individual has the absolute advantage in the production of cheese?

    d. What is the opportunity cost of producing one pound of butter for Joe?

    e. What is the opportunity cost of producing one pound of butter for Betty?

    f. What is the opportunity cost of producing one pound of cheese for Joe?

    g. What is the opportunity cost of producing one pound of cheese for Betty?

    h. Who has the comparative advantage in the production of butter?

    i. Who has the comparative advantage in the production of cheese?

4. George and Kim own a cleaning and yard service business and are its only source of labor. George can rake 1 yard in 1 hour or clean 1 house in 4 hours. Kim can rake 1 yard in 2 hours or clean 1 house in 2 hours.

    a. Fill in the following table for George and Kim.

George		Kim	
Hours to rake a yard	Hours to clean a house	Hours to rake a yard	Hours to clean a house
_____	_____	_____	_____

    b. Fill in the following table showing production possibility combinations that are feasible and efficient for George and Kim if they each work 40 hours.

George's production possibilities		Kim's production possibilities	
Number of yards raked	Number of houses cleaned	Number of yards raked	Number of houses cleaned
0	_____	0	_____
_____	5	_____	10
_____	0	_____	0

On the following graphs, draw George's and Kim's production possibility frontiers if they each work 40 hours.

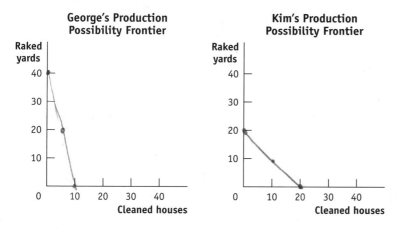

George's Production Possibility Frontier

Kim's Production Possibility Frontier

c. If George and Kim specialize according to their comparative advantages, what will George do?

d. If George and Kim work independently and each cleans and rakes at every house, what is the maximum number of houses they can clean and rake if they each work 40 hours?

e. If George and Kim both agree to work 40 hours, what is the maximum number of houses that can receive both services if they specialize and work cooperatively?

5. Use the simple circular-flow diagram to answer this set of questions.
   a. Firms produce goods and services. What do firms receive when they produce these goods and services?

   b. Firms purchase factors of production from households. What do firms do with these factors of production?

   c. Households purchase goods and services from firms. Where do households acquire the funds to make these purchases?

   d. Households provide factors of production to firms. What motivates households to provide these factors of production?

   e. If firms hire larger amounts of factors of production, what do you anticipate will happen to the level of the production of goods and services?

6. The statements below are either positive or normative. Identify each statement. Explain your answer.

  a. The Canadian welfare system should provide greater monetary support to program participants.

  b. A tax on gasoline will reduce consumption of gasoline.

  c. A tax on gasoline is a more efficient way to finance highway construction than imposing user fees in the form of highway tolls.

7. Consider an economy that produces two goods, X and Y, with all resources fully employed. Use the accompanying table to answer the following questions.

Quantity of X	Quantity of Y
21	0
19	1
17	2
15	3
13	4
11	5
9	6
7	7
5	8
3	9
1	10
0	11

  a. What is the opportunity cost of 11 units of Y? The opportunity cost of one unit of Y? The opportunity cost of 21 units of X? The opportunity cost of one unit of X?

  b. Consider a combination of 5 units of X and 5 units of Y. Do you think that resources are under-utilized? What is the opportunity of adding 3 units of Y, with X staying at 5 units?

  c. What is the shape of the PPF line? Is opportunity cost constant or increasing?

8. Consider the story of two castaways. The accompanying table shows the PPF functions of Tom and Lloyd.

Tom's PPF		Lloyd's PPF	
Coconuts	Fish	Coconuts	Fish
100	0	50	0
80	10	40	10
60	20	30	20
40	30	20	30
20	40	10	40
0	50	0	50

  a. In what line of activity does Tom have the comparative advantage? Why?
  b. In what line of activity does Lloyd have the comparative advantage? Why?

c. If they specialize and agree to trade, what will be the total output of coconuts and fish?

d. Suppose they agree to trade one coconut for 2/3 fish (in other words, 1 fish for 3/2 coconuts). If Tom trades 48 coconuts, how many fish will he get in exchange? Assume that before trade took place, Tom consumed 52 coconuts and Lloyd consumed 18 fish. What will be the combination of consumption after trade and before trade for Tom? What will be the combination of consumption after trade and before trade for Lloyd? Is trade beneficial to both parties? Why?

Answers to How Well Do You Understand the Chapter

1. simplified

2. models, trade-offs, gains from trade, transactions

3. two, feasible, trade-offs

4. production possibility frontier (PPF), efficient, less

5. opportunity costs

6. opportunity costs

7. outward, outward, goods and services

8. comparative advantage, trade, comparative advantage, gains from trade

9. comparative advantage, straight, constant

10. comparative advantage, absolute advantage, comparative advantage, specialization

11. households, transactions, trades

12. circular-flow, input-output, payments

13. circular-flow, goods and services, factor markets, labour, income, income, expenditures

14. positive, normative, forecasts

Answers to Multiple-Choice Questions

1. Funland can increase its production of yo-yos only if it decreases its production of bicycles. Between combinations B and C, Funland can produce 20 yo-yos for every bicycle it does not produce; thus, if Funland produces 1,000 additional yo-yos, it must give up 1,000 divided by 20, or 50 bicycles. **Answer: B.**

2. The opportunity cost of producing an additional bicycle for Funland given its initial production at combination E is 10 yo-yos. If Funland increases its production of bicycles by 200, it must give up 2,000 yo-yos, therefore the opportunity cost of producing these 10 additional bicycles is 100 yo-yos. **Answer: C.**

3. Funland's production possibility frontier illustrates increasing opportunity cost, since as more and more bicycles are produced, increasingly larger amounts of yo-yos must be given up. For example, in order to produce 200 additional bicycles at combination E, Funland must reduce production of yo-yos by 2,000, while in order to produce 200 additional bicycles at combination D, Funland must reduce production of yo-yos by 3,000. Increasing opportunity cost is also true if Funland increases its production of yo-yos; increasing amounts of yo-yo production entail increasingly larger opportunity costs. **Answer: B.**

4. The data in the table tell us Funland can produce 400 bicycles per year while simultaneously producing 15,000 yo-yos per year. When Funland produces 400 bicycles per year and only 12,000 yo-yos, it uses resources inefficiently. Therefore, Funland is producing at a point inside the production possibility frontier. **Answer: D.**

5. Only one of these answers can be correct. The slope of a straight line is constant, and therefore the opportunity cost of producing one more unit of the good, measured by how much of the other good you must give up in order to produce one more unit of the first good, is constant. **Answer: C.**

6. Economic models are an attempt to simplify the real world while allowing economists to focus on the impact of changes in specific variables on economic outcomes. Economic models should be as simple as possible while still providing insight into the economic question they address. **Answer: D.**

7. The other things equal assumption is used in economic models to allow the model builder to focus on the impact of a change in a single variable on the model while all the other variables do not change. **Answer: C.**

8. Only points that lie on a country's production possibility frontier are efficient; points inside the production possibility frontier can be produced (they are feasible) but do not represent the maximum amount of production that is possible given the country's resources and technology; points outside the production possibility frontier cannot be produced with the country's available resources and technology (they are not feasible). **Answer: D.**

9. Production possibility frontiers illustrate scarcity of resources since the frontier acts as a boundary between those production combinations that are feasible and those that are not feasible. However, the bowed-out shape of the production possibility frontier is due to specialization of resources: when small amounts of one good are produced, we can increase the production of that good with a relatively small decrease in the production of the second good since we can use resources that are particularly well suited for the production of the first good. However, when large amounts of a good are produced, resources that are less well suited for that good's production are used, and thus relatively more of the other good's production must be sacrificed. **Answer: B.**

10. The discovery of new resources will make it possible for a country to produce more, causing its production possibility frontier to shift out away from the origin. **Answer: A.**

11. Small Land has a comparative advantage in the production of milk since its opportunity cost of milk production (1/2 unit of bread for every unit of milk it produces) is less than Big Land's opportunity cost of milk production (2 units of bread for every unit of milk it produces). In contrast, Big Land has the comparative advantage in the production of bread since its opportunity cost of bread production (1/2 unit of milk) is less than Small Land's opportunity cost of bread production (2 units of milk). **Answer: B.**

12. Specialization and trade based on comparative advantage is mutually beneficial to both trading partners. **Answer: A.**

13. The benefits from trade arise because of comparative advantage, the ability to produce a good with lower opportunity cost than a competitor can. Countries will mutually benefit from trade provided they have different opportunity costs of production and they each produce according to their comparative advantage. This beneficial trade does not depend upon absolute advantage. **Answer: D.**

14. The circular-flow diagram represents two flows between households and firms: (i) the flow of goods and services as well as the flow of factors of production; and (ii) the flow of money as payment for goods and services or as income received by factors of production. The model provides a simple representation of the equality between expenditure on goods and services and income received by factors of production. **Answer: D.**

15. The absolute advantage in the production of both goods belongs to Ellen. Ruth has the comparative advantage in wrapping presents, while Ellen has the comparative advantage in taking orders. If they each produce 6 orders and 12 wrapped packages, Ellen will work 3.5 hours (1.5 hours taking 6 orders and 2 hours wrapping packages), while Ruth will work 8 hours and 24 minutes (6 hours taking 6 orders and 2 hours and 24 minutes wrapping packages). If they both specialize and produce only one type of good, Ellen can produce 12 orders in 3 hours, while it will take Ruth 4 hours and 48 minutes to wrap 24 packages. **Answer: D.**

16. A positive statement is an objective or descriptive statement, while a normative statement is subjective or prescriptive. Statement D expresses an opinion or a subjective evaluation and is therefore a normative statement. **Answer: D.**

17. The circular flow diagram does not include government, saving, or investment; nor does it allow businesses to make transactions between each other. It provides a simple representation of the economic relationship between households and firms. **Answer: C.**

18. Although forecasting may serve as a guide to policy, it is still a prediction rather than a prescription: a forecast is an example of positive economics. **Answer: B.**

19. Opportunity costs are constant. The opportunity costs of 1 extra unit of fish are 2 coconuts. **Answer: C.**

20. We cannot consider negative costs. **Answer: C.**

21. Adding 2 more units of fish (by drawing unemployed people into gainful employment) will not reduce the output of coconuts. We started with 5 fish and 6 coconuts and now we have 7 fish and 6 coconuts. Therefore, the opportunity cost of 2 extra units of fish is zero. **Answer: D.**

22. Country A has an absolute advantage in wine, because country A can produce 100 bottles of wine, while country B can produce 50 bottles of wine. **Answer: C.**

23. Since the opportunity cost of 10 bottles of beer in country A is 20 bottles of wine, the opportunity cost of 1 bottle of beer is 2 bottles of wine. **Answer: D.**

24. Since the opportunity cost of 10 bottles of beer in country B is 10 bottles of wine, the opportunity cost of 1 bottle of beer is 1 bottle of wine. **Answer: A.**

25. Since 1 < 2, the opportunity cost of beer is less in country B. **Answer: B.**

26. Since opportunity costs are lower in country B, country B has the comparative advantage in beer production. **Answer: B.**

27. Since the opportunity cost of 20 bottles of wine in country A is 10 bottles of beer, the opportunity cost of 1 bottle of wine is 0.5 bottles of beer. **Answer: D.**

28. Since the opportunity cost of 10 bottles of wine in country B is 10 bottles of beer, the opportunity cost of 1 bottle of wine is 1 bottle of beer. **Answer: A.**

29. Since opportunity cost is lower in country A, country A has the comparative advantage in wine production. **Answer: A.**

30. Country A should specialize in wine and country B should specialize in beer. Trading will be beneficial to both countries. **Answer: A.**

Answers to Problems and Exercises

1. a.   The production possibility frontier for Pacifica is shown in the following graph.

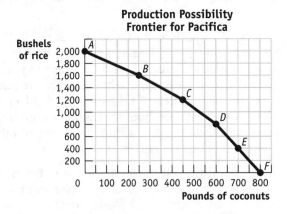

Production Possibility Frontier for Pacifica

b.   In answering this question, you need to decide whether the given point lies on the production possibility frontier (answer I), lies inside the production possibility frontier (answer II), or lies outside the production possibility frontier (answer III).
   i.   Since Pacifica can produce 450 pounds of coconuts and 1,200 bushels of rice, it follows that Pacifica can easily produce 300 pounds of coconuts and 1,200 bushels of rice. **Answer: II.**
   ii.   Since the point corresponding to 450 pounds of coconuts and 1,200 bushels of rice lies on Pacifica's production possibility frontier, it follows that the point corresponding to 450 pounds of coconuts and 1,400 bushels of rice lies outside its production possibility frontier. **Answer: III.**
   iii.   Since Pacifica can produce 800 bushels of rice and 600 pounds of coconuts, it must also be possible for Pacifica to produce 600 bushels of rice and 500 pounds of coconuts (a reduction in the production of both goods). **Answer: II.**
   iv.   Since Pacifica can produce 700 pounds of coconuts and 400 bushels of rice on its production possibility frontier, it must follow that 725 pounds of coconuts and 600 bushels of rice (an increase in the production of both goods) represent a point that lies outside Pacifica's production possibility frontier. **Answer: III.**
   v.   Since this point is given in the table, it represents a point that lies on Pacifica's production possibility frontier. **Answer: I.**
c.   The opportunity cost of moving from one point to another point on the production possibility frontier is measured by how many units of one good are given up in order to increase production of the other good.
   i.   1,200 bushels of rice
   ii.   350 pounds of coconuts
   iii.   1,200 bushels of rice

2. a. Point *A* represents the maximum amount of oats that can be produced by this economy. Any other point on the production possibility frontier relative to point *A* results in some production of cotton and a reduction in oat production.

 b. Point *G* is feasible since it is a production combination that lies inside the production possibility frontier. However, it is not efficient since it would be possible to increase oat or cotton production without decreasing production of the other good.

 c. Point *F* currently is not a feasible point for production for this economy since it lies beyond the production possibility frontier. However, if there is economic growth the production possibility frontier will shift out, resulting in an ability to produce more of both goods.

 d. The opportunity cost of moving from point *C* to point *B* is measured by the units of cotton per year that must be given up in order to increase oat production.

3. a.

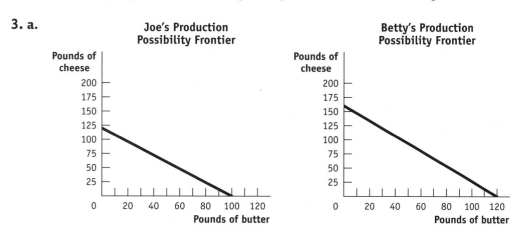

 b. Betty has the absolute advantage in the production of butter since she can produce more butter than Joe (120 pounds versus 100 pounds) from the same amount of resources.

 c. Betty has the absolute advantage in the production of cheese since she can produce more cheese than Joe (160 pounds versus 120 pounds) from the same amount of resources.

 d. The opportunity cost of producing one pound of butter for Joe is 1.2 pounds of cheese.

 e. The opportunity cost of producing one pound of butter for Betty is 4/3 pounds of cheese.

 f. The opportunity cost of producing one pound of cheese for Joe is 0.833 pound of butter.

 g. The opportunity cost of producing one pound of cheese for Betty is 3/4 pound of butter.

 h. Joe has the comparative advantage in the production of butter since his opportunity cost, 1.2 pounds of cheese, is less than Betty's opportunity cost of 4/3 pounds of cheese.

 i. Betty has the comparative advantage in the production of cheese since her opportunity cost of cheese production is lower than Joe's (3/4 pound of butter versus 0.8 pound of butter).

4. a.

George		Kim	
Hours to rake a yard	**Hours to clean a house**	**Hours to rake a yard**	**Hours to clean a house**
1 hour	4 hours	2 hours	2 hours

b.

George's production possibilities		Kim's production possibilities	
Number of yards raked	**Number of houses cleaned**	**Number of yards raked**	**Number of houses cleaned**
0	10	0	20
20	5	10	10
40	0	20	0

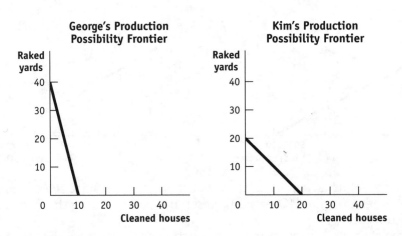

George's Production Possibility Frontier

Kim's Production Possibility Frontier

c. George will rake yards since his opportunity cost of raking yards (1/4 clean house) is smaller than Kim's opportunity cost of raking yards (1 clean house).

d. Working 40 hours, George can clean and rake at 8 houses (he will use 32 hours to clean the 8 houses and another 8 hours to rake their yards). Working 40 hours, Kim can clean and rake at 10 houses (she will use 20 hours to clean the 10 houses and 20 hours to rake their yards). The number of houses independently and completely served by George and Kim is 8 + 10 = 18 houses.

e. Kim will specialize and clean 20 houses using her 40 hours. George will rake the yards of these 20 houses, and that will use 20 of his 40 hours. With his remaining 20 hours George can clean and rake 4 homes. Together George and Kim can provide both services to 24 houses if they specialize and cooperate with one another.

5. a. Firms earn money from selling goods and services to households.

b. Firms use factors of production to produce the goods and services they sell to households.

c. Households purchase goods and services using the income they receive from selling factors of production to firms.

d. Households provide factors of production to firms in order to receive income that they then spend on goods and services.

e. Production of goods and services will increase since firms will have more factors of production available to them to produce goods and services.

6. a. This statement is an example of normative economics since it expresses how one person thinks the world should work rather than expressing a factual, objective statement.

   b. This statement is an example of positive economics since it is a statement that can be analyzed and determined to be either true or false independent of the analyst's values.

   c. This statement is an example of positive economics since the two methods of financing highway construction can be compared as to which method achieves the goal most efficiently.

7. a. 21 units of X; 21/11 units of X; 11 units of Y; 11/21 units of Y

   b. no; zero

   c. straight line; constant opportunity cost

8. a. Coconuts. Tom's opportunity cost for 1 coconut is 1/2 fish, while Lloyd's opportunity cost for 1 coconut is 1 fish. Tom's opportunity cost is relatively lower than Lloyd's opportunity cost.

   b. Fish. Lloyd's opportunity cost for 1 fish is 1 coconut, while Tom's opportunity cost for 1 fish is 2 coconuts. Lloyd's opportunity cost is relatively lower than Tom's opportunity cost.

   c. 100 units of coconuts and 50 units of fish.

   d. 32 units of fish. For Tom, the consumption after the trade, coconuts = 52 and fish = 32. Before trade, coconuts = 52 and fish = 24.
   For Lloyd, the consumption combination after trade, fish = 18, coconuts = 48. Before trade, fish = 18, coconuts = 32.
   Trade is beneficial to both. The consumption basket is higher after trade.

chapter **2** Appendix

Graphs in Economics

This appendix reviews how to look at graphs and simple equations. Some basic math principles and relations between variables help us to understand economic theories and concepts. The authors discuss how graphs describe relationships between variables and how to look at slopes and maximum values.

How Well Do You Understand the Chapter?

Fill in the blanks using the following terms to complete the following statements. Terms may be used more than once. If you find yourself having difficulties, please refer back to the appropriate section in the text.

absolute value	interpretation	pie	two
arc	left	point(s)	unrelated
average	length	positive	value
causality	linear	price	variable(s)
constant	maximum	relationship	vertical
decreases	minimum	right	x-variable
dependent	negative	run	x-axis
graph(s)	non-linear	slope	y-variable
horizontal	numerical	straight	zero
increases	observation	tangent	
independent	omitted	time	
infinity	percentage	truncated	

1. When studying economics, _____ are the visual images used to illustrate ideas and enhance understanding. _____ _____ in economics typically depict the relationship between economic variables. A(n) _____ is a quantity that can take on more than one _____, for example; a person's age, a household's income, and the price of a bicycle are all variables. Most economic models describe the _____ between two economic variables while holding all other _____ constant.

2. In a two-axis _____, one variable is called the *x*-variable and the other variable is called the _____. The *x*-variable is measured along the horizontal axis, while the *y*-variable is measured along the _____ axis. The horizontal axis and the vertical axis intersect at the origin, where both the *x*-variable and the *y*-variable have a value of

_____. As you move to the right along the x-axis, the value of the x-variable _____. As you move up from the origin along the y-axis, the value of the y-variable _____. Graphs often represent a causal relationship: the value of the independent valuable affects the value of the _____ variable.

3. A straight line on a graph depicts a(n) _____ relationship between the two variables. A curved, or _____ line depicts a non-linear relationship. Two variables have a(n) _____ relationship when an increase in one variable leads to an increase in the other variable. Two variables have a negative relationship when an increase in one variable leads to _____ in the other variable. A curve depicting a positive relationship slopes upward to the _____, while a curve depicting a(n) _____ relationship slopes downward to the right. The point at which a curve crosses the _____ axis is called the horizontal intercept. The horizontal intercept shows the value of the _____ when the y-variable equals _____. The point at which a curve crosses the vertical axis is called the _____ intercept; the vertical intercept shows the value of the _____ when the x-variable equals _____.

4. A _____ measures the steepness of the curve and tells you how responsive the y-variable is to changes in the x-variable. On a linear curve, the slope is calculated by dividing the "rise" between two points by the "_____" between these same two points. The rise measures the change in the y-variable, while the _____ measures the change in the x-variable. If two variables have a(n) _____ relationship, the slope of the curve representing this relationship will have a positive value; if two variables have a negative relationship, the slope of the curve representing this relationship will have a(n) _____ value. The slope of a horizontal line is always _____, while the slope of a vertical line is always equal to _____.

5. As you move along the curve, a linear curve has _____ slope. If the curve slopes upward to the right and gets increasingly steeper, it has _____ increasing slope; if the curve slopes upward to the right and gets increasingly flatter, it has _____ decreasing slope.

6. There are _____ methods for calculating the slope of a non-linear relationship. The _____ method of slope measurement calculates a(n) _____ slope of the curve between two points by drawing a straight line between the two points on the curve and calculating the slope of that straight line. The _____ method of slope measurement calculates the slope of the curve at a particular point by finding the slope of the straight line which is _____ to the curve at that point. A tangent line is a straight line that just touches a(n) _____ curve at a particular point.

7. When the slope of a curve changes from positive to negative, it creates a(n) _____ point on the curve; when the slope of a curve changes from negative to positive, it creates a(n) _____ point on the curve.

8. Numerical graphs display numerical information. Time-series graphs, scatter diagrams, pie charts, and bar graphs are examples of _____ graphs. In a time-series graph, _____ is graphed on the horizontal axis, while values of a variable that occurred at those times are graphed on the vertical axis. A scatter diagram consists of a set of _____, where each point corresponds to an actual _____ of the x-variable and y-variable. A(n) _____ chart depicts the share of a total amount that is accounted for by various components, where the share is typically expressed as a(n) _____. A bar graph employs bars of various height or _____ to indicate a variable's values.

9. Graphs can be constructed, intentionally or unintentionally, in ways that are misleading and may lead to inaccurate conclusions. The scale used in constructing a graph can influence your _____ of the data being presented. Sometimes the scale on a graph is _____, where part of the range of values on an axis is omitted; truncation of a scale can influence interpretation of the graph's data. A scatter diagram can lead the viewer to believe that two variables are related, but this may be a misinterpretation of the data if the observed relationship is due to an unobserved effect of a third _____ on each of the other two variables. This _____ variable creates the erroneous appearance of a direct causal relationship between the two represented variables. It is important to understand how graphs may mislead or be interpreted incorrectly since policy decisions, business decisions, and political arguments are often based on the _____ of numerical graphs. The mistake of reverse causality occurs when the dependent variable is erroneously taken as a(n) _____ variable, while the independent variable is erroneously taken as a(n) _____ variable.

Learning Tips

TIP #1: The construction and interpretation of graphs is crucial in economics.

Graphs give the economist a handy way to show relationships between variables. Graphs often present a concept in a clear visual image that can take many words to explain.

TIP #2: There are two methods for calculating the slope of a curved line: the arc method and the point method.

Both methods are used in the book. The arc method calculates an average slope of a curve by drawing a straight line between two points on the curve and calculating the slope of that straight line. The point method calculates the slope of the curve at a particular point by finding the slope of the straight line tangent to the curve at that point.

TIP #3: There are a variety of ways to present data in graphical form.

Economists use two-variable graphs, pie charts, bar graphs, and scatter diagrams. Each of these forms provides insights on the relationship between variables.

TIP #4: Numerical graphs can present data in a misleading manner.

Sometimes graphs can distort relationships, and sometimes this distortion is intentional. Common problems include altering the scale used in the construction of a graph, using a truncated scale, or misrepresenting the direction of causality between variables.

Multiple-Choice Questions

1. A variable
   a. is a numerical value.
   b. is a quantity that can take on more than one value.
   c. has a constant value in economic models.
   d. depicts the relationship between two economic measures.

2. Economic models often use two-variable graphs to portray the relationship between two different variables while allowing other variables that might influence the relationship
   a. to vary.
   b. to increase.
   c. to decrease.
   d. to stay constant.

3. Which of the following statements is true?
   a. In general, the x-axis measures the independent variable and the y-axis measures the dependent variable.
   b. Price, although an independent variable, is by convention always measured on the y-axis.
   c. At the origin, the value of both variables is zero.
   d. All of the above are true.

4. A straight line in a graph
   a. has constant slope.
   b. indicates that the two variables have a linear relationship.
   c. may have a slope that is positive, negative, equal to zero, or equal to infinity.
   d. is all of the above.

5. A curved line in a graph
   a. has constant slope.
   b. must have either positive or negative slope.
   c. has a slope measure that varies as you move along the curve.
   d. has a slope of infinity.

6. Which of the following statements is true?
   a. If the x- and y-variables have a positive relationship, then as the x-variable increases in value the y-variable decreases in value.
   b. The x- and y-variables have no causal relationship to each other when a graph of the two variables is either a vertical or a horizontal line.
   c. If the x- and y-variables have a negative relationship, then as the y-variable decreases in value the x-variable also decreases in value.
   d. The vertical intercept corresponds to that point on the vertical axis where the value of the y-variable equals zero.

7. As you move rightward along the horizontal axis, a curve with positive increasing slope
   a. slopes downward.
   b. slopes upward and gets flatter.
   c. slopes upward and gets steeper.
   d. slopes downward and gets steeper.

8. The arc method of calculating the slope of a curve
   a. involves drawing a straight line between two points on the curve and then calculating the slope of that straight line.
   b. calculates a measure of the average slope of the curve between two points on the curve.
   c. does not require the drawing of a line tangent to the curve at a particular point on the curve.
   d. is all of the above.

9. A maximum point occurs when
   a. the x-variable is maximized.
   b. the x-variable equals zero.
   c. the slope of the curve changes from positive to negative.
   d. the slope of the curve changes from negative to positive.

10. Which of the following types of graphs would be best to use if you wanted to depict the relationship between time and another variable?
   a. time-series graph
   b. scatter diagram
   c. pie chart
   d. bar graph

11. The information in a pie chart represents
   a. different points, where each point corresponds to an actual observation of the x- and y-variables.
   b. the share of a total amount that is accounted for by various components, usually given as percentages.

c. different values of the variables by height or length.

d. different values of the variables as they vary over time.

12. Graphs may be misleading to the viewer because of the

a. choice of scale that is used in creating the graph.

b. truncation of the x- and/or y-axis.

c. lack of clarity about what information is being presented.

d. all of the above.

13. Suppose there is a relationship between two variables. When the researcher wrongly believes that the first variable causes the changes in the second variable, when in fact it is the second variable causing changes in the first variable, we call this a problem of

a. an omitted variable.

b. a truncated graph.

c. reverse causality.

d. misleading scale.

14. Given the equation of $x = 10 - 2y$, where the x-variable is in the horizontal axis,

a. the slope of the graph is -2.

b. the slope of the graph is not constant.

c. the vertical intercept is 10.

d. the vertical intercept is 5.

15. Consider the equation of $x = 20 + 4y$, where the x-variable is in the horizontal axis. Which of the following statements is **false?**

a. The slope of the graph is 1/4.

b. The intercept in the horizontal axis is 20.

c. The intercept in the vertical axis is 5.

d. The slope is positive and constant.

Problems and Exercises

1. Consider the five sets of data below.

Set A		Set B		Set C		Set D		Set E	
X	**Y**	**X**	**Y**	**X**	**Y**	**X**	**Y**	**X**	**Y**
10	1	0	5	5	8	0	10	0	15
10	2	1	4	6	8	1	12	1	10
10	3	2	3	7	8	2	14	2	7
10	4	3	2	8	8	3	16	3	5

Suppose you were to graph each of the data sets in a two-variable graph with the x-variable on the horizontal axis and the y-variable on the vertical axis.

a. Which data set(s) represent(s) a horizontal line?

b. Which data set(s) has/have a slope of infinity?

c. Which data set(s) depict(s) a positive relationship?

d. Which data set(s) depict(s) a negative relationship?

e. Which data set(s) depict(s) a linear relationship?

f. Which data set(s) has/have a slope greater than zero?

g. What is the absolute value of the slope of data set *B*?

h. What is the absolute value of the slope of data set *D*?

2. Use the following graph to answer this question. Note that this graph is not drawn to scale.

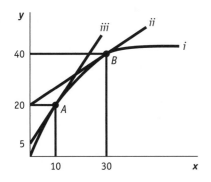

a. What is the y-intercept of line *iii*?

b. Which line is drawn tangent to the curve *i* at point *B*?

c. Using the arc method, calculate the slope between points *A* and *B*.

d. Using the point method, what is the slope at point *A*?

   e. Using the point method, what is the slope at point *B*?

   f. What is the relationship between the slope found in question 2c with the slopes found in questions 2d and 2e?

3. For each of the following pairs of variables, identify the independent variable and explain why you think it is the independent variable.
   a. Price of hamburgers and quantity of hamburgers consumed.

   b. Interest rates and the quantity of loans a bank makes.

4. Study the following four graphs. For each of the following statements, indicate which graph matches the statement. In addition, identify which variable would appear on the horizontal axis and which variable would appear on the vertical axis.

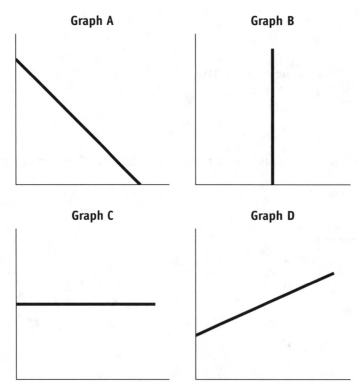

   Graph A   **Graph B**

   Graph C   **Graph D**

   a. If the price of football tickets decreases, more people attend the game.

   b. Older adults have more health problems than younger adults.

   c. No matter the price there are a fixed number of original Vincent van Gogh paintings.

d. Regardless of the quantity of corn a farmer produces, he or she will still sell it for the prevailing market price.

5. Consider the following data.

Year	Number of applications for admission to EastBay University
1980	4,000
1990	6,000
2000	9,000
2005	21,000

a. Graph the preceding data on both of the following graphs, using linear segments to connect the four observations with one another.

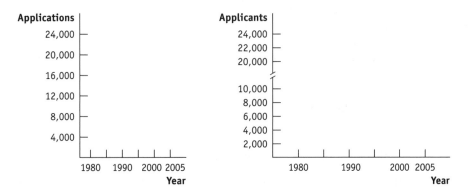

b. Compare and contrast the two graphs you have drawn in part a.

6. Consider the equation of $x = 20 - 0.5y$ and draw the x-variable as the horizontal axis.

a. What is the intercept of the horizontal axis?

b. What is the intercept of the vertical axis?

c. What is the slope of the graph? Is the slope constant, increasing, or decreasing as values of y change?

d. What is the value of x when $y = 12$ and when $y = 8$?

e. Consider the second equation of $x = 10 + 0.5y$. Given both equations, solve for y and for x.

Answers to How Well Do You Understand the Chapter

1. graphs, graphs, variable, values, relationship, variables

2. graph, *y*-variable, vertical, zero, increases, increases, dependent

3. linear, non-linear, positive, decreases, right, negative, horizontal, *x*-variable, zero, vertical, *y*-variable, zero

4. slope, run, run, positive, negative, zero, infinity

5. constant, positive, negative

6. two, arc, average, point, tangent, non-linear

7. maximum, minimum

8. numerical, time, points, observation, pie, percentage, length

9. interpretation, truncated, variable, omitted, interpretation, independent, dependent

Answers to Multiple-Choice Questions

1. A variable is a measure of something, such as price or quantity, that can vary numerically; thus, a variable is a quantity that can take on more than one value. **Answer: B.**

2. Economic models use two-variable graphs in order to present a visual image of the relationship between these two variables. Other variables that might affect the relationship between the two variables are held constant to simplify the analysis. **Answer: D.**

3. Each of these statements is correct. Although the independent variable is typically placed on the horizontal axis, price, by convention, is always placed on the vertical axis. At the origin, where the x-axis intersects the y-axis, both variables have a value of zero. **Answer: D.**

4. By definition a straight line in a graph is linear; it therefore depicts a linear relationship. In addition, a straight line has constant slope since the ratio of the change in the y-variable to the change in the x-variable is constant along the entire line. Straight lines can slope up to the right (positive slope), slope down to the right (negative slope), be horizontal (slope of zero), or be vertical (slope of infinity). **Answer: D.**

5. A curved line's slope varies as you move along the curve since the ratio of the change in the y-variable to the change in the x-variable is not constant. The slope of a curved line is positive if the line curves upward as you move to the right along the x-axis, and negative if the line curves downward as you move to the right along the x-axis. A curved line can contain both positively and negatively sloped segments. **Answer: C.**

6. The x- and y-variables have a positive relationship when both variables move together: if x increases in value, then y increases in value, or if x decreases in value, then y decreases in value. The x- and y-variables have a negative relationship when the variables move in opposite directions: if x increases in value, then y decreases in value, and vice versa. The vertical intercept is the value of y when the x-variable (not the y-variable) equals zero. A vertical or horizontal line indicates that there is no relationship between the two variables: if the line is vertical, the y-variable changes values without affecting the x-variable, and if the line is horizontal, the x-variable changes values without affecting the y-variable. **Answer: B.**

7. A curve with a positive slope slopes upward. If the slope is positive and increasing, this means that the change in the y-variable increases faster than the change in the x-variable. This is true only if the line is upward sloping and gets increasingly steep. **Answer: C.**

8. Drawing a straight line between two points on the curve and then calculating the slope of that straight line is the arc method. The arc method is an approximation of the slope of the curve between the two chosen endpoints: it is an average slope. The tangent line is necessary when calculating slope using the point method, not the arc method. **Answer: D.**

9. A maximum point refers to the point where the y-variable reaches its maximum value; this will occur at that point where the slope changes from positive to negative. **Answer: C.**

10. A time-series graph depicts the value of a variable graphed at different points in time. **Answer: A.**

11. Different points, where each point corresponds to an actual observation of the x- and y-variables, describes a scatter diagram. A bar graph depicts different values of the variables by height or length, while a time-series graph shows different values of the variables as they vary over time. A pie chart is the share of a total amount that is accounted for by various components, usually given as percentages. **Answer: B.**

12. It is important to realize that graphs may be misleading to a viewer because of the scale that is used in constructing the graph, the values omitted from the x-axis or the y-axis (the case of the truncated axis), or because it is not clear what numerical information the graph is providing. **Answer: D.**

13. When two variables are related, researchers need to investigate whether the first variable determines the value of the second variable or vice versa. Getting the direction of causality wrong is termed reverse causality. **Answer: C.**

14. Slope is rise over run and it is constant at −0.5. When x is zero, y is 5. **Answer: D.**

15. Slope is 1/4 and it is constant. When x is zero, y is −5. **Answer: C.**

Answers to Problems and Exercises

1. a. Set C, since the y-variable is constant at 8 while the x-variables change.
   b. Set A has a slope of infinity. Slope is defined as the ratio of the change in the y-variable to the change in the x-variable, and in this case the change in the x-variable is equal to zero.
   c. Set D, since as the x-variable increases in value the y-variable also increases in value.
   d. Set B and set E, since the x-variable and y-variable move in opposite directions: as one variable increases in value the other variable decreases in value.
   e. Sets A, B, C, and D all depict linear relationships, since each of these sets has constant slope.
   f. Set A and set D, since set A has a slope of infinity and set D has a slope of 2.
   g. Set B's slope is −1, so the absolute value of the slope of this set would be 1.
   h. The absolute value of the slope of data set D is 2.

2. a. The y-intercept of line *iii* is the value of y when the x-variable equals zero. In this case the value of the y-intercept is 5.
   b. Line *ii* is drawn tangent to curve *i* at point B since it just touches the curve at point B.
   c. To calculate the slope between points A and B using the arc method, we need to find the change in the y-variable and divide this by the change in the

x-variable. The change in the y-variable equals 20 (40 − 20) and the change in the x-variable equals 20 (30 − 10). The ratio of these changes, or the slope, using the arc method is 20/20, or 1.

d. The slope at point A using the point method is equal to the slope of the line drawn tangent to the curve at point A. The slope of line *iii* is 15/10 = 1.5.

e. The slope at point B using the point method is equal to the slope of the line drawn tangent to the curve at point B. The slope of line *ii* is 20/30 = 0.67.

f. The slope measure found using the arc method is an average slope. When we compare this average slope to the measures of slope we calculated using the point method, we find that the average slope measure's value lies between the more precisely calculated slope measures we found using the point method.

3. a. Price of hamburgers is the independent variable since the price influences the quantity of the good consumed.

b. An interest rate is the price of borrowing funds (money). As a price it is the independent variable that affects the quantity of loans made by an individual or a bank.

4. a. Graph A depicts this situation, with the quantity of people attending the game on the horizontal axis and the price of football tickets on the vertical axis.

b. Graph D depicts this situation, with the age of adults on the horizontal axis and health problems on the vertical axis.

c. Graph B depicts this situation, with the quantity of paintings on the horizontal axis and the price on the vertical axis. (Price, although the independent variable, is placed on the vertical axis by convention.)

d. Graph C depicts this situation, since the farmer can sell as much corn as she or he would like without affecting the market price. Quantity of corn would be on the horizontal axis and price of corn would be on the vertical axis.

5. a.

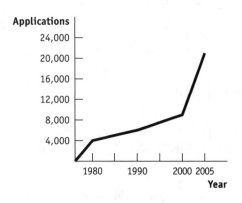 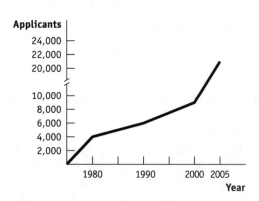

b. The two graphs visually have a different impact on the viewer: the left graph uses a smaller scale on both axes, and this leads the increase from year 2000 to year 2005 to appear quite steep (which it is, since it represents more than a 100% increase in the number of applicants between the year 2000 and the year 2005). The right graph spreads out the scale of the x-axis and also truncates part of the y-axis, and this distorts the data shown in the graph. This example is meant to reinforce the importance of choice of scale in making graphs as well as the potential impact on interpretation when a scale is truncated.

6. a. 20

b. 40

c. −2; constant

d. 14; 16

e. $y = 10$ and $x = 15$

chapter **3**

Supply and Demand

This chapter introduces the economic analysis of demand and supply. After reviewing market demand and market supply, we will be able to see how a competitive market works. The main determinants of demand are the following:

- *price of the product in question*

- *prices of related goods*

- *income of the buyers*

- *tastes of the buyers*

- *expectations*

The main determinants of supply are the following:

- *price of the product itself*

- *prices of inputs*

- *technology*

- *expectations*

After studying this chapter and working out the following problems, you will know how the equilibrium price and quantity are solved. You will also know how new equilibrium is established when either demand or supply change or both change.

How Well Do You Understand the Chapter?

Use the following list of words to complete the blanks in the review of the chapter. Words may be used more than once or not at all. If you find yourself having difficulties, please refer back to the appropriate section in the text.

along	*equal*	*larger*	*positive*
change	*fall*	*left*	*right*
complements	*higher*	*less*	*smaller*
constant	*increase*	*lower*	*smaller*
decrease	*indeterminate*	*more*	*substitutes*
demand	*inferior*	*negative*	*supply*
down	*larger*	*normal*	*up*

1. According to the law of demand, as price increases, the quantities demanded _____, and as price decreases, the quantities demanded _____. Other things being equal, a higher price for a good leads people to demand a(n) _____ quantity of goods. When price falls, we move _____ a given demand curve. A demand curve shows a(n) _____ relationship between price and quantity demanded.

2. The demand curve of a given good will shift to the _____ if the price of a complement good increases. Two goods are _____ if a fall in the price of one good leads consumers to buy less of the other goods. Other things being equal, as the prices of substitute goods increase, people demand a(n) _____ quantity of the other good. Apples and oranges are _____. Oatmeal cookies and tea are _____. If there is an increase in the price of butter, there will be a(n) _____ in the demand for margarine.

3. Assume that peanut butter and bread are complements. If there is an increase in the price of peanut butter, the quantity demanded of peanut butter will _____. As a result, the demand curve of bread will shift to the _____.

4. Assume that the good X is normal. If the income of the consumers increases, the demand curve of good X will shift to the _____. With economic downturns, we observed that the demand curve of a Kraft dinner shifted to the right; therefore, a Kraft dinner is a(n) _____ good.

5. As your student income depletes at the end of the winter term in your university, you buy more macaroni and cheese dinners. Therefore, as far as you are concerned, macaroni and cheese dinners are _____ goods. Inferior goods are not bad goods. Inferior goods are those goods that show a(n) _____ relationship between income and demand.

6. There is a well-founded expectation that Ontario will raise the tax on cigarettes in tomorrow's budget announcement. As a result, demand for cigarettes in Ontario will _____ today.

7. Other things being equal, as price increases, suppliers are willing to supply a(n) _____ quantity of a given good. As price decreases, sellers are willing to supply a(n) _____ quantity of a given good.

8. With technological improvements, the supply curve of digital cameras has shifted to the _____.

9. With increased energy prices, the production costs of goods will _____, and as a result, the supply curve of goods in Canadian markets will shift to the _____.

10. When the equilibrium in a competitive market is established, the quantity demand-ed of a good is _____ to the quantity supplied. Changes in the equi-librium prices will occur if there is a change (shift) in either _____ or _____ .

11. If a severe frost problem damages the production of oranges, the supply curve of oranges will shift to the _____ and the price of oranges will _____ . As a result, the price of apples may increase, because of a(n) _____ in the demand for apples.

12. Consider an initial equilibrium situation. If both demand and supply double, the equilibrium price will remain _____ . If the demand curve shifts to the right and the supply curve shifts to the left, the equilibrium price will _____ , but the effect on equilibrium quantity will be _____ .

13. Consider an initial equilibrium situation of a digital camera. Assume that supply of a digital camera doubled due to great technological improvements, while demand increased by 50%. As a result, the new equilibrium price of a digital camera should be _____ than the old equilibrium price, and the new equilibrium quantity of a digital camera should be _____ than the old equilibri-um quantity.

14. If the demand curve shifts to the left while the supply curve shifts to the right, the new equilibrium quantity is _____ .

Learning Tips

TIP #1: The demand curve shows the relationships between price and quantity demanded.

Other things being equal, as price increases, the quantity demanded of goods decreases. Higher price is associated with lower quantities demanded. The law of demand shows that consumers are willing to buy more at lower prices. The movement along a given demand curves shows the effects of price and price only on the quantities demanded. See Figure 3.1.

Figure 3.1

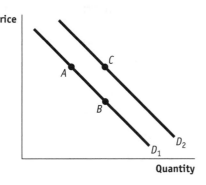

Question: Consider the movement from point *A* to point *B* (in Figure 3.1), which can be explained by

A) higher-consumer income.
B) the higher price of related goods.
C) the higher price of the good itself.
D) the lower price of the good itself.

Answer: D

TIP #2: The shift of demand curve is related to other variables, beside that of price itself. The other variables are: the price of related goods, income, tastes, and expectations.

If the price of **substitutes** increases, the demand curve for the good under consideration will shift to the right. If the price of **complements** increases, the demand curve under consideration will shift to the left. As income increases, the demand curve for **normal goods** will shift to the right.

As income increases, the demand curve for **inferior goods** will shift to the left. Normal goods are those goods that are positively related to income. Inferior goods are those goods that are negatively related to income. Any favorable effects of changes in consumers' tastes shift the demand curve to the right. Expectations regarding future shortages, future taxes, and future price hikes will shift the demand curve to the right at the present time. **Make sure that you know the distinction between moving along a curve and a shift of the curve.**

Question: See Figure 3.1. All of the following will cause a movement from *A* to *C* **except**

A) higher-consumer income.
B) higher price of substitutes.
C) expectation about future shortages.
D) lower price of the good itself.

Answer: D

TIP #3: The supply curve shows the relationships between price and quantity supplied.

The law of supply shows that sellers are willing to supply more when price increases. As price increases, the quantity supplied increases. **Make sure that you know the distinction between moving across a given supply curve and a shift of the supply curve.** The movement up along a given supply curve shows the effects of price and price alone. Across a given supply curve, we see a positive relation between price and quantity supplied. A shift of the supply curve is caused by variables, other than the price itself. Reduced input prices and technological improvements shift the supply curve to the right. See Figure 3.2.

Figure 3.2

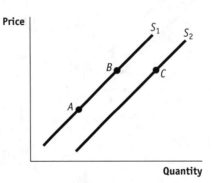

Question: Consider the movement from point A to point B (in Figure 3.2), which can be explained by

A) higher prices.
B) lower prices.
C) lower wages.
D) improved cost-saving technology.

Answer: A

Question: Movement from point A to point C (in Figure 3.2) can be explained by all of the following, **except**

A) the higher price of the good itself.
B) lower wages.
C) improved cost-saving technology.
D) entry of new firms.

Answer: A

TIP #4: A competitive equilibrium is found when quantity demanded is equal to quantity supplied.

At the market-clearing price, the price that consumers are willing to pay is equal to the price that sellers are asking for selling their goods, at the same quantity.

TIP #5: Changes in demand (shift factors), or changes in supply (shift factors), or changes in both demand and supply will bring about new equilibrium outcomes.

If both demand and supply increase, the equilibrium quantity will increase, but the effect on equilibrium price will be indeterminate. We must know the magnitudes of changes in both demand and supply to determine if price increases, decreases, or stays the same. If the increase in demand is greater than the increase in supply, price will increase. If the increase in demand is matched by the increase in supply, then price will not change. If the increase in demand is less than the increase in supply, then price will go down.

If demand increases and supply decreases, the equilibrium price will increase, but the effect on equilibrium quantity will be indeterminate, because we don't know the extent of the shifts.

Figure 3.3

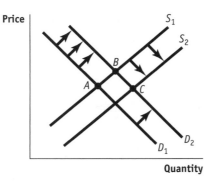

Points to remember:
A) If the demand curve shifts to the right (from D_1 to D_2) and supply curve does not change (the given supply curve is S_1), then both equilibrium price and equilibrium quantity will increase. See the movement from point A to point B in Figure 3.3.
B) If the supply curve shifts to the right (from S_1 to S_2) and demand curve shifts does not change (the given demand curve is D_2), then the equilibrium price will fall and equilibrium quantity will increase. See the movement from point B to point C in Figure 3.3.
C) The movement across a given supply curve is caused by the shift of the demand curve.
D) The movement across a given demand curve is caused by the shift of the supply curve.

TIP #6: A table may help you to identify the change to equilibrium as a result of simultaneous changes to demand and supply.

You can fill in the rows for the change in demand and the change in supply, then just add up the columns. For example, Table 3.1 shows that when there is an increase in both demand and supply in a market, equilibrium quantity definitely increases, but we cannot determine what will happen to equilibrium price.

Table 3.1

	Equilibrium price	Equilibrium quantity
Increase in demand	Increase	Increase
Increase in supply	Decrease	Increase
Net effect	???	Increase

Other possible combinations of changes in demand and supply are shown in Tables 3.2, 3.3, and 3.4.

Table 3.2

	Equilibrium price	Equilibrium quantity
Decrease in demand	Decrease	Decrease
Decrease in supply	Increase	Decrease
Net effect	???	Decrease

Table 3.3

	Equilibrium price	Equilibrium quantity
Increase in demand	Increase	Increase
Decrease in supply	Increase	Decrease
Net effect	Increase	???

Table 3.4

	Equilibrium price	Equilibrium quantity
Decrease in demand	Decrease	Decrease
Increase in supply	Decrease	Increase
Net effect	Decrease	???

Multiple-Choice Questions

The demand and supply schedules in the accompanying table reflect the weekly demand and supply of movie tickets in a small town. Answer the next four questions based on this schedule.

Price	Quantity demanded	Quantity supplied
$4.00	1,200	0
5.00	1,000	200
6.00	800	400
7.00	600	600
8.00	400	800
9.00	200	1,000

1. As the price of movie ticket falls from $8 to $7,
   a. the quantity demanded of movie tickets increases from 400 to 600.
   b. the quantity supplied of movie tickets rises from 600 to 800.
   c. the demand for movie tickets increases from 400 to 600.
   d. the supply of movie tickets decreases from 800 to 600.

2. The market for movie tickets will be in equilibrium when the
   a. equilibrium price is $6.00 and the equilibrium quantity is 400.
   b. equilibrium price is $6.00 and the equilibrium quantity is 800.
   c. equilibrium price is $7.00 and the equilibrium quantity is 600.
   d. equilibrium price is $5.00 and equilibrium quantity is 1,000.

3. If there is an increase in the demand for movie tickets, then at a price of $7
   a. quantity demanded will equal 600.
   b. quantity demanded will be less than 600.
   c. quantity demanded will be more than 600.
   d. it is impossible to tell the level of quantity demanded.

4. At a price of $9, there is a
   a. surplus of 1,000 movie tickets.
   b. shortage of 800 movie tickets.
   c. surplus of 800 movie tickets.
   d. surplus of 200 movie tickets.

5. During the fall of 2002, many vacationers on cruise liners became ill while on board their ships. Consequently, there was a
   a. decrease in the quantity demanded of cruise vacations but no change in demand for cruise vacations.
   b. decrease in the demand for cruise vacations.
   c. increase in the quantity supplied of cruise vacations but no change in supply of cruise vacations.
   d. increase in the supply of cruise vacations.

6. If the market for pencils clears, then we know
   a. that everyone who wanted to buy a pencil can.
   b. that everyone who wanted to sell a pencil can.
   c. that everyone who wanted to buy or sell a pencil at the equilibrium price can.
   d. that the market is not in equilibrium.

7. If there is an increase in the price of chocolate, we know that in response the
   a. demand for chocolate will decrease.
   b. quantity demanded for chocolate will decrease.
   c. supply of chocolate will decrease.
   d. quantity supplied of chocolate will decrease.

8. Which of the following would lower the equilibrium price of tea?
   a. a decrease in the price of coffee
   b. an increase in income and tea is a normal good
   c. an increase in the price of inputs in the production of tea
   d. an increase in a fungus that has destroyed a large proportion of the tea crop

9. As a result of the increased wage package negotiated by the hospital and the hospital workers' union,
   a. quantity supplied of hospital services will increase, with no change in supply.
   b. supply of hospital services will increase.
   c. quantity supplied of hospital services will decrease, with no change in supply.
   d. supply of hospital services will decrease.

10. The Smith family eats both meat and potatoes on a regular basis and we need to know how the family views these goods. If the price of meat rises and the family eats more potatoes, then the two goods must be
    a. substitutes.
    b. complements.
    c. inferior.
    d. normal.

11. Folklore tells us that pregnant women like to eat ice cream with pickles. If they were the only consumers of both goods, an increase in the price of pickles would
    a. decrease the demand for pickles.
    b. increase the demand for ice cream.
    c. increase the demand for pickles.
    d. decrease the demand for ice cream.

12. Toward the end of the month when money gets tight, Sara eats a lot of peanut butter sandwiches. Sara doesn't eat them because she likes them but because they're cheap. If Sara experiences an increase in income, we expect her
    a. demand for peanut butter sandwiches will increase.
    b. demand for peanut butter sandwiches will decrease.
    c. supply of peanut butter sandwiches will increase.
    d. supply of peanut butter sandwiches will decrease.

13. In the market for videotape rentals, the equilibrium price has fallen and the equilibrium output has risen. Which of the following may explain these changes?
    a. Prices of movie tickets have increased.
    b. Royalties paid to actors based on videotape rentals have fallen.
    c. DVD players have fallen in price.
    d. The government has begun to offer free concerts in parks and museums.

14. Equilibrium in the fish market is disturbed by two different events: (i) a report by the Canadian Medical Association announces that increased consumption of fish is associated with lower heart disease, and (ii) fishermen are banned from fishing in environmentally sensitive areas that previously were important sources for their catch. In the market for fish,
   a. equilibrium price will increase and equilibrium output will decrease.
   b. both equilibrium price and output will increase.
   c. equilibrium price will increase but there will be no change in equilibrium output.
   d. equilibrium price will increase but we don't have enough information to determine the change in equilibrium quantity.

15. How will the market for bicycles be affected by an increase in the price of gasoline and an increase in the desire for exercise?
   a. The equilibrium price and quantity of bicycles will increase.
   b. The equilibrium price of bicycles will fall and the equilibrium quantity will increase.
   c. The equilibrium price of bicycles will rise but we don't have enough information to determine the change in equilibrium quantity.
   d. The equilibrium output of bicycles will rise but we don't have enough information to determine the change in equilibrium price.

16. A new fertilizer doubles the grape harvest in the California wine country, while at the same time the government decreases the minimum age to purchase alcoholic beverages to 18. In the market for wine,
   a. both the equilibrium price and quantity of wine will increase.
   b. the equilibrium price will remain the same while the equilibrium quantity will increase.
   c. the equilibrium price of wine will rise but we don't have enough information to determine the change in equilibrium quantity.
   d. the equilibrium quantity will increase but we don't have enough information to determine the change in equilibrium price.

17. People become more conscious about the fat content in fast-food burgers at the same time as fast-food workers' wages decrease. In the market for fast-food burgers,
   a. there is an increase in equilibrium price and a decrease in equilibrium quantity.
   b. there is a decrease in equilibrium price and an increase in equilibrium quantity.
   c. the equilibrium price will fall but we don't have enough information to determine the change in equilibrium quantity.
   d. the equilibrium output will rise but we don't have enough information to determine the change in equilibrium price.

18. Car buyers are increasingly concerned about the low gas mileage associated with sports utility vehicles (SUVs), and the Canadian Auto Workers Union (the union that covers many of the workers producing automobiles in Canada) receives large pay increases for its members. In the market for SUVs,
   a. there is an increase in equilibrium price and a decrease in equilibrium quantity.
   b. there is a decrease in equilibrium price and an increase in equilibrium quantity.
   c. the equilibrium price will rise but we don't have enough information to determine the change in equilibrium quantity.
   d. the equilibrium output will fall but we don't have enough information to determine the change in equilibrium price.

19. If in the market for a particular type of tennis ball the equilibrium price has risen but equilibrium quantity has stayed the same, then
    a. the demand and supply of these tennis balls must have risen.
    b. the demand for these tennis balls must have risen but the supply must have fallen.
    c. the demand and supply of these tennis balls must have fallen.
    d. the supply of these tennis balls must have risen but the demand must have fallen.

20. If in the market for oranges the equilibrium quantity has risen but equilibrium price has stayed the same, then
    a. the demand and supply of oranges must have risen.
    b. the demand for oranges must have risen but the supply must have fallen.
    c. the demand and supply of oranges must have fallen.
    d. the supply of oranges must have risen but the demand must have fallen.

21. Consider the demand and supply graphs of pizza and identify one of the following statements as a "movement along a given demand curve."
    a. lower price of pizza sauce
    b. sudden increase in the number of buyers
    c. increase in consumer income
    d. increase in the prices of the substitutes of pizza

22. According to the law of demand for a given good (as reflected in a given demand curve)
    a. as income increases, consumers buy more of the normal goods.
    b. as price increases, consumers buy less of the given good.
    c. as prices of substitutes increase, consumers buy more of the given good.
    d. as tastes improve, consumers buy more of the given good.

23. An increase in the quantity supplied of pizza can be caused by
    a. a rightward shift of the supply curve.
    b. an increase in income with the assumption that pizza is a normal good.
    c. technological progress in the pizza production.
    d. lower wages of the pizza workers.

24. Which of the following statements is **false**?
    a. At the market-clearing price, the quantity demanded is equal to quantity supplied.
    b. As the price of oranges increases, the demand for oranges decreases.
    c. As income increases, the demand for normal goods increases.
    d. As the number of producers increases, the supply in the market increases.

25. Which of the following statements is true?
    a. If two goods are complements, a decrease in the price of one good will cause the demand for the other good to decrease.
    b. If two goods are substitutes, an increase in the price of one good causes the demand for the other good to increase.
    c. The movement along a demand curve is caused by income changes.
    d. The movement along a supply curve is caused by changes in wages.

26. The likely reason for the scalper's price being higher than the official ticket price for the Calgary Flames playoff game against the Tampa Bay Lightning in the Stanley Cup Final is
    a. an increase in the demand for the playoff game tickets.
    b. an increase in the supply of the playoff game tickets.
    c. an increase in governmental subsidies to sports and entertainment.
    d. an increase in the popularity of Don Cherry, an outspoken CBC commentator in the CBC *Hockey Night*.

27. You expect that you will have less income during the end of the school term (because you have over-spent your beer budget during the term). As a result, the inferior good in your consumption basket is
    a. beer, because you are buying less beer now.
    b. movie tickets, because you are buying less movie tickets now.
    c. a Kraft dinner, because you are buying more Kraft dinners now.
    d. beer, because you hate beer now.

28. During the past year, consumers' income has increased by 5%. Other things being constant, demand for lobster increased by 20%, the demand for steak increased by 18%, demand for tuna increased by 1% and demand for some other products decreased by 15%. Therefore
    a. tuna is an inferior good, because it showed the least increment.
    b. only lobster and steak are normal goods.
    c. only lobster, steak, and tuna are the normal goods.
    d. lobster, steak, tuna, and other goods are normal goods.

29. We have observed that lobster prices in the Atlantic Canada fall during the peak summer-harvest season, even though Atlantic Canada receives the highest number of tourists during the peak harvest season. We can conclude that
    a. the percentage increase in supply of lobster is less than the percentage increase in demand for lobster.
    b. the percentage increase in supply of lobster is greater than the percentage increase in demand for lobster.
    c. the demand curve of lobster has shifted to the left.
    d. the supply curve of lobster has shifted to the right, while the demand curve of lobster has shifted to the left.

30. Your professor used to recommend few textbooks for reading, but students were not required to buy any of them. But this year, your professor has made the textbook by Krugman, Wells, and Myatt the mandatory textbook and students are required to buy it. This year was also a significant year for the company that published this textbook, because the company implemented strategic cost-saving measures. Therefore
    a. the price of the textbook should increase.
    b. the price of the textbook should decrease.
    c. the price of the textbook may increase or decrease.
    d. the demand for the competing textbooks must increase.

31. Increased supply of the textbook by Krugman, Wells, and Myatt is caused by
    a. an increase in the demand for the textbook.
    b. an increase in the price of the textbook.
    c. an increase in the popularity of the textbook.
    d. a decrease in the printing costs of the textbook.

32. The price of movie rentals has gone down recently because
 a. the price of VCRs has gone down significantly.
 b. the price of a movie theatre ticket has gone up.
 c. there is an increase in the number of movie rental stores.
 d. there is an increase in the popularity of the DVDs.

Consider the following market for pita bread and answer Questions 33–34 on the basis of the accompanying table, where the demand schedules of three individuals are given. The market demand is composed of three individuals' demand functions. The market supply at respective prices is given too.

Price per pita bread	Quantity demanded by Sarah	Quantity demanded by Rinku	Quantity demanded by Sholok	Market supply
$0.30	10	15	20	12
0.40	9	13	16	16
0.50	8	11	12	20
0.60	7	9	8	24
0.70	6	7	4	28

33. At a price of $0.30 per pita bread, the market will have a _____ pita breads; as a result, the price of pita bread will go _____.
 a. surplus of 20; down
 b. surplus of 33; down
 c. shortage of 33; up
 d. shortage of 20; up

34. The market-clearing price is
 a. $0.30.
 b. $0.40.
 c. $0.50.
 d. $0.60.
 e. $0.70.

35. Many consumers use carrot muffins and coffee as _____. If the price of coffee increases, then the demand curve of carrot muffins with respect to price of carrot muffin will _____.
 a. substitutes; shift to the right
 b. complements; shift to the right
 c. complements; shift to the left
 d. substitutes; shift to the left

36. Which of the following statements is **false?**
 a. As more buyers enter the market, the market demand curve shifts to the right.
 b. As income falls, the demand for an inferior good increases.
 c. One explanation for a movement up along a given supply curve is that more producers enter the market as price increases.
 d. Higher price of gasoline may reduce the demand for automobiles.

37. Consider the market for recycled products. What will be the outcome if consumer preferences change favorably toward recycled products and if, at the same time, production technology of recycled products has improved?
a. The price of recycled products may increase or decrease.
b. The quantity of recycled products may increase or decrease.
c. The price of recycled products must increase.
d. The quantity of recycled products must increase.

38. For an inferior good, a fall in consumers' income combined with increases in production costs, will lead to a
a. higher price of the inferior good.
b. lower price of the inferior good.
c. higher quantity (bought and sold) of the inferior good.
d. lower quantity (bought and sold) of the inferior goods.

39. The other day you noticed that the price as well as the quantity bought and sold of organic vegetables in the farmers market had recently increased. One possible explanation could be
a. increased production costs of organic vegetables along with an unchanged demand schedule.
b. a shift in consumers preference toward organic vegetables.
c. a fall in income with the assumption that organic vegetables are normal goods.
d. lower production costs of organic vegetables.

40. The price of a ticket to the last hockey game played by Wayne Gretzky in Ottawa Senator's hockey arena increased because
a. scalpers kept the price too high.
b. the ticket supply was reduced drastically.
c. there was an increase in demand.
d. there was an increase in supply.

41. Students are parking in no-parking zones in the street, because of a massive shortage of parking spots on campus. One can conclude that the price for parking on campus is
a. above the equilibrium price.
b. below the equilibrium price.
c. too high.
d. at the equilibrium price.

Answer question 42–43 on the basis of the following graph.

U2 is giving a concert in the Air Canada Centre in September 2005. The seating capacity (20,000 seats) is given by the vertical supply curve. The demand function is given by D_1 line.

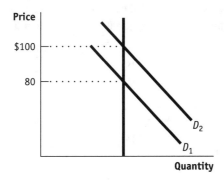

42. The equilibrium price of a ticket to the U2 concert is
  a. $80.
  b. $100.
  c. $120.
  d. $160.

43. If the concert is a sold-out event and if the market demand curve shifts to D_2 on the day of the concert, the scalper's price for a ticket will be
  a. $80.
  b. $100.
  c. $120.
  d. $160.

Optional questions: Answer questions 44–45 on the basis of the following competitive model

$$Q = 400 - 15P + 2Y \quad \text{(Demand function)}$$
$$Q = -100 + 10P \quad \text{(Supply function)}$$

Where P is price, Q is quantity, and Y is income.

***44.** If $Y = 1,000$, the equilibrium P and Q are
  a. 100 and 900, respectively.
  b. 100 and 1,700, respectively.
  c. 180 and 900, respectively.
  d. 180 and 1,700, respectively.

***45.** If income doubles, the new equilibrium P and Q will be
  a. 100 and 900, respectively.
  b. 100 and 1,700, respectively.
  c. 180 and 900, respectively.
  d. 180 and 1,700, respectively.

Problems and Exercises

Read each question carefully and then write your answers in the space provided or on a separate sheet of paper.

1. Answer the following questions based on the weekly market demand schedule for cups of coffee at the College Coffee Shop, as well as the demand schedules for three students, Ann, Brad, and Ceci, shown in the accompanying table.

Price	Ann's demand	Brad's demand	Ceci's demand	Everyone else's demand	Market demand
$0.25	10	5	20	___	8,000
0.50	9	4	19	___	7,000
0.75	8	3	18	___	6,000
1.00	7	2	17	___	5,000
1.25	6	1	16	___	4,000
1.50	5	0	15	___	3,000
1.75	4	0	14	___	2,000
2.00	3	0	13	___	1,000

a. In the table on the previous page, fill in Everyone else's weekly demand for coffee (i.e., the market less Ann, Brad, and Ceci).

b. Draw Ann's, Brad's, and Ceci's weekly demands for coffee. Do the individuals' demand curves and schedules show the "law of demand"?

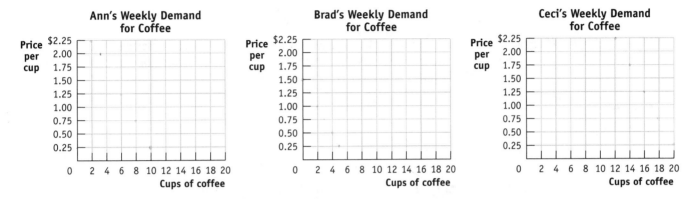

c. Draw the demand curve for the weekly market demand for coffee in the following figure. Do the preceding market demand schedule and the demand curve in the following figure show the law of demand?

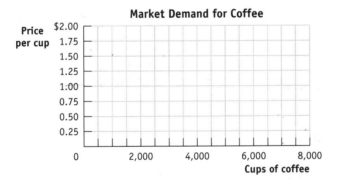

d. If the price of coffee rises from $1.00 to $1.50, will the market demand for coffee or the quantity demanded of coffee change? How will it change?

e. If there is an increase in the price of tea, will the market demand for coffee or the quantity demanded of coffee change? How will it change?

f. If there is an increase in the price of tea but Ceci's demand for coffee does not change, does Ceci see coffee and tea as substitutes?

g. If there is an increase in income and Brad reduces his consumption of coffee (perhaps in favor of espresso), is coffee a normal or inferior good for Brad? How will Brad's demand curve for coffee change?

h. What will happen to Ceci's demand for her new favorite coffee, "April Rain," which is only available during the month of April, as April comes to an end?

2. The Campus Coffee Shop's weekly supply schedule of cups of coffee is shown in the following table. Graph the market supply curve in the following figure and answer the questions below.

Price	Market supply
$0.25	3,500
0.50	4,000
0.75	4,500
1.00	5,000
1.25	5,500
1.50	6,000
1.75	6,500
2.00	7,000

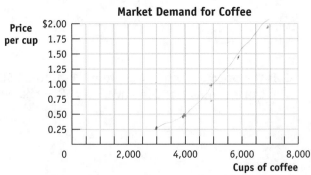

Market Demand for Coffee

a. When the price of a cup of coffee rises, does the quantity supplied of coffee increase or decrease? Describe how an increase in the price of coffee might change the supply curve in the preceding graph.

b. If there is an increase in the wages paid to students who work in the coffee shop, will the supply curve shift to the left or right?

c. If several developing countries begin exporting coffee, will the supply curve shift to the left or right?

3. The following table shows the market demand and supply schedules for cups of coffee at the Campus Coffee Shop. Graph the demand and supply curves in the following figure.

Price	Demand	Supply
$0.25	8,000	3,500
0.50	7,000	4,000
0.75	6,000	4,500
1.00	5,000	5,000
1.25	4,000	5,500
1.50	3,000	6,000
1.75	2,000	6,500
2.00	1,000	7,000

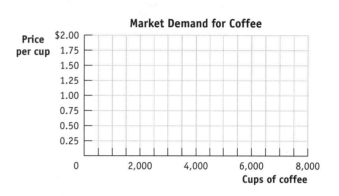

Market Demand for Coffee

a. What is the equilibrium price and equilibrium level of output?

b. What quantity is demanded and what quantity is supplied at a price of $0.75 per cup of coffee? Is there a shortage or surplus at that price? By how much do they differ? Would you expect the price of a cup of coffee to change?

c. What quantity is demanded and what quantity is supplied at a price of $1.75 per cup of coffee? Is there a shortage or surplus at that price? By how much do they differ? Would you expect the price of a cup of coffee to change?

d. If we assume coffee is a normal good, how will an increase in income affect demand? If there is an increase in income and demand increases by 1,500 cups per week at every price, what will be the new equilibrium price and output of coffee?

    e. Returning to the original supply and demand curves, what will happen to demand and/or supply of coffee if there is a decrease in the price of tea? If the price of tea falls and the demand for coffee decreases by 1,500 cups per week at every price, what will be the new equilibrium price and output of coffee?

    f. Returning to the original supply and demand curves, how will an increase in the price of coffee beans affect the demand and/or supply of coffee? If the increase in the price of coffee beans increases such that the supply of coffee falls by 1,500 cups per week at every price, what will be the new equilibrium price and output of coffee?

4. In each of the following markets, explain what will happen, if anything, to supply and demand, and how the new equilibrium price and quantity compare to the initial equilibrium price and output.

    a. Chocolate: Compare the market for chocolate for a week during January and during the week leading up to Valentine's Day. How do the equilibrium price and equilibrium quantity of chocolate compare during the two times of year?

    b. Milk: A ban on the use of certain hormones for cows radically lowers the amount of milk each cow produces.

    c. Tofu: The American Medical Association releases a report extolling the virtues of tofu at the same time as a frost destroys the soybean (main ingredient in tofu) crop.

    d. Economists: More colleges require students to take an economics class, while universities graduate more economists with Ph.D. degrees.

e. Film: The prices of digital cameras fall and film manufacturers develop a new technology that lowers the cost of producing film.

f. Child Car Seats: The number of babies being born falls, while at the same time additional government regulations raise the cost of producing car seats.

5. The following table pertains to hypothetical demand and supply schedules of lobster in Canada. Prices are expressed as dollars per kg of lobster. The quantities are expressed in thousand kg.

Price per kg	Quantity demanded	Quantity supplied
$ 6	140	60
8	120	80
9	110	90
10	100	100
11	90	110
12	80	120
13	70	130
14	60	140
15	50	150
16	40	160
20	0	200

a. Is $6 the market-clearing price? If so, explain why. If not, why not?

b. When price is $8, what is the magnitude of excess demand or shortage? What happens to price when there is an excess demand in the market?

c. When you plot a demand curve, what is the slope ($\Delta P/\Delta Q$) of this demand curve?

d. When price is $14, what is the amount of surplus? What happens to price when there is a surplus in the market?

e. What is the market-clearing price? What is the equilibrium quantity?

6. Consider demand and supply schedules of good X in Canada and in the Rest of the World (ROW).

Price	Demand in Canada	Supply in Canada	Demand in ROW	Supply in ROW
30	70	30	997	762
40	60	40	996	1,016
50	50	50	995	1,270
60	40	60	994	1,524

a. Fill in the columns of world demand and supply schedules.

Price	Demand in the world	Supply in the world
$30	1,067	792
40	____	____
50	____	____
60	____	____

b. Find the equilibrium world price. Is Canada an exporter or importer at the world price? Why?

c. If there is a total ban on foreign imports, what will be the price in Canada? Will the price in ROW be higher or lower than the price in Canada? Why?

7. In 2004, the NHL playoff between the Ottawa Senators and the Toronto Maple Leafs was dubbed as the Battle of Ontario. The 7th and deciding playoff game in Toronto was a sold-out game. Explain why the scalpers' price was significantly higher than the official price.

8. Explain with the help of a graph why the following statement is true or false.

"A recent study showed that eating spinach helps reduce heart attacks, causing an increase in the demand for spinach. This increase in demand caused a higher price for spinach in the market. This higher price will in turn reduce the demand for spinach."

*9. *Optional question:* Consider the following demand equation of spinach.

$Q = 200 - 0.5P + 0.2P^O + 0.3Y$, where Q is the quantity of spinach, P is the price of spinach, P^O is the price of substitutes, and Y is the income.

a. Re-write the above equation assuming that $P^O = 20$ and $Y = 1,000$.

b. In part a, is the equation that is described a demand equation or a supply equation? Why?

c. Is spinach a normal good or an inferior good? Why?

d. Consider the original equation and justify that the other good is not a complement.

*10. *Optional question:* Consider the following competitive model where Q is the quantity and P is the price.

$Q = 100 - P$ (Demand function in Canada)
$Q = P$ (Supply function in Canada)
$Q = 1,000 - 0.1P$ (Demand function in the ROW)
$Q = 25.4P$ (Supply function in the ROW)

a. If Canada is a closed economy (Canada does not engage in trade in the world market), then what will be the equilibrium price in Canada? What will be the equilibrium price in the ROW?

b. Derive the world demand function and the world supply function.

c. Find the equilibrium price and quantity. Is Canada an exporter or importer (circle the correct choice) at the world market price? What is the advantage to consumers in Canada if Canada participates in world trade instead of remaining in isolation?

11. Consider the following demand and supply schedules of PEI potatoes.

Price (P)	Quantity demanded (Q_D)	Quantity supplied (Q_S)
$10	0	15,000
8	2,000	12,000
6	4,000	9,000
4	6,000	6,000
2	8,000	3,000
0	10,000	0

a. What is the equilibrium price and equilibrium quantity?

b. Derive the demand equation.

c. Derive the supply equation.

d. Use the demand and supply equations that you derived and solve for *P* and for *Q*.

e. Draw graphs to show the results for all the equations you just derived.

12. Consider the market for apples (normal good) and assume an initial competitive equilibrium of apples. Trace the effects of the following in the accompanying table.

Cause	Demand curve	Demand curve	Price change	Quantity change
	Specify the shift (*leftward* or *rightward*) of the demand curve, or state that there is *no shift*.	Specify the shift (*leftward* or *rightward*) of the demand curve, or state that there is *no shift*.	Specify *zero* if price does not change, or insert *plus* sign if price increases, or insert *minus* sign if price decreases, or put a *question mark* if price remains the same, or increases or decreases.	Specify *zero* if quantity does not change, or insert *plus* sign if quantity increases, or insert *minus* sign if quantity decreases, or put a *question mark* if quantity remains the same, or increases or decreases.
Early frost damaging the crop.	No shift	Leftward	+	−
New health reports indicate that eating apples helps fight cancer.				
Increase in consumers' income and increase in wages for the workers in apple orchards.				
Increase in the demand for apple ciders and more government subsidies for the apple growers.				

13. The consumer report on the beer industry shows that, during the last year, beer consumption in Ontario has increased by 40%, while average price of beer has gone down by 10%. Explain these statistical results.

14. Explain why each of the following statements is true or false.
a. As price of apples fall, demand for apples increases.

b. As income falls, demand for apples may increase or decrease.

c. (Assume that spinach is a normal good). The demand for spinach increased due to a report linking eating spinach to better health and at the same time, consumers' income falling because of a severe recession. As a result, the demand for spinach must increase.

d. Consider a given demand curve. The reason for a down-sloping demand curve is that as price goes down, more buyers enter the market.

e. When more sellers enter the market, the supply curve shifts to the right.

15. Draw demand-supply graphs for chicken and fish. Consider a drop in the supply of chicken and trace its effect on price and quantity in both markets.

Answers to How Well Do You Understand the Chapter

1. decrease, increase, smaller, along, negative

2. left, substitutes, larger, substitutes, complements, increase

3. fall (decrease), left

4. right, inferior

5. inferior, negative

6. increase

7. larger, smaller

8. right

9. increase, left

10. equal, demand, supply

11. left, increase, increase

12. constant, increase, indeterminate

13. lower, higher

14. indeterminate

Answers to Multiple-Choice Questions

1. As the price of movie tickets falls, only quantity demanded and quantity supplied of tickets per week changes—a change in price will not change the supply or demand of movie tickets. As the price falls from $8 to $7, from the demand schedule we see that quantity demanded rises from 400 to 600 tickets per week, while quantity supplied falls from 800 to 600 tickets per week. **Answer: A.**

2. The market is in equilibrium when quantity demanded equals quantity supplied. This happens in the market for movie tickets at a price of $7.00. At any price higher than $7, quantity supplied is greater than quantity demanded; at any price below $7, quantity demanded is greater than quantity supplied. **Answer: C.**

3. An increase in demand will shift the demand curve to the right. At every price, more will be demanded. Therefore, after an increase in demand, more than 600 tickets will be demanded at a price of $7. **Answer: C.**

4. We know that at a price higher than $7 (the equilibrium price), there will be an excess supply. At $9, quantity supplied is 1,000 tickets and quantity demanded is 200 tickets. Therefore, there is an excess supply, or surplus, of 800 movie tickets. **Answer: C.**

5. As cruise line vacationers became ill, there was a decrease in the demand for cruises (a shift to the left in the demand curve). This created an excess supply of cruises at the initial equilibrium price and the price for cruises fell. As the price fell, there was an increase in quantity demanded of cruises (a movement down the new demand curve) and a decrease in quantity supplied (a movement down the supply curve). **Answer: B.**

6. When the market for pencils clears, the market is in equilibrium. This means that at the market price the quantity demanded of pencils equals the quantity supplied of pencils. Some people may want to buy or sell a pencil but cannot or do not want to at that price. **Answer: C.**

7. If the price of chocolate rises, there will be an increase in the quantity supplied of chocolate and a decrease in the quantity demanded of chocolate. There is no change to either demand or supply of chocolate because of a change in its price. **Answer: B.**

8. The price of tea will fall if there is either a decrease in demand or an increase in supply. If there is a decrease in the price of coffee, quantity demanded of coffee will increase, and since coffee and tea are substitutes, the demand for tea will decrease. On the other hand, an increase in income will increase the demand for tea (tea is a normal good) and the price of tea would rise. Both the increase in the price of inputs and a destruction of the tea crop would decrease the supply of tea and its price would rise. **Answer: A.**

9. Increased wages for hospital workers raises the cost of providing hospital services. The supply of hospital services will decrease. **Answer: D.**

10. As the price of meat rises, the family's quantity demanded of meat will fall. If at the same time it eats more potatoes, the family must be substituting potatoes for meat. The family views the two goods as substitutes. **Answer: A.**

11. Ice cream and pickles are complements for pregnant women. As the price of pickles rises, there will be a decrease in the quantity demanded of pickles and a decrease in the demand for ice cream. **Answer: D.**

12. Since Sara eats peanut butter sandwiches because they're cheap and not because she likes them, a peanut butter sandwich is an inferior good for her. When her income rises, we expect that her demand for peanut butter sandwiches will decrease. **Answer: B.**

13. If the equilibrium price of videotape rentals has fallen and the equilibrium quantity has risen, there must have been an increase in the supply of videotape rentals. This will happen if royalties paid to actors based on videotape rentals fall (a decrease in the price of an input). If the prices of movie tickets rise, there would be an increase in demand of videotape rentals, resulting in an increase in both the equilibrium price and quantity of videotape rentals. If the price of DVD players falls, there would be an increase in quantity demanded of DVD rentals, and since DVD rentals and videotape rentals are substitutes, there would be a decrease in demand for videotape rentals. The decrease in demand would decrease both the equilibrium price and quantity of videotape rentals. There would also be a decrease in demand of videotapes if the government began to offer free concerts—concerts and videotape rentals are substitute goods. **Answer: B.**

14. The report from the American Medical Association will increase the demand for fish because of fish's beneficial health effects, and the ban from fishing in environmentally sensitive areas will decrease the supply of fish. Using the following table, we see that this will definitely increase the equilibrium price of fish, but we cannot determine the effect on the equilibrium quantity. **Answer: D.**

	Equilibrium price	Equilibrium quantity
Increase in demand	Increase	Increase
Decrease in supply	Increase	Decrease
Net effect	Increase	???

15. An increase in the price of gasoline and an increase in the desire for exercise will both increase the demand for bicycles. Consequently, there will be increases in the equilibrium price and quantity of bicycles. **Answer: A.**

16. The doubling of the grape harvest in California will increase the supply of wine, while the reduction in the minimum drinking age will increase the demand for wine. Using the accompanying table, we see that these two changes will increase the equilibrium quantity of wine, but we are not certain if the equilibrium price will rise or fall. **Answer: D.**

	Equilibrium price	Equilibrium quantity
Increase in demand	Increase	Increase
Increase in supply	Decrease	Increase
Net effect	???	Increase

17. As consumers become more fat conscious, there will be a decrease in the demand for fast-food burgers. The decrease in the minimum wage earned by many fast-food workers will increase the supply of fast-food burgers. Using the accompanying table, we see that the decrease in demand and increase in supply will definitely lower the equilibrium price, but the equilibrium quantity may rise, fall, or stay the same. **Answer: C.**

	Equilibrium price	Equilibrium quantity
Decrease in demand	Decrease	Decrease
Increase in supply	Decrease	Increase
Net effect	Decrease	???

18. Concern about low gas mileage with SUVs will decrease the demand for those cars, while the increase in pay for the United Auto Workers will decrease the supply of SUVs. Using the following table, we see that the equilibrium output of SUVs will fall but we can't say what will happen to the equilibrium price. **Answer: D.**

	Equilibrium price	Equilibrium quantity
Decrease in demand	Decrease	Decrease
Decrease in supply	Increase	Decrease
Net effect	???	Decrease

19. If the equilibrium price of a particular type of tennis ball has risen, it must mean that the demand has risen (putting upward pressure on price) but the supply has decreased (also putting upward pressure on price). Since the equilibrium quantity did not change, the pressure for quantity to rise with the increase in demand is offset by the pressure for quantity to fall with the decrease in supply. **Answer: B.**

20. If the equilibrium quantity of oranges has risen, it must mean that the demand and supply have both increased—both put upward pressure on quantity. Since the equilibrium price did not change, the pressure for price to rise with the increase in demand is offset by the pressure for price to fall due to the increase in supply. **Answer: A.**

21. The production costs of pizza will go down due to the lower price of pizza sauce. As a result, the supply curve of pizza will shift to the right and price will go down across a given demand curve. **Answer: A.**

22. According to the law of demand, as price increases, quantity demanded decreases. All other choices, except choice **b**, show shifts of the demand curve. **Answer: B.**

23. This question deals with "movement across a supply curve." An increase in income shifts the demand curve to the right; price increases, and as a result, more quantity is supplied. **Answer: B.**

24. As price increases, "quantity demanded" decreases; price-fall does not lead to the change (shift) of the demand curve. **Answer: B.**

25. For substitutes, an increase in price of one good leads to a rightward shift in the demand curve of the other good. **Answer: B.**

26. An increase (rightward shift) in the demand for playoff game tickets will lead to higher scalper's price. **Answer: A.**

27. An inferior good is exemplified by the fact that a fall in income leads to more demand. A Kraft dinner is an inferior good here. **Answer: C.**

28. A normal good shows that higher income is positively related to greater demand. Lobster, steak, and tuna are normal goods, because they exhibited positive increase in demand along with positive increase in income. **Answer: C.**

29. Increase in supply is greater than the increase in demand, causing a lower price of lobster. **Answer: B.**

30. The question shows that both demand and supply increased. Since we don't know the extent of those increases, we cannot conclude whether price should increase, fall, or remain constant. **Answer: C.**

31. All factors in this question will cause shifts of the demand curve. Increase in supply of the textbooks is caused by fall in the printing costs. **Answer: D.**

32. Lower price of VCRs means more quantity of VCRs demanded, which will cause a rightward shift in the demand for movie rentals and a higher price for them. Higher price of movie theatre ticket means less demand for movie tickets and more demand for movie rentals; as a result, the price for movie rentals should increase. Similarly, increase in the popularity of DVD movies means a higher price of movie rentals. More supply of movie rentals due to more stores will cause a rightward shift of the supply curve and a lower price of movie rentals. **Answer: C.**

33. The market demand at a price of $0.30 is 45 units, while the market supply is 12. Therefore, there is a shortage of 33 and price will go up. **Answer: C.**

34. Quantity demanded is equal to quantity supplied when price is $0.60. **Answer: D.**

35. Coffee and carrot muffins are complements. Higher price of coffee means less coffee demanded, and less demand for coffee means less demand for carrot muffins. **Answer: C.**

36. Across a given supply curve, the number of producers is constant. As more producers enter the market, the supply curve shifts to the right. **Answer: C.**

37. Since both demand and supply curves have shifted to the right, more quantities will be bought and sold. But the effect on price is unknown without knowledge of the extent of the shifts. **Answer: D.**

38. For inferior goods, a fall in income will lead to an increase in demand. Higher production costs mean lower output at given prices (i.e., a leftward shift of the supply curve). Therefore, price will definitely increase, but the effect on quantity is unknown, because we don't know the extent of the shifts. **Answer: A.**

39. The first choice in this question should lead to lower quantity bought and sold with higher price. Fall in income should cause the demand curve to shift to the left and result in a lower price. The fourth choice in this question should cause a lower price. Rightward shift of the demand curve means a higher price and more quantity traded. **Answer: B.**

40. Increase in demand. **Answer: C.**

41. Shortages occur when the price is below the equilibrium price. **Answer: B.**

42. See where the demand curve D_1 intersects the vertical supply curve. **Answer: A.**

43. New equilibrium price is $100. **Answer: B.**

44. When $Y = 1,000$, the demand function is $Q = 2,400 - 15P$

$$-100 + 10P = 2,400 - 15P$$
$$25P = 2,500$$
$$P = 100 \text{ and } Q = 900$$

Answer: A.

45. $-100 + 10P = 4,400 - 15P$

$$25P = 500$$
$$P = 180 \text{ and } Q = 1,700$$

Answer: D.

Answers to Problems and Exercises

1. a. To find Everyone Else's demand, take the total market demand and subtract the demands of Ann, Brad, and Ceci.

Price	Ann's demand	Brad's demand	Ceci's demand	Everyone else's demand	Market demand
$0.25	10	5	20	7,965	8,000
0.50	9	4	19	6,968	7,000
0.75	8	3	18	5,971	6,000
1.00	7	2	17	4,974	5,000
1.25	6	1	16	3,977	4,000
1.50	5	0	15	2,980	3,000
1.75	4	0	14	1,982	2,000
2.00	3	0	13	984	1,000

b. The preceding demand schedules and the demand curves in the following figures show the "law of demand." As the price of the good increases, quantity demanded decreases.

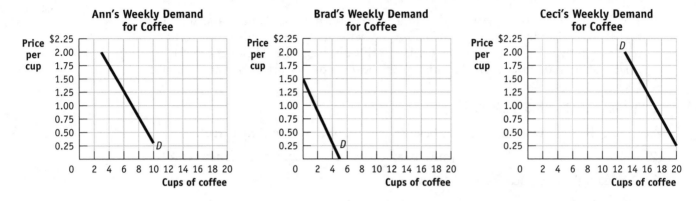

c. The weekly market demand curve for coffee in the following figure shows the law of demand: when price falls, quantity demanded rises.

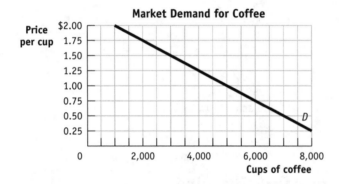

d. As the price of coffee rises from $1.00 to $1.50, there is only a change in quantity demanded. It will fall from 5,000 cups to 3,000 cups.

e. Coffee and tea are substitutes. As the price of tea increases, there will be an increase in the demand for coffee. At all prices, consumers will want to purchase more coffee.

f. If the price of tea does not affect Ceci's demand for coffee, she does not see tea as a substitute for coffee.

g. If Brad reduces his consumption of coffee when there is an increase in income, coffee is an inferior good for Brad. His demand curve for coffee will shift to the left.

h. As the month comes to an end, Ceci's demand for coffee will rise since she expects not to be able to have any more "April Rain" once May arrives.

2. The market supply curve for coffee is shown in the following figure.

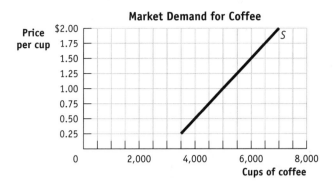

Market Demand for Coffee

a. There is a positive relationship between the price of a cup of coffee and quantity supplied. An increase in the price of coffee will result in a movement up the supply curve but not a shift in the supply curve.
b. An increase in the wages paid to students who work in the coffee shop will decrease supply (less will be supplied at every price) and shift the supply curve to the left.
c. An increase in the number of developing countries exporting coffee will increase supply (more will be supplied at every price), shifting the supply curve to the right.

3. The market supply and demand curves for coffee are shown in the following figure.

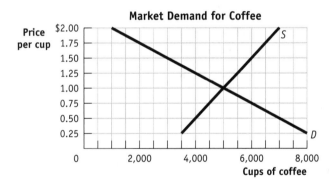

Market Demand for Coffee

a. In equilibrium, the market clears—the amount consumers wish to buy is equal to the amount firms wish to sell. In this case, the equilibrium price is $1.00 per cup and the equilibrium level of output is 5,000 cups of coffee.
b. At a price of $0.75, quantity demanded is 6,000 cups of coffee per week and quantity supplied is 4,500 cups of coffee per week. There is an excess demand of coffee (a shortage) equal to 1,500 cups per week. As a result, the price of a cup of coffee will increase.
c. At a price of $1.75, quantity demanded is 2,000 cups of coffee per week and quantity supplied is 6,500 cups of coffee per week. There is an excess supply of coffee (a surplus) equal to 4,500 cups per week. As a result, the price of a cup of coffee will decrease.

d. If coffee is a normal good, an increase in income will increase the demand for coffee. If the demand for coffee increases by 1,500 cups per week at every price, the new equilibrium price will be $1.25 per cup and the new equilibrium quantity will be 5,500 cups, as shown in the following figure.

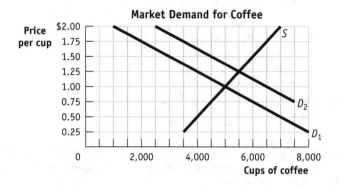

e. Assuming coffee and tea are substitutes, a decrease in the price of tea will lower the demand for coffee but will not affect the supply of coffee. If the demand for coffee falls by 1,500 cups per week at every price, the new equilibrium price will be $0.75 per cup and the new equilibrium quantity will be 4,500 cups, as shown in the following figure.

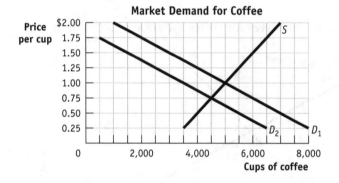

f. Since coffee beans are an input in the production of coffee, an increase in their price will reduce the supply of coffee. If the supply of coffee falls by 1,500 cups per week at every price, the new equilibrium price will be $1.25 per cup and the new equilibrium quantity will be 4,000 cups, as shown in the following figure.

4. a. Chocolate: During the week leading up to Valentine's Day the demand for chocolate increases, and there are increases in the equilibrium price and the equilibrium quantity of chocolate.

b. Milk: If a ban on the use of certain hormones lowers the amount of milk each cow produces, there will be a decrease in the supply of milk. As a result, the equilibrium price of milk will increase and equilibrium quantity will decrease.

c. Tofu: The report extolling the virtues of tofu will increase demand, while the frost that destroys the soybean crop will decrease supply. To see how these two factors affect equilibrium price and equilibrium output, we can look at each effect individually and then find the net effect.

	Equilibrium price	Equilibrium quantity
Increase in demand	Increase	Increase
Decrease in supply	Increase	Decrease
Net effect	Increase	???

Equilibrium price will definitely rise, but we cannot determine what will happen to the equilibrium quantity.

d. Economists: When more colleges require students to take an economics course, the demand for economists to teach those courses will increase. The bumper crop of new economics Ph.D.'s will increase the supply of economists. Again, we need to look at how these two factors affect equilibrium price and equilibrium output. We can look at each effect individually and then find the net effect.

	Equilibrium price	Equilibrium quantity
Increase in demand	Increase	Increase
Increase in supply	Decrease	Increase
Net effect	???	Increase

The equilibrium quantity will definitely increase, but we cannot determine how the equilibrium price will change.

e. Film: Since digital cameras are a substitute for film cameras, as the price of digital cameras fall there will be a decrease in the demand for film. Supply will increase as film manufacturers develop a new technology that lowers the cost of producing film. Here is how each factor affects equilibrium price and equilibrium output:

	Equilibrium price	Equilibrium quantity
Decrease in demand	Decrease	Decrease
Increase in supply	Decrease	Increase
Net effect	Decrease	???

These changes to the film market will definitely decrease equilibrium price, but we cannot determine what will happen to equilibrium quantity.

f. Child car seats: Demand will fall due to the lower birth rate, and supply will decrease as the government regulations increase the cost of producing car seats. Here is how each factor affects equilibrium price and equilibrium output:

	Equilibrium price	Equilibrium quantity
Decrease in demand	Decrease	Decrease
Decrease in supply	Increase	Decrease
Net effect	???	Decrease

These changes to the child car seat market will definitely decrease equilibrium quantity, but we cannot determine what will happen to equilibrium price.

5. a. $6 is not a market-clearing price, because quantity demanded exceeds quantity supplied.
   b. Excess demand is 40 kg. Price will increase.
   c. −1/10.
   d. Surplus is 80 kg. Price will decrease.
   e. $P = \$10$ and $Q = 100$ kg.

6. a. Demand: 1,056, 1,045, and 1,034; Supply: 1,056, 1,320, and 1,584.
   b. Price is $40. Canada imports 20, because the Canadian demand exceeds the Canadian supply.
   c. Price in Canada is $50. The price in ROW should be lower, because the ROW has a larger supply available for the ROW markets (due to zero import by Canada).

7. The 7th playoff game was a sell-out game. There was a huge increase in demand for this deciding game in Toronto. Because of manifold increases in demand, the scalpers had a bonanza; they sold the tickets at about four times higher than the official ticket price.

8. The statement is false. Increase in demand shifts the demand curve to the right. As a result, price increases. Increase in price causes an increase in quantity supplied. See the accompanying graph, where the initial equilibrium point is point A and the new equilibrium point is B.

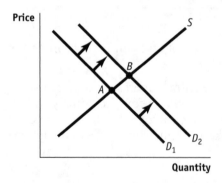

9. a. $Q = 502 - 0.5P$
   b. It is a demand equation, because quantity (Q) is negatively related to price (P) when we consider a demand function.
   c. It is a normal good, because quantity (Q) is positively related to income (Y).
   d. For complements, quantity (Q) is negatively related to price of other goods. In this question, P_O is positively related to Q; that means, we are dealing with substitutes.

10. a. Set Q demanded equal to Q supplied and solve price (P).
   $100 - P = P$. Therefore, in Canada, $P = 50$ and $Q = 50$.
   Use the condition that
   $1000 - 0.1P = 25.4P$
   In ROW, $P = 39.22$ and $Q = 996.19$
   b. $Q = 1100 - 1.1P$ (world demand function)
   $Q = 26.4P$ (world supply function)
   c. World price $= 40$ and equilibrium $Q = 1,056$.
   Canada imports 20 units.
   Consumers benefit due to lower price.

11. a. $P = \$4$ and $Q = 6{,}000$.
   b. $Q_D = 10{,}000 - 1000P$.
   c. $Q_s = 1{,}500P$.
   d. From $1{,}500P = 10{,}000 - 1{,}000P$, we solve P as \$4 and Q as 6,000.

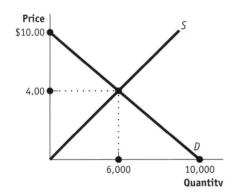

12.

Demand curve	Supply curve	Price change	Quantity change
Rightward	No shift	+	+
Rightward	Leftward	+	?
Rightward	Rightward	?	+

13. The beer industry witnessed an increase in demand. At the same time, supply curve of beer shifted to the right. The increase in supply was greater than the increase in demand and as a result, the price of beer has gone down.

14. a. False. As price of apples fall, the *quantity demanded* for apples increases. This is a movement on a given demand curve. When we say "demand for apples increases," we mean a rightward shift of the demand curve, caused by anything but the price of apples.
   b. True. If apples are considered as normal goods, then demand will fall; but if apples are considered as inferior goods, then demand will increase.
   c. False. The favorable health report will shift the demand curve to the right, but the income effect will shift the demand curve to the left. Since we don't know the extent of these shifts, we cannot conclude that the demand for spinach will increase.
   d. False. On a given demand curve, the number of buyers is fixed.
   e. True.

15.

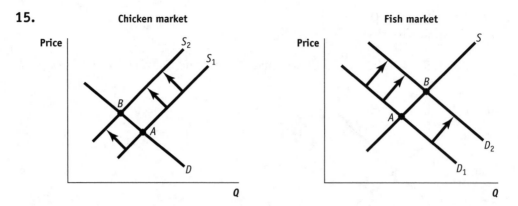

The supply curve in the chicken market will shift to the left, causing a higher price of chicken.

If chicken and fish are substitutes, then an increase in chicken price will cause a rightward shift of the demand curve of fish. As a result, the price of fish will increase.

## chapter 4

The Market Strikes Back

Apply the demand-supply framework that you learned in the last chapter and see how price controls, quotas, and taxes work in our economy in Canada. Generally, the government imposes price controls, quotas, and taxes to protect consumers, to protect producers, or to raise tax-revenues; these measures lead to debates and criticisms. You will see that whenever government does intervene in markets, it causes some inefficiencies, which will be explained in this chapter.

How Well Do You Understand the Chapter?

Fill in the blanks using the following terms, or circle the correct answer to complete the following statements. Terms may be used more than once. If you find yourself having difficulties, please refer back to the appropriate section in the text.

black	greater	license	rent
both	high	less	rise
burden	ignore	minimum	resources
consumers	increase(s)	price ceiling	sales
decrease(s)	illegal	price control(s)	shortage
down	inefficiencies	price floor	surplus
excise	low	producers	up
fall	lower	quota	wedge

1. The government may try to affect markets by imposing _____ that specify either a minimum or maximum price in a market. A(n) _____ is the maximum price that can be charged in a market; price floor is a(n) _____ price. Whenever the government intervenes in markets, inefficiencies such as _____, or black market, prices may develop.

2. The government would impose a ceiling if it believed that the equilibrium price of a(n) good in an uncontrolled (free) market is too _____ for consumers to pay. When the government imposes a ceiling that is lower than the market equilibrium price, quantity demanded will be quantity supplied, resulting in a _____ of the good. Rent control is an example of a(n) _____.

3. The government would impose a(n) _____ if it believed the equilibrium price of a good in an uncontrolled (free) market is too low for producers to earn respectable incomes. This is a way to protect the _____ of a good. When the government imposes a price floor that is higher than the market equilibrium price, quantity demanded will be _____ than quantity supplied, resulting in a(n) _____ of the good. Minimum wage is an example of a(n) _____.

4. In creating either a surplus or shortage of the good, the government creates _____ in the market. With a price ceiling and the resulting _____, consumers waste _____ searching for the good, while producers offer goods of inefficiently _____ quality. With a(n) _____ and the resulting surplus, there will be an inefficient allocation of _____ among sellers, with producers offering goods of inefficiently _____ quality.

5. With price controls, a(n) _____ market, or illegal market, may develop. When either demanders or suppliers are not able to purchase or sell what they wish to at the government-imposed price-ceiling, the illegal price will be _____ than the mandated (official or legal) ceiling price.

6. The government may also affect the market equilibrium price and output by imposing a quantity control. Whenever the government imposes a(n) _____, a limit to the amount that can be sold, or requires a(n) _____, which limits the number of suppliers in a market, it will not only affect the amount of the good that is exchanged but also the price at which it is exchanged.

7. When the government imposes a quantity control it drives a(n) _____ between the demand price, the price that consumers are willing to pay for the amount available under the quantity control, and the supply price, the price at which producers are willing to offer the amount available under the quantity control. The demand price is _____ than the supply price, and this difference is known as the price _____ or quota _____.

8. Quantity controls also may have some _____ associated with them. As long as the demand price of a given quantity is _____ than the supply price, there is a missed opportunity.

9. When government assesses a(n) _____ tax, a per-unit tax on a particular good, it also affects the market equilibrium price, output, and results in _____.

10. If the per-unit tax is collected from the producers, the supply curve will shift _____ by the amount of the tax. Consequently, the price that consumers will pay will _____; but after producers remit the tax revenue to the government, producers will receive a(n) _____ price than before the tax. The _____, or cost, of the tax is borne by _____ the producers, and the consumers when we have normal-looking demand supply graphs.

11. If the tax is collected from the _____, the demand curve will shift _____ by the amount of the tax. Consequently, the price that consumers will pay to the producers will be _____ but they will also have to pay the tax, leading to a total price, the price to producers plus tax, that is _____ than the price before the tax. Again, _____ producers and consumers share the burden of the tax.

12. Since the imposition of the tax _____ the amount of the good exchanged, there is an opportunity cost. Since the tax has discouraged some mutually beneficial transactions, we say that there is an excess _____, or deadweight loss, from a tax.

Learning Tips

TIP #1: When the government imposes a price ceiling, be sure the price ceiling is below the equilibrium price; if it isn't, the price ceiling won't affect the market. Similarly, when the government imposes a price floor, be sure the price floor is above the equilibrium price to affect the market.

If the government sets a price ceiling above the equilibrium price, the price control will not affect the market equilibrium price. See Figure 4.1. At the price ceiling, quantity supplied will be greater than quantity demanded and the price in the market will fall until it returns to its original equilibrium price. The price ceiling only restricts the price from rising.

Figure 4.1

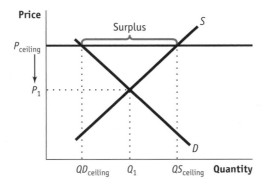

If the government sets a price floor below the equilibrium price, the price control will not affect the market equilibrium price. At the price floor, quantity demanded will be greater than quantity supplied and the price in the market will rise until it returns to its original equilibrium price. The price floor only restricts the price from falling. See Figure 4.2.

Figure 4.2

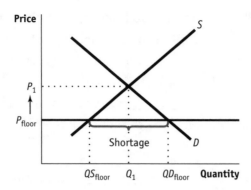

Question: Consider Figure 4.2. Which of the following statements is **incorrect?**

A) Effective ceiling price is set a point below the uncontrolled (free) market equilibrium price.
B) There will a shortage with a ceiling price.
C) Effective floor price is set a point above the uncontrolled (free) market equilibrium price.
D) When the ceiling price is imposed, the black market price is always lower than the uncontrolled (free) market price.

Answer: D

TIP #2: Remember that the government can use either an excise tax or license sales to change the equilibrium price and output in a market. Either way, the government can raise the same amount of revenue.

By imposing an excise tax or a quantity control, the government drives a wedge between the demand price and the supply price. When the government imposes a tax, the price wedge is equal to the amount of the tax. See Figure 4.3a. When the government grants licenses as a means of quantity control, the price wedge is the quota rent. See Figure 4.3b. If the government sells licenses to produce output and sets the price of each license equal to the price wedge, it can generate the same revenue as the excise tax; you can see this by comparing Figure 4.3a with Figure 4.3b.

Figure 4.3a   **Figure 4.3b**

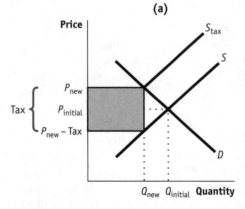

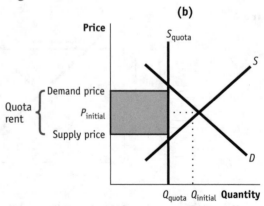

Question: Consider Figure 4.3a. Which of the following statements is **incorrect?**

A) With the per-unit tax, after-tax price exceeds the initial no-tax equilibrium price by the amount of the per-unit tax.
B) Tax reduces the quantity sold.

C) Tax reduces the sellers' income.
D) There is a deadweight loss with tax.

Answer: A

TIP #3: The question of "who pays the tax?" is more than just a question of who remits the tax money to the government. It doesn't matter whether the buyers or the sellers are required to send the tax to the government because the tax burden is usually shared by the buyers and the sellers.

Figure 4.4a illustrates an example of the government imposing a per-unit tax to be paid by the consumers, while Figure 4.4b shows an example of a per-unit tax to be paid by the producers.

Figure 4.4a   **Figure 4.4b**

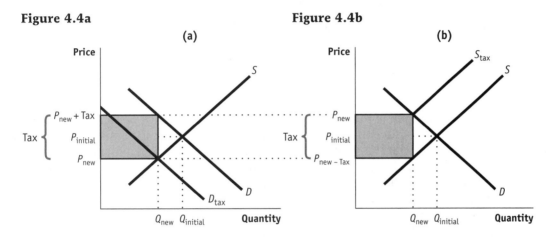

Question: Consider Figure 4.4a. Which of the following statements is **incorrect?**

A) After the per-unit tax is imposed, the seller's price net of tax is higher than the initial no-tax equilibrium price.
B) After the per-unit tax is imposed, the buyer's final price (which includes per-unit tax) is higher than the initial no-tax equilibrium price.
C) Both consumers and producers are worse off as a result of the per-unit tax.
D) Tax reduces quantity sold.

Answer: A

Although the new price falls to P_{new} in Figure 4.4a, where the consumer is required to "pay the tax," that price represents the price that producers receive after the imposition of the tax. Since the consumer must pay that price plus the tax, the cost to the consumer of the good is P_{new} + Tax after the imposition of the tax. The portion of the tax paid by the consumer and the portion paid by the producer does not depend upon who is nominally required to pay the tax. While the producer is nominally responsible for the tax in Figure 4.4b, the market price rises to P_{new} and the consumer pays that price; the producer only receives P_{new} − Tax after the tax is paid to the government. Figure 4.4b shows that the price the consumer pays and the price the producer receives are identical to the prices shown in Figure 4.4a, even though in that figure we assumed that the consumer was nominally responsible for the tax. The price the consumer pays and the price the producer receives is the same whether the consumer or the producer is required to "pay the tax."

TIP #4: You can determine how much of the tax is paid by the consumer and by the producer by comparing the old equilibrium price with the new equilibrium price and the tax.

Since it does not matter who actually "pays the tax," we can look at the burden of the tax assuming the producer pays the tax. Figure 4.5 shows the government's revenue from the tax and the consumer's and producer's share of the tax.

Figure 4.5

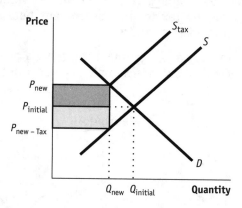

The government's revenue is the amount of the tax (the difference between the supply curves, or $P_{new} - [P_{new} - Tax]$) times the quantity exchanged after the imposition of the tax (Q_{new}). It is the sum of the shaded rectangles. The consumer pays a higher price with the tax (P_{new} versus $P_{initial}$) on the quantity exchanged after the imposition of the tax (Q_{new}), so the consumer's burden is ($P_{new} - P_{initial}$) times Q_{new}. The producer receives a lower price ($P_{new} - Tax$ versus $P_{initial}$) with the tax on the quantity exchanged after the imposition of the tax (Q_{new}), so the producer's burden is ($P_{initial} - [P_{new} - Tax]$) times Q_{new}.

Multiple-Choice Questions

1. The government might impose a price ceiling in a market for a good if it believed that the price in the market was
   a. too high for the consumers of the good.
   b. too low for the consumers of the good.
   c. too high for the producers of the good.
   d. too low for the producers of the good.

2. When the government imposes a price floor in a market, which of the following inefficiencies may occur?
   a. The good may be offered for sale with inefficiently low quality.
   b. The good may be offered for sale with inefficiently high quality.
   c. A shortage of the good may occur.
   d. A black market may develop, where the good or service is exchanged at a price higher than the price floor.

3. Rent controls are inefficient because they result in
   a. cheaper housing for some renters than in the absence of the controls.
   b. lower-quality housing for some renters than in the absence of controls.
   c. shorter waits for rent-controlled housing.
   d. a surplus of rent-controlled apartments.

*The following five questions are based on the demand and supply schedules in the
accompanying table reflecting the weekly demand and supply of movie tickets in a small town.*

Price	Quantity demanded	Quantity supplied
$4.00	1,200	0
5.00	1,000	200
6.00	800	400
7.00	600	600
8.00	400	800
9.00	200	1,000

4. To provide affordable entertainment for teens—and get them off the streets at night—
the local government imposes a price ceiling of $5.00 on movie tickets. Consequently,
  a. there are 1,000 happy patrons who are now able to see movies for only $5.00 per
  ticket.
  b. there are 800 frustrated patrons who would like to buy a ticket at $5.00 but can-
  not get one.
  c. there are 200 frustrated moviegoers who would like to buy a ticket at $5.00 but
  cannot get one.
  d. nothing happens to the equilibrium price or quantity of movie tickets; the price
  ceiling is ineffective.

5. To provide affordable entertainment for teens—and get them off the streets at
night—the local government imposes a price ceiling of $8.00. Consequently,
  a. there are 800 happy patrons who are now able to see movies for only $8.00 per
  ticket.
  b. there are 400 frustrated patrons who would like to buy a ticket at $8.00 but can-
  not get one.
  c. there are 200 frustrated moviegoers who would like to buy a ticket at $8.00 but
  cannot get one.
  d. nothing happens to the equilibrium price or quantity of movie tickets; the price
  ceiling is ineffective.

6. If the government limits the number of movie tickets sold to 400 tickets each week
by requiring a license to sell tickets, the quota rent for the holders of the licenses
would be
  a. $7 per ticket.
  b. $6 per ticket.
  c. $4 per ticket.
  d. $2 per ticket.

7. To raise revenue to improve the parks in the town, the government imposes a tax of
$2 on movie tickets, collected from the theater owners. As a result, the price of
movie tickets rises to
  a. $9 and the equilibrium level of tickets bought and sold is 200 each week.
  b. $9 and the equilibrium level of tickets bought and sold is 1,000 each week.
  c. $8 and the equilibrium level of tickets bought and sold is 400 each week.
  d. $7 and the equilibrium level of tickets bought and sold is 600 each week.

8. If the government imposed a tax of $2 on movie tickets, it would raise revenue
equal to
  a. $400.
  b. $800.
  c. $1,200.
  d. $2,000.

The accompanying figure describes the market for unskilled labor in a particular town. Use this graph to answer the next two questions.

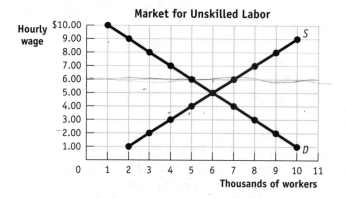

9. If the government imposes a minimum wage of $6.00, then
   a. employment will fall to 5,000 workers and unemployment will be equal to 1,000 workers.
   b. employment will fall to 6,000 workers and unemployment will be equal to 2,000 workers.
   c. employment will fall to 5,000 workers and unemployment will be equal to 2,000 workers.
   d. employment will fall to 6,000 workers and unemployment will be equal to 1,000 workers.

10. At a minimum wage of $6.00, unemployment will result because
   a. 1,000 workers will lose jobs, and 1,000 workers will enter the labor force but not find jobs as the wage rises from $5.00 to $6.00.
   b. 2,000 workers will lose jobs as the wage rate rises from $5.00 to $6.00.
   c. 2,000 workers will enter the labor force but not find jobs as the wage rate rises from $5.00 to $6.00.
   d. 5,000 workers will lose jobs as the wage rate rises from $5.00 to $6.00.

11. Many economists believe that the minimum wage in Canada does not create unemployment (or a surplus of workers) because
   a. the minimum wage is below the equilibrium wage and therefore is ineffective.
   b. the minimum wage is above the equilibrium wage and therefore is ineffective.
   c. most minimum wage workers are teenagers.
   d. the minimum wage is a voluntary program.

12. As long as the demand price of a given quantity exceeds the supply price,
   a. there is a missed opportunity.
   b. there is a shortage of the good.
   c. producers have no incentive to sell the product.
   d. consumers have no incentive to buy the product.

13. When the government imposes a tax in a market and collects the tax from the producers,
   a. the price of the good rises by the full amount of the tax.
   b. the supply curve shifts down by the full amount of the tax.
   c. the supply curve shifts up by the full amount of the tax.
   d. both the demand and supply curves shift up by the full amount of the tax.

14. When the government imposes a tax in a market and collects the tax from the consumers,

a. the price of the good rises by the full amount of the tax.

b. the demand curve shifts down by the full amount of the tax.

c. the supply curve shifts up by the full amount of the tax.

d. both the demand and supply curves shift up by the full amount of the tax.

15. The excess burden, or deadweight loss, of a tax comes about because

a. the consumers pay a higher price than they would without the tax.

b. both producers and consumers are hurt by the tax.

c. the tax lowers the quantity exchanged and some mutually beneficial transactions do not take place.

d. of all of the above.

16. The following figure shows a simplified market for taxi rides during the average evening rush hour in Montreal. Given the number of taxi medallions, the maximum number of rides available during an average rush hour is 20,000. The evening rush-hour quota rent is

a. $4.

b. $6.

c. $8.

d. $12.

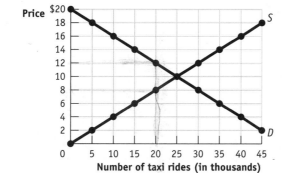

17. The following figure shows a market in which the government has imposed a quota of 1,000 units. The government could also reduce the amount exchanged in the market to 1,000 by imposing a tax equal to

a. $1.

b. $2.

c. $3.

d. $4.

18. The minimum wage has

a. some positive employment effects.

b. some negative employment effects.

c. made all unskilled workers worse off.

d. made all unskilled workers better off.

19. Which of the following statements is true?
  a. Minimum wages in Canada are, on an average, higher (in terms of purchasing power) than at any time in the last 30 years.
  b. Job-training programs can simultaneously increase the equilibrium wage and employment in Canada.
  c. Job-training programs can increase the equilibrium wage but will not affect employment situation in Canada.
  d. Job-training programs cannot increase the equilibrium wage of unskilled workers.

20. The following figure shows a market in which the government has imposed a tax. Which of the following statements about the graph is correct?

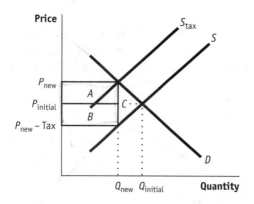

  a. Rectangle A represents the portion of the tax paid by the producers.
  b. Rectangle B represents the portion of the tax paid by the consumers.
  c. The sum of rectangles A and B represents the government's revenue from the tax.
  d. Triangle C represents the government's tax revenue from the tax.

21. Consider the labour market for unskilled workers. With more job-training schemes in Canada, the demand for labour will shift to the _____ and the wage rate as well as employment will _____.
  a. right; increase
  b. left; decrease
  c. right, decrease
  d. left, increase

Answer questions 22–25 on the basis of the following demand and supply schedules of blueberries. Quantities are expressed in thousand kg.

Price per kg	Quantity demanded	Quantity supplied
$1.00	100	20
1.50	90	30
2.00	80	40
2.50	70	50
3.00	60	60
3.50	50	70
4.00	40	80
4.50	30	90
5.00	20	100

22. With a price ceiling of $1.50 per kg, the shortages will be
  a. 30 thousand kg.
  b. 40 thousand kg.
  c. 50 thousand kg.
  d. 60 thousand kg.

23. With a price ceiling of $1.50 per kg, the black market price can be as high as
  a. $5.
  b. $6.
  c. $3.
  d. none of the above.

24. Instead of a ceiling price, the Nova Scotia government imposes a per-unit tax of $1.00 per kg. As a result, the post-tax market price will be
  a. $4.00.
  b. $3.50.
  c. $3.00.
  d. none of the above.

25. As a result of a per-unit tax of $1.00 per kg, total tax revenues will be
  a. $50 thousand.
  b. $60 thousand.
  c. $70 thousand.
  d. none of the above.

Problems and Exercises

Read each question carefully and then write your answers in the space provided or on a separate sheet of paper.

1. The following table shows the market demand and supply curves for 18-hole golf games per week at the golf courses in Midvale City. (For simplicity we're assuming that all golf courses and tee times are equally desirable.) Graph the demand and supply curves in the following figure.

Price per 18-hole golf game	Demand for 18-hole golf games (in thousands)	Supply for 18-hole golf games (in thousands)
$10	10	0
20	9	1
30	8	2
40	7	3
50	6	4
60	5	5
70	4	6
80	3	7
90	2	8
100	1	9
110	0	10

Market for Golf Games

Price of golf game (vertical axis: $110, 100, 90, 80, 70, 60, 50, 40, 30, 20, 10)

Quantity of golf games (in thousands) (horizontal axis: 0 1 2 3 4 5 6 7 8 9 10)

a. The market-clearing price is _____ and the market-clearing level

of output is _____ games.

b. One of the candidates for mayor of Midvale City is running on a platform that proposes to keep the price of an 18-hole golf game affordable to everyone by imposing a price ceiling of $20 for an 18-hole game. If he is elected, what will happen to the price and the number of golf games played? What types of inefficiencies might result?

c. Another candidate for mayor of Midvale City proposes to reward some of her biggest contributors, the owners of the golf courses, by imposing a price floor of $80 per game of golf. If she is elected, what will happen to the price and number of golf games played? What types of inefficiencies might result?

d. A third candidate for mayor is running on a "Family First" platform and is concerned about how golf separates families. He is proposing to limit the number of golf games to 3,000 per week. If he is elected, what will happen to the price and number of golf games played? What types of inefficiencies might result?

2. Canada has a long history of Marketing Boards to protect farm income and farm price.

The province of Prince Edward Island is famous for island spuds. The following table shows the hypothetical demand and supply schedules of PEI potatoes.

Price per kg	Demand (in thousand kg)	Supply (in thousand kg)
$1.00	100	20
1.10	90	30
1.20	80	40
1.30	70	50
1.40	60	60
1.50	50	70
1.60	40	80
1.70	30	90

a. If the Potato Marketing Board in PEI did not intervene, what will be the equilibrium unregulated free market price and quantity?

b. If the Marketing Board imposes a price floor of $1.60 per kg, what will be the surplus in the market? If the government buys this surplus, what will be the cost of buying? What will be the total farm income?

c. Suppose instead of buying surplus potatoes, the government decides to provide farmers with subsidy of $0.40 per kg, what will be the total subsidy payments to the farmers?

3. The Pelmar County supervisor has proposed a tax on beer as a way to both curb excessive drinking and to raise the needed revenue to cover its budget deficit. The monthly supply and demand curves for beer (we're assuming all beer is the same) are shown in the accompanying figure. Answer the following questions assuming the government imposes a tax of $1 per six-pack and collects the tax from the producers.

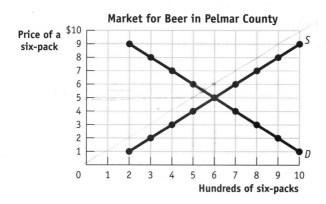

a. After the imposition of a tax of $1 per six-pack, what is the new equilibrium price and output of beer?

b. What is the government's revenue from the tax?

c. How much of the $1 tax is paid by the consumers and how much by the producers?

4. Suppose the Canadian government is considering some price support policies to provide income assistance to Canadian wheat farmers in the prairies. The quantities of demand and supply in bushels are shown in the following table.

Price per bushel	Quantity demanded	Quantity supplied
$10	800	1,200
8	900	1,100
6	1,000	1,000
4	1,100	900
2	1,200	800

a. If the government sets a price-floor of $10.00, how many bushels will be produced? What will be the surplus? If the government buys surplus wheat (to be donated to the Third World countries), how much will it cost the government?

b. Suppose the government sets a target price of $10.00 and output quota at 1,200 bushels. Find the market price at which 1,200 bushels of wheat will be purchased by consumers. If the government gives (as subsidy) to farmers an amount equal to the difference between market price and target price for each bushel of wheat, how much will it cost the government?

c. Which option is cheaper to the government? Which option will be chosen by the farmers?

5. Explain why the following statement is true or false: If the demand curve is vertical, the burden of excise tax is shared by both consumers and producers.

6. The hypothetical demand and supply functions of Atlantic lobsters are the following:

$$Q^D = 220 - 10P$$
$$Q^S = -80 + 20P$$

In the above equations, Q^D is the quantity of lobsters demanded, Q^S is the quantity of lobster supplied, and P is the price of lobsters per kg.

a. Find the equilibrium price and quantity.

b. If output is restricted to 80 kg, what will be the price at which consumers are willing to buy 80 kg, and what will be the price at which lobster fisherman are willing to sell 80 kg?

c. Given your answer in **b,** what will be the quota rent?

d. Instead of using a quota system, find the appropriate per-unit excise tax to ensure that lobster fisheries are limited to 80 kg. What will be the tax revenues? What will be the deadweight loss?

7. Explain with a diagram why the following statement is true or false: "Other things remaining constant, the steeper the demand curve of labour, the less the negative employment effects due to the minimum wage regulations."

Answers to How Well Do You Understand the Chapter

1. price controls, price ceiling, minimum, illegal

2. high, shortage, price ceiling

3. price floor, producers, less, surplus, price floor

4. inefficiencies, shortage, resources, low, price floor, sales, low

5. black, greater

6. quota, license

7. wedge, greater, wedge, rent

8. inefficiencies, greater

9. excise, inefficiencies

10. up, increase, lower, burden, both

11. consumers, down, less, greater, both

12. decreases, burden

Answers to Multiple-Choice Questions

1. When the government imposes a price ceiling (a maximum price), it does so because it believes that the equilibrium price is too high. The producers want a high price but consumers want a low price. By setting a maximum price below the equilibrium price, the government is trying to help the consumers. **Answer: A.**

2. When the government imposes a price floor (a minimum price) in a market, a surplus results. Since producers will be competing with one another for customers but not on the basis of price, they may offer some perks with the good. **Answer: B.**

3. Rent controls are a price ceiling and create shortages of apartments. Owners have little incentive to keep up these apartments, and consequently they are often of lower quality. **Answer: B.**

4. At a price of $5.00 per ticket, 1,000 tickets will be demanded but only 200 will be supplied. Therefore, 200 people will be able to buy tickets and 800 will not. **Answer: B.**

5. When the government imposes a price ceiling of $8 tickets will be demanded, 800 will be supplied, and a surplus will result. The surplus would cause prices to fall—and they can fall because the price ceiling is only a maximum price. The price of a movie ticket will fall back to the equilibrium price of $7. **Answer: D.**

6. If the government limits the number of movie tickets sold to 400, the demand price of those 400 tickets would be $8.00, while the supply price of the tickets would be $6.00. The quota rent is the difference between the demand price and the supply price, or $2 per ticket. **Answer: D.**

7. A tax of $2 on movie tickets will shift the supply curve for movie tickets up by $2, as shown in the following figure. The new equilibrium price will be $8 per ticket and 400 tickets will be bought and sold. **Answer: C.**

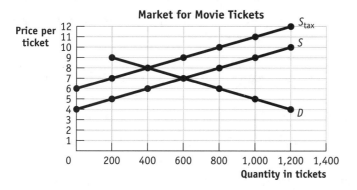

8. From the preceding figure we can see that 400 tickets would be exchanged with the tax and the government would earn $800 from the tax (= $2 × 400). **Answer: B.**

9. At a $6 minimum wage, 7,000 workers will be looking for jobs, but firms will only want to hire 5,000 of them. There will be 2,000 unemployed workers. **Answer: C.**

10. As the wage rises from the equilibrium wage of $5 to the $6 minimum wage, 1,000 workers will lose their jobs (firms would hire 6,000 workers at a wage of $5, but at $6 only 5,000 will be hired). Also, 1,000 workers who were not willing to work at $5 enter the labor force at a wage of $6 but are not able to find jobs. **Answer: A.**

11. If the minimum wage is set below the equilibrium wage, it will have no effect on the market and therefore the minimum wage will not create unemployment. This is the situation that many economists believe exists for the minimum wage in the United States. **Answer: A.**

12. When the demand price exceeds the supply price for a given quantity, there is a shortage of the good and the market would be better off with more exchanged. There is a missed opportunity. **Answer: A.**

13. When the government imposes a tax in a market and the tax is collected from the producers, the supply curve will shift up by the full amount of the tax. Producers want the same price for supplying a particular quantity plus the tax. **Answer: C.**

14. When the government imposes a tax in a market and the tax is collected from the consumers, the demand curve will shift down by the amount of the tax. The demand curve reflects that price paid to the producer. Consumers are only willing to pay the same price for a particular quantity, but now part of the payment is to the government and the rest is to the producer. **Answer: B.**

15. Since a tax lowers the amount of the good exchanged, some mutually beneficial transactions that would have taken place do not. This is the excess burden, or deadweight loss, of a tax. **Answer: D.**

16. The quota rent is the difference between the demand price and the supply price for the quota. At the quota of 20,000 rides, the quota rent is $4 (= $12 − $8). **Answer: A.**

17. If the tax were $4 per unit, the supply curve would shift up by $4 and intersect the demand curve at a price of $8 and quantity of 1,000 units. **Answer: D.**

18. Use given demand-supply curves with wage rate at the vertical axis and quantity of labour at the horizontal axis and set the minimum wage above the free-market wage rate (where demand and supply curves intersect). The gap between demand and supply at the minimum wage is the amount of unemployment. **Answer: B.**

19. A job-training program shifts the demand for labour curve to the right. As a result, both wage and employment increase. **Answer: B.**

20. Rectangle *A* is the portion of the tax paid by the consumers, rectangle *B* is the portion paid by the producers. Together rectangles *A* and *B* represent the government's tax revenue. **Answer: C.**

21. A job-training program shifts the demand for labour curve to the right. **Answer: A.**

22. See the gap between quantity demanded and quantity supplied when the ceiling price is $1.50. **Answer: D.**

23. If the quantity supplied is 30 thousand kg at the ceiling price of $1.50, there are consumers who will be willing to buy 30 thousand kg at a price of $4.50. Therefore, $4.50 is the highest black market price. **Answer: D.**

24. When consumers buy 50 thousand kg at a final (gross) price of $3.50, it is equal to the supply price of $2.50 (net of tax), at which sellers are willing to supply 50 thousand kg of blueberries. **Answer: B.**

25. With *Q* = 50 thousand kg and tax = $1.00, tax revenues = $50 thousand. **Answer: A.**

Answers to Problems and Exercises

1.

Market for Golf Games

Price of golf games — Quantity of golf games (in thousands)

a. The market-clearing price is $60 and the market-clearing level of output is 5,000 games.

b. A price ceiling of $20 for an 18-hole game will insure that the price of an 18-hole game is $20, but only 1,000 games will be offered for sale at that price. There will be an excess demand of 8,000 games—a lot of people who would like to play for $20 a game will be disappointed. We might expect to see golf courses requiring golf carts that would rent for very high rates (wasted resources); certain players might make side payments to employees to ensure that they get to play (wasted resources); and the owners of the golf courses might not keep the greens and fairways in their best condition (inefficiently low quality).

c. A price floor of $80 will insure that the price of a golf game will be $80, but only 3,000 games will be played at that price. Since the owners of the golf courses would like to supply 7,000 games at that price, there will be a surplus in the market. The owners might try to attract more players by offering cheap or free golf cart rentals (wasted resources and inefficiently high quality), lessons by pros (wasted resources and inefficiently high quality), and drinks at the 19th hole (wasted resources).

d. If the mayor imposes a quota of 3,000 games, the price of a golf game will rise to $80 and there will be a price wedge, or quota rent, of $40 (= $80 – $40). Some inefficiencies would include missed opportunities; golfers would be willing to pay $70 per game for 1,000 additional golf games and the golf courses would offer those 1,000 games for $50 per game. Also, there's an incentive on the part of both golfers and golf courses to ignore the law.

2. Use the data in the table.
   a. Price = $1.40, quantity demanded and supplied = 60 thousand kg.
   b. At the floor price, quantity demanded = 40 thousand kg and quantity supplied = 80 thousand kg. Therefore, surplus = 40 thousand kg. Cost of buying this surplus = $1.60 times 40 thousand kg = $64 thousand.
   c. With a subsidy of $0.40 per kg, quantity demanded and supplied will be 80 thousand kg. The total subsidy costs to the government = $32 thousand.

3. a. If the government imposes a tax of $1 per six-pack, the supply curve with the tax will shift up by the amount of the tax. Before the tax, producers were willing to supply 600 six-packs for $5 each; after the tax they require $6 to supply 600 six-packs. The new equilibrium price with the tax is $5.50 per six-pack, and the equilibrium quantity is 550 six-packs per month.

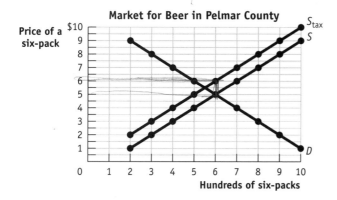

Market for Beer in Pelmar County

b. The government's revenue is the tax, $1, times the new equilibrium quantity, 550 six-packs, or $550 per month.
   c. The consumers were paying $0.50 more per six-pack after the tax on 550 six-packs, or $275. The producers are receiving $0.50 less per six-pack after the tax on 550 six-packs, or $275. The consumers and producers are paying equal amounts of the tax.

4. a. Quantity produced = 1,200 bushels. Since quantity demanded is 800 bushels, surplus equals 400 bushels. The cost of buying this surplus is $4,000.
   b. The difference between target price and market price (when consumers buy 1,200 bushels) is $8. If $8 is subsidized for each bushel, it will cost the government $9,600.
   c. Buying surplus is cheaper for the government. The farmers are indifferent between two options, because they will earn $12,000 in total in both options.

5. False. With a vertical demand curve, an excise tax (which shifts the supply curve), the price increases by the amount of the tax. The total burden of tax falls on consumers.

6. a. $P = $10; Q = 120$
   b. Consumers are willing to pay = $14; producers are willing to sell at = $8.
   c. Quota rent = (80) ($14 – $8) = $480.

d. Appropriate excise tax = \$6
   Tax revenue = \$6(80) = \$480
   Deadweight loss = (1/2)(40)(\$4) + (1/2)(40)(\$2) = \$120

7. True. See the following graph.
   With the demand curve of D_1, the unemployment is $L_1 - L_3$.
   With the steeper demand curve of D_2, the unemployment is $L_2 - L_3$ and it is less than the previous unemployment.

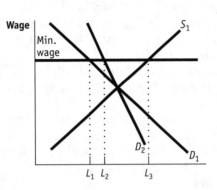

chapter 5

Elasticity

The elasticity of demand deals with the percentage change of the quantity demanded due to the percentage change of the price of the good, the price of the income, or the price of other goods. The elasticity of supply is the percentage change of the quantity supplied due to the percentage change of the price of the good. Elasticity measures the degree of responsiveness; if we know that two variables are related, we can find out the extent by which one variable affects the other variable.

With respect to price elasticity of demand, we show the relationship between elasticity and total revenue. We also investigate how the burden (incidence) of an excise tax as borne by the consumers and producers is dependent on the elasticity of demand and supply.

How Well Do You Understand the Chapter?

Fill in the blanks using the following terms to complete the following statements. Terms may be used more than once. If you find yourself having difficulties, please refer back to appropriate section in the text.

absolute	income	negatively	quantity demanded
cannot	increase(s)	perfectly price elastic	quantity effect
changes	inelastic	perfectly price inelastic	quantity supplied
complements	inferior	price	strength
decrease(s)	initial	price effect	substitute(s)
demand	inputs	price-elastic	supply
dominates	less than	price elasticities	time
elastic	luxuries	price-inelastic	unit-elastic
elasticities	midpoint method	positive	unrelated
equal to	more than	positively	
greater than	negative		

1. Price elasticity of demand is a measure of how _____ responds to a change in price. We know that for most goods quantity demanded is _____ related to price. Price elasticity of demand looks at how much quantity demanded _____ when there is an increase in price.

We measure price elasticity of demand by looking at the ratio of the percentage change in _____ to the percentage change in price. We use the _____ of the price elasticity of demand to avoid the issue of starting and finishing points. Although the price elasticity of demand is negative, it is always reported as a(n) _____ value. The absolute value of the price elasticity of demand can range from zero to infinity.

2. If the value of the price elasticity of demand is greater than 1, we say the demand is price _____ and that the percentage change in quantity demanded is _____ the percentage change in price. If price elasticity of demand is equal to 1, we say the demand is _____ and that the percentage change in quantity demanded will be _____ the percentage change in price. If the elasticity is less than 1, we say the demand is price-_____ and that the percent change in quantity demanded is _____ the percent change in price. If quantity demanded does not respond to a change in price, we say that demand is _____ _____. If quantity demanded responds infinitely to any small change in price, we say that demand is _____.

3. Total revenue may change when there is a change in _____, but how it will change (increase or decrease) depends on the price elasticity of _____. If the price elasticity of demand is greater than 1 (demand is _____), and if producers are interested in raising total revenue, then they must _____ prices. If the price elasticity of demand is equal to 1 (demand is _____), the producers cannot raise total revenue by changing prices. If the price elasticity of demand is less than 1, and producers are interested in raising total revenue, then they must _____ prices.

4. Price elasticity of demand differs from the slope of the demand curve. Whereas slope is constant along a linear demand curve, price elasticity of demand _____ as we move down a demand curve. Demand curves tend to be _____ at high prices and _____ at low prices.

5. Factors affecting elasticity of demand include whether close _____ for the good are readily available, whether the good is viewed as a necessity or as a luxury, and the _____ available to adjust habits or tastes due to the changes in price. The demand for a good will be more price-elastic the greater the availability of close _____. Price elasticity of demand will also be larger for goods that are viewed as _____ as opposed to necessities. The longer the period during which consumers can adjust to the _____ in price, the more likely it is they will find substitutes and therefore that the price elasticity of demand will be larger.

6. Cross-price elasticity of demand measures how responsive demand is to a change in the price of _____ goods or complement goods. We know that demand for a good will _____ if there is a decrease in the price of a complement good or an increase in the price of a substitute good. Also, if the price of a substitute good falls or the price of a complement good rises, demand for the other good will _____. The cross-price elasticity of demand will be _____ for substitute goods and _____ for complement goods. The magnitude of the number indicates the _____ of

the relationship. A large negative number will indicate that the two goods are strong _____, while a large positive number will indicate that the two goods are very close _____. Cross-price elasticities of demand close to zero indicate that the two goods are _____ or only loosely related.

7. Income elasticity of demand measures how quantity demanded of a good responds to a change in _____. As income increases, demand for normal goods _____ but the demand for inferior goods _____. The income elasticity of demand will be _____ for normal goods and negative for _____ goods. The magnitude of the income elasticity of demand indicates how responsive demand is to a change in _____.

8. Price elasticity of supply measures the responsiveness of _____ to change in price. We know that when price increases, quantity supplied increases, so the price elasticity of supply is always _____. If the price elasticity of supply is _____ 1, then the percentage change in quantity supplied is larger than the percentage change in price and we say that supply is price _____. If the price elasticity of supply is _____ 1, then the percent change in quantity supplied is less than the percent change in price and we say that supply is price _____. When the price elasticity of supply is equal to 1, the percentage change in quantity supplied is _____ the percentage change in price and we say that supply is _____. The price elasticity of supply depends on the availability of _____ and the time available to change quantity supplied. Long-run price elasticities of supply tend to be _____ because given a longer time, suppliers can find suitable _____ to expand production.

9. The relative _____ of supply and demand determine whether the demanders or the suppliers will bear more of the burden of a tax. Assuming that the producers remit ("pay") the tax, the burden of a tax paid by the consumer is the difference between the new price and the initial price. The burden of a tax on the producer is the difference between the price that the producer receives after the tax (i.e., the new price *minus* the tax) and the _____ price. Consumers will bear the tax-burden completely, if the demand is _____. If the price elasticity of demand is _____ the price elasticity of supply, the consumers will bear a larger tax burden. If the price elasticity of demand is _____ the price elasticity of supply, then the demanders and suppliers will the tax burden equally.

Learning Tips

TIP #1: From the law of demand we know that the price elasticity of demand must be a negative number (as price rises, quantity demanded falls, and vice versa), but we refer to it as though it were an absolute value.

Since all economists and economics students know the law of demand, we know that the price elasticity of demand is a negative number. Rather than continuously writing and referring to the price elasticity of demand as a negative number, we drop the minus sign and report it as an absolute value. In other words, when we estimate elasticity mathematically it should include a minus sign, but when we describe elasticity in language the sign is ignored.

Question: If the quantity demanded increases by 10%, while price decreases by 5%, we can conclude that the price-elasticity demand is

A) +2%.
B) −2%.
C) +2.
D) −2.

Answer: D

TIP #2: The price elasticity of demand determines how a change in price will affect total revenue.

When a seller raises the price of the good, quantity demanded falls. While the increase in price tends to increase total revenue (price effect), the fall in quantity demanded will tend to decrease it (quantity effect). The price elasticity of demand tells us about the magnitudes of these effects.

$$\text{Price elasticity of demand} = \frac{\%\ \text{change in quantity demanded}}{\%\ \text{change in price}}$$

When the price elasticity of demand is greater than 1, the quantity effect outweighs the price effect and the quantity effect dominates the change in total revenue.

Price elasticity of demand > 1 → Quantity Effect > Price Effect

In this case, if sellers want to increase total revenue, they must increase sales, and they can do that by lowering prices.

However, if the price elasticity of demand is less than 1, the price effect will outweigh the quantity effect.

Price elasticity of demand < 1 → Quantity Effect < Price Effect

In this case, if sellers want to increase total revenue, they must increase price. Although sales will fall, the higher price per unit will result in higher total revenue.

If the price elasticity of demand is equal to 1 (i.e., demand is unit-elastic) then the quantity effect and the price effect will exactly offset one another and a change in price will not change total revenue.

Price elasticity of demand = 1 → Quantity Effect = Price Effect

Question: The price of a movie ticket has increased recently and you have cut down on number of movies you see every month, but your monthly expenditure on movies has remained constant. Therefore, we can conclude that

A) the price elasticity of demand is inelastic.
B) the price elasticity of demand is elastic.
C) the price elasticity of demand is unit-elastic.
D) income elasticity of demand is zero.

Answer: C

TIP #3: Price elasticity of demand is not the same as the slope of the demand curve.

Along a linear demand curve, slope is constant but elasticity is not. In general, elasticity is large at high prices and small at low prices.

Consider a linear demand curve. Which of the following statements about it is **false?**

A) In the mid-point of the linear demand curve, the elasticity of demand is unit elastic.
B) At the price-intercept point in a graph with a linear demand curve, where the quantity demanded is zero, the price elasticity of demand is zero.
C) As we move down a linear demand curve, the absolute value of elasticity becomes smaller.
D) The elasticity of demand of a vertical demand curve is zero.

Answer: B

TIP #4: The formulas to calculate elasticities are similar in many ways: the numerator in each formula indicates whether we are calculating an elasticity of demand or supply and the denominator reflects what type of elasticity.

You can see the similarities and differences in the equations below.

$$\text{Price elasticity of demand} = \frac{\% \text{ change in quantity demanded}}{\% \text{ change in price}}$$

$$\text{Cross-price elasticity of demand} = \frac{\% \text{ change in quantity demanded of A}}{\% \text{ change in price of B}}$$

$$\text{Income elasticity of demand} = \frac{\% \text{ change in quantity demanded}}{\% \text{ change in income}}$$

$$\text{Price elasticity of supply} = \frac{\% \text{ change in quantity supplied}}{\% \text{ change in price}}$$

When we are calculating the income elasticity of demand, for example, since it's an elasticity of demand we know that the numerator will be the percent change in quantity demanded, and since it's an income elasticity the denominator will be the percent change in income.

To calculate the percent change in something, let's say income, using the midpoint method, you divide the change in income by the average income:

$$\% \text{ change in income} = \frac{\text{change in income}}{\text{average income}} \times 100$$

TIP #5: Relative price elasticities determine how consumers and producers will share the burden of a tax.

When the government imposes a tax on a good, it doesn't matter who "pays the tax." Whether the consumers or the producers actually remit or write a check to the government to pay the tax, the burden of the tax will likely be shared by the two groups. If the producer "pays the tax," the supply curve shifts up by the amount of the tax, raising the equilibrium price and lowering the equilibrium quantity. Clearly the consumers are worse off—they are paying more for less. The producers are also hurt because they receive a price that is lower than what the consumer pays with the tax and less than the price they received before the tax on a smaller quantity. If the price elasticity of demand is greater than the price elasticity of supply, then consumers will pay a larger portion of the tax than the producers. If the price elasticity of demand is less than the price elasticity of supply, then the producers will pay a larger portion of the tax. If the price elasticity of demand equals the price elasticity of supply, then the producers and consumers will share the tax equally.

Figure 5.1 shows a graph where the price elasticities of demand and supply are equal at the initial equilibrium price and consumers and producers pay equal portions of a $2 tax.

Figure 5.1

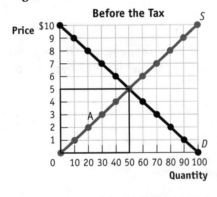

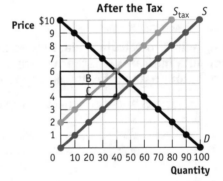

$P_{\text{initial}} = \$5$

$Q_{\text{initial}} = 50 \text{ units}$

Total Cost to Consumers = $250
(rectangle A)

Total Revenue to Producers = $250
(rectangle A)

$P_{\text{new}} = \$6$

$Q_{\text{new}} = 40$

Consumer pays $1 more because of the tax on the new quantity purchased, or $40.
(rectangle B)

Producer receives $1 less because of the tax on the new quantity, or $40.
(rectangle C)

Tax revenue to government = $80
$(P \times Q) = (2 \times 40) = \$80$

Figure 5.2 shows a graph where consumers pay proportionately less of a $3 tax. In this case, at the initial equilibrium price, the price elasticity of demand is more than the price elasticity of supply.

Figure 5.2

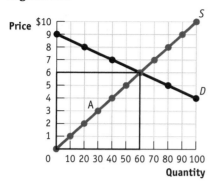

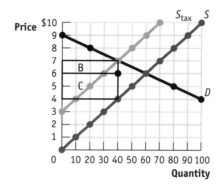

$P_{initial}$ = $6

$Q_{initial}$ = 60 units

Total Cost to Consumers = $360
(rectangle A)

Total Revenue to Producers = $360
(rectangle A)

P_{new} = $7

Q_{new} = 40

Consumer pays $1 more because of
the tax on the new quantity purchased,
or $40.
(rectangle B)

Producer receives $2 less because of the
tax on the new quantity, or $80.
(rectangle C)

Tax revenue to government = $120
$(P \times Q)$ = (3×40) = $120

In Figure 5.3, the consumer pays proportionately more of the tax when, at the initial equilibrium price, the price elasticity of demand is less than the price elasticity of supply. Figure 5.3 illustrates such a market in which the government imposes a $1.50 per unit tax.

Figure 5.3

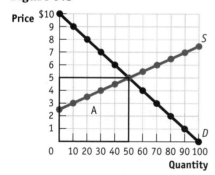

$P_{initial}$ = $5

$Q_{initial}$ = 50 units

Total Cost to Consumers = $250
(rectangle A)

Total Revenue to Producers = $250
(rectangle A)

P_{new} = $6

Q_{new} = 40

Consumer pays $1 more because of
the tax on the new quantity purchased,
or $40.
(rectangle B)

Producer receives $0.50 less because of the
tax on the new quantity, or $20.
(rectangle C)

Tax revenue to government = $60
$(P \times Q)$ = (1.50×40) = $60

Multiple-Choice Questions

1. When the transit authority raises subway fares by 10%, ridership falls by 5%. What is the price elasticity of demand for subway rides?
   a. 1
   b. 0.5
   c. 2
   d. 5

2. The accompanying table shows the weekly demand schedule for ice cream in a particular town. Using the midpoint method, what is the price elasticity of demand between the prices of $2.50 and $3.00 per cone?

Price per cone	Quantity demanded (in cones)
$0.00	1,600
0.50	1,400
1.00	1,200
1.50	1,000
2.00	800
2.50	600
3.00	400
3.50	200
4.00	0

   a. 0
   b. .25
   c. 1
   d. 2.2

3. Given the demand schedule for ice cream in the table above, as the price of a cone rises from $2.50 to $3.00, total revenue
   a. falls from $1,500 to $1,200.
   b. falls from $400 to $600.
   c. rises from $1,500 to $2,000.
   d. rises from $1,000 to $1,200.

4. The demand for enrollment at RTC University is price inelastic. When the board of trustees faces a budget shortfall and needs to increase tuition revenue, they should
   a. raise tuition because the increase in tuition will more than offset the fall in enrollment and total revenue will rise.
   b. lower tuition because the increase in enrollment will more than offset the lower tuition and total revenue will rise.
   c. raise tuition because enrollment will increase along with the tuition.
   d. raise tuition because enrollment will not change and the higher tuition per student will increase total revenue.

5. When the price of insulin rises, even diabetics who do not have insurance and pay the full cost of their medication do not cut back on how much they demand. We describe this type of demand as
   a. perfectly price elastic.
   b. elastic.
   c. unit-elastic.
   d. perfectly price inelastic.

6. Along the demand curve in the accompanying figure, the price elasticity of demand
   a. is constant and equal to its slope.
   b. is larger at P_2 than at P_1.
   c. is smaller at P_2 than at P_1.
   d. is unit-elastic.

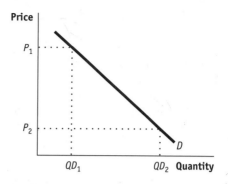

7. If a good has many close substitutes, its price elasticity of demand will be
   a. constant.
   b. larger than if there existed few close substitutes.
   c. smaller than if there existed few close substitutes.
   d. unit-elastic.

8. Since for most people eating in restaurants is a luxury while eating at home is a necessity, the demand for food eaten at home
   a. is less sensitive to changes in price than the demand for food eaten in a restaurant.
   b. is more sensitive to changes in price than the demand for food eaten in a restaurant.
   c. cannot be compared with the demand for food eaten in a restaurant in terms of price elasticity of demand.
   d. has a higher price elasticity of demand than the demand for food eaten in a restaurant.

9. When the price of a good rises, it may take time for consumers to find suitable substitutes. Therefore, as the time available to find substitutes increases, the price elasticity of demand will usually
   a. decrease.
   b. increase.
   c. stay the same.
   d. fall before rising.

10. The cross-price elasticity of demand for Coke and Pepsi is
   a. equal to zero.
   b. larger than zero.
   c. less than zero.
   d. cannot be estimated.

11. When the price of rice rises, quantity demanded of beans falls. The cross-price elasticity of demand for rice and beans must be
   a. equal to zero.
   b. larger than zero.
   c. less than zero.
   d. cannot be estimated.

12. When income rises, the quantity demanded of movie tickets also rises. The income elasticity of demand for movie tickets is
   a. equal to zero.
   b. larger than zero.
   c. less than zero.
   d. cannot be estimated.

13. When there is an increase in income, the percent change in the quantity demanded for food eaten away from home rises more than the percent change in income. Food eaten away from home is a
a. normal good.
b. inferior good.
c. complement of food eaten at home.
d. none of the above.

14. Given the weekly supply schedule for ice cream in a particular town in the table below and using the midpoint method, what is the price elasticity of supply between the prices of $2.50 and $3.00 per cone?

Price per cone	Quantity supplied (in cones)
$0.00	0
0.50	0
1.00	0
1.50	400
2.00	800
2.50	1,200
3.00	1,600
3.50	2,000
4.00	2,400

a. 0
b. .82
c. 1
d. 1.57

15. As soon as the price of a good goes up, suppliers would like to produce more but may not be able to because they cannot immediately hire more skilled laborers and/or purchase new machinery. However, over time firms can hire more workers and purchase more machinery. Consequently, the price elasticity of supply
a. decreases over time.
b. increases over time.
c. remains constant over time.
d. may increase or decrease over time.

16. The accompanying figure shows the weekly demand and supply curves for ice cream that we discussed in earlier questions. If the government imposes a tax of $0.75 per cone collected from the producers, what will be the consumers' burden from the tax?

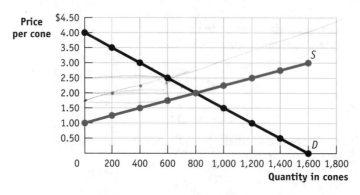

a. The consumers will pay $2.75 for 500 cones after the tax for a burden to them of $0.75 per cone.

b. The consumers will pay $2.50 for 600 cones after the tax for a burden to them of $0.50 per cone.

c. The consumers will pay $2.25 for 700 cones after the tax for a burden to them of $0.25 per cone.

d. The consumers will continue to pay $2.00 for 800 cones after the tax and avoid any burden from the tax.

17. In the problem before, what is the producers' burden from the tax?

a. The producers will receive a price of $1.75 for 600 cones after the tax for a burden to them of $0.25 per cone.

b. The producers will receive a price of $1.50 for 700 cones after the tax for a burden to them of $0.50 per cone.

c. The producers will receive a price of $1.25 for 800 cones after the tax for a burden to them of $0.75 per cone.

d. There is no burden to the producers—the consumers will pay all of the tax.

18. In the accompanying figure, how do the producers and consumers share the burden of the tax?

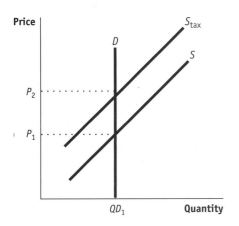

a. The consumers pay most of the tax.

b. The producers pay most of the tax.

c. The consumers pay all of the tax.

d. The producers pay all of the tax.

19. If the government imposes a price ceiling in a market, the resulting shortage will be smaller when demand is _____ and supply is _____.

a. elastic; inelastic

b. inelastic; inelastic

c. elastic; elastic

d. perfectly inelastic; elastic

20. If the government imposes a price floor in a market, the resulting surplus will be smaller when demand is _____ and supply is _____.

a. elastic; inelastic

b. inelastic; inelastic

c. elastic; elastic

d. perfectly inelastic; elastic

21. Which of the following statements is **false?**
    a. If the demand for a good is elastic, a fall in price will increase total revenue, because quantity effect is stronger than the price effect.
    b. If the demand for a good is elastic, an increase in price will reduce total revenue, because quantity effect is stronger than the price effect.
    c. If the demand for a good is inelastic, an increase in price will increase total revenue, because quantity effect is stronger than the price effect.
    d. If the demand for a good is unit-elastic, an increase in price does not change the total revenue, because the quantity effect and price effect offset each other.

22. Assume that the reduction of a given output due to the introduction of a quota restriction has increased its price. As a result, the total revenue of the producers has increased. We can conclude that the demand for the given product is
    a. elastic.
    b. inelastic.
    c. unit-elastic.
    d. perfectly elastic.

23. A higher minimum wage will increase total income of the unskilled labour if the demand for unskilled labour is
    a. elastic.
    b. inelastic.
    c. unit-elastic.
    d. perfectly elastic.

24. Which of the following statements is **false?**
    a. Income elasticity of demand for food is less than 1.
    b. The demand for spinach is more elastic than the demand for vegetables.
    c. The incidence of payroll taxes in Canada falls almost entirely on workers.
    d. The greater the price elasticity of demand, the greater the incidence of an excise tax on consumers.

25. The price of souvenir T-shirts in Charlottetown in PEI has increased from $12 to $18. As a result, total revenue has fallen from $24,000 to $18,000. We can conclude that the price elasticity (based on mid-point method) is _____ and the demand for T-shirt is _____.
    a. −0.25; inelastic
    b. −1.33; elastic
    c. −1.67; elastic
    d. −0.67; inelastic

Problems and Exercises

Read each question carefully and then write your answers in the space provided or on a separate sheet of paper.

1. For each of the following pairs of goods, identify which good in the pair has the higher price elasticity of demand. Explain your answers.
   a. Coke; soft drink industry

b. Visits to the doctor; visits to the baseball stadium

c. Gasoline consumed each year; gasoline consumed each week

d. Insulin for a diabetic; dialysis treatment for someone with kidney disease

e. Water; diamonds

2. For the following pairs of goods, do you think the cross-price elasticity of demand will be positive or negative or zero? How large will the number be? Explain your answers.
   a. videotape rentals; DVD rentals

   b. refrigerators; electricity

c. Coke; Pepsi

d. conventional ovens; microwave ovens

e. water; diamonds

3. For the following pairs of goods, which do you think will have the higher income elasticity of demand? Are any of them negative? Explain your answers.
   a. macaroni and cheese; fettuccine Alfredo

   b. public higher education; private higher education

   c. college textbooks; hardcover bestsellers

d. televisions; computers

e. water; diamonds

4. The weekly supply and demand for movie tickets at the Campus Cinema are shown in the following table. Plot the demand and supply curves in the accompanying figure.

Price	Demand	Supply
$1.00	9,000	0
2.00	8,000	500
3.00	7,000	1,000
4.00	6,000	1,500
5.00	5,000	2,000
6.00	4,000	2,500
7.00	3,000	3,000
8.00	2,000	3,500
9.00	1,000	4,000
10.00	0	4,500

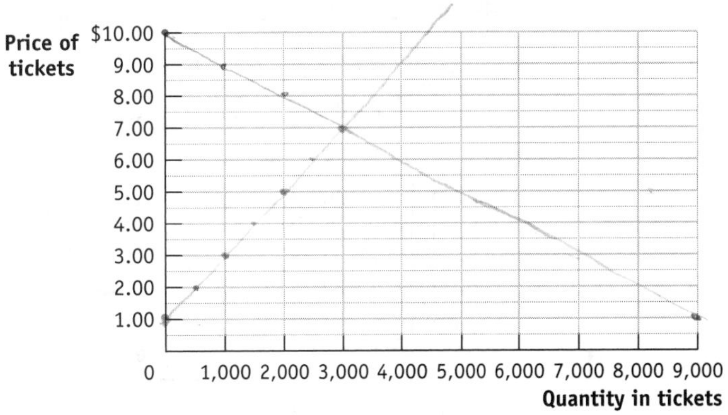

a. The equilibrium price for movie tickets at the Campus Cinema is $ 7.00
and the equilibrium quantity is 3,000 tickets per week.

b. Using the midpoint method, calculate the price elasticity of demand and supply between all prices in the accompanying table. How would you characterize the relative price elasticities of demand and supply around the equilibrium price—inelastic or elastic?

$$e_p^D = \frac{\%\Delta Q_D}{\%\Delta P} = \frac{(Q_2 - Q_1)/(Q_2 + Q_1)/2}{(P_2 - P_1)/(P_2 + P_1)/2} = \frac{(9000 - 8000)/(9000 + 8000)/2}{(2.00 - 1.00)/(2.00 + 1.00)/2} =$$

Price	Demand	Supply	Price elasticity of demand	Price elasticity of supply
$1.00	9,000	0		
2.00	8,000	500		
3.00	7,000	1,000		
4.00	6,000	1,500		
5.00	5,000	2,000		
6.00	4,000	2,500		
7.00	3,000	3,000		
8.00	2,000	3,500		
9.00	1,000	4,000		
10.00	0	4,500		

c. Calculate total revenue along the demand curve for movie tickets in the following table. Copy in your estimates of price elasticity of demand from part b. How do the changes in total revenue compare to the price elasticities of demand?

Price	Demand	Total revenue	Price elasticity of demand
$1.00	9,000		
2.00	8,000		
3.00	7,000		
4.00	6,000		
5.00	5,000		
6.00	4,000		
7.00	3,000		
8.00	2,000		
9.00	1,000		
10.00	0		

d. Redraw the demand curve for movie tickets in the figures below. In the first figure show the price and quantity effect of a decrease in price from $3.00 to $2.00. Do the same in the other figure for a decrease in price from $9.00 to $8.00. Can you explain how these figures relate to the price elasticities of demand?

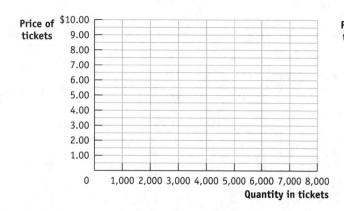

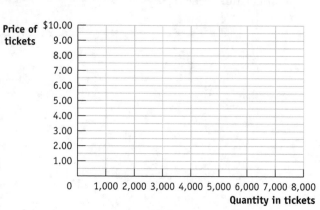

e. If there was an increase in the average income of the patrons of the Campus Cinema from $500 per week to $600 per week and the quantity demanded of tickets each week at a price of $6.00 increased from 4,000 to 5,000 tickets, then the income elasticity of demand for movie tickets would be _____, indicating that movie tickets are a(n) _____ (inferior/normal) good.

f. If there was a decrease in the price of video rentals from $3.00 per rental to $2.00 per rental and quantity demanded of movie tickets fell from 4,000 to 3,500 tickets each week, then the cross-price elasticity of demand for movie tickets would be _____, indicating that movie tickets and video rentals are _____ (substitute, complement, or unrelated) goods.

g. In an effort to both increase revenue and encourage more exercise, the government imposes a tax of $1.50 per movie ticket at the Campus Cinema. Plot the new supply curve on the figure before part a. The new equilibrium price of movie tickets will be $_____ and the new equilibrium quantity will be _____ tickets per week. The government's revenue from the tax will be $_____. Show this area on the graph above. The price to the consumers has risen $_____ per ticket for the new quantity of tickets purchased, so the consumers will be paying $_____ of the tax revenue. The price the producers will receive will be $_____ after the tax or a decrease of $_____ per ticket for the new quantity sold, so the producer will be paying $_____ of the tax revenue. Show the consumers' and producers' burden of the tax graphically above.

5. The following figures show possible demand curves in a market with differing price elasticities. If the government is considering imposing a tax in this market, show the relative burdens for the consumers and the producers of a tax under each of the demand conditions.

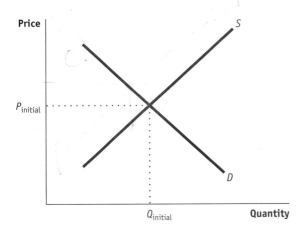

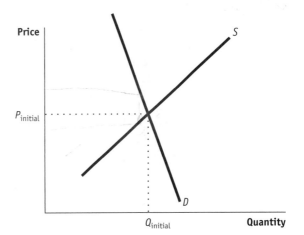

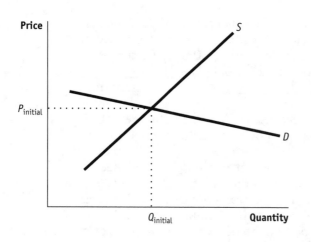

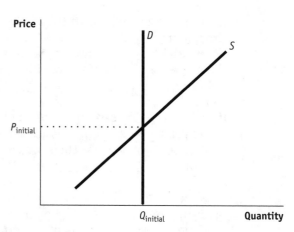

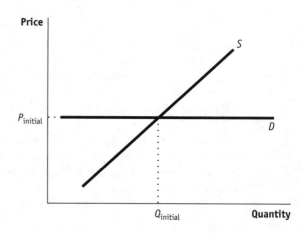

6. Indicate whether each of the following statements is true or false and explain why.
   a. The price elasticity of demand for Ford SUVs will decrease as other car manufacturers decide to make and sell similar SUVs.
   b. Price elasticity of demand of textile products will become more elastic in Canada as the government removes trade barriers to foreign textile products.

7. The Toronto Blue Jays pay all baseball players in U.S. currency. Explain what happens to salary expenses (in terms of the Canadian dollar) when the Canadian dollar becomes stronger relative to the U.S. dollar.

8. Assume that Honda Accord has the following elasticities in Canada.
   Price elasticity of demand of Honda Accord = –0.50
   Income elasticity = +1.5
   If the price of Honda Accord increases by 2%, while income of consumers increases by 4%, what will be the net total percentage change in the quantity demanded of Honda Accord?

*9. The following are the hypothetical demand and supply functions of Atlantic lobsters.
   $Q^D = 220 - 10P$
   In the equation just shown, Q^D is the quantity of lobsters demanded and P is the price of lobsters per kg.
   a. When $P = \$15$, what is total revenue? When $P = \$12$, what is total revenue? In the range just shown, is demand elastic and unit-elastic or inelastic? To increase total revenue, should you increase or decrease price?

b. When $P = \$11$, what is total revenue? Is demand elastic, unit-elastic, or inelastic at that particular point?

c. When $P = \$8$, what is total revenue? To increase total revenue, should you increase or decrease price? At what price, is total revenue maximum?

10. In the following cases, what will be the incidence of an excise tax on consumers and on producers?

a. The demand curve is vertical and supply curve is sloping up.

b. The demand curve is horizontal and the supply curve is vertical.

c. The demand is elastic and the supply is inelastic.

Answers to How Well Do You Understand the Chapter

1. quantity demanded, negatively, decreases, quantity demanded, midpoint method, absolute

2. elastic, greater than, unit-elastic, equal to, inelastic, less than, perfectly price inelastic, perfectly price elastic

3. price, demand, price-elastic, decrease, unit-elastic, increase

4. decreases, elastic, inelastic

5. substitute, time, substitutes, luxuries, changes

6. substitutes, increase, decrease, positive, negative, strength, complements, substitutes, unrelated

7. income, increases, decreases, positive, inferior, income

8. quantity supplied, positive, more than, elastic, less than, inelastic, equal to, unit-elastic, inputs, elastic, inputs

9. elasticities, initial, perfectly price inelastic, less than, equal to

Answers to Multiple-Choice Questions

1. We can measure the price elasticity of demand for subway rides as follows:

$$\text{Price elasticity of demand} = \frac{\% \text{ change in quantity demanded}}{\% \text{ change in price}}$$

$$\text{Price elasticity of demand} = \frac{5\%}{10\%} = 0.5 \qquad \textbf{Answer: B.}$$

2. In this question, we need to calculate the percent change in quantity demanded and the percent change in price for the demand for cones between the prices of $2.50 and $3.00 using the midpoint method. Remember that you will ignore the negative sign in the calculation because price elasticity of demand is always expressed as a number greater than zero. **Answer: D.**

$$\text{Price elasticity of demand} = \frac{\% \text{ change in quantity demanded}}{\% \text{ change in price}}$$

$$= \frac{Q_2 - Q_1/(Q_2 + Q_1)/2}{P_2 - P_1/(P_2 + P_1)/2} = \frac{(600 - 400)/(600 + 400)/2}{(\$2.50 - \$3.00)/(\$2.50 + \$3.00)/2} = 2.2$$

3. At $2.50 per cone, total revenue is $1,500 (= $2.50 × 600) while at $3.00 per cone, total revenue is $1,200 (= $3.00 × 400). **Answer: A.**

4. Since the demand for enrollment is price inelastic, when the board of trustees changes tuition, the price effect will dominate the quantity effect. Therefore, the board should raise tuition, and although enrollment will fall, the increase in tuition per remaining student will more than offset the lower enrollment. **Answer: A.**

5. Since insulin-dependent diabetics will buy insulin at any price, their demand for insulin is completely unresponsive to changes in price. We describe that demand as perfectly price inelastic. **Answer: D.**

6. The demand curve shown is a linear demand curve. Linear demand curves have constant slopes but price elasticity varies along the curve. In particular, the price elasticity of demand is larger at higher prices than at lower prices. Since P_2 is a lower price than P_1, the price elasticity of demand must be smaller at P_2 than at P_1. **Answer: C.**

7. If many close substitutes are available for a good, the quantity demanded for it will be highly responsive to changes in its price. As the price rises, consumers will switch to a substitute good and, as the price falls, they will switch from a substitute good to that good. **Answer: B.**

8. The price elasticity of demand for a necessity is lower than that for a luxury. **Answer: A.**

9. As the time to find substitutes increases, consumers will be able to change quantity demanded more in response to a change in price. **Answer: B.**

10. For most people, Coke and Pepsi are substitute goods. As the price of one rises, demand for the other also rises. The cross-price elasticity of demand is positive. **Answer: B.**

11. As the price of rice rises, quantity demanded of rice will fall. If the quantity demanded of beans also falls as the price of rice rises, then rice and beans must be eaten together and therefore they are complement goods. The cross-price elasticity of demand is negative. **Answer: C.**

12. If there is an increase in the demand for a good when there is an increase in income, then the good is a normal good. The income elasticity of demand for normal goods is positive. **Answer: B.**

13. Since the percent change in quantity demanded for food eaten away from home rises when income rises, the income elasticity of demand is greater than zero and it is defined as a normal good. **Answer: A.**

14. We can use the midpoint method to estimate the price elasticity of supply for ice cream between the prices of $2.50 and $3.00 per cone:

$$\text{Price elasticity of supply} = \frac{\%\text{ change in quantity supplied}}{\%\text{ change in price}}$$

$$= \frac{Q_2 - Q_1/(Q_2 + Q_1)/2}{P_2 - P_1/(P_2 + P_1)/2} = \frac{(1,600 - 1,200)/1,400}{(\$2.50 - \$3.00)/\$2.75} = 1.57 \textbf{ Answer: D.}$$

15. As the firm has more time to change the number of workers and purchase or sell machinery, the more it will be able to change quantity supplied due to a given percent change in price. **Answer: B.**

16. When the government imposes a tax of $0.75, the supply curve shifts up by that amount. The new equilibrium price will be $2.50 per cone and the new equilibrium quantity will be 600 cones. See the following figures.

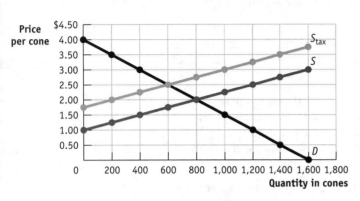
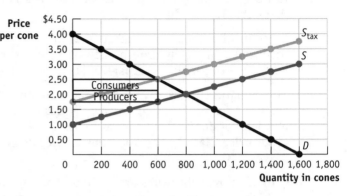

The government's revenue from the tax will be $450 (= $0.75 × 600). The consumers paid $2.00 per cone prior to the tax, so the consumers are paying $0.50 of the tax on the 600 cones or $300. **Answer: B.**

17. The producers' net price is $1.75—compared with the initial price of $2.00. The producers are paying $0.25 of the tax on the 600 cones or $150. **Answer: A.**

18. In the accompanying figure, the demand curve is price inelastic and therefore the consumers will pay all of the tax. **Answer: C.**

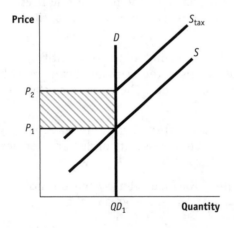

19. The shortage resulting from a price ceiling will be smaller, the smaller the price elasticities of supply and demand. **Answer: B.**

20. The surplus resulting from a price floor will be smaller, the smaller the price elasticities of supply and demand. **Answer: B.**

21. An increase in price increases total revenue, because the negative quantity effect is smaller than the positive price effect. **Answer: C.**

22. When there are simultaneous increases in price (due to imposition of quota) and in total revenue, it means that the demand is inelastic. **Answer: B.**

23. Since both wage rate as well as labour income increased, it is a case of inelastic demand. **Answer: B.**

24. When demand becomes more elastic, the increase in price is less as a result of the excise tax and the burden (incidence) on consumers is less. **Answer: D.**

25. Given the values of price and total revenues, we can calculate the quantities. When $P = 12, $Q = 2,000$; when $P = 18, $Q = 10,000$. With the midpoint method, we get elasticity value as -1.67. The demand is elastic. **Answers: C.**

Answers to Problems and Exercises

1. a. The demand for Coke will have a higher price elasticity than the demand for soft drinks because there are many good substitutes for Coke and far fewer for the soft drink industry. Therefore, the demand for Coke will respond more to a change in price than will the demand for the soft drink industry as a whole.

b. The demand for visits to the baseball stadium will have a higher price elasticity than will the demand for visits to the doctor. Visiting the doctor is a necessity while visiting the baseball stadium is not (you could watch the game on television or listen to it on the radio). Therefore, the demand for visits to the baseball stadium will be more responsive to a change in price than will visits to the doctor.

c. The demand for gasoline consumed each year will have a higher price elasticity of demand than will the demand for it each week. As the price of gasoline rises, it is difficult to substantially reduce the demand for gasoline in a week. It takes time to find ways to conserve gas, such as determine the public transportation schedule, arrange carpools, or buy a more gas-efficient car. However, over the course of a year, you would expect the demand to be more responsive to a change in the price of gasoline.

d. The demand for insulin for a diabetic and dialysis treatment for someone with kidney disease would have similar—and extremely small, if not zero—price elasticities. They are both absolute necessities for the individuals in need of them, so they would have perfectly price inelastic demands.

e. Since water is a necessity for life and diamonds a luxury, the price elasticity of demand for diamonds is much higher than that for water. Also, the price of water tends to be relatively low, so that a large percent change in its price will not radically affect the proportion of income spent on it and quantity demanded will be relatively unresponsive to a change in price. On the other hand, diamonds are so expensive that a small percent change in their price will radically affect the proportion of income spent on them and quantity demanded will be very responsive to a change in price.

2. a. Since videotape rentals and DVD rentals are substitutes, the cross-price elasticity of demand will be positive. Since they are very close substitutes—one can rent almost any movie in either medium—the value of the cross-price elasticity of demand will be high.

b. Refrigerators and electricity are complement goods—you cannot use a refrigerator without electricity—and so the cross-price elasticity of demand is negative. We would expect that the value of the cross-price elasticity is relatively small. A refrigerator is a necessity in today's world, and although as the price of electricity rises we might turn off any extra refrigerators or raise the temperature in the refrigerator so as to not use as much electricity, it is difficult to imagine people abandoning refrigerators.

c. Coke and Pepsi are substitute goods and the cross-price elasticity of demand is positive. As the price of Pepsi rises, people will drink more Coke and vice versa. Some of you may be shocked by this. You may be loyal Coke or Pepsi drinkers and do not see the two goods as substitutes. For you, Coke and Pepsi may be unrelated goods and your cross-price elasticity of demand for the two goods is zero. However, for the market as a whole, they are very close substitutes and the cross-price elasticity of demand will be a large positive number.

d. When microwave ovens were first introduced, some believed that they were an excellent substitute for conventional ovens. Recipes abounded that described how you could bake and roast in a microwave. At that time, you would have predicted a large positive cross-price elasticity of demand. Over time, we realized that microwave ovens, while excellent for quickly heating up and defrosting food, were not substitutes for conventional ovens. The price of microwave ovens has fallen over time, with little, if any, effect on the quantity demanded of conventional ovens. The cross-price elasticity of demand for microwave ovens and conventional ovens is close to zero—they are unrelated goods.

e. Water and diamonds are unrelated goods and the cross-price elasticity of demand is zero. It is hard to imagine anyone increasing or decreasing the quantity demanded of diamonds because of a change in the price of water!

3. a. Fettuccine Alfredo will have a higher income elasticity of demand than macaroni and cheese. Although basically the same—pasta, butter, cream, and cheese—the quality of the ingredients are more expensive for fettuccine Alfredo than for mac'n cheese. As income rises, the quantity demanded of fettuccine Alfredo will also rise and the percent increase may be larger than the percent change in income—the income elasticity of demand for fettuccine Alfredo is definitely positive and may be greater than 1. We usually view macaroni and cheese as an inferior good—as income rises, quantity demanded of macaroni and cheese falls—and the income elasticity of demand will be negative.

b. Public and private higher education are both normal goods but the income elasticity of demand for private education will be higher than that for public education. The major difference between public and private higher education is the cost—the average cost of a private higher education was almost three times that for public education in the academic year 2000–2001. As income changes, we expect there will be a larger percent change in the demand for private education than for public education because the cost of private education is a larger proportion of total income than is public education.

c. The income elasticity of demand for hardcover bestsellers is greater than that for college textbooks. Most people buy college textbooks because they have to—it's a necessary part of taking a college course—and quantity demanded does not respond significantly to change in income. Hardcover bestsellers are usually viewed as a luxury and quantity demanded of them does respond significantly to changes in income.

d. Both the income elasticities of demand for televisions and computers are positive but the income elasticity of demand for computers is higher than that for televisions. It may change in the future, but today televisions are seen as essentials for most families, while computers are still luxuries. In addition, the world of computers changes so rapidly that as income rises, we tend to upgrade the computer to avoid obsolescence. As families experience an increase in income, the percent increase in quantity demanded of computers is greater than the percent increase in quantity demanded of televisions.

e. The income elasticity of demand for water is positive—it's a normal good—but less than the income elasticity of demand for diamonds.

4. The weekly demand and supply curves for movie tickets are shown in the following figure.

Price	Demand	Supply
$1.00	9,000	0
2.00	8,000	500
3.00	7,000	1,000
4.00	6,000	1,500
5.00	5,000	2,000
6.00	4,000	2,500
7.00	3,000	3,000
8.00	2,000	3,500
9.00	1,000	4,000
10.00	0	4,500

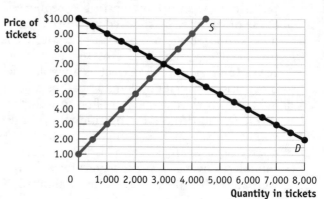

a. The equilibrium price for movie tickets at the Campus Cinema is $\underline{\$7.00}$ and the equilibrium quantity is $\underline{3,000}$ tickets per week. It is where the demand and supply curves intersect.

b. We can calculate the price elasticity of demand between a price of $1.00 and $2.00 per ticket and quantity demanded changes from 9,000 to 8,000 tickets as:

$$\text{Price elasticity of demand} = \frac{\text{\% change in quantity demanded}}{\text{\% change in price}}$$

$$= \frac{Q_2 - Q_1/(Q_2 + Q_1)/2}{P_2 - P_1/(P_2 + P_1)/2}$$

$$= \frac{1,000/(9,000 + 8,000)/2}{1/(1 + 2)/2} = \frac{1,000/8,500}{1/1.5}$$

$$= \frac{0.118}{0.667} = 0.177$$

Similarly, between a price of $1.00 and $2.00 per ticket, quantity supplied increases from 0 to 500 tickets and we can calculate the price elasticity of supply as

$$\text{Price elasticity of demand} = \frac{\text{\% change in quantity demanded}}{\text{\% change in price}}$$

$$= \frac{Q_2 - Q_1/(Q_2 + Q_1)/2}{P_2 - P_1/(P_2 + P_1)/2}$$

$$= \frac{500/(0 + 500)/2}{1/(1 + 2)/2} = \frac{500/250}{1/1.5}$$

$$= \frac{2.00}{0.667} = 3.00$$

Price	Demand	Supply	Price elasticity of demand	Price elasticity of supply
$1.00	9,000	0		
			0.18	3.00
2.00	8,000	500		
			0.33	1.67
3.00	7,000	1,000		
			0.54	1.40
4.00	6,000	1,500		
			0.82	1.29
5.00	5,000	2,000		
			1.22	1.22
6.00	4,000	2,500		
			1.86	1.18
7.00	3,000	3,000		
			3.00	1.15
8.00	2,000	3,500		
			5.67	1.13
9.00	1,000	4,000		
			19.00	1.12
10.00	0	4,500		

c. Total revenue is shown in the accompanying table. In that table, while the elasticity of demand is less than 1, we see that as the price goes up, total revenue also rises—the price effect dominates the sales effect in determining how total revenue changes with a change in price. For example, as the price rises from $2.00 to $3.00, the price elasticity of demand is 0.33 and total revenue rises from $16,000 to $21,000. However, as the price continues to go up and the price elasticity of demand becomes greater than 1, total revenue falls—the sales effect dominates the price effect and total revenue moves in the same direction as quantity. As the price rises from $8.00 to $9.00, the price elasticity of demand is 5.67 and total revenue falls from $16,000 to $9,000.

Price	Demand	Total revenue	Price elasticity of demand
$1.00	9,000		
		$9,000	0.18
2.00	8,000		
		16,000	0.33
3.00	7,000		
		21,000	0.54
4.00	6,000		
		24,000	0.82
5.00	5,000		
		25,000	1.22
6.00	4,000		
		24,000	1.86
7.00	3,000		
		21,000	3.00
8.00	2,000		
		16,000	5.67
9.00	1,000		
		9,000	19.00
10.00	0		

d. The following figures show the effects of a decrease in price from $3.00 to $2.00 and from $9.00 to $8.00. In the first figure, the price elasticity of demand between a price of $3.00 and a price of $2.00 is less than 1 and the quantity effect (A) is smaller than the price effect (C). Total revenue falls as price falls. In the second figure, the price elasticity of demand is greater than 1 and the quantity effect (A) is larger than the price effect (C). Total revenue rises with a decrease in price.

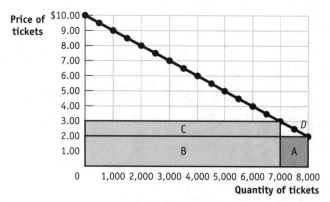

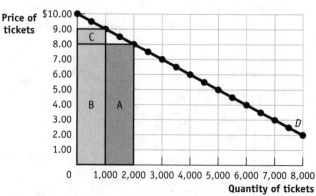

e. If there was a 20% increase in the income of the patrons of the Campus Cinema and the quantity demanded of tickets each week at a price of $6.00 increased from 4,000 to 5,000 tickets, then the income elasticity of demand for movie tickets would be <u>1.22</u>, indicating that movie tickets are a(n) <u>normal</u> good.

$$\text{Income elasticity of demand} = \frac{\text{\% change in quantity demanded}}{\text{\% change in income}}$$

$$= \frac{Q_2 - Q_1/(Q_2 + Q_1)/2}{(\text{Income}_2 - \text{Income}_1)/(\text{Income}_2 + \text{Income}_1)/2}$$

$$= \frac{1{,}000/(5{,}000 + 4{,}000)/2}{100/(600 + 500)/2} = \frac{0.22}{0.18}$$

$$= 1.22 > 0 = > \text{Normal good}$$

f. If there was a decrease in the price of video rentals from $3.00 per rental to $2.00 and quantity demanded of movie tickets fell from 4,000 to 3,500 tickets each week, then the cross-price elasticity of demand for movie tickets and video rentals would be <u>0.333</u>, indicating that movie tickets and video rentals are <u>substitute</u> goods.

$$\text{Cross-price elasticity of demand} = \frac{\text{\% change in quantity demanded of movie tickets}}{\text{\% change in the price of video rentals}}$$

$$= \frac{Q_{MT2} - Q_{MT1}/(Q_{MT2} + Q_{MT1})/2}{(P_{VR2} - P_{VR1})/(P_{VR2} + P_{VR1})/2}$$

$$= \frac{-500/(4{,}000 + 3{,}500)/2}{-1/(3 + 2)/2} = \frac{-0.133}{-0.400}$$

$$= 0.333 > 0 = > \text{Movie tickets and video rentals are substitute goods.}$$

Note: Remember that in this case the sign of the elasticity matters and we cannot ignore it. A positive value means the goods are substitutes; a negative value means the goods are complements.

g. If the government imposes a tax of $1.50 per movie ticket at the Campus Cinema, the accompanying figure shows the new supply curve.

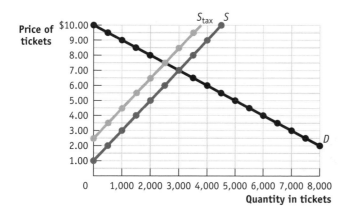

The new equilibrium price of movie tickets will be <u>$7.50</u> and the new equilibrium quantity will be <u>2,500</u> tickets per week. This is where the supply curve with the tax intersects the original demand curve. The government's revenue from the tax will be <u>$3,750</u>—the government will receive $1.50 on each of the 2,500 tickets sold. This is the shaded rectangle in the following figure.

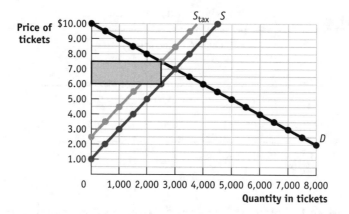

The price to the consumers has risen $0.50 per ticket—from $7.00 to $7.50—for the new quantity of tickets purchased (2,500 tickets), so the consumers will be paying $1,250 of the tax. The price the producers will receive will be $6.00 after the tax—the new price $7.50 less the $1.50 tax—or a decrease of $1.00 per ticket for the new quantity sold, so the producer will be paying $2,500 of the tax. The consumers' and producers' burden of the tax are shown in the following figure.

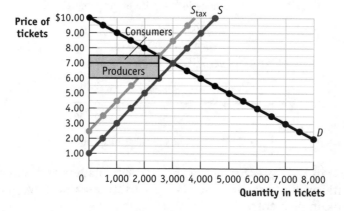

5. In each of these graphs, the supply curve is the same but the demand curve changes. The accompanying figure shows a market where the price elasticities of supply and demand are approximately equal at equilibrium. In this case the consumers and the producers bear equal burdens from the tax.

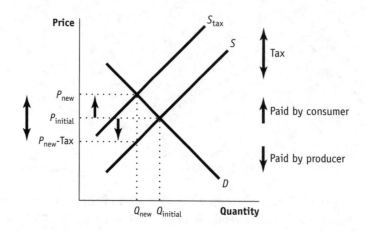

The following figures differ in that the price elasticity of demand is less elastic than that of supply in the first panel and it is the price elasticity of supply that is less elastic in the second panel. Here we see that both the consumers and the producers pay some portion of the tax, but it is the group with the less price elastic curve that pays more of the tax.

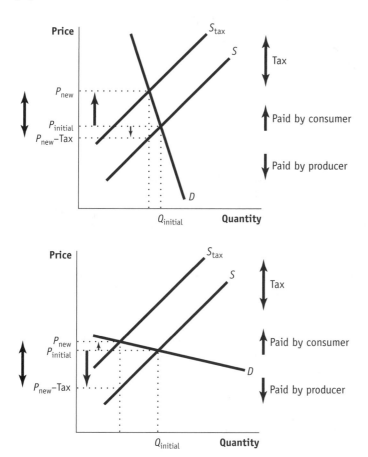

The following figures show perfectly price inelastic and perfectly price elastic demand curves. In these cases, the burden of the tax is not shared but is borne by only one group. In the first panel where the demand curve is perfectly price inelastic, the price rises by the full amount of the tax and the consumers pay all of the tax. In the second panel where the demand curve is perfectly price elastic, the price is unaffected by the tax and the producers pay all of the tax.

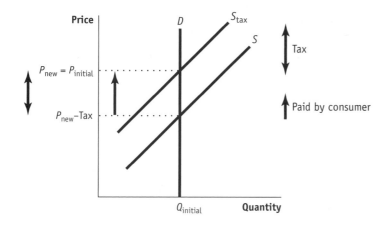

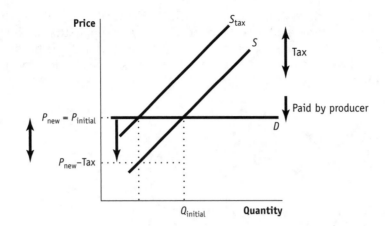

6. a. False. When other car manufacturers produce and sell similar SUVs, there are more substitutes in the market. More substitutes mean more elastic demand.

   b. True. Removal of trade barriers means more foreign textile products and more substitutes competing against Canadian products. Therefore, demand will become more elastic.

7. All Toronto Blue Jays players are paid in U.S. dollars. Since the Canadian dollar is stronger, the Toronto Blue Jays are spending fewer Canadian dollars for a given fixed quantity of U.S. dollars.

8. Since price elasticity is –0.5, we can see that 2% increase in price will bring down quantity demanded by 1%. Since income elasticity is 1.5, we can see that a 4% increase in price will increase quantity demanded by 6%. Therefore, the net percentage increase in quantity demanded is 5%.

9. a. When $P = \$15$, $Q = 70$, and $TR = \$1{,}050$.
   When $P = \$12$, $Q = 100$, and $TR = \$1{,}200$
   Elastic.
   Reduce price.

   b. When $P = \$11$, $Q = 110$, and $TR = \$1{,}210$
   Unit-elastic.

   c. When $P = \$8$, $Q = 140$, and $TR = \$1{,}120$
   Increase price.
   $P = \$11$

10. a. The burden (incidence) of the excise tax is solely on consumers with none on producers, because the price increases by the amount of the tax.

   b. The burden (incidence) of the excise tax is solely on producers with none on consumers, because the price stays the same after the tax.

   c. The burden (incidence) of the excise tax is relatively less on consumers and relatively more on producers.

chapter 6

Consumer and Producer Surplus

This chapter provides a detailed analysis of consumer surplus and producer surplus. To understand consumer surplus, we need to see that an individual's demand curve reflects his or her willingness to pay for a given amount of a good. We assume that an individual will be willing to pay less and less for an additional quantity of a given good. Consumer surplus is the difference between what a buyer is willing to pay and what he or she actually pays. To understand producer surplus, we need to see that an up-sloping supply curve represents the producers' supply price, which in turn represents their costs. Producer surplus is the difference between what producers receive for quantities sold and what it costs at various quantities of output. Generally, an unregulated free market brings an equilibrium outcome where quantity demanded is equal to quantity supplied at the market clearing price. This equilibrium is considered an efficient outcome because it maximizes the combined consumer and producer surplus. This chapter explains why there is a loss of surplus if we are not at the efficient point and why gains in trade exist. We also measure the deadweight loss of an excise tax as the loss of surplus.

How Well Do You Understand the Chapter?

Fill in the blanks using the terms below to complete the following statements. Terms may be used more than once. If you find yourself having difficulties, please refer back to the appropriate section in the text.

above	*deadweight loss*	*larger*	*sum*
below	*decrease(s)*	*lowest*	*surplus*
beneficial	*efficient*	*market(s)*	*total*
best	*enough*	*market failure*	*total surplus*
better	*excise tax*	*minimum*	*triangle*
cannot	*externality*	*price*	*under*
consumer(s)	*gains*	*price elasticities*	*willingness to pay*
consumer surplus	*government*	*producer*	*worse off*
costs	*increase(s)*	*producer surplus(es)*	

1. We can view a demand curve as the _____ curve of each potential consumer. Each consumer will benefit if the _____ is less than his or her willingness to pay. We measure that benefit (the individual consumer surplus) by the difference between the consumer's _____ and the market price. Total consumer surplus is just the _____ of the individual consumer surpluses, and we measure it graphically as the area _____ the demand curve and _____ the market price. The term _____ refers to both individual and to total consumer surplus.

2. A(n) _____ in price increases consumer surplus via two channels: a gain to consumers who would have bought at the original price and a gain to consumers who are persuaded to buy by the lower price. A(n) _____ _____ in the price of a good reduces consumer surplus in a similar fashion.

3. There is a similar distinction between a firm's individual producer surplus and total producer surplus. An individual firm benefits from selling a good in a(n) _____ as long as it can cover their _____. The cost of each potential producer is the _____ price at which he or she is willing to supply a unit of that good. The difference between the price received and the seller's costs is its _____. Total producer surplus is just the sum of all individual _____. We can measure total producer surplus as the area _____ the supply curve and below the market _____.

4. When the price of a good _____, producer surplus increases through two channels: the gains of those who would have supplied the good in the original, lower price and the gains of those who are induced to supply the good by the higher price. A(n) _____ in the price of a good similarly leads to a fall in producer surplus. The term _____ is often used to refer to both the individual and to the total producer surplus.

5. Markets make everyone _____ off, and we can measure this by the total _____ in a market (the total net gain to society from the production and consumption of a good). The _____ surplus represents the _____ from trade. Some markets are efficient and maximize _____. Any possible rearrangement of consumption or sales, or a change in the quantity bought and sold, _____ total surplus. Another way to look at the efficiency of markets is to say that we _____ make anyone better off without making someone else _____.

6. If we try to reallocate equilibrium output in a market among consumers, consumer surplus will _____. The market allocates the good to those consumers who have the highest _____. If we try reallocating equilibrium output in a market among sellers, _____ will fall. The market allocates the right to sell the good to the producers with the _____ cost.

7. In perfectly competitive markets, the market equilibrium is the _____ outcome for every individual consumer and producer. It maximizes _____ and _____ surplus. However, sometimes _____ occurs when markets fail to be efficient. Markets may fail to be efficient in a sense that there may not be _____ buyers and/or sellers in a market, and therefore either one or more buyers or sellers can influence the market _____. Also, it is possible that the actions of buyers and/or sellers affect others (this is called a(n) _____), and the market equilibrium

may not maximize consumer and producer surplus. Finally, it may be that some goods, by their very nature, are unsuited for efficient management by

_____.

8. In Chapter 5, we saw that both producers and consumers bear the burden of a(n) _____ and that the relative burden depends on the _____ of the supply and demand curves. We also saw that there was an excess burden or _____ of a tax because some mutually _____ transactions did not take place. The deadweight loss can be measured as a loss of both consumer surplus and _____ _____ surplus. Some of the loss of the total surplus becomes revenue to the _____. The difference between the loss of _____ and the tax revenue is the excess burden or _____ of the tax. We measure it graphically as the _____ representing the potential surplus of the mutually beneficial transactions that did not take place. The larger the elasticity of demand or elasticity of supply, the _____ is the deadweight loss of the tax.

Learning Tips

TIP #1: You can only measure consumer surplus as the triangle under the demand curve and above the market price if there are a large number of buyers. You can only measure producer surplus as the triangle above the supply curve and under the market price if there are a large number of sellers.

If you only have a few buyers or a few sellers, as in Figure 6.1 (Figures 6-2 and 6-7 in the text), you must calculate each individual's surplus and then add them together to get the market consumer or producer surplus. Each individual's consumer surplus is measured as the difference between that individual's willingness to pay and the market price. Each individual's producer surplus is measured as the difference between the market price and the individual's cost.

Figure 6.1

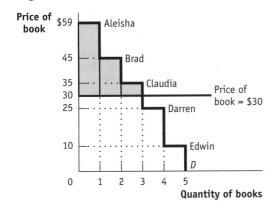
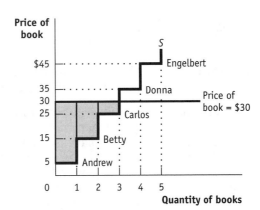

Question: Consider Figure 6.1. Assume that the price of each book is $30, the total consumer surplus is

A) $59.
B) $49.
C) $45.
D) $30.

TIP #2: Producer and consumer surplus changes when the price of a good changes.

As the price of a good rises, quantity demanded will fall. Since consumers buy fewer goods at higher prices, and on those goods there is a smaller difference between willingness to pay and the market price, consumer surplus must decline. The reverse is true for a decrease in price.

As the price of a good rises, quantity supplied will rise. Since producers supply more goods at higher prices, and on those goods and the others that had been supplied there is a larger difference between market price and cost, producer surplus must increase. The reverse is true for a decrease in price.

TIP #3: The combined loss in consumer and producer surplus exceeds the revenue to the government when the government imposes a tax in the market.

Since fewer units of the good are exchanged, the consumer and producer surplus earned on those units no longer sold is lost to everyone. In Figures 6.2 and 6.3, consumer surplus is shown as triangle A, producer surplus as triangle B; rectangle C represents the government's revenue and triangle F is the total loss (deadweight loss) in producer and consumer surplus because of the tax.

Figure 6.2

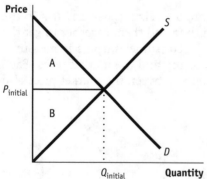

Figure 6.3

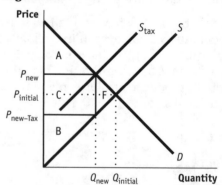

TIP #4: The excess burden or deadweight loss of a tax will be greater the larger the price elasticities of demand and supply.

The excess burden or deadweight loss of the tax comes about because of the loss of total surplus that results when transactions that are mutually beneficial to consumers and producers do not take place. A tax will discourage a larger number of transactions when the demand and supply curves are relatively price elastic. Compare Figures 6.4 and 6.5. In Figure 6.4, the demand and supply curves are relatively price inelastic when compared with Figure 6.5. If the government imposes the same per-unit tax in both markets, the loss of consumer and producer surplus will be much larger in Figure 6.5 than in Figure 6.4. This is because when the supply and demand curves are relatively price elastic, the tax will discourage more transactions than when the curves are relatively price inelastic. (The more elastic curves indicate that the consumers and producers are more responsive to changes in prices.)

Figure 6.4

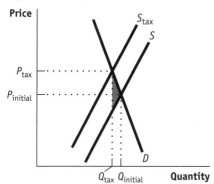

Figure 6.5

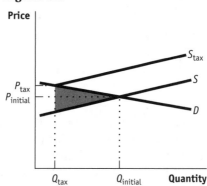

Multiple-Choice Questions

1. The demand curve shows
   a. the maximum amount consumers are willing to pay for particular units of a good.
   b. the minimum amount consumers are willing to pay for particular units of a good.
   c. the average amount consumers are willing to pay for particular units of a good.
   d. that consumers want to pay the lowest price possible.

Answer the next three questions based on the following demand schedule and curve for six buyers of tickets to a dress rehearsal of a new play at the local college.

Potential buyer	Willingness to pay
A	$10
B	9
C	7
D	6
E	5
F	2

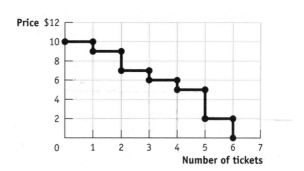

2. If the price of a ticket to the dress rehearsal is $6, how many tickets will be sold?
   a. 1
   b. 3
   c. 4
   d. 5

3. At a price of $5 per ticket, total consumer surplus would equal
   a. $2.
   b. $4.
   c. $12.
   d. $24.

4. If the college imposed a price ceiling of $2 for the dress rehearsal, the number of tickets sold would be _____ and consumer surplus would equal
_____.
   a. 4; $5
   b. 5; $15
   c. 5; $6
   d. 6; $27

5. When the quantities we are dealing with are relatively large, we can identify total consumer surplus on a graph as the
   a. area above the demand curve and below the price.
   b. area above the demand curve and above the price.
   c. area below the demand curve and below the price.
   d. area below the demand curve and above the price.

6. As the price of a good increases, consumer surplus
   a. increases.
   b. decreases.
   c. stays the same.
   d. may increase, decrease, or stay the same.

7. As the price in a market falls,
   a. consumer surplus decreases because some consumers leave the market, reducing consumer surplus.
   b. consumer surplus decreases because the consumers who remain in the market receive a lower consumer surplus.
   c. consumer surplus increases because consumers who would have bought the good at the higher price earn more consumer surplus, and new consumers enter the market who also earn consumer surplus.
   d. consumer surplus may increase, decrease, or stay the same.

8. If the demand curve is perfectly price elastic,
   a. consumer surplus will equal zero.
   b. consumer surplus will equal producer surplus.
   c. consumer surplus will equal total surplus.
   d. consumer surplus will be greater than producer surplus.

9. After waiting in line for three hours to buy two $50 tickets for a concert, someone offered Agnes $160 for her two tickets. Agnes refused even though she knew that comparable seats were still available for $50 per ticket if she waited in line again for three hours. We know that the opportunity cost of Agnes's time is
   a. greater than or equal to $60 per hour.
   b. less than or equal to $60 per hour.
   c. greater than or equal to $20 per hour.
   d. less than or equal to $20 per hour.

10. We measure total producer surplus as the
   a. area above the supply curve and below the price.
   b. area above the supply curve and above the price.
   c. area below the supply curve and below the price.
   d. area below the supply curve and above the price.

11. As the price of oranges rises, the producer surplus in the orange market
   a. increases.
   b. decreases.
   c. does not change.
   d. may increase, decrease, or stay the same.

12. Economists say markets are efficient when
   a. opportunity costs are minimized.
   b. total revenue is maximized.
   c. total surplus is maximized.
   d. it is possible to make someone better off while making another worse off.

13. If the free-market equilibrium price of an orange is $0.50, Lucy is willing to buy an orange but Liam is not. If we let Lucy buy the orange but then take it away from her and give it to Liam,
   a. consumer surplus will rise.
   b. consumer surplus will fall.
   c. producer surplus will rise.
   d. producer surplus will fall.

14. Markets may not be efficient if
   a. opportunity costs are present.
   b. only monetary costs are present.
   c. no monetary costs are present.
   d. externalities are present.

15. When the government imposes a price floor above the equilibrium price in a market, consumer surplus _____ and total surplus _____.
   a. may fall; may rise
   b. will fall; will fall
   c. will rise; will rise
   d. may rise; may fall

16. When the government imposes a price floor above the equilibrium price in a market, producer surplus
   a. will rise.
   b. will fall.
   c. will not change.
   d. may rise, fall, or stay the same.

17. If the demand curve for a good is perfectly price inelastic and the government imposes a tax in the market,
   a. there will be no deadweight loss.
   b. the government's tax revenue will equal the loss in producer surplus.
   c. the government's tax revenue will be more than the loss in producer surplus.
   d. the government's tax revenue will be less than the loss in producer surplus.

Use the accompanying figure to answer the next three questions.

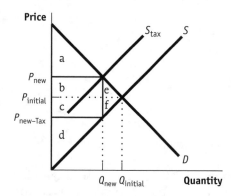

18. Before the government introduces a tax in the market, consumer surplus is represented by
a. areas a, b, and c.
b. areas a, b, and e.
c. areas e and f.
d. areas c, f, and d.

19. After the government introduces a tax in the market, the government's revenue is represented by
a. areas a, b, and c.
b. areas a, b, c, and d.
c. areas e and f.
d. areas b and c.

20. The deadweight loss from the tax is equal to
a. areas a, b, and c.
b. areas a, b, and e.
c. areas e and f.
d. areas b, c, e, and f.

21. Assume that the market demand curve is perfectly price inelastic and the supply curve is up-sloping. When an excise tax is imposed, the deadweight loss will be
a. the maximum positive value.
b. zero.
c. more than zero.
d. less than zero.

Answer questions 22–23 on the basis of the following:

There are 4 consumers willing to pay the following prices for 1-hour of Internet games in an Internet café. Andrew is willing to pay $10, Sarah is willing to pay $8, Rinque is willing to pay $6, and Sholok is willing to pay $4.

22. If the price of the Internet game is $5, the total consumer surplus will be
a. $24.
b. $20.
c. $18.
d. $9.

23. If the price of the Internet game decreases to $3, the total consumer surplus will increase by
   a. $16.
   b. $9
   c. $7.
   d. $2.

*24. When the demand function is $Q^D = 100 - P$ and the supply function is $Q^S = 4P$, the maximum total surplus is gained when the amount bought and sold is
   a. 20.
   b. 40.
   c. 80.
   d. 100.

*25. When the demand function is $Q^D = 100 - P$ and the supply function is $Q^S = 4P$ and the market equilibrium is an efficient outcome, the total surplus will be
   a. $8,000.
   b. $6,400.
   c. $5,200.
   d. $4,000.

Problems and Exercises

Read each question carefully and then write your answers in the space provided or on a separate sheet of paper.

1. There are five signed lithographs of Picasso's *Peace Dove* in excellent condition. Abner, Buddy, Carlos, Dylan, and Edgar currently own them but would be willing to sell if the price were right (higher than their opportunity cost). Lydia, Mira, Nicole, Olivia, and Pia would all like to buy one of those lithographs but each has a different willingness to pay. The accompanying table shows the willingness to pay (maximum price) of the buyers and the opportunity costs (minimum price) of the sellers.

Seller	Minimum price	Buyer	Maximum price
Abner	$1,200	Lydia	$1,000
Buddy	4,500	Mira	5,000
Carlos	3,000	Nicole	2,500
Dylan	2,500	Olivia	1,500
Edgar	2,800	Pia	2,000

a. Draw figures similar to Figures 6-1 and 6-6 in your text showing the willingness to pay for the Picasso lithograph of the buyers and the cost for the lithograph of the sellers.

b. All lithographs sell for the same price. How many lithographs will be bought and sold? What will be the price of the lithographs? Who will sell and who will buy the lithographs?

c. What is the total amount of consumer surplus? producer surplus? total surplus?

d. Show consumer and producer surplus graphically.

e. If there were more interested buyers for lithographs of Picasso's *Peace Dove* and the market price of the lithograph rose to $3,000, calculate the new values of consumer and producer surplus for the above individuals. Why have they changed?

f. If there were more lithographs of Picasso's *Peace Dove* in excellent condition available and the market price of the lithograph fell to $2,000, calculate the new values of consumer and producer surplus for the above individuals. Why have they changed?

2. The following table shows the market demand and supply schedules for cups of coffee at the Campus Coffee Shop. Graph the demand and supply curves and find the equilibrium price and equilibrium output.

Quantity	Supply price	Demand price
0	$0.00	$3.00
1,000	0.50	2.00
2,000	1.00	1.00
3,000	1.50	0.00
4,000	2.00	
5,000	2.50	

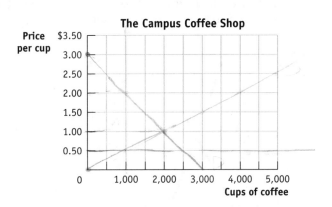

a. At the equilibrium price, graphically show consumer surplus, producer surplus, and total surplus.

CS = A

PS = B

=> Total surplus = A+B

b. If the government imposed a quota on the Campus Coffee Shop such that they could not sell more than 1,000 cups of coffee, what will be the new price and output at the shop? How will the quota affect consumer, producer, and total surplus?

① $2.00/cup

② 1000 cups

TS, PS, CS ↓

c. If the government imposed a $0.50 price ceiling in the market for coffee, what will be the new price and output at the Campus Coffee Shop? How will the price ceiling affect consumer, producer, and total surplus?

P = 0.50 $/cup

Q = 1000 cups

CS, PS, TS ↓

3. The government is considering imposing the same tax in the markets shown in the following figures. Which of the markets will have the largest deadweight loss? Which will have the smallest deadweight loss? Since governments would like to minimize the deadweight loss associated with a tax, can you advise the government as to what types of price elasticities of demand will minimize the deadweight loss?

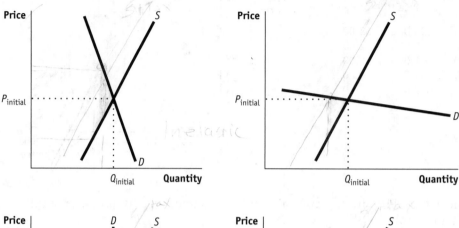

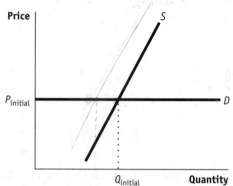

4. In each of the following markets explain what will happen, if you can, to consumer, producer, and total surplus. Show your answers graphically.
a. Bottled Water: A newspaper reports an unhealthy level of bacteria in tap water.

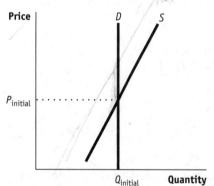

ALL go up

b. Milk: A ban on the use of certain hormones for cows radically lowers the amount of milk each cow produces.

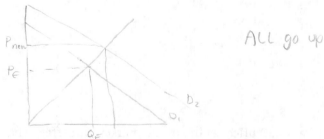

c. Gasoline: The government lowers the excise tax on gasoline products.

5. Consider the following table.

Units of goods	Willingness to pay by Sarah	Willingness to pay by Prima
1	$50	$40
2	$40	$35
3	$30	$30
4	$20	$25
5	$10	$20
6	$ 0	$15
7	$ 0	$10
6	$ 0	$ 5

a. If the price is $14 per unit, how many units of goods will be bought by Sarah and by Prima? What will be the total consumer surplus?

b. If the price goes down to $6, how many units of goods will be bought by Sarah and by Prima? What will be the total consumer surplus?

6. Consider the following schedule of demand and supply of pizza in Hamilton, Ontario.

Price of pizza	Quantity of pizza demanded	Quantity of pizza supplied
$8	1	7
7	2	6
6	3	5
5	4	4
4	5	3
3	6	2
2	7	1

a. Find the equilibrium price, equilibrium quantity, consumer surplus, producer surplus, and total surplus.

b. Hamilton City decided to impose an excise tax of $2 per pizza. Find the equilibrium price, equilibrium quantity, consumer surplus, producer surplus, and total surplus.

*7. Consider the following equations.

$P = 10 - Q$ [Price (P) that consumers are willing to pay for a given quantity (Q)]
$P = Q$ [Price (P) that producers are asking for a given quantity (Q)]

We assume that, in an equilibrium situation, the price that consumers are willing to pay is equal to the asking price of producers.

a. Find the equilibrium P and Q. Find the total surplus.

b. If the excise tax is $4 per unit of output, what will be the total surplus, total tax collections, and deadweight loss?

Answers to How Well Do You Understand the Chapter

1. willingness to pay, price, willingness to pay, sum, under, above, consumer surplus

2. decrease, increase

3. market, costs, minimum, producer surplus, producer surpluses, above, price

4. increases, decrease, producer surplus

5. better, surplus, total, gains, total surplus, decreases, cannot, worse off

6. decrease, willingness to pay, producer surplus, lowest

7. efficient, consumer, producer, market failure, enough, price, externality, markets

8. excise tax, price elasticities, deadweight loss, beneficial, producer, government, total surplus, deadweight loss, triangle, larger

Answers to Multiple-Choice Questions

1. The demand curve reflects the highest amount that consumers are willing to pay for particular units of a good. **Answer: A.**

2. At a price of $6, consumers are only willing to purchase 4 tickets. **Answer: C.**

3. At a price of $5, consumers are willing to purchase 5 tickets. The consumer surplus will equal the sum of $5 (the surplus earned on the first ticket), $4 (the surplus earned on the second ticket), $2 (the surplus earned on the third ticket), and $1 (the surplus earned on the fourth ticket) for a total of $12. There is no consumer surplus earned on the fifth ticket. **Answer: C.**

4. At a price ceiling of $2, the college will sell 6 tickets and the ticket buyers will earn a surplus of $27. Compared with the answer for a price of $5, consumer surplus increases by $3 on each of the original 4 tickets sold and $3 on the fifth ticket sold. **Answer: D.**

5. Consumer surplus is the difference between what consumers are willing to pay for particular units and what they actually pay. We measure this as the area under the demand curve (willingness to pay) and above the market price. **Answer: D.**

6. As the price of a good increases, some consumers leave the market and those who remain earn a lower consumer surplus on each unit that they continue to buy—both lead to a decrease in consumer surplus. **Answer: B.**

7. As the price of a good falls, more consumers enter the market, and those who were already in the market earn a higher consumer surplus on each unit that they continue to buy—both lead to an increase in consumer surplus. **Answer: C.**

8. If the demand curve is perfectly price elastic, consumers are only willing to buy units of the good at one particular price. That price must be the market price. Since there is no difference between the price consumers are willing to pay and the market price, there is no area below the demand curve and above the market price and consumer surplus is zero. The figure below shows the answer graphically. **Answer: A.**

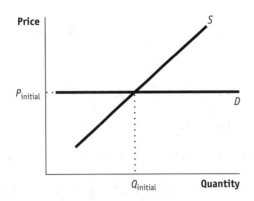

9. Agnes would earn $60 for the three-hour wait to get additional tickets, or $20 per hour. Since she chooses not to sell her tickets, $160 must be equal to or lower than the price of the tickets plus the opportunity cost of her time. Agnes values her time at a rate equal to or greater than $20 per hour. **Answer: C.**

10. Producer surplus measures the difference between the market price of a good and the price at which producers are willing to sell particular units. We measure producer surplus as the area under the market price and above the supply curve. **Answer: A.**

11. As the price of oranges rises, more sellers enter the market and those who were already in the market earn a higher producer surplus—both lead to an increase in producer surplus. **Answer: A.**

12. Markets are efficient when they allocate goods in such a way that no one can be made better off without someone else being made worse off. This is true in equilibrium because the total surplus is maximized. **Answer: C.**

13. Since Lucy is willing to buy an orange at a price of $0.50, that price must reflect at least the value that Lucy attributes to oranges. Since Liam does not buy an orange at a price of $0.50, he values the orange at something less than $0.50. When we take an orange away from Lucy and give it to Liam, consumer surplus must fall. **Answer: B.**

14. Markets may not be efficient if an individual buyer or seller does not take the market price as given (for example, a monopolist) and/or if there are welfare effects influencing individuals other than the market participants (an externality). **Answer: D.**

15. The government imposes a price floor above the market price. As the accompanying figures show, as the price rises, both consumer surplus (triangle A) and total surplus (triangle A plus area with diagonal lines) will fall. **Answer: B.**

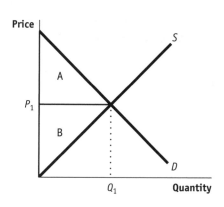
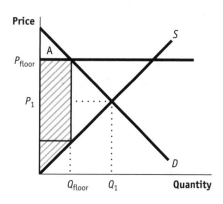

16. The government imposes a price floor above the market price. As the price rises, the number of units sold declines. Producers will earn a larger producer surplus on each unit it sells but they will sell fewer units. Producer surplus may rise, fall, or stay the same. **Answer: D.**

17. The figure below shows that as the government imposes a tax in a market where the demand curve is perfectly price inelastic, there will be no deadweight loss. Triangle B is the producer surplus both before and after the tax and rectangle C is the government's revenue from the tax. **Answer: A.**

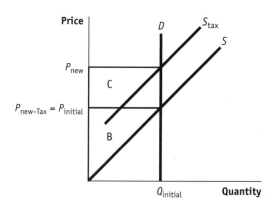

18. Consumer surplus is the area under the demand curve and above the market price. This includes areas a, b, and e. **Answer: B.**

19. The government's revenue is the per-unit tax (= $P_{new} − [P_{new} − Tax]$) times the new quantity exchanged (Q_{new}). This area is represented by areas b and c. **Answer: D.**

20. The deadweight loss is the combined loss of consumer and producer surplus when the government imposes the tax. This is areas e and f. **Answer: C.**

21. With the vertical demand curve, the price increases by the amount of the excise tax. The total loss of surplus is equal to the total tax revenues. Therefore, there is zero deadweight loss. **Answer: B.**

22. $P = \$5$, the consumer surplus for Andrew is $5, for Sarah, $3 and for Rinque, $1. The total consumer surplus is $9. **Answer: D.**

23. When $P = \$3$, the consumer surplus for Andrew is $7, for Sarah, $5, for Rinque, $3, and for Sholok, $1. The total consumer surplus is $16. The increase in consumer surplus is $16 − $9 = $7. **Answer: C.**

24. When $Q^D = Q^S$, the equilibrium P is $20 and the equilibrium Q is 80 units. **Answer: C.**

25. At the equilibrium outcome, the total consumer surplus is $3,200 and the total producer surplus is $800. Therefore, the total surplus is $4,000. **Answer: D.**

Answers to Problems and Exercises

1. a.

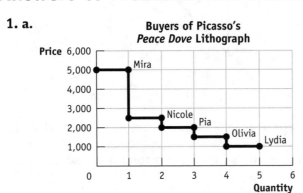

Buyers of Picasso's
***Peace Dove* Lithograph**

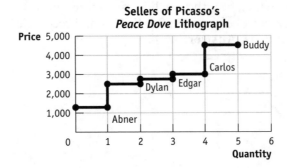

Sellers of Picasso's
***Peace Dove* Lithograph**

b. Abner and Dylan sell their lithographs to Mira and Nicole for $2,500. See the following figure.

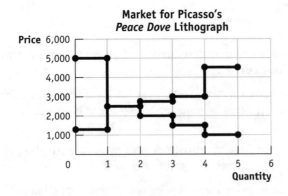

Market for Picasso's
***Peace Dove* Lithograph**

c. Consumer surplus is $2,500: Mira earns $2,500 in consumer surplus (she was willing to pay $5,000 but only pays the market price of $2,500), but Nicole does not earn anything (she was only willing to pay the market price of $2,500). Producer surplus is $1,300: Abner earns $1,300 in producer surplus (his costs were only $1,200 but he received $2,500), but Dylan does not earn any (his costs equaled the market price of $2,500). Total surplus is $3,800.

d.

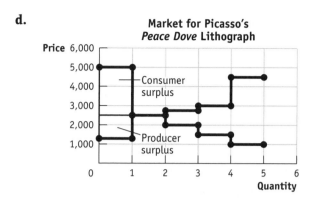

Market for Picasso's
Peace Dove **Lithograph**

e. At a price of $3,000, only Mira (out of our five buyers) would buy the lithograph and she would earn consumer surplus of $2,000. Abner, Dylan, and Carlos would sell their lithographs and they would earn producer surplus of $2,300 ($1,800 for Abner, $500 for Dylan, and nothing for Carlos). As the price rose, consumer surplus fell because Nicole dropped out of the market and Mira earned a smaller consumer surplus, while producer surplus rose because both Abner and Dylan earned a larger producer surplus and Carlos came into the market.

f. At a price of $2,000, Mira, Nicole, and Pia would buy the lithograph and they would earn consumer surplus of $3,500 ($3,000 for Mira, $500 for Nicole, and nothing for Pia). Only Abner would sell the lithograph and he would earn producer surplus of $800. As the price fell, producer surplus fell because Dylan no longer sells his lithograph and Abner receives a smaller producer surplus, while consumer surplus rose because Pia came into the market and both Mira and Nicole earned a larger consumer surplus.

2.

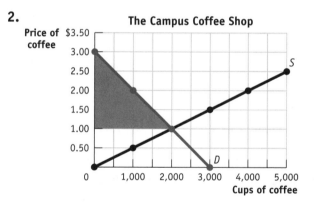

The Campus Coffee Shop

a. The equilibrium price is $1.00 per cup of coffee and the equilibrium output is 2,000 cups of coffee per week. Consumer surplus is the area below the demand curve and above the price—the upper triangle. Producer surplus is the area above the supply curve and under the price—the bottom triangle. Total surplus is the sum of consumer and producer surplus, or the two triangles combined.

b. At a quota of 1,000 cups of coffee, the Campus Coffee Shop will sell the 1,000 cups at $2.00 per cup. Consumer surplus will fall under the quota to the triangle above $2.00 and below the demand curve—the shaded triangle. Consumer surplus will always fall when a quota is imposed.

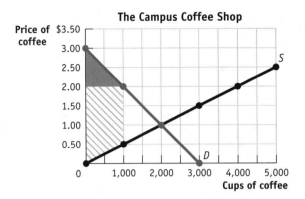

In this situation, producer surplus will increase under the quota to the area under $2 and above the supply curve up to a quantity of 1,000 cups—the area with diagonal lines. However, in general producer surplus may be higher or lower under a quota depending on how the gain in producer surplus on the quantity sold with the quota compares to the loss of producer surplus on the units that were sold initially but not under the quota.

Total surplus in the coffee market is definitely lower compared with the original equilibrium in the market. Total surplus will always decrease when a quota is imposed.

c. With a $0.50 price ceiling, the Campus Coffee Shop will sell 1,000 cups of coffee at $0.50 per cup.

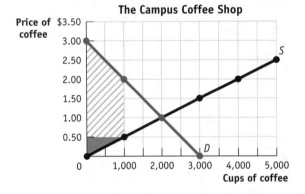

Comparing the market equilibrium with no government intervention with the $0.50 price ceiling, producer surplus will definitely be lower; it is represented by the shaded triangle. If a price ceiling is effective, producer surplus will definitely decrease. Consumer surplus (represented by the area with diagonal lines) appears to be the same with the price ceiling. In this case, it appears that the gain in consumer surplus on the first 1,000 cups equals the loss of consumer surplus on the 1,000 cups not consumed. However, in general, under an effective price ceiling, consumer surplus may increase, decrease, or stay the same. Total surplus is definitely lower compared with the original equilibrium in the coffee market. Total surplus always decreases with a price ceiling.

3. In the graphs below, the supply curve is the same but the demand curve shows differing price elasticities of demand. When the government imposes the same tax in the market, the supply curve shifts up by the same amount in each graph to S_{tax}. In the top two graphs, we see that when the price elasticity of demand is larger (the graph on the right), the deadweight loss due to the tax is larger than it is when the price elasticity of demand is smaller (the graph on the left). In the two bottom graphs, the one on the left shows a perfectly price inelastic demand curve (price elasticity of demand equals 0), while the one on the right shows a perfectly price elastic demand curve (price elasticity of demand is infinite). When the price elasticity of demand is zero, there is no deadweight loss for the tax. As the demand curve has greater elasticity, the deadweight loss gets larger and it is at its largest when the price elasticity of demand is infinite.

We could show a similar relationship between the price elasticity of supply and the deadweight loss if we held the demand curve constant and allowed the price elasticity of supply to vary. When the price elasticity of supply is zero (supply curve is vertical), there will be no deadweight loss, and the deadweight loss will get larger as the price elasticity of supply gets larger (as the supply curve becomes more horizontal).

If the government wants to minimize the deadweight loss from a tax, it should impose a tax in a market where the relative price elasticities of demand and supply are small.

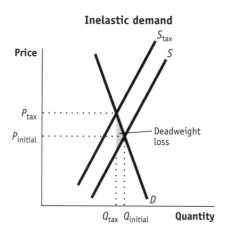

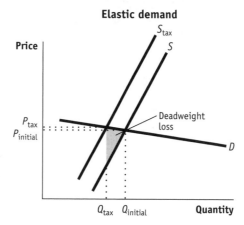

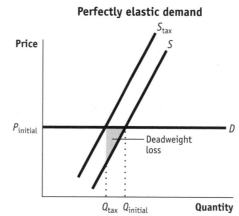

4. a. The demand for bottled water rises, increasing price and quantity. As price and quantity rise, producer surplus definitely rises but we can't say what will happen to consumer surplus. Consumer surplus may rise or fall—price has risen but so has the consumer's willingness to pay. From the graph below, we see that total surplus must rise.

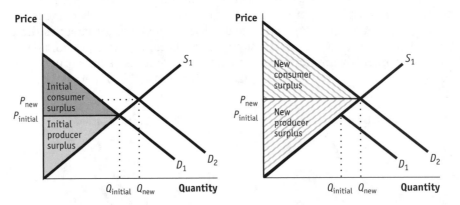

b. The ban on hormones will decrease the supply of milk, increasing price and lowering output. As shown in the graphs below, as price rises, consumer surplus definitely falls (fewer units are purchased and there is a lower surplus on those units consumers still buy). We can't tell what will happen to producer surplus—price has risen but so have costs. Total surplus definitely falls.

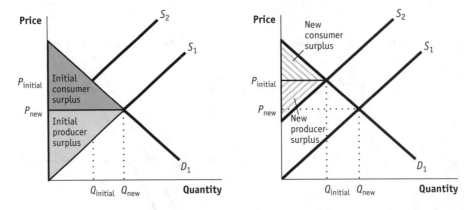

c. As the government lowers the excise tax, the supply of gasoline will increase, lowering price and raising output. As illustrated in the graphs below, consumer surplus will definitely increase—more consumers will enter the market and consumer surplus on the initial units sold will increase. Producer surplus may rise, fall, or stay the same—prices fall but so do costs. Total surplus increases.

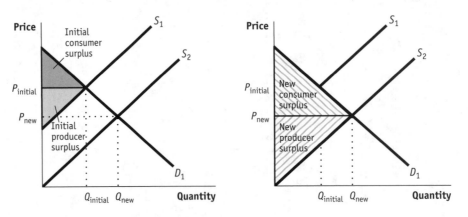

5. a. Sarah buys 4 units. Her total consumer surplus = $36 + $26 + $16 + $6 = $84

Prima buys 6 units. Her total consumer surplus = $26 + $21 + $16 + $11 + $6 + $1 = $81

Total surplus = $84 + $81 = $165

b. Sarah buys 5 units. Her total consumer surplus = $44 + $34 + $24 + $14 + $4 = $120

Prima buys 7 units. Her total consumer surplus = $34 + $29 + $24 + $19 + $14 + $9 + $4 = $133

Total surplus = $253

6. a. $P = \$5$, $Q = 4$, consumer surplus = $6, producer surplus = $6, and total surplus = $12

b. $P = \$6$, $Q = 3$, consumer surplus = $3, producer surplus = $3, and total surplus = $6

7. a. $Q = 5$, $P = \$5$, and total surplus = ($12.50 + $12.50) = $25. At the market equilibrium, the supply-price is equal to the demand-price; using this condition, we can solve equilibrium output, where quantity demanded is equal to quantity supplied. From $Q = 10 - Q$, we can solve $Q = 5$ and $P = \$5$.

b. $Q = 3$, $P = \$7$, total surplus = ($4.50 + $4.50) = $9, total tax collections = $12, and deadweight loss = $4. With tax, the after-tax supply-price is $4 + Q$. Set the new supply-price equal to the demand price and solve new Q. $Q + 4 = 10 - Q$. Therefore, $Q = 3$ and the after-tax $P = \$7$. The total tax revenue = $(3(\$4)) = \$12$. To find the deadweight loss, we need to find out pre-tax total surplus and after-tax total surplus. At the initial equilibrium, the consumer surplus = $[(\$5(5))/2]$ = $12.5 and producer surplus = $[(\$5(5))/2] = \$12.5$. Therefore, the total surplus is $25. After the tax, the consumer surplus = $[(\$3(3))/2] = \$4.5$ and producer surplus = $[(\$3(3))/2] = \$4.5$.

Therefore, the total surplus is $9.

The loss of total surplus = $25 − $9 = $16.

The deadweight loss = Loss of total surplus − tax revenue = $16 − $12 = $4.

## chapter 7

Making Decisions

This chapter surveys the principles involved in making economic decisions by individuals and firms. In making economic decisions, we need to look at the opportunity costs (the real or true costs), which are different from simple monetary or accounting costs. We need to understand the difference between explicit cost and implicit cost. It is important that we know the difference between accounting profit and economic profit so we can see why economic profit is the appropriate basis for economic decisions. Marginal analysis involving marginal cost and marginal benefit is highlighted to show how optimal quantity of output can be determined. We need to know the meaning of sunk costs and see why sunk costs are ignored when we make economic decisions in an incremental (marginal) sense. The present value concepts are analyzed for making decisions that involve costs and benefits over time.

How Well Do You Understand the Chapter?

Fill in the blanks using the terms below to complete the following statements. Terms may be used more than once. If you find yourself having difficulties, please refer back to the appropriate section in the text.

alternative	future	marginal	principle
benefits	highest	marginal benefit	reduction
decreasing	ignored	marginal cost	sell
difference	implicit	more than	time
different	increasing	non-recoverable	times
economic	interest rate	opportunity	total revenue
equal to	intersects	optimal	upward-sloping
explicit	less than	present value	

1. The true cost of anything is its _opportunity_ cost (what you have to give up to get something), and it is often more than the simple monetary cost. The monetary costs are _explicit_ costs, but there may be costs that do not require any outlay of money. These costs, implicit costs, are measured by the value of the _benifits_ that are forgone. For example, the explicit costs of an additional year of college and tuition, cost of books and supplies, and so forth; the _implicit_ cost is what you could have earned by taking a job for the year instead of studying. The sum of explicit and implicit costs is called the _economic_ cost. Often, people underestimate their costs because they ignore _implicit_ costs.

2. Firms are concerned with making a profit, but we can distinguish between two types of profits: accounting and _economic_ profits. An accounting profit is the difference between total _revenue_ and total explicit costs; it does not take into consideration implicit costs. It does include depreciation, which reflects the _reduction_ in the value of the machines that the firm owns due to wear and tear. An economic profit is the _difference_ between total revenue and all costs, both explicit and implicit. An important component of a firm's implicit costs is the implicit cost of capital, which is the value of its assets, such as equipment, buildings, tools, inventory, and financial assets. Even if a firm owns its own machinery, there is a(n) _implicit_ cost for using it. If the firm owns the machinery but didn't produce, it could either lease the machinery to other firms or _sell_ it and then invest the proceeds in another moneymaking venture. The implicit cost of capital is the cost of the capital used by a business. It is also important to consider the opportunity cost of the owner's _time_ as an implicit cost.

3. When making decisions about "how much" to work, "how much" to produce or "how much to buy," we use an approach known as _marginal_ analysis. When we take on an activity, we expect to benefit from it but recognize that there is a(n) _opportunity_ cost associated with it. The _marginal benefit_ is the benefit associated with doing a little bit more; the _m. cost_ is the cost associated with doing a little bit more. Although marginal cost may be constant, it typically is not. It is more typical that when we do 1 more unit of an activity, the marginal cost associated with the additional unit may be _increasing_. The marginal cost curve is graphically represented as _upward sloping_. The _m. benefit_ curve represents the marginal benefit of an activity. The downward-sloping marginal benefit curve reflects a(n) _decreasing_ marginal benefit, which occurs when each additional unit of the activity produces less marginal benefit than did the previous unit.

4. As long as the marginal benefit is _above_ the marginal cost, we should take on an additional unit of that activity; an additional unit adds more to benefit than to cost. However, if the marginal cost is _below_ the marginal benefit, we would be better off doing a little bit less; an additional unit adds more to cost than to benefit. When the marginal benefit is _equal_ the marginal cost, we have generated the maximum amount of total gain from the activity; it is the _optimal_ quantity of an activity. At the optimal quantity, the marginal cost curve _intersects_ the marginal benefit curve.

5. We should not consider sunk costs, costs that are _lost_ when applying the principle of marginal analysis. Since a sunk cost occurred in the past, it does not affect the cost associated with doing a little bit more of an activity and therefore should be _ignored_ in decisions about future actions.

6. When someone borrows money for a year, the ___*interest*___ is the price, calculated as a percentage of the amount borrowed, charged by the lender. In addition, the interest rate can be used to convert future benefits and costs into what economists call ___*present value*___.

7. When we have to make decisions that involve future costs and benefits, we need to compare the present value of the costs with the _____ of the benefits. Time is money; a dollar today is worth _____ a dollar a year from now. If you have a dollar today, you could lend it to someone for a time who will give you _____ a dollar back. In the same way, if you expected to receive $1 in the future, it would only be worth something _____ $1 to you today. Based on that $1 in the future, you could only borrow something _____ $1 to you today. In particular, the present value of $1 to be received one year from now is _____ $1/(1 + r) and the present value of $1 to be received n years from now is equal to $1/(1 + r)^n$.

8. By using present value, you can compare the cost and benefit of any activity received at a(n) _____ time. The net present value of an activity equals the present value of future benefits less the _____ of future costs of the activity. When choosing among activities, you would choose the activity that has the _____ net present value.

Learning Tips

TIP #1: Economic profit is the difference between total revenue and total costs. Total costs include opportunity costs, which can be explicit or implicit costs. The accounting profit is different than the economic profit. It is possible to have a positive accounting profit and, at the same time, a negative economic profit. If the firm is earning zero economic profit, it means that the firm is earning enough to be content with.

Question: Sholok, who has an undergraduate degree in Economics, is running a small dry-cleaning business that provides him with total revenue of $100,000 a year. His operating expenses are $40,000 a year. He could have earned $40,000 a year, if he worked in an economic consulting firm. Based on this information, which of the following statements is **false**?

A) His accounting profit is $60,000.
B) His economic profit is $20,000.
C) He should not continue this business, because his economic profit is less than what he could have earned in the consulting firm.
D) His income tax is based on his accounting profit of $60,000.

Answer: C.

TIP #2: Remember that total benefits may be increasing even when marginal benefits are diminishing; total benefits will decrease only when marginal benefits are negative.

Marginal benefit is the additional benefit derived from taking on one more unit of an activity. If the additional benefit (marginal benefit) is positive, that means that the additional unit is adding to total benefit—that is, total benefit must be rising. However, it is possible that so much of an activity is undertaken that the marginal benefit actually lowers total benefit. In this case, the marginal benefit must be negative. No one will pursue an activity to the point at which marginal benefit is negative. According to the principle of marginal analysis, an individual or firm will pursue an activity up until the point at which marginal benefit equals marginal cost.

Tip #3: Sunk costs influence only the "either-or" decision but not the "how much" decision.

When you are trying to decide whether to take on a project or activity (the "either-or" decision), you look at the present value of all costs and benefits and decide whether to undertake the project or activity based on a higher net present value. Once you've undertaken the project and paid the sunk cost, you make the "how much" decision by comparing marginal costs with marginal benefits. At that point, you ignore sunk costs. If marginal benefit exceeds marginal cost, you should undertake an additional unit of activity; if marginal cost exceeds marginal benefit, you should reduce your activity by one unit. The optimal amount of an activity will occur when the marginal benefit of the last unit of activity equals the marginal cost of that unit.

Tip #4: When choosing among projects based on net present value, the level of interest rates will influence which project will have the highest net present value.

One project may be preferred at a low interest rate and another at a high interest rate. It is also possible that we will be indifferent between two projects at a particular interest rate. Let's assume that you are trying to choose between two projects and the costs and benefits of the projects will occur over the next five years, as shown in the Table 7.1.

Table 7.1

	Project A	Project B
Dollars realized today	−$90,000.00	−$90,000.00
Dollars realized one year from now	25,000.00	5,000.00
Dollars realized two years from now	25,000.00	15,000.00
Dollars realized three years from now	25,000.00	35,000.00
Dollars realized four years from now	25,000.00	35,000.00
Dollars realized five years from now	25,000.00	52,766.35

If you calculate the net present value of the two projects at annual interest rates of 3% to 10%, you will see that at low interest rates you will prefer Project B, and at high interest rates you will prefer Project A. Figure 7.1 shows the net present values of the two projects at annual interest rates from 3% to 10%. The figure also shows that at an interest rate of 7%, we are indifferent between the two.

Figure 7.1

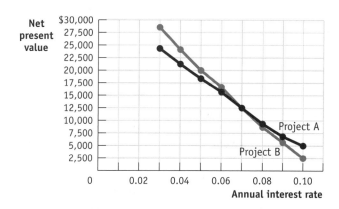

We prefer Project B to Project A at low interest rates because Project B yields larger benefits in later years. At lower interest rates, these larger benefits become higher present values. However, as interest rates rise, the present values of these larger and later benefits result in smaller present values.

Multiple-Choice Questions

1. One reason that there is so little agricultural land left in Ontario is that
   a. the government is reclaiming the land for urban development.
   b. the land has been contaminated by pesticides.
   c. there is a large implicit cost of capital in not selling agricultural land to real estate developers.
   d. all of the above.

Answer the next four questions based on the following information:

Juan Gonzalez saved $50,000 to start the J.G. Home Remodeling Company. He quit a job that paid $60,000 per year, rented a furnished showroom for $15,000 for the year, purchased $50,000 in capital equipment (an amount that could have earned an annual rate of interest of 5%), and incurred costs of $25,000 for secretarial help and advertising. In his first year, his revenue was approximately $100,000.

2. The accounting profit of the J.G. Home Remodeling Company is
   a. $100,000.
   b. $60,000.
   c. $40,000.
   d. $0.

3. The implicit cost of capital for the J.G. Home Remodeling Company is
   a. $0.
   b. $2,500.
   c. $5,000.
   d. $50,000.

4. What are the implicit costs of the J.G. Home Remodeling Company?
   a. $5,000.
   b. $25,000.
   c. $60,000.
   d. $62,500.

5. The economic profit of the J.G. Home Remodeling Company is
   a. $60,000.
   b. $40,000.
   c. $0.
   d. -$2,500.

6. Which of the following statements is incorrect?
   a. Although marginal costs may initially rise, as more and more of an activity is undertaken, it is usually the case that marginal costs eventually decrease.
   b. Although marginal benefits may initially rise, as more and more of an activity is undertaken, it is usually the case that marginal benefits eventually decrease.
   c. It is possible for marginal costs to be positive.
   d. It is possible for marginal benefits to be negative.

7. You should undertake an activity until the point where
   a. marginal benefit is zero.
   b. marginal cost is zero.
   c. marginal benefit equals marginal cost.
   d. total benefit equals total cost.

8. If the marginal benefit is decreasing,
   a. total benefit must be decreasing.
   b. total benefit must be negative.
   c. total benefit may be increasing.
   d. it is impossible to determine anything about total benefit.

9. Sara loves to eat cookies. Her first cookie normally yields a marginal benefit of $4. Each additional cookie creates a declining marginal benefit by $.50 per cookie. If her favorite cookie store charges $3 per cookie, how many cookies should she eat?
   a. 1
   b. 3
   c. 5
   d. 8

Answer the next five questions based on the following information:

Ian runs a personal car washing service. He will come to your home or office and wash your car. He has six customers and each will hire him at a different price to wash their car. These prices are shown in the following table.

Customer	Price
Monica	$30
Phoebe	5
Rachel	20
Joey	15
Chandler	10
Ross	25

Ian has figured out his costs of providing car washes (he has no sunk costs) and they appear in the following table. Ian's marginal cost is constant at $17.50.

# of Washes	Total cost
1	$17.50
2	35.00
3	52.50
4	70.00
5	87.50
6	105.00

10. Ian's optimal number of car washes is
   a. 5.
   b. 6.
   c. 2.
   d. 3.

11. Ian faces
   a. increasing marginal benefit.
   b. constant marginal benefit.
   c. increasing marginal cost.
   d. constant marginal cost.

12. At the optimal level of car washes, Ian's net gain from washing cars is   30 + 25 + 20 = 75
   a. $13.   — Total C = 52.50
   b. $22.50.   _____
   c. $50.   22.50.
   d. $73.50.

13. If the government requires all car washers to be licensed and charges $20 for a license, Ian's optimal number of car washes will   b/c $20 is a sunk cost.
   a. fall to 1 car wash.
   b. fall to 2 car washes.
   c. fall to 4 car washes.
   d. not change.

14. If the government requires all car washers to be licensed and charges $10 for a license, Ian's net gain from washing cars is   22.50
   a. $0.   — 10.00
   b. $12.50.   _____
   c. $32.50.   12.50.
   d. $50.

Answer the following question based on the table below. The table represents Raul's marginal benefit and marginal cost of making silk ties.

Number of ties	Marginal benefit	Marginal cost
1	$60	$10
2	50	20
3	40	30
4	30	40

(handwritten: 40 ⟩10 ; 30)

(handwritten box: 40 − 30 = 10)

15. If Raul increases the number of ties he makes from 2 to 3, his net gain will increase by
   a. $0.
   b. $10.
   c. $20.
   d. $30.

16. You have been hired as a motivational speaker to talk to a group attending a conference in another city. The group offers you $1,000 for your speech and you buy your airline ticket (your only expense for giving the speech) for $500, but it is nonrefundable. Shortly after buying the ticket, the group tells you that attendance at the conference will be much lower than anticipated and therefore they can only pay you $450 for the speech. You should
   a. not give the speech since you are losing $50 traveling to this other city.
   b. refuse to give the speech and stay home.
   c. refuse to give the speech but take the flight to the other city so as to not waste the airline ticket.
   d. give the speech anyway.

(handwritten: b/c = lost.)

17. If the one-year rate of interest is 10%, the present value of $300 to be received one year from now is
   a. $300.
   b. $272.73.
   c. $252.26.
   d. $200.

18. Which of the following statements is correct?
   a. As the interest rate increases, the present value of a future sum decreases.
   b. As the interest rate increases, the present value of a future sum increases.
   c. There is no relationship between the interest rate and the present value of a future sum.
   d. None of the above is correct.

19. What is the net present value of a project that costs $2,500 today but will pay $4,000 in four years assuming that the rate of interest is 5%?
   a. $567.22
   b. $1,500
   c. $790.81
   d. $3,290.81

20. Wilbur is 65 years old and about to retire. His employer presents him with three pension payout options. Option I is an immediate lump-sum payment of $1 million. Option II is to receive $250,000 at the end of each year for the next five years (a total of $1.25 million). Option III is to receive $150,000 at the end of every year for the next ten years (a total of $1.5 million). If Wilbur expects to live to age 85, wants to choose the pension payout that has the highest present value, and assumes a rate of interest of 10%, which option should he take?
a. He should take the lump-sum payment of $1 million.
b. He should take the $250,000 each year for the next five years.
c. He should take the $150,000 each year for the next ten years.
d. He is indifferent among the three because they all have the same present value.

21. Which of the following statements is true?
a. Positive accounting profit implies positive economic profit.
b. Negative economic profit implies negative accounting profit.
c. It is possible to have a negative economic profit as well as a positive accounting profit.
d. If the firm earns zero economic profit, it is illogical to continue the business.

Answer question 22 on the basis of the following information:

Sarah is running a business that promotes live concerts, and it provides her with $200,000 a year. Before she started her business, she was earning $60,000 working for an information and technology firm. Her yearly operating expenses are $100,000. She can count $10,000 a year as depreciation costs for office equipment, which includes computers. If she did not use her savings to buy office equipment, she could have earned $1,000 as interest income.

22. Which of the following statements is incorrect?
a. Sarah's accounting profit is $90,000.
b. Sarah's economic profit is $30,000.
c. Sarah's economic profit is $29,000.
d. Sarah's accounting profit is higher than her economic profit.

***23.** If your marginal benefit (*MB*) function is *MB* = 120 − 5Q, where Q is the number of concerts and your marginal cost of attending concert is constant at $100, the optimal quantity of concerts that you should attend is
a. 1.
b. 2.
c. 3.
d. 4.

***24.** If your marginal benefit (*MB*) function is *MB* = 120 − 4Q, where Q is the number of concerts and your marginal cost of attending concert is constant at $80, your total net benefit at the optimal point is
a. $100.
b. $200.
c. $300.
d. $400.

25. Which of the following statements is true?
a. If sunk costs double, the marginal cost will double.
b. An increase in sunk costs will not affect the optimal outcome.
c. Depreciation costs are counted in accounting costs, but they are not counted when we calculate economic profit.
d. If the marginal cost curve shifts to right, it will reduce economic profit.

Problems and Exercises

Read each question carefully and then write your answers in the space provided or on a separate sheet of paper.

1. Fern has just quit her job at the university, where she was an instructor of economics (a job that paid $52,000 per year). After receiving a $500,000 inheritance from her long-lost aunt, she opened Fern's Friendly Floral Shop. The inheritance allowed her to buy a small shop in the center of town, the refrigerators necessary for storing flowers, a computer, and a delivery van; she even had $200,000 left to deposit in her bank account, which earns 3% per year. Fern has two employees each earning $32,000 per year, and the cost of flowers, packaging materials, etc., equals $30,000 per year. If Fern's revenue from her first year in business is $150,000, calculate Fern's accounting profit (assume depreciation on the refrigerators, computer, and van equals $2,000 that year), implicit cost of capital, cost of Fern's time, and her economic profit. Should Fern remain in business?

2. While attending college, Julia runs a business baking birthday cakes on weekends. She knows the total benefits she receives from baking from 0 to 6 cakes per weekend, as well as the total costs associated with baking the cakes, and these are shown in the accompanying table. How many cakes should Julia bake each weekend? What is her total benefit from baking the cakes? What are her total costs? What is her net gain?

Number of cakes	Total benefit	Total cost	Total net benefit
0	$0	$25	
			-25
1	30	30	
			0
2	55	40	
			15
3	75	55	
			20
4	90	75	
			15
5	100	100	
			0
6	105	130	
			-15

As the summer approaches, there is an increase in demand for birthday cakes because students want to celebrate all the summer birthdays before school gets out. The total benefits for Julia of baking this weekend are as shown in the accompanying table. How many should Julia bake this weekend? What is her net gain?

Number of cakes	Total benefit	Total cost	Total net benefit
0	$0	$25	
			-25
1	40	30	
			10
2	75	40	
			35
3	105	55	
			50
4	130	75	
			55
5	150	100	
			50
6	165	130	
			35

3. In each of the following situations, explain whether the individual or firm should undertake more of the activity, less of the activity, or quit the activity outright.
   a. Kit is at an all-you-can-eat hot dog party and the marginal benefit of another hot dog is less than that of the previous hot dog.

   b. Kanta paid $25 to get into an amusement park where she can enjoy all of the rides without any additional cost or ticket. She expects that the total benefits of her visit will exceed $50. After being at the park for less than 20 minutes, it begins to rain and shows no sign of letting up and the marginal benefit from going on any of the rides is negative.

   c. Tom is considering seeing the latest Harry Potter movie for the tenth time when the price of a ticket is $8. He assessed his total benefit from seeing the movie nine times was $200 and that seeing it ten times would be worth $205.

4. A new technology firm is trying to decide which of three projects to undertake. The costs and benefits associated with each project are shown in the following table. If the firm anticipates an annual rate of interest of 10%, which project has the highest net present value? How will your answer change if the rate of interest is 5%? How can you explain why a change in the interest rate affects which project has the highest net present value?

	Project A	Project B	Project C
Dollars realized today	–$1,000,000	–$500,000	–$100,000
Dollars realized one year from now	–500,000	250,000	100,000
Dollars realized two years from now	500,000	125,000	200,000
Dollars realized three years from now	1,600,000	250,000	200,000

5. Mrs. Cat owns an Internet café in Toronto. Her costs and revenue estimates for a year are given in the accompanying table.

Revenue:	$200,000
Rent:	$64,000
Wages paid to workers:	$60,000
Depreciated value of equipment costs:	$20,000
Lost interest income:	$5,000

Forgone income of Mrs. Cat (who worked as an administrative assistant in a law firm): $40,000
The total accounting cost =
The total economic costs =
The total accounting profit =
The total economic profit =

6. Anushka loves going to concerts. Her yearly marginal benefit function for attending the number of concerts that she goes to is: $MB = 120 - 8Q$, where Q is the number of concerts. Her marginal cost of attending concert is constant at $80.
   a. Draw the marginal benefit (MB) curve and the MC cost curve.
   b. Find the optimal number of concerts for Anushka.
   c. What is her net benefit?

7. A pharmaceutical company is planning to invest $7 million to develop a new cancer drug. Profits are known and expected to decline due to substitutes developed in future years. The annual profit will be $4 million after 1 year, $3 million after 2 years, $2 million after 3 years, $1 million after 4 years, and then be zero in subsequent years. Find the net present value with a 10% interest rate.

Answers to How Well Do You Understand the Chapter

1. opportunity, explicit, benefits, implicit, economic, implicit

2. economic, total revenue, reduction, difference, implicit, sell, time

3. marginal, opportunity, marginal benefit, marginal cost, increasing, upward-sloping, marginal benefit, decreasing

4. greater than, greater than, equal to, optimal, intersects

5. non-recoverable, ignored

6. interest rate, present value

7. present value, more than, more than, less than, less than, equal to

8. future, present value, highest

Answer to Multiple-Choice Questions

1. During the last 20 years, the metropolitan areas in Ontario have expanded rapidly, resulting in increasing land values. For farmers who rent land, this is an explicit cost of business and many find they are unable to pay these rents. For farmers who own their land, the implicit cost of the land is rising. Consequently, many areas that were formerly farms have been turned over to real estate developers. **Answer: C.**

2. Accounting profit is equal to total revenue minus explicit (monetary) costs. Total revenue is $100,000 and explicit costs are $15,000 (rent) and $25,000 (secretarial help and advertising). Accounting profit is $100,000 less $40,000, or $60,000. **Answer: B.**

3. The implicit cost of capital is the opportunity cost of capital used by the business. If Juan Gonzalez did not buy the capital equipment, he would have had $50,000 that could be earning an annual rate of interest of 5%. The implicit cost of capital is $2,500 (= $50,000 × 0.05). **Answer: B.**

4. The implicit costs are the implicit cost of capital and the cost of the owner's time. Juan Gonzalez's implicit costs are $2,500 (implicit cost of capital) and the cost of his time, which is the salary that he gave up to start the J.G. Home Remodeling Company, $60,000. His implicit costs are $62,500. **Answer: D.**

5. Economic profit is the difference between total revenue and all costs, explicit and implicit. Juan Gonzalez's economic profit is $100,000 (total revenue) less $40,000 (explicit costs) less $62,500 (implicit costs), or –$2,500. **Answer: D.**

6. Although marginal costs may fall for a time, they are never negative and usually increase—not decrease—as more and more of an activity is undertaken. Although marginal benefits may rise for a time, they can be negative and usually decrease as more and more of an activity is undertaken. Therefore the only statement that is incorrect is "Although marginal costs may initially rise, as more and more of an activity is undertaken, it is usually the case that marginal costs eventually decrease." **Answer: A.**

7. According to the principle of marginal analysis, you should undertake an activity until the point where marginal benefit equals marginal cost. This is the point at which you have maximized your net gain. **Answer: C.**

8. Marginal benefit is the change in total benefit that occurs from undertaking just a little bit more of an activity. It may be that marginal benefit is decreasing, but as long as it is still positive, total benefit will be increasing. **Answer: C.**

9. Sara will eat cookies until the marginal benefit of the cookie equals the marginal cost. All cookies cost $3 each. The marginal benefit of the first cookie to Sara is $4, the second is $3.50, and the third is $3. Sara should eat 3 cookies. **Answer: B.**

10. Since Ian will wash the cars by first washing the car of the person who will pay the most and then the next, we can see the marginal benefit and marginal cost of washing each car in the figure below. Ian will wash 3 cars (Phoebe, Chandler, and Joey will have dirty cars) because at that number of car washes the marginal benefit equals the marginal cost at $17.50. **Answer: D.**

11. Ian faces constant marginal costs. Each additional car wash costs the same as the previous car wash, $17.50. **Answer: D.**

12. The total benefit from washing 3 cars is the sum of the prices he will receive for the first 3 cars washed, or $75 (= $30 + $25 + 20). The total cost is $52.50 (= $17.50 × 3). Therefore, the net gain is $22.50 (= $75 – $52.50). **Answer: B.**

13. When the government charges $20 for a license, it is a sunk cost; to wash cars, Ian has to pay for a license. Sunk costs do not affect marginal costs. Therefore, neither Ian's marginal benefit nor marginal cost of car washes will change. Consequently, Ian has no incentive to change the number of car washes he undertakes. **Answer: D.**

14. When the government charges $10 for a license, Ian's net gain from washing cars will fall by $10. Since before the license fee he was earning a net gain of $22.50, with the license fee he will earn a net gain of $12.50. **Answer: B.**

15. The marginal benefit to Raul from making the third tie is $40 and the marginal cost is $30. Therefore, his net gain increases by $10 when he increases production from 2 ties to 3. **Answer: B.**

16. The price of the airline ticket is nonrefundable; it is a sunk cost. It will not influence your decision whether to speak at the conference or not. The marginal cost of the trip is now $0, and the marginal benefit is $450. You will give the speech anyway. **Answer: D.**

17. To calculate the answer to this problem, we must use the following:

$$PV = \frac{300}{(1 + .10)^1} = \$272.73$$

Answer: B.

18. As the interest rate rises, the present value of a future sum decreases. It is sometimes easier to see it from a different perspective: $1 will grow to a larger amount in one year if there is a higher interest rate. With a higher interest rate, the present value of a future sum falls. **Answer: A.**

19. Net present value is the present value of today's and future benefits minus the present value of today's and future costs. There is just one cost, $2,500, and it is paid today. The benefit, however, will be received in four years. We can calculate the present value of $4,000 to be received four years from now when the interest rate is 5% as

$$PV \text{ of benefit} = \frac{4,000}{(1 + .05)^4} = \$3,290.81$$

Therefore, the net gain is $790.81 (= $3,290.81 – $2,500). **Answer: C.**

20. Wilbur should take the immediate $1 million lump-sum payment; the other options have present values less than $1 million. The present value of the lump-sum payment is $1 million—it is received today. The other two are more complicated: Option II has a present value of $947,696.69, while Option III has a present value of $921,685.07. The following tables show the present values of the different payout plans for Options II and III. **Answer: A.**

Years till payment	Payment	Present value of payment
1	$250,000.00	$227,272.73
2	250,000.00	206,611.57
3	250,000.00	187,828.70
4	250,000.00	170,753.36
5	250,000.00	155,230.33
Total	$1,250,000.00	$947,696.69

Years till payment	Payment	Present value of payment
1	$150,000.00	$136,363.64
2	150,000.00	123,966.94
3	150,000.00	112,697.22
4	150,000.00	102,452.02
5	150,000.00	93,138.20
6	150,000.00	84,671.09
7	150,000.00	76,973.72
8	150,000.00	69,976.11
9	150,000.00	63,614.64
10	150,000.00	57,831.49
Total	$1,500,000.00	$921,685.07

21. Check numerical examples to see that the firm can have positive accounting profit as well as negative economic profit. **Answer: C.**

22. Accounting profit = $200,000 − $100,000 − $10,000 = $90,000.
Economic profit = $200,000 − $100,000 − $10,000 − $60,000 − $1,000 = $29,000.
Answer: B.

23. Take $MC = MB$ and solve optimal $Q = 4$ from $100 = 120 - Q$. **Answer: D.**

24. Take $MC = MB$ and solve optimal $Q = 10$. The total net benefit = $200. See the accompanying graph. **Answer: B.**

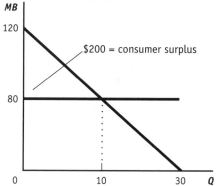

25. Depreciation costs are counted in both accounting and economic costs. If the MC curve shifts to the right, economic profit will increase. Sunk costs have no effect on MC and on optimal outcome. **Answer: B.**

Answers to Problems and Exercises

1. Fern's explicit costs are the costs of her two employees ($64,000), depreciation on her capital ($2,000), and the cost of flowers, packaging, and other ($30,000), or $96,000. Given that she earned revenue equal to $150,000, her accounting profit is $54,000 (= $150,000 − $96,000). The implicit cost of capital is the interest she could have earned on the $300,000 of the inheritance that she used to buy the store, refrigerators, computer, and van. We can calculate that as 3% times $300,000, or $9,000. The cost of her time is what she could have earned at the university had she not quit her job, $52,000. Fern's economic profit is total revenue ($150,000) less explicit costs ($96,000), less the implicit cost of capital ($9,000), less the cost of her time ($52,000), or −$7,000. Since she is earning an economic loss, Fern should not remain in business if she feels that this year's finances will continue in the future.

2. Julia will choose to bake the number of cakes for which the principle of marginal analysis holds; she will produce where marginal benefit equals marginal cost. The accompanying table shows Julia's benefits and costs associated with each cake that she bakes.

Number of cakes	Total benefit	Total cost	Total net benefit
0	$0	$25	−$25
1	30	30	0
2	55	40	15
3	75	55	20
4	90	75	15
5	100	100	0
6	105	130	−25

Julia will bake 3 cakes. Her total benefit from producing cakes is $75, and her total costs are $55. Her net gain is $20 (= $75 − $55).

When the demand for birthday cakes increases as summer approaches, Julia will now bake 4 cakes during the weekend (at 4 cakes, marginal benefit = marginal cost = $22.50) and her net gain will equal $55.

Number of cakes	Total benefit	Total cost	Total net benefit
0	$0	$25	−$25
1	40	30	10
2	75	40	35
3	105	55	50
4	130	75	55
5	150	100	50
6	165	130	35

3. a. Although the marginal benefit of another hot dog is less than that of the previous hot dog, as long as the marginal benefit is still positive, Kit should eat another hot dog because the marginal cost of another hot dog is zero.

b. Kanta should leave the park. The $25 admission fee is a sunk cost. Since the marginal cost of a ride is zero but the marginal benefit is negative, she should not go on any rides.

c. Tom should not go to see Harry Potter for the tenth time. The marginal benefit is only $5, while the price of the ticket is $8.

4. The first step to determine which project should be undertaken is to calculate the present value of the future costs and benefits from each of the projects using the following formula:

$$PV = 1 \Big/ (1 + r)^n$$

where PV represents present value, r is the rate of interest, and n is the number of years until the benefit is received or the cost imposed. The following table shows the present values of the costs and benefits of each project when the rate of interest is 10%. Project C has the highest net present value.

PV (rate of interest) = 10%

Year	Project A Dollar flow	Project A Present value	Project B Dollar flow	Project B Present value	Project C Dollar flow	Project C Present value
Dollars realized today	−$1,000,000	−$1,000,000	−$500,000	−$500,000	−$100,000	-$100,000
Dollars realized one year from now	−500,000	−454,545	250,000	227,273	100,000	90,909
Dollars realized two years from now	500,000	413,223	125,000	103,306	200,000	165,289
Dollars realized three years from now	1,600,000	1,202,104	250,000	187,829	200,000	150,263
Net Present Value		$160,782		$18,408		$306,461

The following table shows the present values of the costs and benefits of each project when the rate of interest is 5%. At this lower rate of interest, Project A has the highest net present value.

PV (rate of interest) = 5%

Year	Project A Dollar flow	Project A Present value	Project B Dollar flow	Project B Present value	Project C Dollar flow	Project C Present value
Dollars realized today	−$1,000,000	−$1,000,000	−$500,000	−$500,000	−$100,000	−$100,000
Dollars realized one year from now	−500,000	−476,190	250,000	238,095	100,000	95,238
Dollars realized two years from now	500,000	453,515	125,000	113,379	200,000	181,406
Dollars realized three years from now	1,600,000	1,382,140	250,000	215,959	200,000	172,768
Net Present Value		$359,465		$67,433		$349,412

Project A has the highest net present value of the three projects at lower interest rates, while Project C has the highest net present value of the three projects at higher interest rates. Project A has high monetary benefits but the firm has to wait until the second year for any benefit and it will receive most of the benefit three years from now. On the other hand, Project C yields benefits for the firm in just one year and the benefits are more evenly spread over the three years. Since the present value decreases with the length until the benefit is received and is inversely related to the interest rate, Project A will realize a higher net present value when interest rates are low, while Project C will realize a higher net present value when interest rates are high.

5. Accounting costs = $64,000 + $60,000 + $20,000 = $144,000.
Economic costs = $64,000 + $60,000 + $20,000 + $5,000 + $40,000 = $189,000.
Accounting profit = $200,000 − $144,000 = $56,000.
Economic profit = $200,000 − $189,000 = $11,000.

6. a.

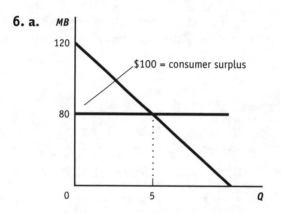

b. Set $MC = MB$. From $80 = 120 − 8Q$, we get optimal $Q = 5$.
c. The total net benefit = ($40)(5)(1/2) = $100.

7. Net present value = $7 million − ($4 million/1.1) − ($3 million/ (1.1)^2
     −($2 million/ (1.1)^3 − ($1 million/(1.1)^4
     = $1.3 million

chapter **8**

Behind the Supply Curve: Inputs and Costs

To see what is behind the supply curve, we need to understand production and cost function. Production depends on inputs, like raw materials, labour, machinery, and so forth. Production costs depend on the quantity of inputs being employed and input prices. In this chapter, we see the relation between total product and marginal product. We also see the implication of diminishing marginal product returns. This chapter explains all cost functions and cost curves. We see the difference between short run and long run and explain how economies or diseconomies of scale affect the long-run average total cost curve.

How Well Do You Understand the Chapter?

Fill in the blanks using the terms below to complete the following statements. Terms may be used more than once. If you find yourself having difficulties, please refer back to the appropriate section in the text.

average total	*fixed*	*output*	*sum*
average total cost	*fixed cost*	*product*	*total cost*
constant	*fixed input*	*production*	*total product*
cost(s)	*inputs*	*quantity*	*variable*
diminishing	*land*	*scale*	*variable cost*
diminishing returns	*long run*	*set-up costs*	*variable input*
diseconomies	*marginal product*	*short run*	*vertical*
economies	*minimize*	*slope*	
equal(s)	*minimum-cost*	*specialization*	

1. Firms are organizations that transform inputs into _____ to maximize profit. The technical relationship between the quantity of inputs a firm utilizes and the quantity of output it produces is its _____ function. In production, we distinguish between fixed inputs and variable inputs. A fixed input is an input whose _____ is fixed and cannot be varied. A fixed input may be _____ or physical capital. An input whose quantity can vary is known as a(n) _____ input. Labour is an example of variable input. However, if the time period under consideration is long enough, all factors are _____. We distinguish between the short run and the _____ for a firm, depending on whether the firm has time to change the quantity of any input. If the quantities of all inputs can be adjusted, then we

are considering the _____ time-period. If the firm does not have time to vary at least one input, then we are considering the _____ time-period.

2. The total _____ curve shows how much output a variable input can produce, given that another input is fixed. When constructing a total product curve, we measure the _____ on the horizontal axis and total product on the vertical axis. We are interested in how a change in the variable input affects a change in the _____. The marginal product is the change in the _____ when there is a change in the variable input. The slope of the total product curve is the _____ of the variable input. The average product of an input is the total product divided by the quantity of variable input. For example, average product of labour is the _____ divided by the quantity of labour.

3. Although total product may expand at an increasing rate when the firm first starts to produce, as more and more of the variable input is added to a(n) _____, total product eventually increases at a diminishing rate. This is known as the _____ to an input.

4. Once we understand the production function, we can use that information to understand the _____ functions of the firm. The prices of the _____ in the production process are the costs of production. The costs of the fixed inputs are the total _____. The total costs of the _____ input will change with changes in output. When we multiply the quantity of variable input by the per-unit cost of the variable input, we get the total _____. Total cost is just the sum of the total fixed cost and total _____. The _____ curve demonstrates how total cost depends on the quantity of output. When constructing a total cost curve, we measure the quantity of output on the horizontal axis and total cost on the _____ axis. The total cost curve slopes upward and, as more _____ is produced, the total cost curve becomes steeper.

5. We can use total cost to determine marginal cost and average cost. Marginal cost is the change in total cost due to a change in _____ produced; it is the _____ of the total cost curve. The _____ curve becomes steeper as the firm produces additional output because the marginal cost of production increases. The increasing marginal costs of production arise because the variable input is subject to _____ marginal product. Each additional unit of the _____ input produces less output than the previous input; therefore, each additional unit of output costs more than the previous unit. Since at low levels of output marginal product may be increasing, at low levels

of output marginal cost may be _____. The marginal cost curve may be sloping downward at low levels of output, but once _____ marginal returns set in, the marginal cost curve is sloping upward. This gives the marginal cost curve its U-shape.

6. It is also helpful for a firm to know its average _____ of production. There are three relevant average cost measures: average total cost, average _____ cost, and average variable cost. We measure average total cost as _____ divided by the level of output produced, average fixed cost as total fixed cost divided by the level of _____ produced, and average variable cost as the total _____ divided by the level of output produced.

7. Since the total fixed costs are the same regardless of the level of output, average fixed costs decrease as _____ increases. This is known as the spreading effect: the larger the output, the more the fixed costs are spread over a larger quantity of output. The average fixed cost curve slopes downward. Average variable costs are the variable costs per unit of output, and they increase because of _____ average product. However, at low levels of output, just as average product may rise as production begins, so average variable costs may fall. The average variable cost curve is shaped like a "U".

8. Average total cost is just the _____ of average fixed cost and average variable cost and is influenced by both the spreading effect and the _____ effect. As the firm begins production, the spreading effect dominates the diminishing returns effect because small increases in output result in big reductions in average _____ cost and average total cost decreases. However, eventually the increase in output does not have such large effects on average fixed cost, and the increasing average _____ cost starts to dominate. At this point, average total cost begins to increase. Consequently, _____ is also U-shaped, since it falls at low levels of output then rises at higher levels.

9. The quantity at which the average total cost curve is at minimum, the bottom of the U-shaped average total cost, is called the _____ per output. It is also the point where marginal cost _____ average total cost. There is a very clear relationship between marginal cost and average total cost. If the marginal cost is less than the average total cost, the _____ must be falling. If the marginal cost is more than the average total cost, the _____ must be rising. If the marginal cost is equal to the average total cost, the _____ is at a minimum.

10. In the long run, all inputs and costs are _____. Since capital and land are usually the fixed input in the short run, in the long run the firm chooses the amount of capital and land that will _____ average total cost for a particular level of output. The long-run average total cost is the _____ for each level of output in the long run.

11. The shape of the long-run average total cost curve depends on how costs change when the firm's _____ (the size of the firm's operations) changes. For some firms, as scale increases, long-run _____ costs fall. This may be due to increased economies of _____. Factors that lower long-run average total cost as output increases are known as _____ of scale (increasing returns to _____). It is also possible that problems of coordination and communication, or _____ of scale (decreasing returns to scale), will increase long-run average total costs for large firms. Finally, it may be that there are no economies or diseconomies of _____ available to the firm. In this case, long-run average total costs are constant as output changes; we say that there are _____ returns to scale.

Learning Tips

TIP #1: As long as marginal product is positive, even if it's declining, total product is increasing.

This is similar to the tip about marginal benefit from Chapter 7. Marginal product is the change in total product due to an additional unit of a variable input; it is the slope of the total product curve. As we add more and more of the variable input to the fixed input, eventually the next unit of the variable input will add less to total product than the previous one—diminishing marginal product. As long as the variable input *adds* to total product, total product will be increasing. If marginal product is positive and diminishing, the total product curve will rise but get flatter and flatter. If marginal product becomes negative, then the total product will be decreasing and the total product curve will slope downward. Figure 8.1 shows a total product curve and explains the ranges in which marginal product is increasing, diminishing, and negative.

Figure 8.1

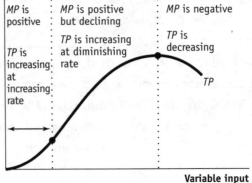

TIP #2: Be careful when drawing short-run average cost curves to show that the marginal cost curve goes through the minimum points of both the average total cost curve and the average variable cost curve.

Both the average total cost and average variable cost curves are U-shaped, and we refer to the minimum point on the average total cost curve as the minimum-cost output. Remember:

- If marginal cost is below average total cost, average total cost is falling.
- If marginal cost is above average total cost, average total cost is rising.
- If marginal cost is equal to average total cost, average total cost is constant and at its minimum level.

Similarly:

- If marginal cost is below average variable cost, average variable cost is falling.
- If marginal cost is above average variable cost, average variable cost is rising.
- If marginal cost is equal to average variable cost, average variable cost is constant and at its minimum level.

Finally, since average total cost equals average variable cost plus average fixed cost, as long as average fixed cost is greater than zero, average total cost must be higher than average variable cost. Therefore, average variable cost must reach its minimum point at a lower level of output than does average total cost. Figure 8.2 shows the relationship between short-run average variable cost and marginal cost, Figure 8.3 shows the relationship between short-run average total cost and marginal cost, and Figure 8.4 shows the relationship between all three of the cost curves.

Figure 8.2

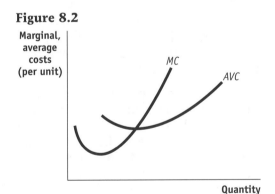

Figure 8.3

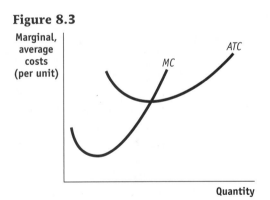

Figure 8.4

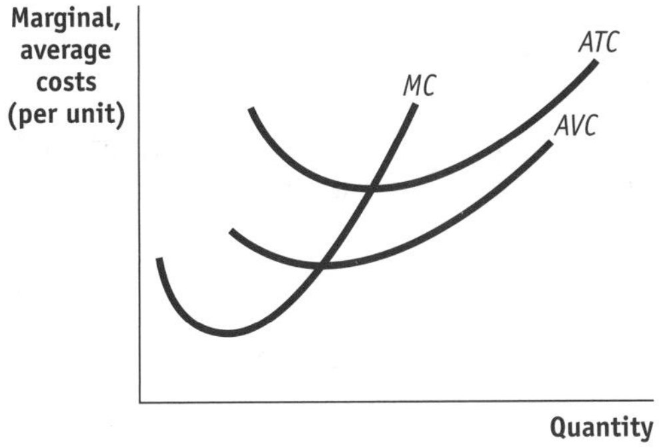

TIP #3: When the firm chooses a point on the long-run average total cost curve that minimizes long-run average costs, it may not be at the minimum point on the short-run average total cost curve for that scale of production.

Figure 8.5 (Figure 8-12 from your text) shows the long-run average total cost curve and three possible short-run average total cost curves for the firm Ben's Boots. If the firm decides to produce 3 pairs of boots in the long run, it will choose the fixed cost associated with ATC_3. This is not the minimum point along ATC_3; the minimum point of ATC_3 occurs at 4 pairs of boots. However, if the firm chooses to produce 4 pairs of boots in the long run, it would choose to build a slightly bigger plant. (The short-run average cost curve for this plant is not shown in the figure.) Similarly, if the firm decides to produce 9 pairs of boots, it will choose the fixed cost associated with ATC_9. This is not the minimum point along ATC_9; the minimum point of ATC_9 occurs at 8 pairs of boots. Only when the firm chooses to produce 6 pairs of boots in the long run will the firm produce at the minimum point along both a short-run ATC curve and $LRATC$.

Figure 8.5

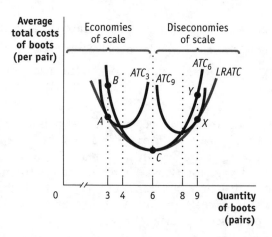

TIP #4: As firms expand the scale of their operations it is possible that they will experience economies of scale at low levels of output and diseconomies of scale when increasing production at high levels of output.

Economies of scale arise because as firms get larger and produce more, workers can limit themselves to more specialized tasks, and also because some industries require large set-up costs, and as production increases, average total cost falls. However, at high levels of output, problems of coordination and communication may arise, and therefore average total cost will increase. Figure 8.5 shows that Ben's Boots experiences economies of scale as output increases to 6 pairs of boots, but then diseconomies of scale set in. It is possible for firms to experience constant returns to scale; long-run average total cost remains constant as the scale of production increases.

Multiple-Choice Questions

1. In the short run, Fern's Floral Shop has a 1,000-square-foot shop, two computers, two full-time employees, and one part-time employee. Which of the following is most likely a fixed input?
   a. 1,000-square-foot shop
   b. two computers
   c. two full-time employees
   d. one part-time employee

2. If we compare the total product curves of two firms that are identical in all ways except that one has more of the fixed input than the other,
   a. the marginal product curve for the firm with more of the fixed input will lie above that of the other firm.
   b. the marginal product curve for the firm with more of the fixed input will lie below that of the other firm.
   c. the marginal product curves for the two firms will be identical.
   d. we cannot say how the marginal product curve for one firm will compare to the other.

Answer the following six questions based on the short-run production function for homemade fudge at Sally's Sweet Shop, shown in the accompanying table.

# of Workers	Fudge per day (in pounds)
0	0
1	10
2	22
3	32
4	40
5	46
6	50

3. The marginal product of the third worker is
   a. 6.
   b. 8.
   c. 10.
   d. 12.

4. The marginal product of the third worker
   a. is equal to that of the second worker.
   b. is less than the marginal product of the second worker.
   c. is greater than the marginal product of the second worker.
   d. cannot be compared to the marginal product of the second worker.

5. After the second worker is hired, the marginal product of each additional worker
   a. decreases.
   b. increases.
   c. remains the same.
   d. may increase or decrease.

6. If Sally must pay $50 per day for each worker and she has a fixed cost of $200, what is the cost of producing 40 pounds of fudge?
   a. $50
   b. $200
   c. $250
   d. $400

7. If Sally must pay $50 per day for each worker and she has a fixed cost of $200, the marginal cost of the 40th pound of fudge is approximately
   a. $5.00.
   b. $6.25.
   c. $7.50.
   d. $10.50.

8. If Sally must pay $50 per day for each worker and she has a fixed cost of $200, the average variable cost of the 40th pound of fudge will be _____ and the average total cost of the 40th pound will be _____.
   a. $5.00; $8.00
   b. $6.25; $10.50
   c. $5.00; $10.00
   d. $10.50; $15.00

9. If the long-run average cost curve is flat over a large range of output, we say that the firm
   a. is experiencing economies of scale.
   b. is experiencing diseconomies of scale.
   c. faces constant returns to scale.
   d. faces diminishing marginal product.

10. When the firm is operating on the long-run average total cost curve, the firm
   a. must be operating at minimum short-run average total cost.
   b. may be operating at minimum short-run average total cost.
   c. must be operating where short-run average variable cost is greater than short-run average total cost.
   d. may be operating where short-run average variable cost is greater than short-run average total cost.

11. A firm expects to produce a given level of output in the long run and operates on the long-run average cost curve. Suddenly demand for the good increases and the firm has to increase production. How will the change in production affect short-run average total costs?
   a. They will not change because the firm will not be able to change the amount of its fixed input.
   b. They will increase because it is hard to get extra production out of the existing facilities.
   c. They will decrease because as the firm expands production they will experience economies of scale.
   d. It is impossible to tell what will happen to short-run average total costs.

12. There are diminishing returns to an input because
   a. as you add more and more of a variable input to less and less of the fixed input, total product decreases.
   b. as you add more and more of a variable input to the fixed input, total product decreases.
   c. as you add more and more of a variable input to the fixed input, the marginal product of the last unit of the variable input will decrease.
   d. as you add more and more of a variable input to less and less of the fixed input, the marginal product of the last unit of the variable input will decrease.

13. Diminishing returns affect all of the following except
   a. marginal product.
   b. average total cost.
   c. average variable cost.
   d. average fixed cost.

14. The average total cost curve for a firm is U-shaped because
    a. at low levels of output, the diminishing returns effect dominates the spreading effect, while at high levels of output the reverse happens.
    b. at low levels of output, the spreading effect dominates the diminishing returns effect, while at high levels of output the reverse happens.
    c. at low levels of output, there are diminishing returns to the variable input, while at high levels of output the reverse happens.
    d. none of the above.

15. If Julia knows the average total cost of baking 12 dozen muffins is $6 and the average total cost of producing 13 dozen muffins is $7, then the marginal cost of producing the 13th dozen muffins is
    a. $1.
    b. $13.
    c. $19.
    d. $31.

16. As Julia produces more and more muffins in the short run, she knows that the
    a. marginal product of the variable input will eventually decline.
    b. marginal cost of production will eventually increase.
    c. average fixed cost will decrease.
    d. all of the above.

17. Ian's fixed cost of mowing lawns is $250 and his marginal cost is constant at $10 per lawn. If Ian mows 5 lawns in one day, what is Ian's average total cost?
    a. $25
    b. $50
    c. $60
    d. $300

18. If the marginal cost curve is above the average variable cost curve,
    a. the average variable cost curve must be falling.
    b. the average total cost curve must be rising.
    c. the average total cost curve may be at a minimum.
    d. none of the above.

19. Economies of scale arise from which of the following?
    a. adding more and more of a variable input to a fixed input
    b. increased specialization of labour
    c. low set-up costs
    d. problems of coordination and communication

20. As a firm increases production in the long run, average total costs may rise due to
    a. problems of coordination and communication (diseconomies of scale).
    b. diminishing marginal product.
    c. increasing set-up costs.
    d. all of the above.

21. Assume that the total fixed cost is $500. If the marginal cost of the first unit of output is $60 and the marginal cost of the 2nd unit of output is $80, then the average total costs of 2 units of output is
    a. $640.
    b. $320.
    c. $140.
    d. $70.

22. Which of the following statements is false when we consider short run?
    a. The marginal cost curve intersects the average variable cost curve when the average variable cost is at minimum.
    b. The marginal cost curve intersects the average total cost curve when the average total cost is at minimum.
    c. When the total fixed cost increases, the marginal cost also increases.
    d. When input price increases, the marginal cost curve shifts up.

23. Assume that the total fixed cost is $500. If the total cost of the 10th unit of output is $1,100 and the total cost of the 11th unit of output is $1,180, then the marginal cost of the 11th unit of output is
    a. $80.
    b. $100.
    c. $180.
    d. $280.

24. If all inputs are reduced by 10% and output falls by 15%, then the firm is operating in the long run with
    a. decreasing returns to scale.
    b. increasing returns to scale.
    c. constant returns to scale.
    d. diminishing marginal product.

25. With decreasing returns to scale, the long-run average total cost curve will be
    a. downward sloping.
    b. upward sloping.
    c. horizontal.
    d. vertical.

26. Which of the following is **incorrect?**
    a. $TC = FC + VC$.
    b. $MP_L = \Delta Q / \Delta L$.
    c. $ATC = FC + AVC$.
    d. $ATC = AFC + AVC$.

27. Which of the following is **incorrect?**
    a. $AVC = ATC - AFC$.
    b. $AFC = ATC - AVC$.
    c. $ATC = AFC + AVC$.
    d. $MC = \Delta ATC / \Delta Q$.

28. Which of the following is **incorrect?**
    a. $MC = \Delta TC / \Delta Q$.
    b. $MC = \Delta VC / Q$.
    c. $MC = \Delta FC / \Delta Q$.
    d. $AVC = \Delta VC / Q$.

29. Which of the following is correct?
  a. $MP_L = \Delta Q/L$.
  b. $MP_L = \Delta Q/\Delta L$.
  c. $MP_L = \Delta L/\Delta Q$.
  d. $MP_L = Q/L$.

30. Which of the following statements is **incorrect?**
  a. When the ATC is at minimum, $ATC = MC$.
  b. When the ATC curve in the long run is horizontal, there are no economies or diseconomies of scale.
  c. When the MC is at minimum, $ATC = MC$.
  d. When the ATC curve is horizontal, $ATC = MC$.

Problems and Exercises

Read each question carefully and then write your answers in the space provided or on a separate sheet of paper.

1. Bob's Recycle-Bicycle Shop builds bicycles out of recycled materials; its production function is shown in the accompanying table. Bob owns a small shop with four machines for taking recyclable materials and turning them into steel for bicycle frames and rubber for tires. He also uses up to ten workers, paint, seats, and wires in the production process.

# of Workers	Total product per month
0	0
1	200
2	500
3	700
4	800
5	850
6	875
7	890
8	900

  a. What are Bob's fixed inputs? What are his variable inputs?

b. Using the following table and figures, calculate Bob's marginal product.

# of Workers	Total product	MP
0	0	
1	200	____
2	500	____
3	700	____
4	800	____
5	850	____
6	875	____
7	890	____
8	900	____

c. What is the marginal product of the first worker Bob hires? What is the marginal product of the second worker? Calculate the marginal product, MPL, of each worker. What principle explains why the marginal product per worker declines as the number of workers employed increases?

2. Using the production function for Bob's Recycle-Bicycle Shop above, and knowing that he has fixed costs of production equal to $2,000 and his variable costs are $400 per worker, calculate the relevant cost data for Bob.

# of Workers	Total product	FC	VC	TC	AFC	AVC	ATC	MC
0	0	____	____	____				
1	200	____	____	____	____	____	____	____
2	500	____	____	____	____	____	____	____
3	700	____	____	____	____	____	____	____
4	800	____	____	____	____	____	____	____
5	850	____	____	____	____	____	____	____
6	875	____	____	____	____	____	____	____
7	890	____	____	____	____	____	____	____
8	900	____	____	____	____	____	____	____

a. Fill in the blanks in the above table.

b. Why does average fixed cost fall continuously?

c. Why may average variable cost fall and then definitely rise?

d. Why does average total cost fall and then rise?

e. How does marginal cost of production relate to the marginal product of each worker?

3. Given the following total production curve and the average total cost curve for Gwen's Great Gyros and knowing that her fixed costs equal $125 and she pays each worker $50 per day (her only variable cost), answer the following questions. The questions may require a specific numerical answer, a range of numbers, or you may answer "less than" or "greater than" some number, "does not exist," or "impossible to determine."

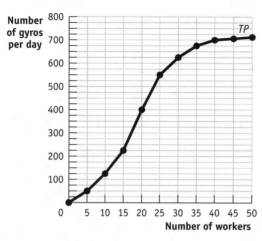

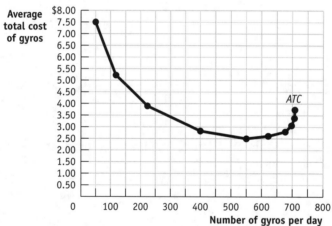

a. At what levels of employment does the marginal product of the workers increase?

b. At what level of employment do diminishing marginal returns occur?

c. At what level of employment does total product increase?

d. At what level of employment does total product decrease?

e. At what level of output is average total cost minimized?

f. At what level of output is average variable cost minimized?

g. At what level of output are average fixed costs minimized?

h. What is the marginal cost of 550 gyros?

4. You have been hired as an economic consultant to Ben's Boots to advise on how much of their fixed input they should use in the long run to lower average total costs. The chief operating officer does not understand why long-run average total costs fall at low levels of production and then rise again with high levels of production. He also does not understand why the firm should not choose the amount of the fixed input that provides the lowest possible overall long-run average total costs of all levels of production. How would you explain these concepts to him?

5. The following table is an incomplete table of various estimates of cost functions of Ben's Boots. Fill in the blanks in the following table.

Output	Total Fixed cost	Total variable cost	Total cost	Average fixed cost	Average variable cost	Average total cost	Marginal cost
0	$100	0		___	___	___	___
1	100	$100	$200	$100	$100	$200	$100
2				50	90	140	
3	100		400	33.33	100		120
4	100		540			135	
5	100		700	20	120		160
6		780			130		180

6. Martha's firm has the following production function in the short run.

# of workers (L)	Units of K	Output (Q)
1	5	10
2	5	18
3	5	24
4	5	28
5	5	30

a. Find the column of marginal product (MP_L).

L	MP_L
1	
2	
3	
4	
5	

b. Assume that each machine costs $6 and each worker costs $100.

Find the column of total fixed cost *(TFC)*, total variable cost *(TVC)*, total cost *(TC)* and average total cost *(ATC)*.

Q	TFC	TVC	TC	ATC
10				
18				
24				
28				
30				

c. What will be the effect on *MC* if total fixed cost doubles?

d. At what level of *L* (and beyond) do we see that diminishing returns dominate more than the spread effect?

*7. Suppose *TVC = WL*, where *TVC* is total variable cost and *W* is the wage rate per labour, and *L* is the quantity of labour. Show that the marginal cost is inversely related to the marginal product of labour.

Answers to How Well Do You Understand the Chapter

1. output, production, quantity, land, variable, variable, long run, long run, short run

2. product, variable input, total product, total product, marginal product, total product

3. fixed input, diminishing return

4. cost, inputs, fixed cost, variable, variable cost, variable cost, total cost, vertical, output

5. output, slope, total cost, diminishing, variable, diminishing, diminishing

6. total cost, fixed, total cost, output, variable cost

7. output, diminishing

8. sum, diminishing return, fixed, variable, average total cost

9. minimum cost, equals, average total cost, average total cost, average total cost

10. variable, minimize, minimum cost

11. scale, average total scale, economies, scale, diseconomies, scale, constant

Answers to Multiple-Choice Questions

1. Fern's 1,000-square-foot shop is most likely a fixed input. Either she owns the shop, in which case it would take some time to sell it or buy an additional shop, or she rents the shop and has a lease (contract) that specifies a time before which she could not stop paying the rent. Since it is fairly easy to buy or sell computers and to hire or fire labour, those inputs are variable. **Answer: A.**

2. If two firms are identical except that one firm has more of the fixed input than the other, the firm with more of the fixed factor will have a higher marginal product (each variable input has greater access to the fixed input) than that of the firm with the smaller fixed input, and therefore its marginal product curve will lie above the other. **Answer: A.**

3. The marginal product is just the change in total product due to an additional unit of the variable input. The marginal product of the third worker is 10 (= [32 – 22]/1). **Answer C.**

4. The marginal product of the second worker is 12 (= [22 – 10]/1); since we just calculated that the marginal product of the third worker is 10, marginal product is declining. **Answer: B.**

5. Although the marginal product of labour increases as employment rises from 1 to 2 workers, marginal product declines after the second worker is hired. **Answer: A.**

6. To produce 40 pounds of fudge, Sally must hire 4 workers and pay each of them $50 for the day for a variable cost of $200. Since her fixed cost is $200, her total cost is $400 (= $200 + $200). **Answer: D.**

7. The marginal cost of producing the 40th pound of fudge is approximately $6.25. The total cost of producing 32 pounds of fudge is $350, and 40 pounds is $400. The marginal cost of producing the 40th pound is the change in total cost divided by the change in output, or $6.25 (= $50/8). **Answer: B.**

8. The total cost of producing 40 pounds of fudge is the variable cost, $200 (= 4 × $50), plus the fixed cost, $200, for a total of $400. The average variable cost will be $5 (= $200/40) and the average total cost will be $10 (= $400/40). **Answer: C.**

9. If the long-run average cost curve is flat over a large range of output, this tells us that there are no cost advantages or disadvantages to having a small scale or a large scale of production. In this case, we say that the firm faces constant returns to scale. **Answer: C.**

10. Only when the firm is producing the level of output that minimizes long-run average total costs will it produce where short-run average total cost is minimized. At any other point on the long-run average total cost curve the firm will be operating at a short-run average total cost that is higher than the minimum for that fixed input. **Answer: B.**

11. If the firm is operating in a region where it is experiencing economies of scale in the long run, or if the firm has to increase production in the short run, short-run average total costs will fall but not by as much as in the long run, when all inputs are variable. On the other hand, if the firm is operating in a region where it is experiencing diseconomies of scale in the long run, and the firm has to increase production in the short run, short-run average total costs will rise. Finally, if the firm is operating in a region where it is experiencing constant returns to scale in the long run, and the firm has to increase production in the short run, short-run average total costs will rise because it will be harder to get extra production out of its existing facilities. **Answer: D.**

12. Diminishing returns explain that as you add more and more of a variable input to a fixed input, eventually the marginal product of the last unit of the variable input decreases. **Answer: C.**

13. Diminishing returns do not affect average fixed costs. Average fixed costs are just fixed costs divided by output and fixed costs are not affected by diminishing returns. **Answer: D.**

14. The average total cost is the sum of average fixed cost and average variable cost. At low levels of output, average fixed cost (the spreading effect) falls substantially while average variable cost may fall or rise slightly (diminishing returns effect), so average total cost decreases. As the firm continues to increase output, average fixed cost does not fall as much, while average variable cost begins to rise. Eventually, the diminishing returns effect dominates the spreading effect and average total cost rises. This gives the average total cost curve its U shape. **Answer: B.**

15. If the average total cost of baking 12 dozen muffins is $6, the total cost of producing 12 dozen muffins must be $72 (= 12 × $6). If the average cost of baking 13 dozen is $7, the total cost of producing 13 dozen muffins must be $91 (= 13 × $7). The marginal cost of the 13th dozen is the change in total cost, $19 (= $91 – $72), divided by the change in dozens of muffins, 1 (= 13 – 12), or $19. **Answer: C.**

16. Due to the diminishing returns to an input in the short run, as she produces more and more muffins in the short run the marginal product of the variable input will eventually decline and the marginal cost of production will increase. Also, as production increases, average fixed cost will decrease. **Answer: D.**

17. Ian will have variable cost of $50 (= 5 × $10) and fixed costs of $250, for a total cost of $300. Average total cost is total cost, $300, divided by output, 5 lawns, for an average total cost of $60. **Answer: C.**

18. When marginal cost is above average variable cost, all we know is that average variable cost must be rising. Average total cost may be rising, falling, or at its minimum level. **Answer: C.**

19. Economies of scale can arise either from increased specialization of an input or set-up costs of production in the long run. Adding more and more of a variable input to a fixed input results in diminishing marginal product in the short run. Problems of coordination and communication result in diseconomies of scale. **Answer: B.**

20. Problems of coordination and communication may increase average total costs in the long run. These are the primary reasons for diseconomies of scale. **Answer: A.**

21. Total costs = $500 + $140 = $640. Average total cost = ($640/2) = $320. **Answer: B.**

22. Changes in fixed costs do not affect marginal costs. **Answer: C.**

23. Marginal cost of the 11th unit = $180 − $100 = $80 **Answer: A.**

24. Since percentage change in output is greater than percentage in all inputs, we have increasing returns to scale. **Answer: B.**

25. The long-run average total cost is upward slowing with decreasing returns to scale. **Answer: B.**

26. ATC is not equal to $FC + AVC$. In fact, $ATC = AFC + AVC$. **Answer: C.**

27. MC is not equal to $\Delta ATC / \Delta Q$. In fact, $MC = \Delta TC/\Delta Q$. **Answer: D.**

28. ΔTFC has no effect on MC. **Answer: C.**

29. Marginal product of labour is $\Delta Q/\Delta L$. **Answer: B.**

30. When MC is at minimum, ATC is not equal to MC; in fact, ATC is greater than MC. **Answer: C.**

Answers to Problems and Exercises

1. **a.** Bob's fixed inputs are his shop and the four machines for taking recyclable materials and turning them into steel for bicycle frames and rubber for tires. The workers, paint, seats, and wires are his variable inputs.
   b. The accompanying table shows the marginal product schedule, while the figures show the total product and marginal product curves for Bob's bike shop.

Number of workers	Total product	Marginal product of labour
0	0	
		200
1	200	
		300
2	500	
		200
3	700	
		100
4	800	
		50
5	850	
		25
6	875	
		15
7	890	
		10
8	900	

c. The marginal product of the first worker is the change in total product, 200, as the first worker is hired. The marginal product of the second worker is 300. The marginal products of the remaining workers are shown in the previous table. The principle of diminishing returns to an input explains why as we add additional units of a variable input to a fixed input, eventually the marginal product attributable to the last unit of the variable input will be less than that of the previous unit.

2.

# of Workers	Total product	FC	VC	TC	AFC	AVC	ATC	MC
0	0	$2,000	$0	$2,000				
								$2.00
1	200	2,000	400	2,400	$10.00	$2.00	$12.00	
								1.33
2	500	2,000	800	2,800	4.00	1.60	5.60	
								2.00
3	700	2,000	1,200	3,200	2.86	1.71	4.57	
								4.00
4	800	2,000	1,600	3,600	2.50	2.00	4.50	
								8.00
5	850	2,000	2,000	4,000	2.35	2.35	4.71	
								16.00
6	875	2,000	2,400	4,400	2.29	2.74	5.03	
								26.67
7	890	2,000	2,800	4,800	2.25	3.15	5.39	
								40.00
8	900	2,000	3,200	5,200	2.22	3.56	5.78	

a. See the table above.
b. Average fixed costs are fixed costs divided by level of output. Since fixed cost by definition does not change, the numerator is always constant but the denominator always increases. Therefore, *AFC* falls continuously. This is called the spreading effect.
c. Average variable cost may fall at first when adding a variable input to a fixed input because there may be some increasing returns to an input. However, as you add more and more of a variable input to a fixed input, diminishing marginal returns set in, resulting in higher variable costs and average variable costs of production. This is called the diminishing returns effect.
d. Average total cost is the sum of average fixed costs and average variable costs. Since average fixed costs fall as output increases (the spreading effect), this puts downward pressure on average total cost. This effect is most significant at low levels of output. Average variable costs may fall at low levels of output (if there are increasing returns to an input), or they may rise slightly at low levels of output. As more and more of a variable input is added to a fixed input, diminishing returns set in. Therefore, the spreading effect dominates at low levels of output and the average total cost curve falls, but then as output expands, the diminishing returns effect dominates the spreading effect and average total costs begin to rise.
e. The marginal cost of production decreases if there is an increasing marginal product of an input—this would only happen at low levels of the variable input and of output. Eventually, as diminishing marginal product sets in, marginal cost must rise. Each additional unit of the variable input costs the same but produces less output. Therefore the marginal cost of producing the additional unit of output increases.

3. a. The marginal product of the workers increases as Gwen hires the first 20 workers. As we look at the production function, the slope of the segments of the curve increases up to the point where the 20th worker is hired.
  b. Diminishing marginal returns set in as we begin to hire after the 20th worker.
  c. Total product is always increasing. The total product curve always slopes upward.
  d. Total product does not decrease with employment. After the 20th worker, total product rises by smaller and smaller amounts, but it still rises. The curve gets flatter, but it is not negative.
  e. Average total cost is minimized when output equals 550 gyros.
  f. All we know is that average variable cost hits its minimum at a level of output less than the level of output at which average total cost is minimized. Therefore, average variable cost is minimized at a level of output less than 550 gyros.
  g. Average fixed costs fall continuously; therefore, they are never minimized.
  h. Since at 550 gyros average total cost is minimized, we know that at that point marginal cost must equal average total cost. From the graph, we can see that at 550 gyros the average total cost, and therefore marginal cost, must be $2.50.

4. You would explain to the COO that in the long run as the firm is able to increase the amount of its fixed input, its scale of operations, there will be greater opportunities for Ben's Boots to allow workers to specialize in particular tasks, so that they may become more skilled and efficient in those tasks. Also, in the case where expensive equipment is required for any level of production, the higher the level of production for Ben's Boots, the lower will be average total cost. These are called economies of scale. However, you also need to remind him that if the firm should get too big, problems of communication and coordination may result in higher long-run average costs. These are diseconomies of scale. The firm does not want to choose to produce at the point at which long-run average cost is minimized because it may not be able to sell all of that output. The decision to produce a certain level of output is not related to the shape of the long-run average cost curve. Once the firm decides on a level of production, they should choose that scale of operations that will minimize long-run average total costs.

5.

Output	Total Fixed cost	Total variable cost	Total cost	Average fixed cost	Average variable cost	Average cost	Marginal cost
0	$100	0	___			___	___
1	100	$100	$200	$100	$100	$200	$100
2	100	180	280	50	90	140	80
3	100	300	400	33.33	100	133.33	120
4	100	440	540	25	110	135	140
5	100	600	700	20	120	140	160
6	100	780	880	16.57	130	146.67	180

6. a.

L	MP_L
1	10
2	8
3	6
4	4
5	2

b.

Q	TFC	TVC	TC	ATC
10	$30	$100	$130	$13.00
18	30	200	230	12.78
24	30	300	330	13.75
28	30	400	430	15.36
30	30	500	530	17.67

c. If total fixed costs double, the marginal cost does not change.

d. Diminishing returns dominate more than the spread effect at output level 24 and beyond.

7. Since $TVC = WL$ and since wage rate (W) is constant, $\Delta TVC = W\Delta L$.

Therefore, $\Delta TVC/\Delta Q = W\Delta L/\Delta Q$.

Since $\Delta L/\Delta Q$ is inverse of MP of labour, we can write $\Delta TVC/\Delta Q = MC = W/MP$.

## chapter 9

Perfect Competition and the Supply Curve

The information about costs and production can be used to explain the profit-maximizing behavior of firms in a perfectly competitive industry. Since a firm is a price-taker (not price-maker), its price is equal to its marginal revenue. The optimal profit-maximizing rule is: **price is equal to marginal cost.** In the short run, a firm can make an economic profit, break even, or suffer losses. If the firm suffers economic losses, it will continue to produce as long as it covers total variable costs. In the long run, due to the assumption of free entry or exit, all firms break even and price reaches its lowest level where the price is equal to the lowest level of long-run and short-run average total cost. We also derive the industry supply curve in both short run and long run.

How Well Do You Understand the Chapter?

Fill in the blanks using the terms below to complete the following statements. Terms may be used more than once. If you find yourself having difficulties, please refer back to the appropriate section in the text.

above	fall	market price	produce
average profit	fixed cost	market share	producer's
average total cost	horizontal	maximize	profit
average variable cost	identical	maximum	quantity supplied
below	industry	minimum	revenue
break(s) even	larger	more than	rise
buyers	leave	negative	short run
difference	less than	optimal	shut down
downward	loss	optimal output	smaller
enter	marginal analysis	output	supply
entry	marginal cost	perfectly price elastic	total revenue
equal to	marginal revenue	price	total variable cost
exit	market	price takers	upward

1. A perfectly competitive market is one in which there are many

_____ and many sellers of a standardized (identical) product. There are so many buyers and so many sellers that all producers and consumers are

_____. There are two necessary conditions for perfect competition:

- The market must have so many producers that no one of them has a large

_____.

- The consumers see the products of all producers as ___equal substitutes___. Perfectly competitive markets are also characterized by the ease with which firms can ___enter___ and leave the industry; no obstacles, such as government regulations or limited access to key resources, prevent new producers from entering the ___market/industry___.

2. Perfectly competitive producers want to maximize total ___profit___; it is the ___difference___ between total revenue and total cost. For any producer, total revenue is just the market price multiplied by units of ___output___. Since perfectly competitive producers are price takers, marginal revenue, the change in ___TR___ due to a change in output, will equal the market price. A firm's marginal revenue curve in a perfectly competitive market is a(n) ___horizontal___ line. We can find the level of output at which total profit is maximized by using the principle of ___marginal___. Remember from Chapter 7 that the ___optimal___ amount of activity is the level at which marginal benefit equals marginal cost. For producers, the marginal benefit is marginal ___revenue___. The ___marginal revenue___ curve graphically shows how marginal revenue varies as output changes. Therefore, the producer will ___maximize___ total profit by producing a level of output at which marginal cost equals marginal revenue. We call this the ___optimal output___ rule. Since for perfectly competitive producers marginal revenue is ___equal to___ market price, they will maximize profit by producing where marginal cost is ___equal to___ the market price. The ___optimal___ output rule of MR = MC can be re-written as P = MC when firms (producers) produce in a perfectly competitive market.

3. When the producer chooses the level of output at which marginal cost equals price, he or she will ___maximize___ profit (or minimize losses). However, it may be that total cost is ___more than___ total revenue at all levels of output and the maximum profit is an economic loss. In this case, the firm may choose not to ___produce___ at all. To determine whether profit is positive (total revenue exceeds total cost), or ___negative___ (total cost exceeds total revenue), or equal to zero (total revenue equals total cost), we compare average total cost with the ___market price___. As long as price is greater than or equal to ___ATC___, the firm does not earn a loss. Therefore, one of the following three situations may arise in the short run.

   - If the market price ___>___ average total cost, the firm will earn an economic profit.

   - If the market price is equal to average total cost, the firm will ___break even___.

   - If the ___price___ is less than average total cost, the firm incurs a loss.

4. Since profit is total revenue minus total cost, we can measure _____ as average revenue minus average total cost. Again, because the perfectly competitive firm is a price taker, average revenue also equals the _____. So we can measure average profit as the _____ less average total cost.

5. The perfectly competitive producer may choose to produce in the _____, even if it is earning a loss, if the loss is smaller than its total _____. If the firm does not produce in the short run, it still must pay its fixed cost; if it shuts down, its _____ is fixed cost. A firm will cease production in the short run if the market price falls below the _____. If by continuing to produce the firm earns a loss that is _____ than fixed cost, the firm should produce in the short run even while earning a loss. Since average revenue equals _____ for a perfect competitor and average variable cost is variable cost divided by _____, as long as price exceeds average variable cost, total revenue will exceed _____, and the firm should produce in the short run even if earning a loss. The lowest price at which the firm will produce in the short run is the _____ point on the average variable cost curve; this is also called the shutdown point.

6. Remember the following conditions when even the firm incurs losses in the short run:

- If the market price exceeds _____, the firm should continue to produce in the short run even while earning a loss.

- If the market price is less than average variable cost, the firm should _____ in the short run to minimize its loss.

- If _____ equals average variable cost, the firm's loss is the same if it continues to produce or if it shuts down in the short run.

7. Since the firm will only produce if the market price is greater than or equal to _____ and since the profit-maximizing rule is marginal cost being _____ price, the firm's short-run supply curve is the marginal cost curve _____ the minimum point of the average variable cost curve. The short-run individual _____ curve shows how an individual producer's optimal output quantity depends on the market price, taking fixed cost as a given. The short-run _____ supply curve shows the relationship between the price of a good and the total output of the industry as a whole, when the number of producers is constant. When we look at the perfectly competitive industry as a whole, the industry is in short-run market equilibrium when quantity demanded is _____ quantity supplied when holding the number of producers constant.

8. In the perfectly competitive industry in the long run, all firms will
_____. Since there is easy _____entry_____ into the perfectly
competitive industry, if the producers in that industry earn profits in the short run,
other firms will enter, and the price will _____ until the firms just
break even. If the producers in the industry are earning a(n) _____
but continuing to produce in the short run, firms will leave the industry in the
long run, and the market price will _____ until the remaining firms
just _____. Long-run market equilibrium occurs when quantity
demanded equals _____ and enough time has passed for all entry
into and exit from the industry to occur.

9. We can understand the industry's long-run _____ curve (how
quantity supplied changes with changes in the price in the long run). If demand
decreases (remember that it means a leftward shift of the demand curve), the market price will decrease, leading the firms in the industry to reduce output and earn
a _____ in the short run. Over time, some firms will
_____ the industry, market supply will decrease, and market price
will _____ until the remaining firms in the industry just break even.
In the long run, the industry will have fewer firms, output will be lower, and the
firms in the industry will just ____break even____. If costs fall due to lower wages,
for example, when firms leave the industry, it may be that the new long-run market
equilibrium will be at a higher _____ than the original, and the
long-run supply curve will be _____ sloping but more elastic than
the short-run supply curve. However, if costs remain the same as firms leave the
industry, the long-run market equilibrium will be at the original market price and
the long-run supply curve will be a(n) _____ curve.

10. If demand increases (remember that it means a rightward shift of the demand
curve), the market price will _____, leading the firms in the industry to expand output and earn an economic ____profit____ in the short run.
Over time, as other firms enter the industry, supply will increase and prices will
_____ until the remaining firms in the industry just break even. In
the long run, the industry will have more firms, industry _____ will
be higher, and finally, all firms in the industry will just _____. If
costs rise when firms _____ the industry, it may be that the new
long-run market equilibrium will be at a higher price than the original and the
long-run supply curve will be _____ sloping but more elastic than
the short-run supply curve. However, if costs remain the same as firms enter the
industry, the long-run supply curve will be a(n) _____ curve.

11. In long-run equilibrium, the value of marginal cost is the same for all firms in a perfectly competitive industry, each firm will just _____, and there is an efficient output because price equals marginal cost. The value of marginal cost is the same for all firms because all firms will produce where marginal cost equals the _____. All firms will break even because of easy entry into and _____ from the industry. Since price (what consumers are willing to pay) equals _____, we know that no mutually beneficial transaction remains unexploited. In the long-run, $P = MC = ATC$ and average total cost is at a(n) _____ point.

Learning Tips

TIP #1: We determine the level of output that maximizes profit for a firm in a perfectly competitive industry by finding where marginal cost equals the market price.

From the principle of marginal analysis we know that the firm should produce where marginal revenue equals marginal cost. This is the optimal output rule. Marginal revenue is just the change in total revenue in response to a change in output; for a perfect competitor, marginal revenue is the market price. The marginal revenue curve is the firm's perfectly elastic demand curve. A firm will maximize profit by finding the level of output at which marginal cost equals price. Figure 9.1 shows the profit-maximizing level of output for a perfectly competitive firm at various prices: if the price is P_1, the firm should produce Q_1; if the price is P_2, the firm should produce Q_2, and if the price is P_3, the firm should produce Q_3.

Figure 9.1

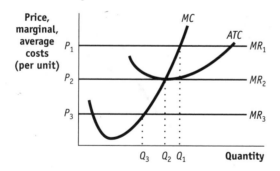

Question: Consider Figure 9.1. If the market price jumps to P_1 from P_2, the profit-maximizing output for a firm in the short run will be

A) Q_1.
B) Q_2.
C) Q_3.
D) above Q_1.

Answer: A.

TIP #2: We can measure the firm's per unit profit by comparing price and average total cost.

Total profit is total revenue minus total cost, or

$$Profit = TR - TC.$$

If we divide through the equation by quantity, we can see that average profit equals average revenue minus average total cost, and we know that average revenue is the market price:

$$\text{Profit}/Q = TR/Q - TC/Q = P - ATC$$

or

$$\text{Profit} = (P - ATC) \times Q.$$

If the price is greater than average total cost, the firm will earn an economic profit. If the price equals average total cost, the firm will just break even. However, if the price falls short of average total cost, the firm will earn a loss.

In Figure 9.2a we can see that at a price of P_1 the firm will earn a profit of $(P_1 - ATC_1) \times Q_1$ (the shaded rectangle). Similarly, at P_2 (see Figure 9.2b), the firm will just break even: $P_2 = ATC_2$. At P_3 in Figure 9.2c, the firm will earn a loss because ATC_3 is greater than P_3, and the loss will equal $(ATC_3 - P_3) \times Q_3$ (the shaded rectangle).

Figure 9.2a

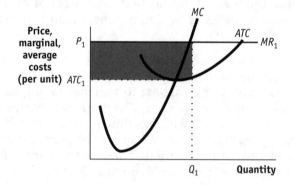

Figure 9.2b

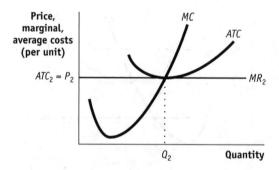

Figure 9.2c

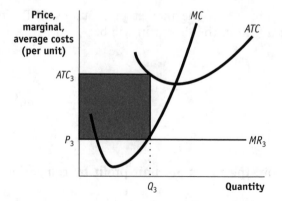

Question: Assume that the short-run equilibrium output for a competitive firm is 20 units, where the firm's average revenue is $10, the firm's marginal cost *(MC)* is $10, and the firm's average total cost *(ATC)* is $8. Therefore, we can conclude that

A) *P* is not equal to *MC*.
B) The output where *ATC* is at minimum occurs at a point where output is more than 20 units.
C) The firm's economic profit is $40, but the economic profit will increase if the firm produces at a point where *ATC* is at a minimum point.
D) The firm's economic profit is $40, but the economic profit will decrease if the firm produces more than 20 units of output.

Answer: D. We know that economic profit will be less than maximum when *MC* is equal to *P*. The option *C* is not correct, because, given the previous information, *P* > *MC* and profit will less than maximum.

TIP #3: To determine if a perfect competitor will continue to produce or shut down in the short run when earning a loss, we need to compare price with average variable cost.

If the price is greater than average variable cost, the firm will continue to produce in the short run, but if the price is less than average variable cost, the firm will shut down. When a firm is earning a loss it will choose to continue to produce or shut down depending on which option will minimize the loss. If the firm shuts down, its loss equals total fixed cost. If the firm earns a loss smaller than total fixed cost by producing, it will continue to produce in the short run. Fixed cost equals total cost less variable cost:

$$FC = TC - VC.$$

Or, average fixed cost equals average total cost less average variable cost:

$$AFC = ATC - AVC.$$

We can find total fixed cost by multiplying *AFC* by output:

$$FC = AFC \times Q = (ATC - AVC) \times Q.$$

The two panels of Figure 9.3 show a situation where the firm is earning a loss and should shut down to minimize its loss. In this case, price is less than the minimum average variable cost. If the firm shuts down, its loss will equal the shaded rectangle in Panel A (this is just fixed costs; fixed costs are always the difference between average total cost and average variable cost multiplied by output), and if it chooses to produce, its loss will equal the rectangle with diagonal lines in Panel B. Since the shaded rectangle is smaller than the one with diagonal lines, the firm should shut down.

Figure 9.3

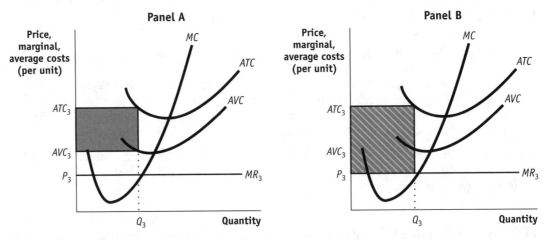

In Figure 9.4, we see a firm that should continue to produce even though it is earning a loss. If the firm shuts down, its loss (fixed costs) will equal the shaded rectangle in Panel A, and if it chooses to produce, its loss will equal the rectangle with diagonal lines in Panel B. Since the rectangle with diagonal lines is smaller than the shaded rectangle, the firm should continue to produce.

Figure 9.4

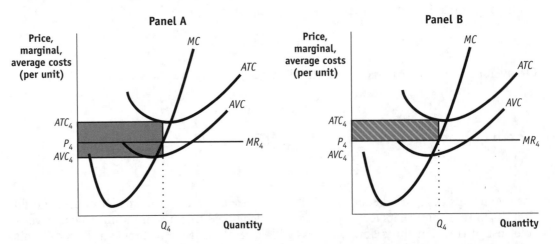

Anytime the price is less than minimum average variable cost, the firm should shut down to minimize its loss in the short run. If the price exceeds minimum average variable cost, the firm should continue to operate in the short run to minimize its loss. This also explains why the firm's short-run supply curve is the marginal cost curve above the minimum point of the average variable cost curve.

Question: Assume that Q_4 in Figure 9.4 equal to 10 units, where $ATC = \$9$, $AVC = \$6$ and $P = MC = \$7$. We can conclude that

A) the firm's economic profit is −$10.
B) the firm's loss is $20, which is less than the total fixed cost of $25.
C) the firm's loss is $20, which is less than the total fixed cost of $30.
D) the firm's loss is $30.

Answer: C.

TIP #4: The long-run adjustment in the perfectly competitive market will always result in all firms breaking even.

In long-run market equilibrium, all producers will break even. If there is some change to the market, for example if demand changes, the industry will adjust in the long run such that all firms once again break even. If long-run market equilibrium is disturbed by an increase in demand, in the short run all firms will expand output and earn economic profits. The economic profits attract new firms into the industry in the long run. As these firms come into the industry, the prices of inputs may rise. As this happens, the market price will come down as firms produce more output, and costs will increase as more firms need inputs. Firms will break even at a higher price than the original long-run equilibrium price and the industry will return to long-run equilibrium. The long-run industry supply curve will be upward-sloping. If the new firms do not bid up the prices of inputs, then the long-run market equilibrium price will be the same as the original price and the long-run industry supply curve will be perfectly elastic.

If long-run equilibrium is disturbed by a decrease in demand, in the short run firms will contract output (some may even shut down) and earn economic losses. The economic losses will encourage some firms to leave the industry in the long run. As firms leave and there is a reduction in the demand for inputs, the prices of the inputs may fall. As this happens, the market price will rise and costs will fall. Firms will break even at a lower price than the original long-run equilibrium price and the industry will return to long-run equilibrium. If the prices in inputs do not fall as firms leave the industry, then the long-run equilibrium price will be the same as the original price and the long-run industry supply curve will be perfectly elastic.

Multiple-Choice Questions

1. In a perfectly competitive market,
   a. there are many buyers and many sellers.
   b. the goods for sale from one producer are perfect substitutes for those produced by another.
   c. there is perfect entry into and exit from the industry.
   d. all of the above.

2. There are many sellers in a perfectly competitive market. So many that
   a. there is tremendous rivalry between firms.
   b. if any one of them produced more or less, there would be a change in market prices.
   c. one producer may have a large market share.
   d. each one is a price taker.

3. Perfectly competitive firms produce where
   a. profit is maximized.
   b. $MR = MC$.
   c. $P = MC$.
   d. all of the above.

4. Which of the following goods are standardized products or commodities?
   a. automobiles
   b. corn
   c. computers
   d. DVD players

5. The marginal revenue curve of a perfectly competitive firm is
   a. equal to the marginal cost curve.
   b. below the marginal cost curve.
   c. above the marginal cost curve.
   d. perfectly elastic at the market price.

Use the following information to answer the next four questions.

Pat owns a potato farm on Price Edward Island called Pat's Potato Patch (PPP). PPP's cost data is given below:

Output (in thousand bushels)	AVC	ATC	MC
1.5	$2,000	$6,000	$1,750
5	2,400	3,600	3,600
6	3,000	4,000	5,000
6.5	3,177	4,100	6,000

6. At what price will PPP just break even?
   a. $1,750
   b. $3,600
   c. $5,900
   d. $10,000

7. At what price will PPP shut down?
   a. $1,750
   b. $3,600
   c. $5,900
   d. $10,000

8. If the market price is $5,000, PPP will produce _____ thousand bushels of potatoes and earn an economic _____.
   a. 2; profit
   b. 4; loss
   c. 6; profit
   d. 9; profit

9. If the market price is $6,000 per thousand bushels, PPP will produce _____ and _____.
   a. 2 thousand bushels; earn an economic loss
   b. 4.5 thousand bushels; break even
   c. 6.5 thousand bushels; earn an economic profit
   d. 10 thousand bushels; earn an economic profit

10. In the perfectly competitive market for tomatoes in the long run, tomato farms will all
   a. break even.
   b. earn an economic loss.
   c. earn an economic profit.
   d. earn an economic loss but continue to produce.

11. Laverne and Shirley run a bed-and-breakfast near the Blue Mountain ski resort in Ontario. During the winter business is great, but the summer is another story. Although they get some tourists exploring the mountain during the warm weather, business is very slow. Laverne and Shirley are trying to decide whether to shut down during the summer months. They should shut down if
    a. total revenue exceeds total fixed cost.
    b. total revenue exceeds total variable cost.
    c. total revenue is less than total cost.
    d. price is less than average variable cost.

12. If a perfect competitor knows that its minimum average total cost is $2, minimum average variable cost is $1.50, and marginal revenue is $3,
    a. the firm will earn an economic profit.
    b. the firm will break even.
    c. the firm will earn an economic loss but continue to produce in the short run.
    d. the firm will earn an economic loss and shut down in the short run.

13. Nila works in the perfectly competitive manicure industry. Although she was hoping to break even, given the market price of $10 for a manicure, she is earning a loss. Nila should
    a. continue to do manicures in the short run as long as her minimum average total costs are more than $10.
    b. continue to do manicures in the short run as long as her minimum average variable costs are more than $10.
    c. continue to do manicures in the short run as long as her minimum average variable costs are less than $10.
    d. shut down.

14. Mila also works in the perfectly competitive manicure industry. The market price is $10 and she does 12 manicures a day. Given that her average total cost is $12, her total revenue is $120, and fixed costs are equal to $24, we know that Mila's
    a. average fixed cost is $1.50.
    b. average profit is –$4.00.
    c. average variable cost is $10.
    d. marginal revenue is $12.

15. A perfectly competitive firm is operating at a loss when
    a. $P = MC$.
    b. $P < ATC$.
    c. $P > ATC$.
    d. $ATC = MC$.

16. A perfectly competitive firm's supply curve is the
    a. marginal revenue curve.
    b. marginal cost curve.
    c. average variable cost curve above the market price.
    d. marginal cost curve above the minimum point on the average variable cost curve.

17. As firms enter a perfectly competitive industry in the long run, the short-run industry supply curve will shift to the _____ and the market price will _____ until all firms _____.
    a. left; rise; break even
    b. right; fall; earn an economic profit
    c. right; fall; break even
    d. left; rise; earn an economic loss

18. In the perfectly competitive market for tomatoes, long-run market equilibrium is disturbed by an increase in demand. In the short run, firms will _____ output and earn a _____.
    a. contract; profit.
    b. expand; profit.
    c. contract; loss.
    d. expand; loss.

19. If firms in a perfectly competitive market in the short run are earning losses but continuing to produce, in the long run
    a. firms will enter the industry and prices will fall.
    b. firms will exit the industry and prices will rise.
    c. firms will enter the industry and prices will rise.
    d. firms will exit the industry and prices will fall.

20. In a perfectly competitive market in the long run, all firms will produce where the market price equals
    a. marginal cost.
    b. average total cost.
    c. average variable cost.
    d. both a and b.

21. Assume that the short-run equilibrium output for a competitive firm is 50 units, where the firm's average revenue is $10, firm's marginal cost (MC) is $10 and the firm's average total cost (ATC) is $8. Which of the following statements is correct?
    a. The minimum point of ATC occurs at an output above 50 units.
    b. The minimum point of ATC occurs at an output below 50 units.
    c. P is unknown.
    d. The minimum MC occurs at 50 units of output.

22. Assume that the short-run equilibrium output for a competitive firm is 15 units, where the firm's average revenue is $10, the firm's marginal cost (MC) is $10, and the firm's average total cost (ATC) is $8. Which of the following statements is correct?
    a. At output = 15 units, ATC is at minimum.
    b. At output = 15 units, MC may not equal to price.
    c. At output = 15 units, the total economic profit is $30, which may not be the maximum profit.
    d. At output = 15 units, the total economic profit is $30, which is the maximum profit.

23. Assume that the profit-maximizing output for a competitive firm in the short run is equal to 10 units, where ATC = $10, AVC = $6, and P = MC = $7. Which of the following statements is correct?
    a. Economic profit is zero.
    b. The firm should produce more.
    c. The firm should produce less.
    d. The firm should not alter the production, because loss is $30, whereas total fixed cost is $40.

24. Assume that the profit-maximizing output for a competitive firm in the short run is equal to 20 units, where AFC = $4, ATC = $8, and $P = MC$ = $10. Which of the following statements is correct?
  a. The firm should produce more.
  b. The minimum economic profit for this firm is $40.
  c. The maximum economic profit for this firm is $40.
  d. The total variable cost is $80.

25. Currently, a competitive firm in the short run is producing 20 units of output, where the ATC is at a minimum point and it is equal to $8. Assume that the current market price is $10. Which of the following statements is correct?
  a. The firm's economic profit of $40 is the maximum economic profit.
  b. The firm should produce more than 20 units of output and earn more than $40 of economic profit.
  c. The firm should not change the output.
  d. The firm should raise the market price and earn more economic profit.

Answer Questions 26–30 on the basis of the following data for a given firm in a competitive market. Assume that the marginal cost increases as output increases. The asterisk (**) indicates the given values as the **minimum** values.

In the following table, P = price, Q = quantity of output, TR = total revenue, TC = total costs, TVC = total variable costs, AC = average total costs, AVC = average variable costs and MC = marginal costs.

	P	Q	TR	TC	TFC	TVC	ATC	AVC	MC
Situation 1	$12	50	$600	$600	$150	$450	$12**	$9	$12
Situation 2	10	200			300		8**		8
Situation 3	10	100	1,000		200			4	10
Situation 4	10	100			100	1,100		11	10
Situation 5	10	100			300			9**	9

26. In Situation 1, the correct response is
  a. the firm should increase the output.
  b. the firm should decrease the output.
  c. the firm should not change the output.
  d. the firm should close down the operation.

27. In Situation 2, the correct response is
  a. the firm should increase the output.
  b. the firm should decrease the output.
  c. the firm should not change the output.
  d. the firm should close down the operation.

28. In Situation 3, the correct response is
  a. the firm should increase the output.
  b. the firm should decrease the output.
  c. the firm should not change the output.
  d. the firm should close down the operation.

29. In Situation 4, the correct response is
  a. the firm should increase the output.
  b. the firm should decrease the output.
  c. the firm should not change the output.
  d. the firm should close down the operation.

30. In Situation 5, the correct response is
   a. the firm should increase the output.
   b. the firm should decrease the output.
   c. the firm should not change the output.
   d. the firm should close down the operation.

Problems and Exercises

Read each question carefully and then write your answers in the space provided or on a separate sheet of paper.

1. Ian offers his mowing services in the perfectly competitive lawn mowing industry. He has fixed cost of $7 per day (the cost of renting the mower) and variable costs as shown in the accompanying table.

Number of lawns mowed per day	Total variable costs	Total costs	Profit when price = $9	Profit when price = $3.60
0	$0.00			
1	2.00			
2	3.50			
3	5.50			
4	8.00			
5	11.00			
6	15.00			
7	21.00			
8	29.00			
9	39.00			

a. What are Ian's total costs of production? Fill in the Total Costs column of the table.

b. Calculate Ian's profit when the market price is $9 per lawn. If the market price of mowing lawns is $9 per lawn, how many lawns will Ian mow? What is his profit? Will he continue to mow lawns in the short run?

c. Calculate Ian's profit when the market price is $3.60 per lawn. If the market price of mowing lawns is $3.60 per lawn, how many lawns will Ian mow? What is his profit? Will he continue to mow lawns in the short run?

2. Ian's fixed costs are $7 per day, and his variable costs are provided in the following table. Complete the table by finding Ian's total costs, average total costs, average variable costs, and his marginal costs of production.

Q	VC	TC	ATC	AVC	MC
0	$0.00				
1	2.00				
2	3.50				
3	5.50				
4	8.00				
5	11.00				
6	15.00				
7	21.00				
8	29.00				
9	39.00				

a. If the market price of mowing lawns is $9 per lawn, how many lawns will Ian mow? What is his profit?

b. At what price will Ian just break even?

c. At what prices for lawn mowing will Ian earn a loss but continue to produce in the short run?

d. At what prices for lawn mowing will Ian shut down his lawn mowing service?

3. In the four panels in the following figure, show a perfect competitor in the short run earning an economic profit (Panel A), breaking even (Panel B), earning an economic loss but continuing to produce (Panel C), and earning an economic loss and shutting down (Panel D). In each graph, be sure to identify a market price, a quantity of output, average total cost, average variable cost (if relevant), and show profit or loss as a rectangle.

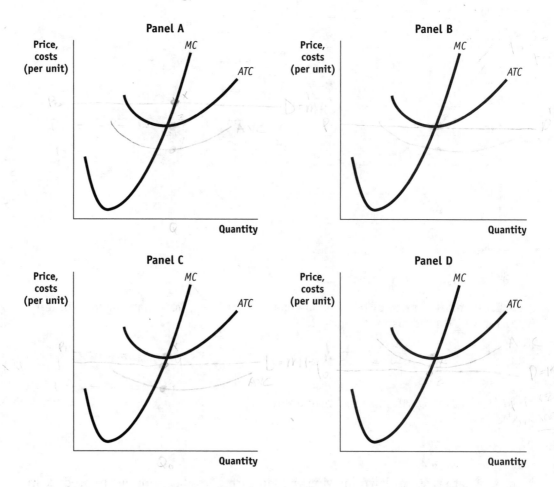

4. Let's return to Ian's lawn mowing service from problems 1 and 2 on pages 216–217.
  a. If Ian is just one of 1,000 lawn mowers in the market, each of which has costs identical to Ian's, draw the industry supply curve in the following figure.

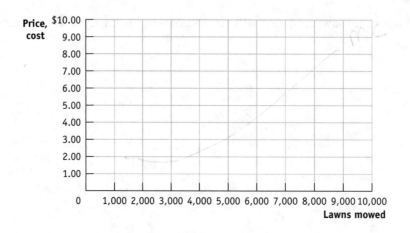

b. If the following table is the market demand schedule, what will be the short-run market equilbrium price? Illustrate this with a graph.

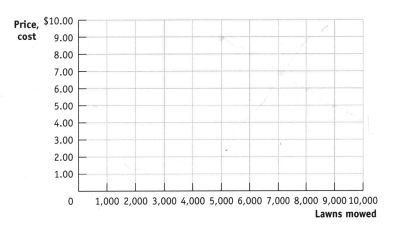

Price	Quantity demanded
$5.00	9,000
6.00	8,000
7.00	7,000
8.00	6,000
9.00	5,000

c. At the short-run market equilibrium price, how much in profit will Ian's lawn mowing service earn?

d. If input prices do not change as firms enter and exit the industry, what will happen in the long run in this market? How is each individual lawn mowing service affected? What is the price elasticity of supply along the long-run industry supply curve? Show the long-run industry supply curve in the accompanying figure.

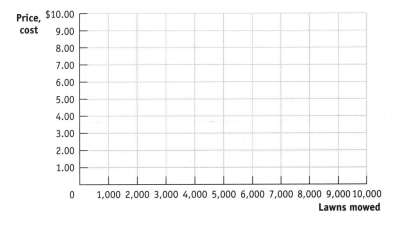

5. Consider the following data for a given firm in a competitive market.

Assume that the marginal cost increases as output increases.

The asterisk (**) indicates the given values as the ***minimum*** values.

In the following table, P = price, Q = quantity of output, TR = total revenue, TC = total costs, TVC = total variable costs, AC = average total costs, AVC = average variable costs and MC = marginal costs.

	P	Q	TR	TC	TFC	TVC	ATC	AVC	MC
Situation 1	$12	50	$600	$600	$150	$450	$12**	$9	$12
Situation 2	10	200			300		8**		8
Situation 3	10	100	1,000		200			4	10
Situation 4	10	100			100	1,100		11	10
Situation 5	10	100			300			9**	9

a. Fill in the above table.

b. Find the situation or situations where the firm should increase output and explain why.

c. Find the situation or situations where the firm should not change output and explain why.

d. Find the situation or situations where the firm should shut down.

*6. You are hired as a consultant. You are given the following current data pertaining to a firm in a competitive industry in the short run.

Market price = $2.00.

Firm's output = 100 units.

Firm's ATC = $1.60.

Firm's ATC of $1.60 at an output of 100 units is the minimum ATC.

(Assume that ATC, AVC and MC curves are U-shaped).

a. Do you think that the firm is making an economic profit? Why or why not?

b. Do you think that the firm can increase its total profit? Should you recommend an increase or decrease of output?

c. What will be the firm's economic profit in the long run? Why?

7. Consider the following cost figures of a representative firm in a perfectly competitive industry in the short run.

Output	Total costs (TC)	Marginal costs (MC)
0	$10	
1	22	
2	36	
3	52	
4	70	
5	90	

a. Fill in the MC column.

b. Assume that there are 1,000 firms. Fill in the column of market supply.

Price (P)	Market demand	Market supply
$12	5,000	
14	4,000	
16	3,000	
18	2,000	
20	1,000	

c. Find the equilibrium P, equilibrium output of a firm, and equilibrium industry output.

d. What is the equilibrium profit for each firm? What will be the likely effect on P in the long run? Why?

Answers to How Well Do You Understand the Chapter

1. buyers, price-takers, market share, identical, enter, industry

2. profit, difference, output, total revenue, horizontal, marginal analysis, optimal, revenue, marginal revenue, maximize, optimal output, equal to, equal to, optimal

3. maximize, more than, produce, negative, market price, average total cost, more than, break even, market price

4. average profit, price, price

5. short run, fixed cost, loss, average variable cost, less than, price, output, total variable cost, minimum

6. average variable cost, shut down, market price

7. average variable cost, equal to, above, supply, market, equal to

8. break even, entry, fall, loss, rise, break even, quantity supplied

9. supply, loss, leave, fall, break even, price, upward, horizontal

10. rise, profit, fall, output, break even, enter, upward, horizontal

11. break even, market price, exit, marginal cost, minimum

Answers to Multiple-Choice Questions

1. In a perfectly competitive market there are many buyers and many sellers exchanging a commodity (a standardized product) and there is perfect entry and exit from the industry. **Answer: D.**

2. There are so many producers in a perfectly competitive market that if any one of them changed their level of production, there wouldn't be any change in price. Therefore, each perfect competitor sells at the market price; each one is a price taker. **Answer: D.**

3. All firms want to produce where profit is maximized, and according to the principle of marginal analysis, this occurs where $MR = MC$. For a perfectly competitive firm, marginal revenue equals price. **Answer: D.**

4. A standardized product or commodity is one for which the output of one producer is a perfect substitute for the output of another. We can distinguish among automobiles, computers, and DVD players by lots of different characteristics, including by producer. However, for a particular type of corn, the output of one producer is a perfect substitute for another. **Answer: B.**

5. For a perfect competitor, marginal revenue equals price. Therefore, the marginal revenue curve is constant at the market price; it is perfectly elastic at the market price. **Answer: D.**

6. A firm breaks even when price equals average total cost. Since price equals marginal revenue for a perfectly competitive firm and firms also produce where marginal revenue equals marginal cost, a perfectly competitive firm will break even when price equals marginal cost and also equals the average total cost. This will happen at minimum average total cost. For PPP, this will occur at a price of $3,600. **Answer: B.**

7. A perfectly competitive firm will shut down when price equals minimum average variable cost. For PPP this occurs at a price of $1,750. **Answer: A.**

8. At a market price of $5,000, PPP will produce 6 thousand bushels (that is where $P = MC$) and earn an economic profit. **Answer: C.**

9. If the market price is $6,000, PPP will produce 6.5 thousand bushels (that's the level of output where $MR = MC$) and earn an economic profit (price exceeds average total costs). **Answer: C.**

10. In the long run, due to easy entry and exit from the market, all firms will break even. **Answer: A.**

11. They should shut down if the loss when they shut down is smaller than the loss they would have if they kept the bed-and-breakfast open. When total revenue is less than total costs, the firm earns a loss, but we don't know if they should shut down or continue in business. If total revenue exceeds total fixed costs or total variable costs, the firm will minimize its loss by continuing in business. However, if price is less than average variable cost, they should shut down. **Answer: D.**

12. Since marginal revenue equals the market price, we know that the market price is $3. Since the market price exceeds minimum average total costs, we know that the firm is earning an economic profit. **Answer: A.**

13. When earning a loss, a perfectly competitive firm should continue in business as long as the loss is smaller than fixed costs (the loss if the firm shuts down). As long as the price exceeds minimum average variable costs, Nila should continue manicuring nails. **Answer: C.**

14. Average fixed costs are fixed costs divided by output: $AFC = \$24/12 = \$2.00$. Her average profit is price less average total costs: Average Profit $= \$10 - \$12 = -\$2.00$. If her average total cost is $12 when she does 12 manicures, then her total costs are $144. Given fixed costs of $24, variable costs are $120 (= $144 − $24), and average variable costs are $10 (= $120/10). In a perfectly competitive industry, price equals marginal revenue and therefore Mila's marginal revenue is $10. **Answer: C.**

15. When average total costs exceed price, the firm is operating at a loss. **Answer: B.**

16. Since a perfectly competitive firm will produce in the short run as long as price exceeds minimum average variable cost and produces at the output level where price equals marginal cost, the marginal cost curve above the minimum average variable cost is the firm's short-run supply curve. **Answer: D.**

17. As firms enter a perfectly competitive industry (presumably because the existing firms in the industry are earning an economic profit in the short run), the short-run industry supply curve shifts to the right, lowering the market price, until all firms break even. When the firms break even, there is no longer any incentive for other firms to enter the industry. **Answer: C.**

18. If long-run equilibrium in a perfectly competitive industry is disturbed by an increase in demand, the market price will rise and the firms in the industry will increase output and earn an economic profit. **Answer: B.**

19. If firms are earning a loss but continuing to produce in the short run, then in the long run some firms will leave the industry (perfectly competitive industries have easy entrance and exit from the industry). As firms leave the industry, the short-run industry supply curve will shift to the left and the market price will rise. The market price will rise until the remaining firms again break even. **Answer: B.**

20. In the long run, all perfectly competitive firms produce where price equals marginal cost (the optimal level of output) and earn a normal profit (price equals minimum average total cost). **Answer: D.**

21. Since $MC > ATC$ at output 50, we are beyond the point where ATC is minimum. **Answer: B.**

22. Since $P = MC$, the firm is at an optimal point and earning maximum profit. **Answer: D.**

23. Since $P = MC$ and since $P > AVC$, the firm should continue to produce 10 units of output. **Answer: D.**

24. At output of 20 units, $P = MC$ and total economic profit is $40. **Answer: C.**

25. Since $P > MC$ at current output, the firm should produce more and earn more profit. **Answer: B.**

26. Since $P = MC$, the firm should not change output. **Answer: C.**

27. Even though $MC = AC$ and the firm is making an economic profit at current output, the firm can increase profit, because at current output $P > MC$. **Answer: A.**

28. Since $P = MC$, the firm should not alter output. **Answer: C.**

29. The firm should shut down, because $P < AVC$. If the firm continues to produce, it will lose $200, but if the firm is shut down, it will lose its total fixed cost of $100. **Answer: D.**

30. Since $P > MC$, the firm should produce more. **Answer: A.**

Answers to Problems and Exercises

1. a. Ian's total cost of production is shown below.

Q	TVC	TC	Profit when price = $9	Profit when price = $3.60
0	$0.00	$7.00	−$7.00	−$7.00
1	2.00	9.00	0.00	−5.40
2	3.50	10.50	7.50	−3.30
3	5.50	12.50	14.50	−1.70
4	8.00	15.00	21.00	−0.60
5	11.00	18.00	27.00	0.00
6	15.00	22.00	32.00	−0.40
7	21.00	28.00	35.00	−2.80
8	29.00	36.00	36.00	−7.20
9	39.00	46.00	35.00	−13.60

b. To answer this question, we need to find profit at each level of output when price is $9. It is shown in the previous table. Ian will mow 8 lawns and earn a profit equal to $36. He will definitely continue to mow lawns in the short run.

   c. The previous table shows Ian's profit at each level of production if the price of lawn mowing falls to $3.60. Ian will mow 5 lawns and just break even. He will continue to produce in the short run.

2. Ian's total costs, average total costs, average variable costs, and marginal costs of production are shown in the following table.

Q	VC	TC	ATC	AVC	MC
0	$0.00	$7.00			
					$2.00
1	2.00	9.00	$9.00	$2.00	
					1.50
2	3.50	10.50	5.25	1.75	
					2.00
3	5.50	12.50	4.17	1.83	
					2.50
4	8.00	15.00	3.75	2.00	
					3.00
5	11.00	18.00	3.60	2.20	
					4.00
6	15.00	22.00	3.67	2.50	
					6.00
7	21.00	28.00	4.00	3.00	
					8.00
8	29.00	36.00	4.50	3.63	
					10.00
9	39.00	46.00	5.11	4.33	

   a. If the market price of mowing lawns is $9, marginal revenue equals $9 at all levels of production. Marginal revenue equals marginal cost when Ian mows 8 lawns. When he mows 8 lawns, his average profit is $4.50 and his total profit is $36 (= $4.50 × 8).

   b. Ian will break even when price equals the minimum point on the average total cost curve—that occurs at a price of $3.60.

   c. Ian will earn a loss at any price less than $3.60 but will continue to produce as long as price exceeds the minimum average variable cost, $1.75.

   d. Ian will shut down his lawn mowing service at any price less than $1.75.

3. Panel A shows a firm earning an economic profit in the short run. To show a firm earning an economic profit, the price must be above the minimum average total cost. The economic profit is average profit (= price − average total cost) multiplied by output; it is shown as the shaded rectangle.

   Panel B shows a firm breaking even in the short run. In this case, price equals minimum average total cost; economic profit is zero.

Panel C shows a firm earning an economic loss but continuing to produce in the short run. The market price in Panel C is less than minimum average total cost (firm earns a loss) but greater than minimum average variable cost (firm continues to produce in the short run). The firm will earn a loss equal to average loss (= average total cost − price) multiplied by output; the loss is shown as the shaded rectangle. This is less than total fixed cost. We can measure total fixed cost at any level of output as the difference between average total and average variable costs multiplied by that level of output. So if we measure at output level Q_c, total fixed costs are $(ATC_c - AVC_c) \times Q_c$.

Panel D shows a firm earning an economic loss and shutting down in the short run. The market price in this case is less than minimum average variable cost. The firm will minimize its loss by shutting down and paying its total fixed cost. Total fixed cost is shown as the rectangle with diagonal lines in Panel D. The loss if it continued to produce would be $(ATC_d - P_d) \times Q_d$, which is greater than total fixed costs $(ATC_d - AVC_d) \times Q_d$.

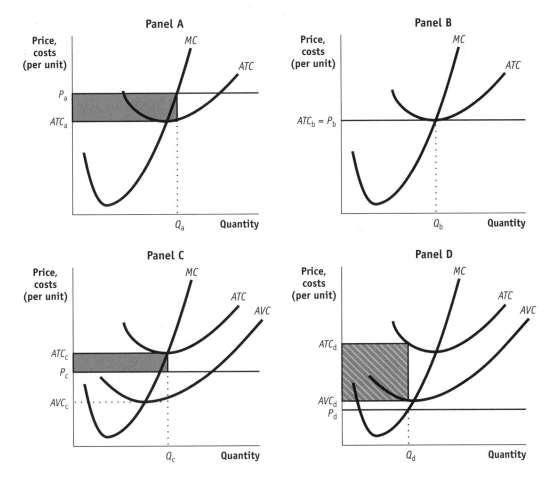

4. a. The industry supply curve is shown in the following figure.

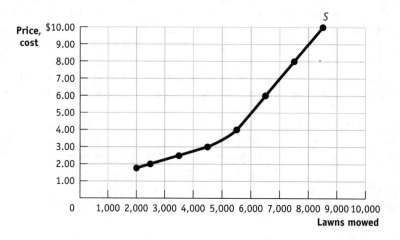

b. Given the market demand, the short-run market equilibrium price will be $7.00, as shown in the following figure.

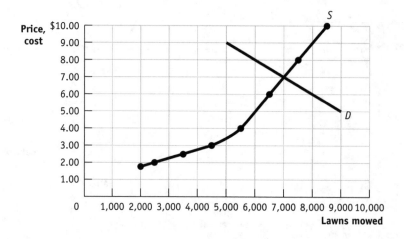

c. At the short-run market equilibrium price, Ian's lawn mowing service will earn a profit of $21—profit is the shaded rectangle in the following figure.

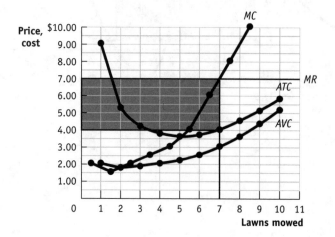

d. Because firms are earning a profit mowing lawns, more firms will come into the industry. As this happens the short-run industry supply curve will shift to the right until the new equilibrium price is equal to the minimum *ATC*, or $3.60—we've assumed that as new firms come into the industry, input prices do not change. At that price, all firms will just break even and there will be no incentive for additional firms to enter the industry. The long-run industry supply curve will be perfectly elastic at a price of $3.60, as shown in the accompanying figure.

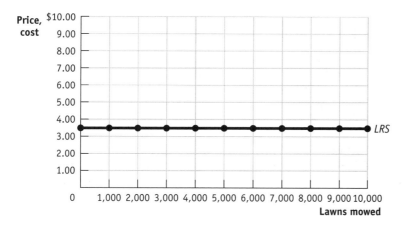

5. a.

	P	Q	TR	TC	TFC	TVC	ATC	AVC	MC
Situation 1	$12	50	$600	$600	$150	$450	$12**	$9	$12
Situation 2	10	200	2,000	1,600	300	1,300	8**	6.50	8
Situation 3	10	100	1,000	600	200	400	6	4	10
Situation 4	10	100	1,000	1,200	100	1,100	12	11	10
Situation 5	10	100	1,000	1,200	300	900	12	9**	9

b. The firm should increase output in Situation 2 and in Situation 5. In situation 2, the price ($10) is greater than the marginal cost ($8). By increasing output (until the point where *P* = *MC*), the firm will make more economic profit. In Situation 5, the price ($10) is greater than the marginal cost ($9). By increasing output (until the point where *P* = *MC*), the firm will lose less.

c. The firm should not change output in Situation 1 and in Situation 3. In situation 1, the price ($12) is equal to the marginal cost ($12). In Situation 3, the price ($10) is equal to the marginal cost ($10).

d. In Situation 4, the firm should shut down, because the price is less than *AVC*. If the firm continues to produce, it will lose $200. If the firm shuts down, it will lose $100. Loss is minimized when the firm shuts down.

6. a. Yes.

The total revenue equals $200, while total cost equals $160. The economic profit is $40.

b. Yes.

Increase output, because at current output, *P* is greater *MC*.

c. Since each firm will make economic profit at the optimal output in the short run, new firms will enter the market, the market supply will increase, and price will fall until economic profit is zero.

7. a.

Output	Total costs (*TC*)	Marginal costs (*MC*)
0	$10	
1	22	$12
2	36	14
3	52	16
4	70	18
5	90	20

b.

Price (*P*)	Market demand	Market supply
$12	5,000	1,000
14	4,000	2,000
16	3,000	3,000
18	2,000	4,000
20	1,000	5,000

c. $P = \$16$, firm's output = 3 and industry output = 3,000.

d. Profit = $48 − $52 = −$4. In the long run, some firms will exit, market supply will decrease, and price will increase until all firms make zero economic profit.

chapter 10

The Rational Consumer

In this chapter, we deal with utility functions and analyze behaviours of consumers who are rational utility-maximizing individuals. We look at how people make choices between different consumption bundles and how price and income affect those choices. We see the application of marginal analysis with the principle of diminishing marginal utility (*MU*). The budget line is introduced in this chapter and we show the meaning of income and substitution effects. In this chapter, we also derive individual and market demand curves.

How Well Do You Understand the Chapter?

Fill in the blanks using the terms below to complete the following statements. Terms may be used more than once. If you find yourself having difficulties, please refer back to the appropriate section in the text.

above	equal	market	purchasing power
all below	flatter	maximize(s)	rational
budget constraint	function	measure	relative
budget line	good A	more	relative prices
bundle	income	negative	satiation
chooses	income effect	none	satisfaction
combination(s)	increase	normal	slope
consumption possibilities	individual	opposite	some
	inverse	optimal	steeper
decrease	large	original	utility
demand	less	$-P_A/P_B$	utils
dollar	marginal utility	positive	upward
dominated	marginal utility per dollar	potatoes	
downward			

1. When economists think about consumer choice, they assume a(n)

_____ utility-maximizing consumer. Utility is measured in hypothet-

ical units called _____. Although we don't _____

utility in practice, the concept is helpful when trying to understand consumer

behaviour. We can think of consumers as having a consumption

_____ (the set of all goods and services they consume) and compare

the utility derived from different consumption bundles. If an individual likes a

good, the total utility curve will be _____ sloping for some levels of

consumption of that good. We define _____ as a change in the total utility due to a change in the consumption of a particular good. We assume that marginal utility (MU) will eventually _____. As marginal utility diminishes, the total utility curve will become _____.

Although marginal utility may _____ over some range of a good, eventually, each successive unit of a good or service consumed adds _____ to total utility than the previous unit; this is known as principle of diminishing _____. It is possible that marginal utility can be _____ (meaning the last unit of a good could lower your total utility). When this occurs, the total utility curve will be _____ sloping.

2. A(n) _____ requires that the cost of a consumer's consumption bundle be no more than the consumer's total income. A consumer's _____ is the set of all consumption bundles that can be consumed given the consumer's income and prevailing prices. If we limit our discussion to how a consumer _____ between various combinations of two goods (A and B), we can see the choice graphically. Given a certain income or budget (N) for the two goods and the prices of the two goods (P_A and P_B), we can draw the _____ for the consumer. The budget line shows the _____ available to a consumer who spends all of his or her income. Graphically, the consumer will be able to consume all combinations of two goods that lie on or below his or her _____, where the budget line is

$$(Q_A \times P_A) + (Q_B \times P_B) \leq N$$

When the consumer is on the budget line, he or she is spending _____ of his or her budget on the two goods. If the consumer is at a point _____ the budget line, he or she is not spending all of his or her income. However, as long as the consumer is not satiated, marginal utility is still _____, and he or she is not getting any utility from saving _____ rather than spending it, the consumer will always choose a consumption bundle on the budget line.

The slope of the budget line is minus the _____ price of one good in terms of the other. If we measure good A on the horizontal axis and good B on the vertical axis, the slope will be _____, or minus the relative price of good A in terms of good B.

3. If the consumer experiences a(n) _____ in income or devotes more of his or her budget to the two goods, the consumer's consumption possibilities have increased and the budget line shifts outward. There is no change to the _____ of the budget line or the relative prices of the goods; the new budget line has the same slope as the _____. If there is a(n) _____ in income or less of the budget is devoted to goods A and B,

the consumption possibilities will decrease and the budget line will shift inward. Again, with no changes in the prices of the two goods, there is no change to the _____ of the budget line.

4. If there is an increase in the price of one good, then the _____ of the two goods will change, as will the slope of the budget line. If we again measure good A on the horizontal axis and good B on the vertical, as the price of good A rises (or the price of good B falls), _____ will become steeper. If the price of good A falls (or the price of good B increases), the _____ becomes flatter.

5. Given the budget constraint and the consumption possibilities, the consumer will choose the _____ of goods on the budget line that _____ his or her utility. This bundle is known as the _____ consumption bundle. The _____ spent on a good or service is the additional utility from spending one more dollar on that good or service. When consumers are choosing among goods, we can thing of them as spending the marginal (or extra) dollar on the good that will bring the most utility for that dollar. In allocating their budget in this way, consumers will _____ total utility given their income. Also, when they've allocated all their income in this way, they will find that the marginal utilities of the last dollar spent on all goods are _____. Returning to our two-good example, the _____ consumption rule says that a consumer will _____ total utility, consuming good A and good B, when the marginal utility of the last dollar spent on the two goods is the same:

$$MU_A/P_A = MU_B/P_B$$

6. The optimal consumption rule helps us understand the individual's _____ curve. If the price of good A rises, then the marginal utility per dollar spent on good A will be less than _____ per dollar spent on good B. The consumer should take one dollar that was spent on good A and spend it on good B. In that way, the consumer's utility will _____. As the consumer spends more on good B and less on good A, the _____ of the last dollar spent on good B will decrease and the marginal utility of the last dollar spent on good A will increase, moving him or her back to the _____ consumption rule. So as the price rises, the individual will buy _____ of that good; this explains the law of demand. We can conclude the following:

- The _____ demand curve is the relationship between quantity demanded and price for a consumer.

- The _____ demand curve is the horizontal sum of the individual demand curves for all consumers. It shows how the quantity demanded by all consumers relates to the price of the good.

- There are two reasons that explain why there is a(n) _____ relationship between price and quantity demanded: the substitution effect and the _____.

7. The optimal consumption rule explains the substitution effect; when the price of one good rises, you consume _____ of it. The substitution effect explains the _____ relationship between price and quantity demanded for most goods. However, for goods that account for a _____ share of a consumer's income, the income effect also plays a role.

8. The income effect explains that, as the price of a given good changes, it also affects the overall _____ of a consumer, and that change in purchasing power affects quantity demanded. For a(n) _____ good, the income effect just reinforces the substitution effect. For an inferior good, however, the income effect and the substitution effect move in _____ directions. If there is a good for which the (opposite) income effect dominates the substitution effect, there would be a _____ relationship between price and quantity demanded. There are some hypothetical cases for which this may happen. For example, this occurred for _____ in Ireland during the famine; but for almost all inferior goods, either the income effect is so small or is _____ by the substitution effect that there is an inverse relationship between price and quantity demanded.

Learning Tips

TIP #1: Although marginal utility may increase at low levels of consumption, as you consume more of a good the marginal utility will eventually decrease.

For some goods, it may require experience to enjoy them. Some examples may include skiing, coffee, and opera. For these goods, as you begin to consume them, total utility will rise but only by a little bit. After you have gained some experience, your appreciation for the next unit of the goods grows and total utility begins to rise at a faster rate. Region I of Figure 10.1 shows total utility rising at an increasing rate; marginal utility is increasing. However, as you continue consuming more, eventually each unit will add less and less to total utility. Region II shows total utility increasing at a decreasing rate; marginal utility is decreasing but positive. You will finally get to a point where any additional units of the goods will reduce total utility. Region III of Figure 10.1 shows total utility decreasing; marginal utility is negative.

Figure 10.1

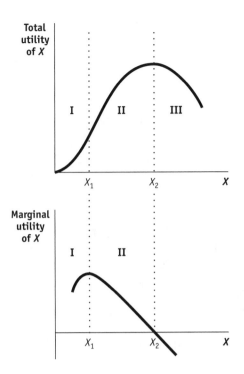

TIP #2: The budget line changes whenever there is a change in income or in the prices of either of the two goods.

If we have two goods, F and G, and we measure F on the horizontal axis and G on the vertical axis, we know that the budget line shows the maximum amounts of the two goods that the consumer can purchase given income (N) and the prices of the two goods (P_F and P_G). The vertical intercept of the budget line will be N/P_G (the maximum amount of G the consumer can purchase if he or she chooses to consume only G), and the horizontal intercept will be N/P_F (the maximum amount of F the consumer can purchase if he or she chooses to consume only F). The slope of the budget line is $-(P_F/P_G)$. Figure 10.2 shows the budget line for a particular level of income ($N=N_1$) and particular prices for the two goods (P_{F1} and P_{G1}).

Figure 10.2

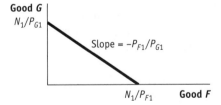

If there is a change in income, the budget line will shift either to the right (if income rose) or to the left (if income fell). In either case, the new budget line will be parallel to the original since there is no change to relative prices. Figure 10.3a shows an increase in income, from N_1 to N_2, and Figure 10.3b shows a decrease, from N_1 to N_3.

Figure 10.3a

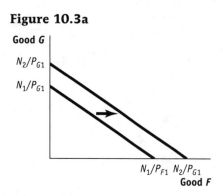

Figure 10.3b

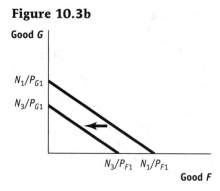

If there is only a change in the price of F, the budget line will pivot around the vertical intercept. There is no change in the amount of good G a person can purchase if he or she only purchases good G. If there is an increase in the price of F, the budget line will pivot to the left, and if there is a decrease in the price of F, the budget line will pivot to the right. Figure 10.4a and 10.4b show an increase in the price of F (the price of F rises to P_{F2}) and a decrease in the price of F (the price of F falls to P_{F3}), respectively.

Figure 10.4a

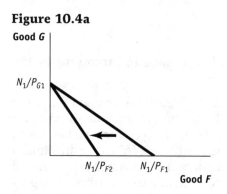

Figure 10.4b

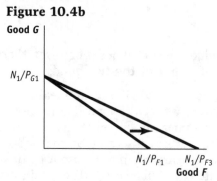

If there is only a change in the price of good G, the budget line will pivot around the horizontal intercept. There is no change in the amount of good F that an individual can purchase if he or she only consumes good F. If there is an increase in the price of G, the budget line will pivot to the left, and if there is a decrease in the price of G, the budget line will pivot to the right. Figure 10.5a and 10.5b show an increase in the price of G (the price of G rises to P_{G2}) and a decrease in the price of G (the price of G falls to P_{G3}), respectively.

Figure 10.5a

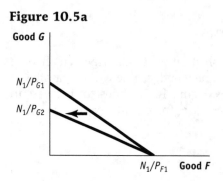

Figure 10.5b

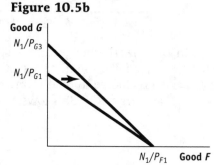

TIP #3: The optimal consumption rule helps us understand the inverse relationship between price and quantity demanded.

According to the optimal consumption rule, the consumer maximizes utility from a given income when the marginal utility of the last dollar spent on all goods is the same. If we only consider two goods, F and G, utility will be maximized when the marginal utility of the last dollar spent on good F equals the marginal utility of the last dollar spent on good G:

$$MU_F/P_F = MU_G/P_G.$$

If there is an increase in the price of good F, the consumer will receive less marginal utility per dollar from good F than from good G:

$$MU_F/P_F < MU_G/P_G.$$

If the consumer reduces her spending by \$1 on good F and buys \$1 more of good G, she will gain more utility from good G than she loses on good F. Her utility will increase by buying more G and less F. As the consumer does this, according to the principle of diminishing marginal utility the marginal utility of G will fall and the marginal utility of F will rise, eventually returning her to the point at which the marginal utility per dollar of each good is the same once again.

TIP #4: When the price of a good changes, there are two effects influencing quantity demanded: the substitution effect and the income effect.

The substitution effect was explained in the previous tip. As the price of a good falls, the marginal utility per dollar spent on that good rises, leading to increased consumption of that good—an inverse relationship between price and quantity demanded. For most goods this is the whole story. However, if the price of a good represents a large proportion of a consumer's income, then the income effect comes into play. As the price of a good falls, the consumer experiences an increase in purchasing power. This increase in purchasing power will increase quantity demanded for normal goods, adding to the substitution effect. However, for inferior goods the decrease in price and consequent increase in purchasing power will decrease quantity demanded. So while the substitution effect encourages the consumer to buy more of the good, the income effect discourages the consumer from the good. Except for the theoretical inferior goods called Giffen goods, the substitution effect dominates the income effect and there is still an inverse relationship between price and quantity demanded.

Multiple-Choice Questions

1. The accompanying figure shows the total utility associated with various combinations of apples and bananas available to a consumer given his or her income and the prices of the two goods. The optimal consumption bundle is where the consumer buys
   a. 2 apples and 9 bananas.
   b. 2 apples and 2 bananas.
   c. 9 apples and 2 bananas.
   d. 0 apples and 15 bananas.

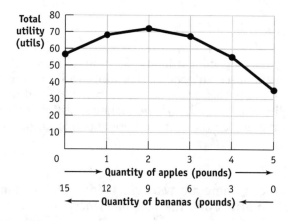

2. Mary Moneybags doesn't really face a budget constraint but she does face a time constraint. Mary has ten hours each week to spend either taking dance classes (each class lasts one hour) or watching movies (the movies run two hours). One possible consumption bundle for Mary is
   a. taking 10 dance classes and watching 5 movies.
   b. taking 5 dance classes and watching 6 movies.
   c. taking 2 dance classes and watching 4 movies.
   d. taking 8 dance classes and watching 2 movies.

3. Charlie gets 10 utils from 1 can of tuna and 18 utils from 2 cans of tuna. If Charlie experiences diminishing marginal utility for tuna, his total utility from 3 cans of tuna will be
   a. 8 utils.
   b. 26 utils.
   c. more than 26 utils.
   d. less than 26 utils.

4. Harry Hollywood loves watching movies. When he watches one movie per week, his total utility is 50 utils, and when he watches two movies, his total utility is 95 utils. Harry faces _____ marginal utility for movies.
   a. increasing
   b. diminishing
   c. positive
   d. both b and c

5. Sam the swimmer enjoys swimming laps in an outdoor pool during the summer. This summer it has rained a lot and Sam has not been able to swim as many laps as he usually does. Sam's marginal utility per lap this year compared with last year is
a. higher.
b. lower.
c. about the same.
d. impossible to determine.

6. Keisha spends all her income on food and transportation, and her budget line for the two goods is $10F + 5T = 500$. Which of the following consumption bundles can Keisha choose?
a. 150 units of transportation and 0 units of food
b. 0 units of transportation and 100 units of food
c. 50 units of transportation and 50 units of food
d. 50 units of transportation and 25 units of food

Use the following information to answer the next three questions.

Harry Hollywood has $50 per week to spend on movie tickets and rentals; the price of a movie ticket is $10 and the price of a movie rental (DVD or video) is $5.

7. Which of the following is one of the consumption bundles Harry can choose?
a. 10 movie rentals and 2 movies tickets
b. 5 movie tickets and no movie rentals
c. 4 movie tickets and 3 movie rentals
d. All of the above.

8. If we measure movie rentals on the horizontal axis and movie tickets on the vertical axis, what is the slope of the budget line?
a. 1/5
b. 1/2
c. −1/2
d. −2

9. If we measure movie rentals on the horizontal axis and movie tickets on the vertical axis, what is the vertical intercept of the budget line?
a. 50
b. 10
c. 5
d. None of the above.

10. Which of the following statements explains what has changed in the following figure?

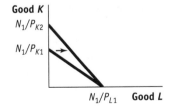

a. There has been an increase in income.
b. There has been a decrease in income.
c. There has been an increase in the price of good K.
d. There has been a decrease in the price of good K.

11. When there is an increase in income, the budget line
    a. has a steeper slope.
    b. has a flatter slope.
    c. shifts to the right with no change in slope.
    d. shifts to the left with no change in slope.

12. Donna spends $30 on milk and honey each month. Each cup of milk costs $1 and each cup of honey costs $3. If the marginal utility she receives from the last cup of milk is 10 utils and from the last cup of honey is 20 utils,
    a. Donna could increase her total utility by increasing her consumption of milk and reducing her consumption of honey.
    b. Donna could increase her total utility by decreasing her consumption of milk and increasing her consumption of honey.
    c. Donna should keep her consumption of milk and honey the same because she is maximizing utility.
    d. It is impossible to determine if Donna is maximizing her utility.

13. Donna spends $30 on milk and honey each month. Each cup of milk costs $1 and each cup of honey costs $3. If her optimal consumption bundle is 9 cups of milk and 7 cups of honey and the marginal utility she receives from the last cup of honey is 15 utils, then the marginal utility of the last cup of milk is
    a. 15 utils.
    b. 9 utils.
    c. 5 utils.
    d. 1/3 of a util.

14. If Marquis is consuming the optimal bundle of pickles and onions and the price of pickles falls, Marquis should
    a. increase his consumption of pickles and decrease his consumption of onions.
    b. decrease his consumption of pickles and increase his consumption of onions.
    c. increase his consumption of pickles but not change his consumption of onions.
    d. decrease his consumption of onions but not change his consumption of pickles.

15. Marquis likes both pickles and onions. However, in equilibrium Marquis receives twice as much marginal utility from the last pickle than from the last onion. It must be that
    a. the prices of pickles and onions are the same.
    b. pickles are twice as expensive as onions.
    c. the price of a pickle is half the price of an onion.
    d. Marquis would be better off consuming more pickles.

16. Tom has recently changed jobs and doubled his income. According to the optimal consumption rule, Tom will now receive
    a. a lower marginal utility from goods than he did before his income rose.
    b. a higher marginal utility from goods than he did before his income rose.
    c. the same marginal utility from goods that he did before his income rose.
    d. twice as much marginal utility from goods than he did before his income rose.

17. Tony and Maria are the only consumers of plaid baseball caps. At a price of $5 per cap, Tony would buy 8 caps per month, and at a price of $10 per cap, he would buy 4 caps per month. Maria will buy 4 caps each month at $5 per cap and 2 caps per month at $10 per cap. At a price of $10, the market demand for plaid baseball caps will be
 a. 2 caps.
 b. 6 caps.
 c. 8 caps.
 d. 12 caps.

18. The quantity demanded of an inferior good increases as its price falls because
 a. the substitution effect and income effect move in the same direction.
 b. the substitution effect dominates the income effect.
 c. the income effect dominates the substitution effect.
 d. none of the above.

19. Which of the following statements is true?
 a. The substitution effect is much more important for goods that take up a substantial share of a consumer's spending.
 b. The substitution effect explains why the demand curve slopes downward for goods that are relatively inexpensive.
 c. The income effect essentially explains the law of demand for most goods.
 d. The income effect always dominates the substitution effect for inferior goods.

20. If a good absorbs a large proportion of a consumer's spending and the price of the good rises, the consumer's purchasing power _____, causing the consumer to buy more of it if the good is _____.
 a. increases; a luxury
 b. increases; inferior
 c. decreases; normal
 d. decreases; inferior

21. Consider a budget line with goods X and Y (good X is the horizontal axis). If P_X/P_Y is 5, then the price of Y is
 a. $10.
 b. $5.
 c. $1.
 d. indeterminate.

22. Consider a budget line with goods X and Y (good X is the horizontal axis.). If the slope of the budget line is –4 and the price of X is $10, the price of Y is
 a. $2.50.
 b. $2.00.
 c. $3.50.
 d. none of the above.

23. If the price of both goods double and income doubles, the budget line will
 a. shift to the right.
 b. shift to the left.
 c. be steeper.
 d. will not change.

*24. Consider an equilibrium situation with a budget line with goods X and Y (good X is drawn in the horizontal axis). If the slope of the budget line is −5 and $MU_X = 10$ utils, then the MU_Y is
   a. impossible to determine.
   b. 2 utils.
   c. 5 utils.
   d. 10 utils.

*25. If $MU_X > MU_X$, but $P_X = P_Y$, one should buy
   a. more X and less Y.
   b. less X and more Y.
   c. a greater proportion of good X compared to the units of good Y.
   d. equal amounts of good X and good Y.

Answer questions 26–29 on the basis of the following table, which shows Sarah's utilities of consumption from goods A and B (utilities are expressed as units of utils). Sarah's daily income (N) is $10 and she spends her entire income on goods A and B.

Units of good A	Total utils (U_A) from A	Marginal utility (MU_A) from A	MU_A/P_A	Units of good B	Total utils (U_B) from B	Marginal utility (MU_B) from B	MU_B/P_B
1	10			1	18		
2	18			2	30		
3	24			3	38		
4	28			4	44		
5	30			5	46		

26. If Sarah is facing a price of A as $1 and a price of B as $2, Sarah will buy
   a. 5 units of A and 5 units of B.
   b. 4 units of A and 3 units of B.
   c. 3 units of A and 2 units of B.
   d. none of the above.

27. If Sarah is facing a price of A as $1 and a price of B as $2, Sarah will buy goods A and B in a way that MU_A/MU_B is
   a. +2.0.
   b. +0.5.
   c. −2.0.
   d. −0.5.

28. If Sarah is facing prices of goods A and B in a way that $P_A = 1 and $P_B = 2, her equation of budget line is (where N is her daily income)
   a. $N = 1 + 2$.
   b. $N = A + B$.
   c. $N = A + 2B$.
   d. $N = 2A + B$.

29. If Sarah is facing prices of goods A and B in a way that $P_A = P_B = 1, Sarah will buy
   a. 5 units of A and 5 units of B.
   b. 4 units of A and 3 units of B.
   c. 3 units of A and 2 units of B.
   d. none of the above.

30. After spending all her income on 10 units of good *A* and 10 units of good *B*, Mrs. Myatt finds that her $MU_A = MU_B = 10$ utils. Therefore,
   a. Mrs. Myatt is maximizing her utility.
   b. Mrs. Myatt is buying the correct combination of *A* and *B*.
   c. Mrs. Myatt should buy more of *A* and *B*.
   d. Mrs. Myatt is maximizing her utility if we assume that $P_A = P_B$.

Problems and Exercises

Read each question carefully and then write your answers in the space provided or on a separate sheet of paper.

1. Hortense likes opera and hamburgers, and her total utility (*TU*) functions for both goods per week are shown in the following table. Graph her two total utility functions and their corresponding marginal utility functions in the accompanying figures. How are the two functions/curves similar and how are they different? At how many operas and hamburgers per week is Hortense satiated?

Units	TU from Opera	TU from Hamburgers
1	3	10
2	7	15
3	17	19
4	21	22
5	24	24
6	26	25
7	27	24

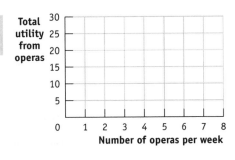

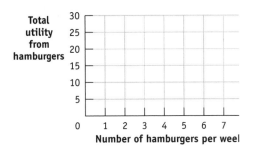

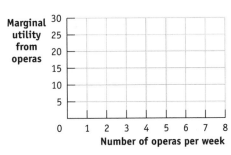

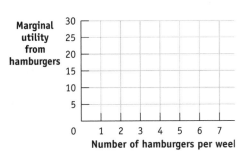

2. Bob likes both hummus and falafels and spends $24 per week on them. The price of hummus is $4 per pound and falafels cost $2 each. Show the budget line and consumption possibilities of hummus and falafels for Bob in the following figure. Show the budget lines for the following changes to income and/or the price of hummus and falafel. (Only consider the change specified in each part below—all other variables return to their original values.)

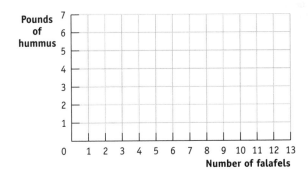

a. Bob's income increases to $28.

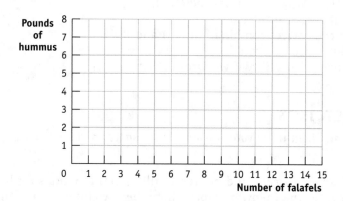

b. Bob's income decreases to $18.

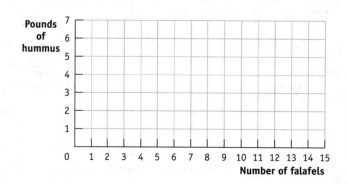

c. The price of hummus goes up to $6 per pound.

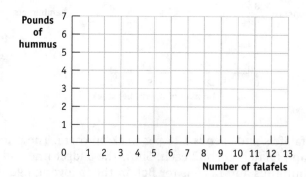

d. The price of hummus falls to $2 per pound.

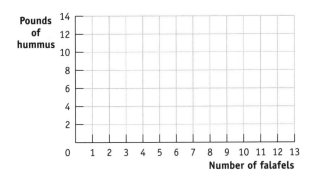

e. The price of a falafel rises to $4.

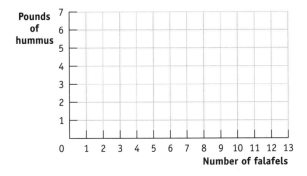

f. The price of a falafel falls to $1.

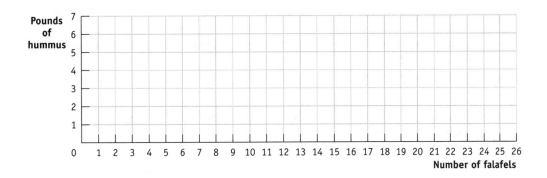

g. Bob's income increases to $48, the price of hummus rises to $8 per pound and the price of a falafel rises to $4.

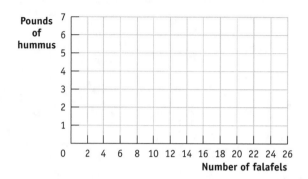

h. Bob's income decreases to $12, the price of hummus falls to $2, and the price of a falafel falls to $1.

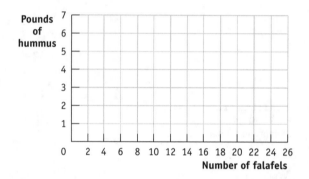

3. If Bob's total utilities are as shown in the following table and Bob still has $24 to spend on falafels that cost $2 each and hummus that costs $4 per pound, what is the optimal consumption bundle? Show how total utility changes with different consumption bundles. How much utility is Bob getting from hummus and falafels when he is consuming the optimal bundle? What is the marginal utility per dollar spent on falafels and the marginal utility per dollar spent on hummus when he is consuming the optimal bundle?

Pounds of hummus per week	Total utility from hummus	Number of falafels per week	Total utility from falafels
0	0	0	0
0.5	10.5	1	19
1	20	2	36
1.5	28.5	3	51
2	36	4	64
2.5	42.5	5	75
3	48	6	84
3.5	52.5	7	91
4	56	8	96
4.5	58.5	9	99
5	60	10	100
5.5	60.5	11	99
6	54.25	12	96

4. If Sara is consuming tea and scones according to the optimal consumption rule, explain how she will react to an increase in the price of scones? How would she have reacted if instead of an increase in the price of scones there was a decrease in the price of tea? How does this help us understand the inverse relationship between price and quantity demanded?

5. Sarah's utilities (utilities are expressed as units of utils) from consumption of two goods, A and B, are given in the accompanying table. Sarah's daily income (N) is $23 and she spends her entire income on goods A and B. Assume that $P_A = \$2$ and $P_B = \$5$.

Units of good A	Total utils (U_A) from A	Marginal utility (MU_A) from A	MU_A/P_A	Units of good B	Total utils (U_B) from B	Marginal utility (MU_B) from B	MU_B/P_B
1	10			1	20		
2	18			2	35		
3	24			3	45		
4	28			4	50		
5	30			5	52		

a. Fill in the columns of the preceding table.

b. What is Sarah's budget constraint equation? What is $\Delta B/\Delta A$? What is P_A/P_B?

c. What is Sarah's equilibrium consumption of A and B? What is her marginal utility per dollar on each good? What is Sarah's total utility per dollar?

d. If income increases to $30, how many goods are bought by Sarah?

*6. Consider the following total utility (U) functions of good X and find with numerical examples if marginal utility is increasing, decreasing or constant.

   a. $U = 10X^{0.5}$.

   b. $U = 10X$.

   c. $U = 10X^2$.

7. Despite that the price of a movie theater ticket has doubled, Sam is seeing more movies each month, even though his monthly income has not changed. Is a movie a normal good or inferior good for Sam?

Answers to How Well Do You Understand the Chapter

1. rational, utils, measure, bundle, upward, marginal utility, diminish, flatter, increase, less, marginal utility, negative, downward

2. budget line, consumption possibilities, chooses, budget line, combinations, budget line, all, below, positive, income, relative, $-P_A/P_B$

3. increase, slope, original, decrease, slope

4. relative price, budget line, budget line

5. combination, maximizes, optimal, marginal utility per dollar, maximize, equal, optimal, maximize

6. demand, marginal utility, increase, marginal utility, optimal, less, individual, market, inverse, income effect

7. less, inverse, large

8. purchasing power, normal, opposite, positive, potatoes, dominated

Answers to Multiple-Choice Questions

1. Total utility is maximized when the consumer buys 2 pounds of apples and 9 pounds of bananas. **Answer: A.**

2. Mary's constraint is time; she has only ten hours a week and is choosing among different combinations of taking dance classes and watching movies. Since each dance class (D) lasts one hour and each movie (M) lasts two hours, her time constraint is

$$10 = 1D + 2M.$$

   We can see the different combinations of dance classes and movies that are available to Mary in the following figure.

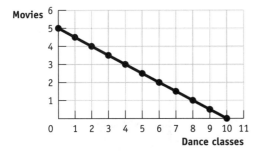

   Mary's only possible consumption bundle is to take 2 dance classes and watch 4 movies. All the other bundles are not possible for Mary given the time each activity takes and the amount of time she has to allocate to them. **Answer: C.**

3. The marginal utility of Charlie's first can of tuna is 10 utils and his utility from the second is 8 utils. If Charlie experiences diminishing marginal utility, then the third can of tuna will add something less than 8 utils to his total utility. His total utility will increase to something less than 26. **Answer: D.**

4. Marginal utility is the change in total utility due to a change in consumption. As Harry watches his first movie, total utility rises by 50 utils, and when he watches a second movie, his total utility rises by 45 utils. Therefore, the marginal utility of the first movie is 50 and of the second is 45—Harry faces diminishing marginal utility. Since each movie adds to total utility, we know that Harry's marginal utility is positive but that Harry faces diminishing marginal utility for movies. **Answer: D.**

5. Due to the principle of diminishing marginal utility, as Sam swims fewer laps this year than last, his marginal utility per lap this year must be higher than it was last year. **Answer: A.**

6. Keisha can choose any combination of food and transportation that lies on the budget line shown in the following figure. The only one of the choices on the line is 50 units of transportation and 25 units of food. Each of the other combinations lies outside Keisha's consumption possibilities. **Answer: D.**

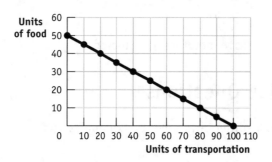

7. Harry can choose any combination of movie tickets and movie rentals that lie on the budget line shown in the following figure. The only option available to him is to purchase 5 movie tickets and no movie rentals. All of the other options lie outside his consumption possibilities. **Answer: B.**

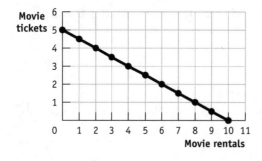

8. If we measure movie rentals on the horizontal axis and movie tickets on the vertical axis, then the slope of the budget line is $-P_{rentals}/P_{tickets}$, or $-1/2$. **Answer: C.**

9. If we measure movie rentals on the horizontal axis and movie tickets on the vertical axis, the vertical intercept will be that amount of movie tickets Harry can purchase if he chooses not to do any movie rentals. We can find that by taking his spending and dividing by the price of a movie ticket. The vertical intercept is 5 ($= 50/10$). **Answer: C.**

10. The figure shows the shift in the budget line if there is a decrease in the price of K. If there is a decrease in the price of K, the horizontal intercept of the budget line (how much of good L the consumer can purchase if he or she devotes all spending to L) doesn't change, but the vertical intercept (how much of good K the consumer can purchase if he or she devotes all spending to K) increases. **Answer: D.**

11. Since the slope of the budget line is the negative of the ratio of the prices of the two goods, if only income changes, the slope of the budget line does not change. As income increases, the consumer's consumption possibilities and the budget line shift outward, or to the right. **Answer: C.**

12. If Donna receives 10 utils from the last cup of milk she buys and milk costs $1 per cup, then she receives 10 utils on the last dollar from milk. If she receives 20 utils from the last cup of honey and honey costs $3, then she receives 6.67 utils per dollar from honey. Since the marginal utility per dollar spent on milk is higher than the marginal utility per dollar spent on honey, she could increase her total utility by buying less honey and more milk. **Answer: A.**

13. If Donna's optimal consumption bundle is 9 cups of milk and 7 cups of honey, then we know that the marginal utility per dollar spent on milk equals the marginal utility per dollar spent on honey:

$$\frac{MU_{milk}}{P_{milk}} = \frac{MU_{honey}}{P_{honey}}$$

Therefore,

$$\frac{MU_{milk}}{1} = \frac{15}{3}$$

Answer: C.

14. If Marquis is consuming the optimal bundle of pickles and onions and there is a decrease in the price of pickles, the marginal utility per dollar spent on pickles will be higher than the marginal utility per dollar spent on onions. To maximize utility, Marquis should buy more pickles and fewer onions. Doing that, the marginal utility of pickles will fall and the marginal utility of onions will rise until the optimal consumption rule again holds. **Answer: A.**

15. If Marquis receives twice as much marginal utility from the last pickle than from the last onion, the pickle must be twice as expensive. Only if pickles cost twice as much as onions will Marquis be achieving the optimal consumption rule. **Answer: B.**

16. When Tom's income increases, the optimal consumption rule tells us that he will buy more of all goods (the optimal consumption rule does not distinguish between normal and inferior goods). As he consumes more of all goods, according to the principle of diminishing marginal utility his marginal utility will decrease. **Answer: A.**

17. The market demand curve is the horizontal sum of the individual demand curves. At each price, we add up quantity demanded by each individual. At a price of $10 per cap, the market demand is Tony's 4 caps plus Maria's 2 caps, or 6 caps. **Answer: B.**

18. As the price falls, the substitution effect encourages an increase in quantity demanded whether for a normal or an inferior good. As price falls, purchasing power increases. The increase in purchasing power will also result in an increase in quantity demanded for normal goods but a decrease in quantity demanded for inferior goods. However, for almost all inferior goods, the substitution effect dominates the income effect and there is an inverse relationship between price and quantity demanded. **Answer: B.**

19. For most goods, the substitution effect explains the whole relationship between price and quantity demanded. This is especially true for goods that are inexpensive. For some goods whose purchase represents a substantial portion of a consumer's spending, the income effect also plays a role. **Answer: B.**

20. As the price of a good rises, the consumer's purchasing power will decrease. If this good represents a large proportion of the consumer's spending, he or she will buy more of it if it is inferior. **Answer: D.**

21. We need to know the price of X. **Answer: D.**

22. Since the slope of the budget line is equal to P_X/P_Y and since $P_X = \$10$, P_Y has to be $2.50. **Answer: A.**

23. If both prices and income double, the budget line is unaffected. **Answer: D.**

24. Since the slope of the budget line is equal to MU_X/MU_Y and since MU_X is 10 utils, MU_Y has to be 2 utils. **Answer: B.**

25. Buy more of X and buy less Y (this will bring more total utility per dollar), until $MU_X = MU_Y$. **Answer: A.**

26. When Sarah buys 4 units of X and 3 units of Y, her marginal utility per dollar on each good is equal to each other and she has also spent her income. **Answer: B.**

27. Since $(MU_A/MU_B) = P_A/P_B$ and since P_A/P_B is 0.5, (MU_A/MU_B) is equal to 0.5. **Answer: B.**

28. Since $N = P_A A + P_B B$ and given the prices, the budget line equation is $N = A + 2B$. **Answer: C.**

29. When Sarah buys 5 units of X and 5 units of Y, her marginal utility per dollar on each good is equal to each other and she has also spent her income. **Answer: A.**

30. Since $(MU_A/MU_B) = P_A/P_B$ and since $MU_A = MU_B$, P_A has to equal P_B. **Answer: D.**

Answers to Problems and Exercises

1. To find Hortense's marginal utility function, we need to calculate what each unit adds to total utility. The accompanying table shows the total utility functions and marginal utility functions for opera and hamburgers.

Units	Total utility from operas	Total utility from hamburgers	Marginal utility of opera	Marginal utility of hamburgers
0	0	0		
			3	10
1	3	10		
			4	5
2	7	15		
			10	4
3	17	19		
			4	3
4	21	22		
			3	2
5	24	24		
			2	1
6	26	25		
			1	-1
7	27	24		

The total utility and marginal utility curves are shown in the following figure.

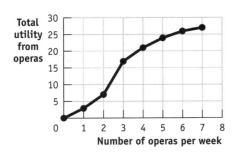

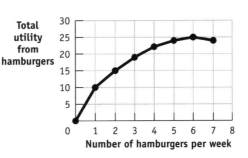

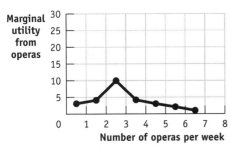

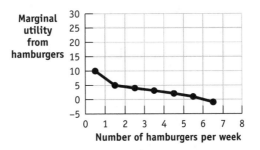

Hortense's total utility from opera is increasing at an increasing rate—each opera adds more to total utility than the previous one—for the first three operas. Only after Hortense has seen three operas in one week does she begin to experience diminishing marginal utility. Hortense may be satiated at seven operas in one week but we do not know for sure. To determine if she was satiated, we would need to know that an eighth opera would bring down her total utility. Hortense's total utility from hamburgers shows total utility increasing at a decreasing rate as soon as she has one hamburger per week. She is satiated when she has had 6 hamburgers; at six burgers, her utility is maximized.

2. If Bob has $24 per week to spend on hummus (H) and falafels (F), the price of hummus is $4 per pound and falafels cost $2 each, his budget line is

$$\$24 = \$4H + \$2F.$$

The following figure shows the budget line.

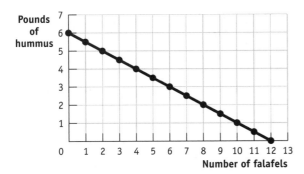

a. The following figure shows his budget line when Bob's income increases to $28.

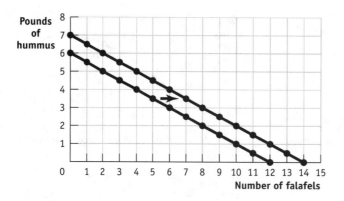

b. The following figure shows the shift in the budget line when Bob's income decreases to $18.

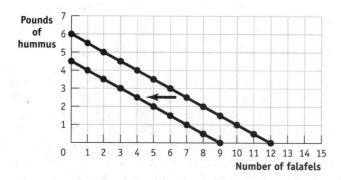

c. The following figure shows the change in the budget line when the price of hummus goes up to $6 per pound.

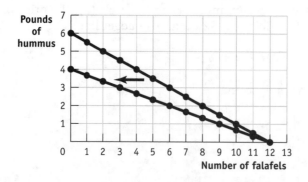

d. If the price of hummus falls to $2 per pound, Bob's budget line will rotate as shown in the following figure.

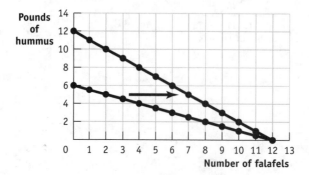

e. If the price of a falafel rises to $4, Bob's budget line will change as shown in the following figure.

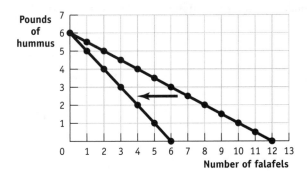

f. If the price of a falafel falls to $1, Bob's budget line will be as shown in the following figure.

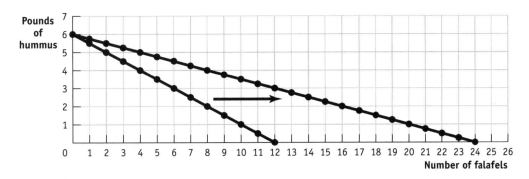

g. If Bob's income increases to $48, the price of hummus rises to $8 per pound and the price of a falafel rises to $4, the budget line will remain the same as the original. In this case, income and the prices of the two goods doubled. The new budget line is

$$\$48 = \$8H + \$4F.$$

We can divide both sides by 2 and go back to the original budget line:

$$\$24 = \$4H + \$2F.$$

h. If Bob's income decreases to $12, the price of hummus falls to $2 per pound and falafels cost $1 each, again there will be no change in the budget line. In this case, income and the prices of the two goods fell by one-half. The new budget line is

$$\$12 = \$2H + \$1F.$$

If we multiply both sides by 2, we go back to the original budget line:

$$\$24 = \$4H + \$2F.$$

3. To find Bob's optimal consumption bundle we need to find where the marginal utility of the last dollar spent on falafels is equal to the marginal utility of the last dollar spent on hummus. To do this we need to calculate the marginal utilities for various units of both goods and then find the marginal utility per dollar associated with various units of both goods. The following table shows this information for falafels and hummus.

Quantity of hummus	Total utility from hummus	Marginal utility of hummus	Marginal utility of hummus/price of hummus	Falafels	Total utility from falafels	Marginal utility of falafels	Marginal utility of falafels/price of falafels
0	0			0	0		
		21	5.25			19	9.5
0.5	10.5			1	19		
		19	4.75			17	8.5
1	20			2	36		
		17	4.25			15	7.5
1.5	28.5			3	51		
		15	3.75			13	6.5
2	36			4	64		
		13	3.25			11	5.5
2.5	42.5			5	75		
		11	2.75			9	4.5
3	48			6	84		
		9	2.25			7	3.5
3.5	52.5			7	91		
		7	1.75			5	2.5
4	56			8	96		
		5	1.25			3	1.5
4.5	58.5			9	99		
		3	0.75			1	0.5
5	60			10	100		
		1	0.25			−1	−0.5
5.5	60.5			11	99		
		−12.5	−3.125			−3	−1.5
6	54.25			12	96		

The following figure shows the above data graphically.

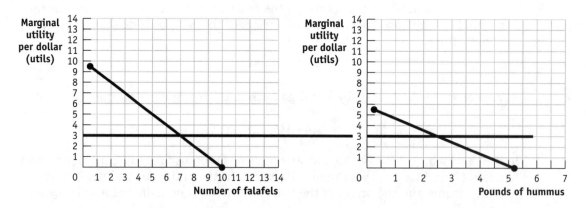

The marginal utility per dollar spent on hummus and falafels is the same and all of Bob's income is spent on the two goods when Bob consumes 7 falafels and 2.5 pounds of hummus. The total utility equals 133.5. We can also see that this is the combination of falafels and hummus that maximizes utility by looking at the total utility from different consumption bundles on the budget line in the following figure.

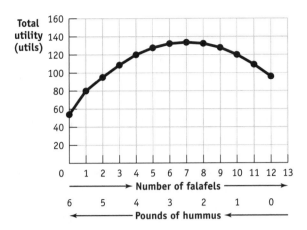

4. If Sara is consuming her optimal consumption bundle of tea and scones, that must mean that she has allocated her income such that the marginal utility of the last dollar spent on tea equals the marginal utility of the last dollar spent on scones:

$$\frac{MU_{tea}}{P_{tea}} = \frac{MU_{scones}}{P_{scones}}$$

When the price of scones rises, the marginal utility of the last dollar spent on scones will fall and will be less than the marginal utility of the last dollar spent on tea:

$$\frac{MU_{tea}}{P_{tea}} > \frac{MU_{scones}}{P_{scones}}$$

This will encourage Sara to buy more tea and fewer scones. As she does that, the marginal utility of tea will fall and the marginal utility of scones will rise until once again the optimal consumption rule holds.

  If there had been a decrease in the price of tea, the marginal utility per dollar spent on tea would rise and be larger than the marginal utility per dollar spent on scones. Again, Sara would buy more tea and fewer scones.

  This helps us understand the inverse relationship between price and quantity demanded because as the price of scones rose, Sara bought fewer scones, and as the price of tea fell, Sara bought more tea.

5. a. See the table below

Units of good A	Total utils (U_A) from A	Marginal utility (MU_A) from A	MU_A/P_A	Units of good B	Total utils (U_B) from B	Marginal utility (MU_B) from B	MU_B/P_B
1	10	10	5	1	20	20	4
2	18	8	4	2	35	15	3
3	24	6	3	3	45	10	2
4	28	4	2	4	50	5	1
5	30	2	1	5	52	2	2/5

b. $10 = 2A + 5B$.

Since income is constant, we can show the following.

$0 = 2\Delta A + 5\Delta B$. Therefore, P_A/P_B is equal to $-\Delta B/\Delta A$, which is 2/5.

c. $A = 4$ and $B = 3$. Marginal utility per dollar is 2. Total utility per dollar = 29.

d. $A = 5$ and $B = 4$.

6. a. When you use more and more X, you will notice that U increases at a diminishing rate. Therefore, marginal utility is decreasing.

b. Marginal utility is constant at 10.

c. When you use more and more X, you will notice that U increases at an increasing rate. Therefore, marginal utility is increasing.

7. The price of a movie theater ticket has doubled and, according to substation effect, Sam should see fewer movies in movie theaters. Since the price increase, Sam's real income has decreased. If a movie is a normal good, then less real income will lead to fewer movie theater tickets being bought. If a movie is an inferior good, less real income will cause more of that being bought. In Sam's case, income effect is going in the opposite direction of the substitution effect. Sam is seeing more movies, because his income effect dominates his substitution effect. Therefore, a movie is an inferior good.

chapter 11

Consumer Preferences and Consumer Choice

In this chapter, we continue with utility functions and show how consumer equilibrium is achieved with budget lines and indifference curves. We see the effects of price changes and income changes on consumer equilibrium. We also look at the significance and meaning of diminishing marginal rate of substitution. And we add here more discussions on income effect and substitution effects within indifference curve frameworks.

How Well Do You Understand the Chapter?

Fill in the blanks using the terms below to complete the following statements. Terms may be used more than once. If you find yourself having difficulties, please refer back to the appropriate section in the text.

above	falls	lower	rises
below	flatter	more	shift
bundles	higher	on	slope
constant	hill	optimal	substitution
consumption rule	income	ordinary	substitution effect
corner	increase	ordinary goods	tangency
curve map	indifference	perfect complements	tangent
decrease	inferior	perfect substitutes	undefined
demand	left	relative price	unique
diminishing	less	right	utility
equals	line	right angle	

1. Consumers choose from a vast array of consumption _____ to find the one that maximizes utility, given their income. A consumer may be indifferent between some bundles that yield the same level of _____ to the consumer and prefer some bundles to others because they give a higher utility to the consumer. If we limit our discussion to just two goods and show the combination of goods among which the consumer is indifferent, we can identify a consumer's _____ curve, the line that shows all the consumption bundles that yield the same amount of total utility for an individual. Since consumers prefer more to less, any combination of the two goods that lies _____ a given indifference curve will yield more utility to the consumer, while any point below a given indifference curve will yield a(n) _____ level of utility to the consumer. The collection of indifference curves that represents a consumer's entire utility function is known as an indifference _____. Every

consumer has a(n) _____ indifference curve map; yet all indifference curve maps share four important properties. They never cross, and those that are farther away from the origin yield a(n) _____ level of total utility than those that are closer. Most indifference curves also slope _____ and are convex to the origin. If a good satisfies all four properties, it is called a(n) _____ good.

2. The _____ of the indifference curve is known as the marginal rate of substitution. Along any one indifference curve, total utility is _____, and the slope of the curve represents the rate at which the consumer can substitute one good for the other without any change in total _____. If we are measuring the quantity of good A on the horizontal axis and the quantity of good B on the vertical axis of an indifference curve, as we move down the curve we know that the marginal utility associated with the additional consumption of good A is exactly offset by the marginal utility associated with the _____ consumption of good B:

$$MU_A \times \Delta A = -MU_B \times \Delta B$$

The _____ of the indifference curve is the negative of the ratio of the marginal utilities:

$$-\frac{MU_A}{MU_B} = \frac{\Delta B}{\Delta A}$$

If goods A and B are _____, then the consumer requires additional units of A to compensate for less B (and vice versa), and the consumer experiences a diminishing marginal rate of _____ in substituting one good for another.

3. Since the indifference curve is convex to the origin, the marginal rate of substitution _____ as we move down an indifference curve. The principle of _____ marginal rate of substitution states that the more of good A one consumes in proportion to good B, the less of good B he or she is willing to substitute for another unit of A. As the consumer moves down an indifference curve, consuming more of good A and less of good B, the marginal utility associated with good A _____ and the marginal utility of good B _____. To remain at the same level of utility, the consumer gives up _____ of good B for good A. The indifference curve gets _____; the marginal rate of substitution falls. As the consumer moves up an indifference curve, consuming _____ of good B and _____ of good A, the marginal utility associated with good A rises and the marginal utility of B good falls. The consumer is _____ willing to give up good A for good B. The indifference curve gets steeper; the marginal rate of substitution _____.

4. The consumer will be maximizing utility given his or her budget constraint when the budget line is _____ to the highest possible indifference curve; this is the _____ condition. The slope of the budget line _____ the slope of the indifference curve (the marginal rate of substitution). From the previous chapter, we know that the slope of the budget line is minus the ratio of the prices ($-P_A/P_B$). Therefore, in equilibrium the following condition holds:

Slope of indifference curve = Slope of budget line

$$\frac{MU_A}{MU_B} = \frac{P_A}{P_B}$$

This is known as the _____ rule. We can transform the relative price rule, which states that at the _____ bundle of goods A and B the marginal rate of substitution between two goods is equal to their relative price, to get the optimal _____ from the previous chapter:

$$\frac{MU_A}{P_A} = \frac{MU_B}{P_B}$$

5. Two goods are _____ if the marginal rate of substitution of one good in place of the other good is constant, regardless of how much each individual consumes. If two goods are perfect substitutes, each indifference curve will be a downward-sloping straight _____ and the marginal rate of substitution is _____. The budget line will touch the _____ possible indifference curve at a point where the consumer consumes only one good or is indifferent among the different bundles on the budget line.

6. Two goods are _____ when a consumer wants to consume the goods in the same ratio regardless of their price. If two goods are perfect complements, each indifference curve will be a(n) _____ (or L-shaped), with the corner at the ratio of good B to good A which the consumer must use together. In this case, the tangency point will always occur at a(n) _____ of the highest indifference curve and the marginal rate of substitution is _____ because the individual's preferences don't allow substitution between goods.

7. We can understand how income affects the _____ for goods by looking at what happens to the consumption of two goods when income changes. An increase in income will shift the budget line to the _____, and the consumer will be able to choose a consumption bundle that yields a higher level of utility that the previous one.

8. When there is a change in the price of a good, both the _____ and the income effect influence how quantity demanded will respond. We can explain the substitution effect by looking at what happens when there is a change in the

_____ of the budget line. An increase in the price of one good (good A) affects relative prices, which is the slope of the budget line ($-P_A/P_B$). Consumers want to buy _____ of good A and _____ of good B (it's relatively less expensive). We can explain the income effect by looking at what happens when there is a(n) _____ in the budget line. An increase in the price of good A lowers the consumer's purchasing power, and this results in a shift to the left in the budget line. If goods A and B are both normal goods, the consumer will buy _____ of both goods. However, if either good A or good B is _____, the consumer will respond to a lower income by increasing the amount of the good purchased. As we saw in the previous chapter, as the price rises, the substitution effect encourages the consumer to buy _____of that good; however, if the good is inferior, as the price rises, the consumer buys _____ of the good due to the income effect. For almost all inferior goods, the _____ effect dominates the _____ effect and an increase in price will result in a decrease in quantity demanded.

Learning Tips

TIP #1: The optimal consumption rule and the tangency condition are comparable ways of viewing the consumer in equilibrium.

In Chapter 10 we learned the optimal consumption rule: the consumer is maximizing utility given a spending constraint when the marginal utility of the last dollar spent on all goods is the same:

$$\frac{MU_A}{P_A} = \frac{MU_B}{P_B}$$

In this chapter, we learned that the consumer is maximizing utility given a spending constraint when the budget line is tangent to the highest possible indifference curve. At that point, the slope of the indifference curve ($-MU_A/MU_B$) will equal the slope of the budget line ($-P_A/P_B$):

$$\frac{MU_A}{MU_B} = \frac{P_A}{P_B}$$

If we take either equation and multiply both sides by the denominator of the term on the left side of the equation and divide both sides by the numerator of the term on the right side of the equation, we can turn one equation into the other.

TIP #2: If two goods are perfect substitutes, the indifference curve map will be a set of straight lines, and the consumer will either consume only one good or be indifferent among any of the combinations on the budget line.

Goods are perfect substitutes if a consumer is always willing to substitute a given amount of one good for the other. It may be that a consumer is indifferent between sugar and Sweet'N Low—he is willing to substitute 2 packets of sugar for one packet of Sweet'N Low. Figure 11.1 shows three indifference curves from that consumer's indifference curve map.

Figure 11.1

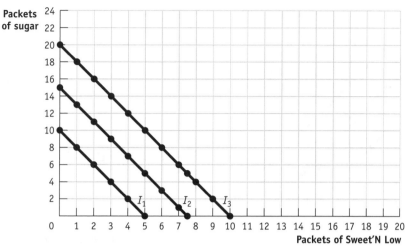

If the consumer has $3.00 to spend on Sweet'N Low and sugar, and a packet of sugar costs $0.20 and Sweet'N Low costs $0.60 per packet, then we can add his budget line for the two goods to his three indifference curves to get Figure 11.2.

Figure 11.2

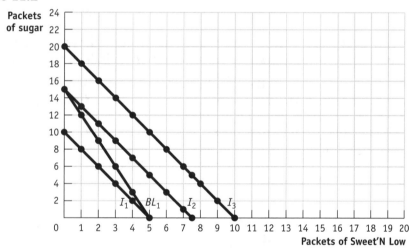

The consumer will maximize consumption given his budget line when he consumes 15 packets of sugar and no Sweet'N Low. He will prefer this bundle as long as the slope of the budget line (minus the ratio of the price of Sweet'N Low to the price of sugar) is more than 2 in absolute value. Therefore, as long as the price of Sweet'N Low is more than twice the price of sugar, the consumer will buy only sugar.

If the price of Sweet'N Low is less than twice the price of sugar, the consumer will only buy Sweet'N Low. Figure 11.3 shows the budget line for the consumer when he has $3.00 to spend on both goods and the price of a packet of sugar is $0.20 and the price of Sweet'N Low is $0.30. Note that in this case the price of Sweet'N Low is only 1.5 times the price of sugar. Under these conditions, the consumer will choose to consume 10 packets of Sweet'N Low and no sugar.

Figure 11.3

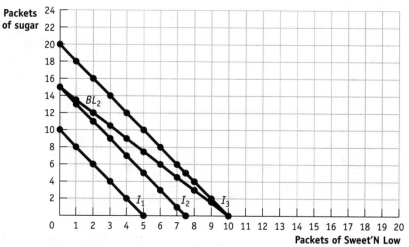

If the price of Sweet'N Low is exactly twice the price of sugar—for example, the consumer has $3.00 to spend on Sweet'N Low and sugar, the price of sugar is $0.20 and the price of Sweet'N Low is $0.40—then the budget line will be the same as the second indifference curve. The consumer can afford all points on that line and any point on that line has the same level of utility as any other. We cannot determine an optimal consumption bundle.

TIP #3: When two goods are perfect complements, the consumer's optimal consumption bundle will always be at the corner of an indifference curve.

When goods are perfect complements, they must be used together in specific proportions. It may be that you must have exactly two teaspoons of sugar in one 8-ounce glass of iced tea. If you have two glasses of tea but only two teaspoons of sugar, you have the same level of utility as if you only had one glass of tea and two teaspoons of sugar. If you have four tablespoons of sugar but only one glass of iced tea, you still only have the same utility as if you had one glass of iced tea and two teaspoons of sugar. Figure 11.4 shows some of your indifference curves for iced tea and sugar.

Figure 11.4

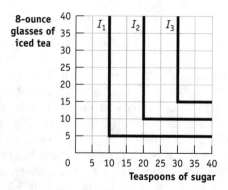

Since every point on a particular indifference curve gives you the same utility, you will always choose the combination of goods on the indifference curve that minimizes the cost of that level of utility. For all indifference curves, that point is the corner of the indifference curve. No matter what the shape of the budget line, the consumer will always choose the point at which the budget line is tangent to the highest possible indifference curve. That will always occur at a corner. At the corner, the consumer will always consume the perfect complements in their specific proportions.

TIP #4: When separating the income and substitution effects of a change in the price of a good, remember that the substitution effect comes from the change in slope of the budget line (the change in relative prices), while the income effect comes from the shift in the budget line (change in purchasing power).

Figure 11.5 shows a consumer's optimal bundle of good L and good M at point A. If there is a decrease in the price of L, this will change the slope of the budget line ($-P_L/P_M$) and will shift the budget line out. If we only allowed for the change in the slope of the budget line but did not allow the consumer to move to a different indifference curve, we could isolate the substitution effect. Figure 11.5 does this.

Figure 11.5

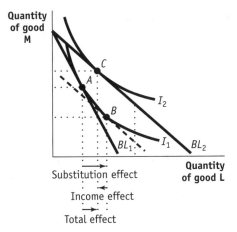

We begin with the consumer in equilibrium at point A. When the price of good L falls, the budget line shifts out to BL_2 and the consumer will be in equilibrium at point C. To isolate the substitution effect of the decrease in the price of L, we move the budget line back until it is just tangent to the first indifference curve (I_1) at point B. This hypothetical budget line appears as the diagonal dashed line in Figure 11.5. The movement from A to B represents the substitution effect. As we expect, a decrease in the price of L will lead the consumer to substitute good L for good M—good L is now relatively less expensive—and point B shows the consumer purchasing more L than at point A. The movement from point B to point C shows the consumer's increased purchasing power due to the decrease in the price of good L, which allows the consumer to reach a higher indifference curve. However, point C shows the consumer purchasing less of good L than at point B. As the consumer's purchasing power increased, the consumer buys less of good L. Good L must be an inferior good. Comparing point A to point C, the consumer responds to a decrease in the price of L by consuming more L, but that is because the substitution effect dominated the income effect.

Multiple-Choice Questions

1. If indifference curves are convex, then we know that they
  a. get flatter as you move down the curves to the right.
  b. are downward-sloping straight lines.
  c. may cross but only at consumption bundles that have small amounts of both goods.
  d. will never be tangent to a budget line.

2. An indifference curve shows all the consumption bundles
   a. that an individual can purchase with a given income.
   b. that yield the same total utility for an individual.
   c. that yield the same marginal utility.
   d. that have the same marginal rate of substitution.

3. In equilibrium, a consumer purchases quantities of the two goods where
   a. the marginal rate of substitution equals the slope of the budget line.
   b. the budget line is tangent to the highest possible indifference curve.
   c. the ratio of the marginal utilities is equal to the ratio of the prices of the goods.
   d. all of the above.

4. When Eve is consuming her optimal consumption bundle, the marginal rate of substitution between apples and bananas is –2. Assuming that apples are measured on the horizontal axis and bananas on the vertical axis, if the price of a banana is $0.25, the price of an apple must be
   a. $0.25.
   b. $0.50.
   c. $1.00.
   d. $2.00.

5. Two bundles on one of Larry's indifference curves are 4 waffles and 5 bowls of cereal and 7 waffles and 3 bowls of cereal. If waffles are measured on the horizontal axis and bowls of cereal on the vertical axis, the marginal rate of substitution between these two bundles of waffles and cereal is
   a. –1/3.
   b. –2/3.
   c. –2.
   d. –3.

6. Zenia spends all her income on two goods: books and DVDs. Measuring books on the horizontal axis and DVDs on the vertical axis, Zenia is currently consuming a bundle of the two goods where the indifference curve is flatter than the budget line. To increase total utility given her income, Zenia should
   a. increase her consumption of books and decrease her consumption of DVDs.
   b. increase her consumption of DVDs and decrease her consumption of books.
   c. do nothing—she is consuming a bundle on her budget line.
   d. None of the above—not enough information is given.

7. If goods C and D are ordinary (or normal) goods, an individual will be willing to
   a. give up more of good C as he or she gives up additional units of good D.
   b. give up less of good C as he or she gives up additional units of good D.
   c. give up more of good C as he or she gains additional units of good D.
   d. give up less of good C as he or she gains additional units of good D.

Answer the following five questions based on Charlie's indifference curves for brownies and cookies shown in the following figure.

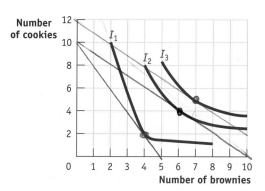

8. Charlie has $10 to spend on cookies and brownies and the prices of brownies and cookies are $1 each. What is Charlie's optimal consumption bundle?
a. 4 brownies and 2 cookies
b. 4 brownies and 8 cookies
c. 6 brownies and 4 cookies
d. 7 brownies and 5 cookies

9. Charlie has $10 to spend on cookies and brownies and the prices of brownies and cookies are $1 each. What is the marginal rate of substitution when Charlie is consuming his optimal bundle?
a. −1/10
b. −1/2
c. −1
d. −2

10. Charlie's spending on cookies rises to $12 with no change in the price of cookies or brownies. What is Charlie's optimal consumption bundle?
a. 4 brownies and 2 cookies
b. 4 brownies and 8 cookies
c. 6 brownies and 4 cookies
d. 7 brownies and 5 cookies

11. Charlie has $10 to spend on cookies and brownies, the price of a brownie is $2, and the price of a cookie is $1. What is Charlie's optimal consumption bundle?
a. 4 brownies and 2 cookies
b. 4 brownies and 8 cookies
c. 6 brownies and 4 cookies
d. 7 brownies and 5 cookies

12. Charlie has $20 to spend on cookies and brownies and the prices of brownies and cookies are $2 each. What is Charlie's optimal consumption bundle?
a. 4 brownies and 2 cookies
b. 4 brownies and 8 cookies
c. 6 brownies and 4 cookies
d. 12 brownies and 8 cookies

13. Cecilia sees hamburgers and hot dogs as perfect substitutes. She will always substitute one hamburger for one hot dog regardless of how many hot dogs or hamburgers she is already purchasing. If the price of a hamburger is greater than the price of a hot dog, Cecilia will
    a. buy mostly hot dogs and very few hamburgers.
    b. buy all hot dogs and no hamburgers.
    c. buy mostly hamburgers and very few hot dogs.
    d. be indifferent to the combination of hamburgers and hot dogs that she buys.

14. Cecilia sees hot dogs and chili as perfect complements. She will always eat one hot dog with half a cup of chili. If she has four hot dogs and three cups of chili, she has the same utility as if she had four hot dogs and two cups of chili. If she has six hot dogs and two cups of chili, she has the same utility as if she had four hot dogs and two cups of chili. At Cecilia's optimal consumption bundle, the marginal rate of substitution is
    a. zero.
    b. one hot dog for half a cup of chili.
    c. one.
    d. undefined.

Use the following figures to answer the following four questions.

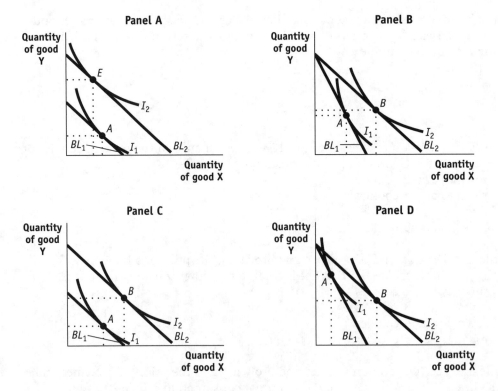

15. Which panel shows an increase in income when good X and good Y are both normal goods.
    a. Panel A
    b. Panel B
    c. Panel C
    d. Panel D

16. Which panel shows an increase in income when good X is an inferior good and good Y is a normal good?
   a. Panel A
   b. Panel B
   c. Panel C
   d. Panel D

17. Which panel shows a decrease in the price of good X when good Y is a normal good?
   a. Panel A
   b. Panel B
   c. Panel C
   d. Panel D

18. Which panel shows a decrease in the price of good X when good Y is an inferior good?
   a. Panel A
   b. Panel B
   c. Panel C
   d. Panel D

19. The following figure shows the income and substitution effects of an increase in the price of good S. The graph indicates that

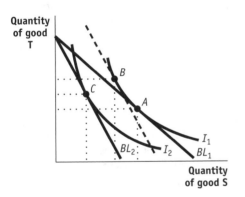

   a. both goods S and T are normal goods.
   b. both goods S and T are inferior goods.
   c. good S is a normal good but good T is an inferior good.
   d. good S is an inferior good but good T is a normal good.

20. Consumers are buying high-fat and low-fat foods. If the government tries to discourage people from eating high-fat foods by imposing an excise tax on them but gives them an income subsidy to eliminate the tax's effect on purchasing power (keeping the consumers on their original indifference curves), what will happen to consumption of high-fat and low-fat foods?
   a. The same amount of both goods will be consumed.
   b. Fewer high-fat foods and more low-fat foods will be consumed.
   c. More high-fat foods and fewer low-fat foods will be consumed.
   d. It is impossible to determine what will happen to the consumption of high-fat and low-fat foods.

21. The tangency condition (when the budget line with goods *A* and *B* is tangent with the highest indifference curve) is comparable with all of the following **except**
a. the relative price rule.
b. optimal consumption rule.
c. $\dfrac{MU_A}{MU_B} = \dfrac{P_A}{P_B}$.
d. the equal marginal utility rule.

22. Consider a consumer with an indifference curve map with two goods (*X* and *Y*) which are perfect substitutes. The horizontal axis represents quantities of *X* and the vertical axis represents quantities of *Y*. If the (absolute) slope of a given budget line is steeper than the (absolute) slope of the indifference curve, the utility-maximizing consumer
a. should buy only *Y* and zero *X*.
b. should buy only *X* and zero *Y*.
c. the consumer should buy both *X* and *Y*.
d. the consumer should buy the maximum amount of *X* and *Y*.

23. Zia Mahmood is a charismatic bridge player who likes to eat nachos and drink red wine in fixed proportion (2 glasses of wine with 1 plate of nachos) after the bridge game. The price of nachos is $15 per plate and the price of red wine is $20 per glass. Zia's budget for spending in a given night is $65. To maximize utility, Zia should buy
a. 3 glasses of wine and 1 nachos.
b. 2 glasses of wine and 1 nachos.
c. 2 glasses of wine and 3 nachos.
d. 1 glass of wine and 4 nachos.

24. Which of the following statements is **false?**
a. All Giffen goods are inferior goods, but all inferior goods are not Giffen goods.
b. All goods can be normal goods, but all goods cannot be inferior goods.
c. All goods can be inferior goods, but all goods cannot be normal goods.
d. For Giffen goods, the demand curve slopes upward.

25. Ryan spends his income on gasoline (represented by the horizontal axis) and other goods (represented by the vertical axis). If the government imposes an additional gasoline tax and also provides income subsidies to Ryan in a way that he could as happy as he was before the tax change, then
a. Ryan buys the same amount of gasoline that he has bought before.
b. Ryan buys less gasoline than he has bought before and buys more of the other goods.
c. Ryan buys less of other goods, but buys the same amount of gasoline.
d. Ryan buys the same amount of other goods that he has bought before.

26. Consider ordinary (normal) goods and find which of the following statements is **false.**
a. Two indifference curves cannot intersect each other.
b. Indifference curve slopes downwards.
c. $\dfrac{MU_A}{MU_B} = \dfrac{P_A}{P_B}$.
d. As we move upward on a given indifference curve, the total utility may increase.

27. If the price of good X goes down, the demand curve will be
   a. flatter, greater the substitution effect (other things remaining constant).
   b. steeper, greater the income effect (assuming normal goods and other things remain constant).
   c. flatter for inferior goods than for than normal goods.
   d. none of the above because income effect does not arise when the prices of goods change.

28. If government gives more income subsidies to students
   a. students will reach a higher level of utility and enrolment at universities will increase.
   b. students will reach a higher level of utility and enrolment at universities will decrease.
   c. students will reach a higher level of utility and enrolment at universities will increase if university education is considered as a normal good.
   d. students will reach a higher level of utility and enrolment at universities will increase if university education is considered as an inferior good.

29. Even though you have lost 10% of your income due to an increase in income tax rates, yet you are taking more public transportation than taxis. Therefore
   a. public transit is a superior good to you.
   b. public transit is a normal good to you.
   c. public transit is an inferior good to you.
   d. public transit is neither a normal or inferior good to you.

30. Draw a graph with good X on the horizontal axis and good Y on the vertical axis. You like good X, but having an additional unit of Y does not make you happy or unhappy. Therefore, we can say that
   a. $MU_X > 0$ and $MU_Y > 0$.
   b. the indifference curve does not exist.
   c. the indifference curve is sloping downward.
   d. the indifference curve is a vertical line for a given amount of X.

Problems and Exercises

Read each question carefully and then write your answers in the space provided or on a separate sheet of paper.

1. Juan Ramon eats tacos and enchiladas for lunch every day. The following tables show three of his indifference curves for tacos and enchiladas each week. Plot the three indifference curves in the figure provided.

Indifference Curve 1		Indifference Curve 2		Indifference Curve 3	
Enchiladas	Tacos	Enchiladas	Tacos	Enchiladas	Tacos
2	32	3	32	4	32
3	16	4	21	5	24
4	11	5	16	6	19
5	8	6	13	7	16
6	6	7	11	8	14
7	5	8	10	9	12.5
8	4.6	9	9.5		
9	4				

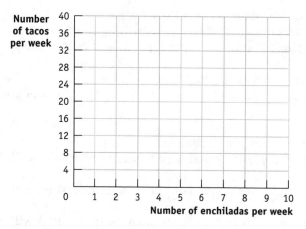

a. Which indifference curve yields the highest level of utility?

b. Do the indifference curves illustrate the four properties that we associate with indifference curves? Are tacos and enchiladas ordinary goods for Juan Ramon?

c. What is the marginal rate of substitution between the different consumption bundles on Indifference Curve 2? Does Indifference Curve 2 show a diminishing marginal rate of substitution?

d. What is the ratio of the marginal utility of enchiladas to the marginal utility of tacos between the different consumption bundles on Indifference Curve 2? Does the ratio diminish as you move down Indifference Curve 2?

2. Juan Ramon has $18 to spend on tacos and enchiladas each week and tacos cost $0.50 each while enchiladas cost $2.00 each.
   a. What is the equation for Juan Ramon's budget line? What is the vertical intercept of the budget line? What is the horizontal intercept of the budget line? What is the slope of the budget line?

b. Plot the budget line on the indifference curve map in Problem 1.

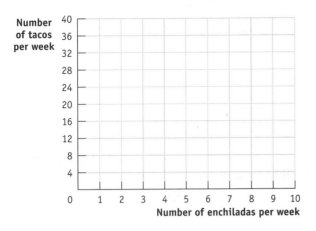

c. What is the optimal consumption bundle for Juan Ramon?

d. What is the marginal rate of substitution when Juan Ramon consumes his optimal bundle?

3. Sally Sportslover enjoys college basketball games. The following figure shows Sally's indifference curve map for basketball games per season.

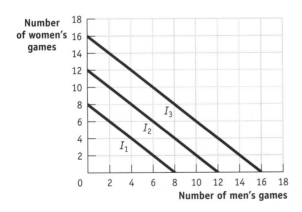

a. What is the marginal rate of substitution along any of the indifference curves? How does Sally see the relationship between men's and women's basketball games?

b. If Sally has $80 per season to buy tickets to basketball games and the price of a ticket to each women's game is $10 and the price of a ticket to each men's game is $5, what is Sally's optimal consumption bundle of men's and women's games? Show your answer graphically on the previous figure.

c. If Sally has $80 per season to buy tickets to basketball games and the price of a ticket to each women's game is $5 and the price of a ticket to each men's game is $10, what is Sally's optimal consumption bundle of men's and women's games? Show your answer graphically on the following figure.

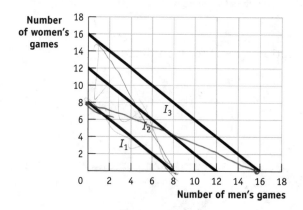

d. If Sally has $80 per season to buy tickets to basketball games and the price of a ticket to the women's and men's games is $10 each, what is Sally's optimal consumption bundle of men's and women's games? Show your answer graphically on the following figure.

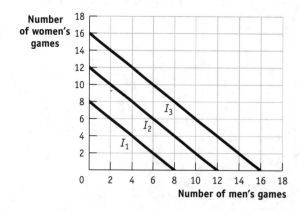

4. Violet buys milk and espresso beans each week to make cappuccino. To make cappuccino, she needs one tablespoon of espresso beans and 4 ounces of milk. The accompanying figure shows her indifference curve map.

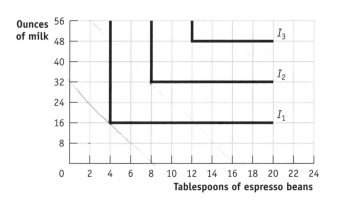

a. Why do her indifference curves look like right angles?

b. What is the marginal rate of substitution at the corner of any one indifference curve?

c. If Violet has $12 to spend each week on espresso beans and milk, and the price of espresso beans is $0.50 per tablespoon and the price of an ounce of milk is $0.25, what is Violet's optimal consumption bundle of espresso beans and milk?

5. Let's return to the problem of choosing the optimal consumption bundle of tacos and enchiladas for Juan Ramon. In problems 1 and 2 we found the optimal consumption bundle for Juan Ramon given his indifference curve map and knowing that the price of an enchilada was $2, the price of a taco was $0.50, and he had $18 to spend on tacos and enchiladas. The following figure shows Juan Ramon's budget line and indifference curve map.

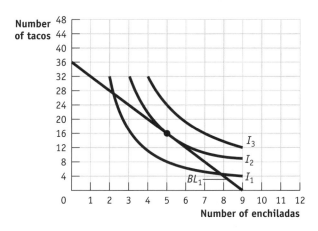

a. What will happen to Juan Ramon's optimal consumption bundle if his income increases to $21.50? What does the change in consumption of tacos and enchiladas due to the increase in income indicate about the goods?

b. What will happen to Juan Ramon's optimal consumption bundle if he has $18 to spend on tacos and enchiladas but the price of a taco rises to $1? What does the change in consumption of tacos and enchiladas due to the increase in the price of a taco indicate about the goods?

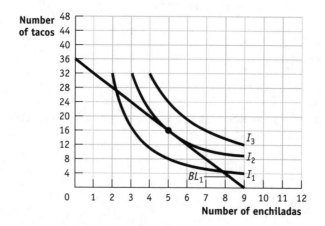

c. In the following graph, show the substitution and income effects when the price of a taco rises to $1.

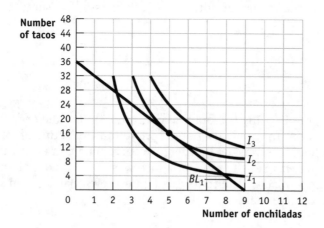

6. Jason likes two goods (X and Y) and his entire income (N) is spent on those goods. Jason's utility function is represented by the following indifference curves (I_1 and I_2). His original budget line is BL_1 with original tangency point as E_1. His new budget line is BL_2 with new equilibrium at E_2.

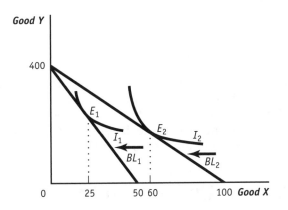

a. If the price of good Y is $1, what is Jason's income? What is the price of good X when we consider the budget line BL_1?

b. At the original equilibrium, what is Jason's total spending on good X and his total spending on good Y?

c. What is the new price of X when we consider BL_2? What is Jason's total spending on good X and his total spending on good Y?

7. Linda Chan earns $100 a week and spends all her income on good A and good B. The price of good A is $5 and that of good B is $10.
a. Derive the budget line equation.

b. What is P_A/P_B? What is $\Delta B/\Delta A$? What is the market rate of exchange between good A and good B?

   c. Assuming that the indifference curve is convex and the tangency takes place at
   the given budget line, what is the marginal rate of substitution at the equilibrium? If MU_A is 16 utils at the equilibrium, what is MU_B?

8. Ingrid spends all her income on popcorn and movie rentals. Consider an initial
equilibrium situation where Ingrid's budget line is tangent to a convex indifference
curve and she ends up renting 10 movies. Even though the price of movie rentals
has increased by 10%, Ingrid still rents 10 movies. Is movie rental a normal good or
an inferior good? Is popcorn a normal good or an inferior good?

Answers to How Well Do You Understand the Chapter

1. bundles, utility, indifference, above, lower, curve map, unique, higher, downward,
ordinary (normal)

2. slope, constant, utility, lower, slope, ordinary (normal) goods, substitution

3. decreases, diminishing, falls (decreases), rises (increases), less, flatter, more, less,
less, increases

4. tangent, tangency, equals, relative price, optimal, consumption rule

5. perfect substitutes, line, constant, highest

6. perfect complements, right angle, corner, undefined

7. demand, right

8. substitution, slope, less, more, shift, less, inferior, less, more, substitution, income

Answer to Multiple-Choice Questions

1. If an indifference curve is convex, then as you move down an indifference curve
the curve gets flatter. **Answer: A.**

2. An indifference curve shows all the consumption bundles that yield the same total
utility for an individual. It does not show the combinations that an individual can
purchase (that is the budget line), the consumption bundles do not yield the same
marginal utility, and the marginal rate of substitution usually diminishes as we
move down an indifference curve. **Answer: B.**

3. A consumer is in equilibrium when the slope of the indifference curve (the marginal
rate of substitution) equals the slope of the budget line. This occurs where the budget line is just tangent to the highest possible indifference curve. Since the marginal
rate of substitution equals the ratio of the marginal utilities, in equilibrium it must
equal the ratio of the prices of the goods (slope of the budget line). **Answer: D.**

4. When Eve is consuming her optimal bundle of apples and bananas, the slope of the
indifference curve (the marginal rate of substitution between A and B) must be
equal to the slope of the budget line ($-P_A/P_B$). Therefore, $-P_A/P_B = -2$. Since the
price of a banana is \$0.25, the price of an apple must be \$0.50. **Answer: B.**

5. If waffles are measured on the horizontal axis and bowls of cereal on the vertical axis, then the marginal rate of substitution between waffles and cereal is $\Delta cereal / \Delta waffles$, or $-2/3$. **Answer: B.**

6. If Zenia's indifference curve is flatter than her budget line, as shown by point A in the following figure, then the marginal rate of substitution between books and DVDs is less than (in absolute value) the ratio of the price of books to the price of DVDs.

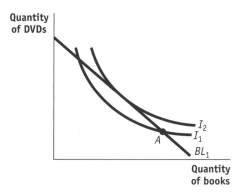

Since the marginal rate of substitution equals the ratio of the marginal utilities,

$$MRS = MU_{books}/MU_{DVDs} < P_{books}/P_{DVDs}$$
or
$$MU_{books}/P_{books} < MU_{DVDs}/P_{DVDs}$$

Zenia should consume more DVDs and fewer books. **Answer: B.**

7. When goods are ordinary, we know that the marginal rate of substitution must be diminishing. So as the individual gains additional units of good D (the marginal utility of D is decreasing), he or she will only be willing to give up less C for it. **Answer: D.**

8. The following figure shows Charlie's budget line with his three indifference curves. Charlie will maximize utility given his budget line when he consumes 6 brownies and 4 cookies. **Answer: C.**

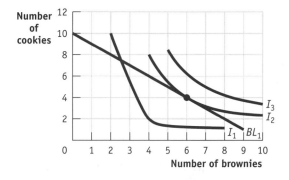

9. When Charlie purchases his optimal consumption bundle the marginal rate of substitution equals (in absolute value) the ratio of the price of brownies to the price of cookies. Charlie's marginal rate of substitution must be -1. **Answer: C.**

10. When Charlie's spending rises to $12, the budget line shifts out as shown in the following figure. Charlie's optimal consumption bundle is 7 brownies and 5 cookies. **Answer: D.**

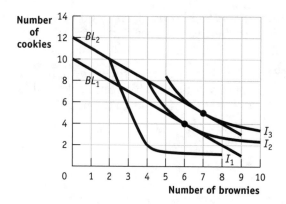

11. The following figure shows what will happen to Charlie's budget line as the price of a brownie rises from $1 to $2 while his income is $10 and the price of a cookie is $1. Charlie's optimal consumption bundle is 4 brownies and 2 cookies. **Answer: A.**

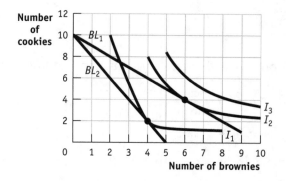

12. If Charlie's income and the prices of the two goods double, his budget line does not change from the original budget line of question 9. The following figure shows the budget line for Charlie when he has $20 to spend on brownies and cookies and the prices of the two goods are each $2. His optimal consumption bundle will be 6 brownies and 4 cookies. **Answer: C.**

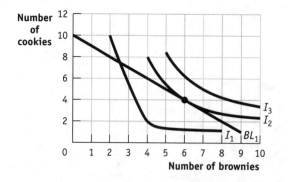

13. Since Cecilia will always substitute one hamburger for one hot dog, her indifference curve map is a series of downward-sloping lines with a slope of −1. If the price of a hamburger is higher than the price of a hot dog, Cecilia will only eat hot dogs. If the price of a hamburger is less than the price of a hot dog, Cecilia will only eat hamburgers. If the price of a hamburger equals the price of a hot dog, Cecilia will be indifferent between all the bundles of hamburgers and hot dogs on her budget line. **Answer: B.**

14. Since Cecilia sees hot dogs and chili as perfect complements, her indifference curve map is a series of right-angle curves. Her optimal consumption bundle will be where the indifference curve just touches the budget line—that will always happen at the corner. At the corner of the indifference curve, the slope or marginal rate of substitution is undefined. **Answer: D.**

15. Panels A and C show the effects of an increase in income on the consumption of good X and good Y. In Panel C, an increase in income results in the consumer buying more of both goods. Both goods are normal goods. **Answer: C.**

16. Panels A and C show the effects of an increase in income on the consumption of good X and good Y. In Panel A, an increase in income results in the consumer buying more of good Y but less of good X. Good X is an inferior good and good Y is a normal good. **Answer: A.**

17. Panels B and D show the effects on the budget line of a decrease in the price of good X. Panel B shows that the decrease in the price of good X and the consequent increase in purchasing power increases quantity demanded of good X and the demand for good Y. Good Y must be a normal good. **Answer: B.**

18. Panels B and D show the effects on the budget line of a decrease in the price of good X. Panel D shows the decrease in the price of good X and the consequent increase in purchasing power, increasing quantity demanded of good X but decreasing the demand for good Y. Good Y must be inferior. **Answer: D.**

19. The substitution effect (movement from point *A* to point *B*) and the income effect (movement from point *B* to point *C*) both tend to decrease quantity demanded of good S as the price of good S rises. Good S must be a normal good. The consumer also decreases his or her purchases of good T as the price of S falls and purchasing power rises; good T must also be a normal good. **Answer: A.**

20. The tax on high-fat foods will change relative prices while the income subsidy keeps consumers on the same indifference curve. As relative prices change, consumers will consume more low-fat goods (they are relatively less expensive) and fewer high-fat foods (they are relatively more expensive). **Answer: B.**

21. The equal marginal utility rule with differential prices of two goods will not lead to optimal consumption. **Answer: D.**

22. To maximize utility, the consumer will buy only Y, because the highest possible indifference curve is reached at the corner where we find the Y-intercept. **Answer: A.**

23. Given his income, Zia buys only 2 glasses of red wine and 1 nachos. **Answer: B.**

24. Since consumer cannot save money, he or she must buy more of something as income increases. Therefore, all goods cannot be simultaneously inferior. **Answer: C.**

25. Since the after tax-price of gas is higher, Ryan's budget line is steeper. Since the steeper budget line (with income-subsidies) is tangent with the old indifference, Ryan is buying less of gasoline and more of other goods. **Answer: B.**

26. A given indifference curve has equal utility at every points on the curve. **Answer: D.**

27. Given others things constant, the greater is the substitution effect, the flatter is the demand curve. Negative income-effect (with inferior goods) will make the demand curve steeper. **Answer: A.**

28. With subsidies, the budget line will shift to the right. If enrolment is an inferior good, the income-effect will be negative and enrolment will decrease. If enrolment is a normal good, the income-effect will be positive and enrolment will increase. **Answer: C.**

29. For normal goods, a fall in income reduces consumption. For inferior goods, a fall in income increases consumption. In this question, public transit is an inferior good. **Answer: C.**

30. Since MU_Y is zero, the indifference curve at a given X is a vertical line. The given amount of X and various quantities of Y provide equal utility. **Answer: D.**

Answers to Problems and Exercises

1. The three indifference curves are plotted in the following figure.

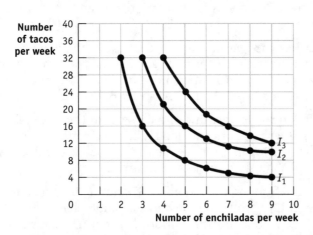

a. Indifference Curve 3 (I_3) yields the highest level of utility.

b. The map does show all four properties usually associated with indifference curves: they do not cross, those farther away from the origin yield a higher level of utility, they are downward-sloping, and they are convex to the origin. Since the indifference curves for tacos and enchiladas share all four properties, they are ordinary goods.

c. The marginal rates of substitution along Indifference Curve 2 are shown in the following table. The marginal rate of substitution is the slope of the indifference curve, rise/run = $\Delta T/\Delta E$. The indifference curve does show diminishing marginal rates of substitution; as Juan Ramon consumes more enchiladas, the marginal rate of substitution between enchiladas and tacos in absolute value falls.

Enchiladas	Tacos	Marginal Rate of Substitution
3	32	
		−11
4	21	
		−5
5	16	
		−3
6	13	
		−2
7	11	
		−1
8	10	
		−0.5
9	9.5	

d. The marginal rate of substitution between enchiladas and tacos equals the ratios of the marginal utility of enchiladas to the marginal utility of tacos. Therefore the ratio of the marginal utilities between every two points is the marginal rate of substitution. We've already calculated it in part c. Since the marginal rate of substitution diminishes as Juan Ramon moves down Indifference Curve 2, so does the ratio of the marginal utilities.

2. a. Juan Ramon's budget line is

$$\$18.00 = (\$2.00 \times \text{enchiladas}) + (\$0.50 \times \text{tacos})$$

The vertical intercept is 36; it is how many tacos Juan Ramon can eat if he only eats tacos (= \$18/\$0.50). The horizontal intercept is 9; it is how many enchiladas Juan Ramon can eat if he only eats enchiladas (= \$18/\$2). The slope of the budget line is –4, or minus the ratio of the price of an enchilada to the price of a taco (= –\$2.00/\$0.50 = –4).

b. The following figure shows Juan Ramon's budget line and the indifference curve map for enchiladas and tacos.

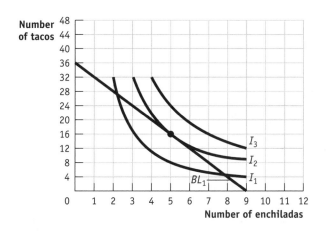

c. Juan Ramon's optimal consumption bundle is 5 enchiladas and 16 tacos; it is at that combination that the budget line is tangent to the highest possible indifference curve.

d. The marginal rate of substitution equals –4. Since we know that Juan Ramon is consuming his optimal consumption bundle, it must be that the slope of the indifference curve (the marginal rate of substitution) equals the slope of the budget line (minus the ratio of the price of enchiladas to the price of tacos).

3. a. The marginal rate of substitution along any of the indifference curves is –1. Sally is always willing to substitute 1 women's game for 1 men's game. She sees them as perfect substitutes at a ratio of one to one.

b. If Sally has \$80 to buy tickets and the price of a ticket to each women's game is \$10 and the price of a ticket to each men's game is \$5, her optimal consumption bundle is 16 men's games and no women's games. In the following figure, we see that combination maximizes Sally's utility given her budget constraint.

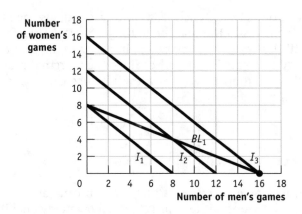

c. If Sally has $80 to buy tickets and the price of a ticket to each women's game is $5 and the price of a ticket to each men's game is $10, her consumption bundle is 16 women's games and no men's games. In the figure below, we see that combination maximizes Sally's utility given her budget constraint.

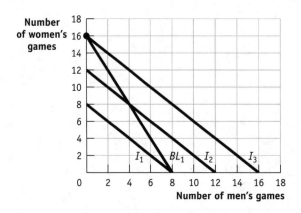

d. If Sally has $80 to buy tickets and the price of a ticket to the women's and the men's games is $10 each, we can't determine an optimal consumption bundle. Her budget line will lie on top of her first indifference curve—any of those combinations yield the same level of utility and no other combination provides a higher level of utility.

4. a. Violet's indifference curves look like right angles because she sees milk and espresso beans as perfect complements. If she has 4 tablespoons of espresso beans, she can make 4 cups of cappuccino and therefore needs 16 ounces of milk. If she has more milk but only 4 tablespoons of espresso, the extra milk does not give her any more utility. If she has more espresso beans but only 16 ounces of milk, again the extra espresso beans do not give her any more utility.

b. At the corner of an indifference curve the marginal rate of substitution is undefined. The marginal rate of substitution is equal to the slope of the indifference curve, but at a corner of an indifference curve it is impossible to measure the slope of the curve.

c. If Violet has $12 to spend each week on espresso beans and milk, and the price of espresso beans is $0.50 per tablespoon and the price of an ounce of milk is $0.25, she will consume 8 tablespoons of espresso beans and 32 ounces of milk.

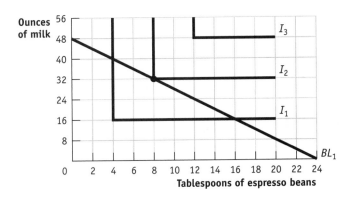

5. a. If Juan Ramon's income increases to $21.50, his optimal consumption bundle will be 6 enchiladas and 19 tacos. Since consumption of both goods increases with an increase in income, both enchiladas and tacos are normal goods.

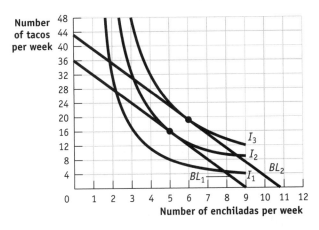

b. If the price of a taco rises to $1, Juan Ramon's optimal consumption bundle will be 5 enchiladas and 8 tacos. The change in the price of a taco does not change the consumption of enchiladas; the goods are neither substitutes nor complements.

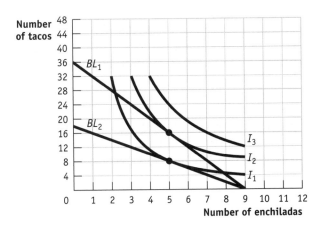

c. We know that when the price of a taco rises from $0.50 to $1, quantity demanded of tacos falls from 16 tacos to 8 tacos. To find the change in quantity demanded due to the substitution effect (the change in relative prices), we can shift the new budget line back to where it is tangent to the original indifference curve. When we do that, we get the dashed line in the following figure.

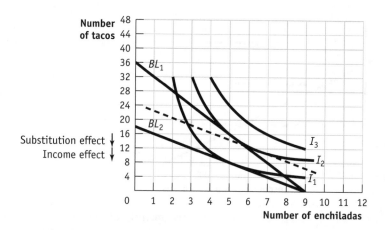

If there were just a change in relative prices, Juan Ramon's optimal bundle would be 6 enchiladas and 13 tacos. As the price of a taco rose, the substitution effect reduced Juan Ramon's taco consumption from 16 to 13. The rest of the change in quantity demanded as the price of a taco rose must be due to the change in purchasing power. As purchasing power fell, Juan Ramon further reduced his taco consumption to 8 tacos; tacos must be a normal good for Juan Ramon.

6. a. Since the most Y that Jason can buy is 400 units, given P_Y of \$1, Jason's income is \$400. Given income as \$400 and given BL_1, the most X that Jason can buy is 50 units, the price of X is \$8.
 b. Spending on X = (\$8)(25) = \$200 and spending on Y = (\$1)(200) = \$200.
 c. With BL_2, the most X that Jason can buy is 100 units, the price of X (given income of \$400) is \$4. Spending on X = (\$4)(60) = \$240 and spending on Y = (\$1)(160) = \$160.

7. a. Linda Chan's budget line equation is 100 = 5A + 10B.
 b. (P_A/P_B) = 5/10; $(\Delta B/\Delta A)$ = −0.5; and the market exchange rate is 0.5 unit of B for 1 unit of A.
 c. The marginal rate of substitution is 0.5 unit of B for 1 unit of A. Since MRS = (MU_A/MU_B) and since MU_A is 16, we can find MU_B is 32.

8. With a 10% increase in the rental price of movie, Ingrid should rent fewer movies due to substitution effect. However, a higher rental price means less purchasing power and less real income. With normal goods, less purchasing power means fewer movie rentals (due to normal income effect). With inferior goods, less purchasing power means more movie rentals (due to opposite income effect). Since Ingrid is renting as many movies as she rented before, the substitution effect is offset by the opposite income effect. Therefore, the movie rental is an inferior good. Since Ingrid is spending more money on movie rentals and since Ingrid's income is fixed, she is buying less popcorn. Therefore, popcorn is a normal good.

chapter 12

Factor Markets and the Distribution of Income

The examples of factors of production are: labour, land, physical capital and human capital. The analysis of factor markets, specially the labour market, is the focus of this chapter. We develop the firm's demand curve for labour, which is derived from the marginal productivity of labour. We show how the market demand curve for labour is derived. Once we know the labour supply function (which depends on income and substitution effect) in conjunction with labour demand function, we can solve equilibrium wage. The authors discuss the issues related to wage differentials and discrimination.

How Well Do You Understand the Chapter?

Fill in the blanks using the terms below to complete the following statements. Terms may be used more than once. If you find yourself having difficulties, please refer back to the appropriate section in the text.

above	*equals*	*labour demand*	*physical capital*
benefit	*factor*	*labour supply*	*profits*
compensating	*factor markets*	*last*	*proprietors' income*
differentials	*fall*	*leisure*	*rental rate*
compensation	*gender*	*less*	*resource*
decrease(s)	*good*	*marginal benefit*	*shifts*
demand	*horizontal*	*marginal cost*	*supply*
derived	*human capital*	*marginal product*	*technology*
discriminate	*improve*	*market power*	*time allocation*
discrimination	*income*	*market price*	*upward*
disparities	*income effect*	*moral*	*utility*
distribution	*increase(s)*	*more*	*wealth*
efficiency wage	*inputs*	*normal*	*wrongly*
efficiency wage model			

1. As we learned in Chapter 2, a factor of production is any _____ that is used by firms to produce goods and services. In this chapter, we investigate _____, the markets in which factors of production are traded. We divide factors of production into four categories: labour, land, _____, and human capital. All natural resources are considered as land. Physical capital and human capital are the assets used by a firm in producing output. Physical capital is primarily plant and equipment; _____ is the improvement in labour created by education and knowledge. Factors of production differ from

_____ in the production process in that a factor of production is a lasting source of income, but an input is used up in the production process.

2. The demand for a factor of production is a(n) _____ demand; it is derived from the optimal output for a firm. The prices of the factors of production determine the factor distribution of _____ which is the division of total income among labour, land, and capital. The largest component of Canada's factor distribution of income is _____ for labour services (i.e., wages and benefits). In 2003, the labour-income was 67% of the total income in Canada. Measured wages and benefits, however, don't capture the full income of "labour," because a large portion of total income is _____, the earnings of people who run their own businesses.

3. Given the importance of the labour income (which demands on the price of labour) in the distribution of _____, we will focus our discussion on labour and derive the demand and supply functions of labour. However, we could have a similar discussion using any of the other factors of production. The firm decides how much labour to hire in a manner similar to its deciding how much of a(n) _____ to produce. From Chapter 9 and the discussion of perfect competition, we remember that a price-taking firm will maximize profit by producing where the _____ equals the marginal cost of the last unit produced. When focusing on labour, the firm compares the marginal benefit (additional revenue) associated with employing an additional unit of labour with the _____ of hiring that labour. The marginal benefit of hiring an additional unit of labour equals the _____ of labour multiplied by the price of output. This is known as the value of the marginal product. If the firm is a price-taker in the product market, the value of the marginal product of labour will _____ as more of the labour is employed because of the diminishing marginal product of labour. If the firm can hire as many units of labour as it wants without increasing wages, the firm will hire up to the point where the value of the marginal product of labour _____ the wage. The value of the marginal product curve demonstrates how the value of the marginal product of labour depends on the quantity of labour employed, and it is the firm's _____ curve for labour. The market demand curve for labour is just the _____ sum of the individual firms' demand curves.

4. The firm's demand curve for labour will shift if there is a change in the price of the output, a change in the _____ of other factors of production, or a change in _____.

Since the demand for labour is a derived demand, any change in the output-price will change the demand for _____. An increase in the output-price will cause a(n) _____ in the demand for labour (a rightward shift of the labour demand curve). A decrease in the output-price will cause a(n)_____ in the demand for labour (a leftward shift of the labour demand curve).

An increase in the supply of other factors of production will increase the productivity of labour and therefore _____ the demand for labour (a rightward shift of the labour demand curve). A decrease in the supply of other factors of production will _____ the productivity of labour and the demand for labour will decrease (a leftward shift of the labour demand curve).

A change in technology can either increase or decrease the _____ for a factor of production. It is possible that the technological change can either increase the marginal productivity of a factor or replace one factor with another. Although it has long been feared that machines would reduce the demand for labour, increases in wages in employment in the long run seem to indicate that technological progress has led to a(n) _____ in the demand for labour.

5. Whether or not the firm owns its factors of production, it will employ factors of production up to the point where the value of the output produced by the last unit _____ the marginal cost of using that factor. The marginal productivity theory of income distribution states that every factor of production is paid its equilibrium value of the _____, which is the additional value produced by the last unit of that factor employed in the factor market as a whole. Whether we consider individual firms or the market, firms will hire up to the point at which the value of the marginal product of labour _____ the equilibrium wage rate. This theory is important because it explains the _____ of income among the economy's factors of production. Each factor's share reflects the value of the marginal product generated by the _____ unit of that factor.

6. Two main objections to the marginal productivity theory of income distribution are:

- In real world we see large _____ in income between factors of production that some think should receive the same payment; and

- Many people _____ believe that the marginal production theory of income distribution gives _____ justification for the distribution of income.

In reality, there is evidence of systematic wage differences across _____, race, and ethnicity, with white males having the highest wages. Some of the wage disparities can be explained by compensating differentials, differences in talent or in human capital, _____ and efficiency wages. _____ explain that some differences in wages reflect differences in on-the-job aesthetics. Differences in wages can also be due to differences in talent or in the quantity of human capital. The marginal productivity theory of income distribution states that every factor of production is paid its equilibrium value of the marginal product. The theory is based on the assumption that factor markets are perfectly competitive, and it may be that employees and employers organize to obtain the _____ necessary to influence wages. It may be that some employers pay an above-equilibrium or _____ to retain workers and encourage performance; this is also known as the

_____.

7. However, some wage differentials may be due to _____. This discrimination is not a natural consequence of market competition. In fact, market competition should penalize discrimination by reducing _____ to those firms that discriminate. However, if labour markets don't work well, either because of market power or efficiency wages, wages may be _____ their equilibrium levels, leading to an excess supply of workers. When this happens, firms may _____ with little or no reduction in profits. There are differences in wages between union-workers and otherwise similar workers in the non-unionized sectors. Unions are organizations of workers that try to _____ wages and _____ working conditions for their members.

8. Individuals decide how much to work as part of their _____ decision, how many hours to spend on different activities. Individuals can spend their time in many different ways, but we are interested in their decision to work for pay or take _____ (the time available for purposes other than earning money to buy marketed goods). To make this decision, the individual uses a version of the optimal consumption rule and compares the marginal _____ of an additional hour worked (the goods that he or she can buy if she works) to the _____ of an additional hour of leisure (time spent with family, friends, on hobbies, etc.)

9. As the wage rises, there are two factors influencing whether an individual will work more hours or fewer hours: the substitution effect and the _____. As the wage rate rises, an individual wants to work _____ because the reward for working (goods that he or she can buy) _____. However, if we consider leisure is a(n) _____ good, and wages increase, the demand for leisure _____. Therefore, the individual wants to work less. The individual _____ curve shows the relation between the quantity of his or her labour supply and the wage rate. If leisure is an inferior good, and wage increases, the supply curve will definitely slope _____. If leisure is normal, and the substitution effect dominates the income effect, the individual's labour supply curve will be _____ sloping. However, in the special case where the income effect (when leisure is normal) dominates the substitution effect, the individual _____ curve will be downward sloping.

10. The market supply curve of labour is the _____ sum of the individual labour supply curves. The market supply curve will shift when there are changes in preferences and social norms that affect willingness to work, changes in population, changes in opportunities, and changes in _____.

Learning Tips

TIP #1: The value of the marginal product of labour is the firm's demand curve for labour.

Firms will always hire up to where the value of the marginal product of labour equals the marginal cost of labour. This is the principle of marginal analysis applied to the hiring decision. If the firm is a perfect competitor in the labour market—the firm is a price taker in the labour market—the marginal cost of labour is the market wage rate. The firm will hire labour up to the point where the wage equals the value of the marginal product of labour. Figure 12.1 shows the value of the marginal product of labour per week for Heather's Hat Emporium.

Figure 12.1

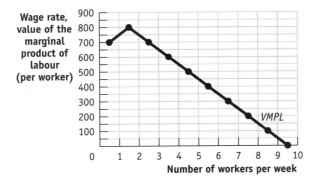

If the market wage per week for hat makers is $650, Heather will hire 3 workers. If the market wage is $550, Heather will hire 4 workers. If the market wage is $150, Heather will hire 8 workers. The value of the marginal product of labour curve is the firm's demand curve for labour. The demand curve slopes downward because there are diminishing marginal returns to labour. Whenever there is a change in the wage rate, there is a change in quantity demanded of labour.

TIP #2: Anything that changes the value of the marginal product of labour will change the firm's demand for labour.

Since the firm's demand curve for labour is the value of the marginal product of labour, if there is a change in either the price of the good that labour is producing or a change in the marginal product of labour, the demand curve for labour will change. For Heather's Hat Emporium, a change in the supply or demand for hats will change the price of a hat and there will be a change in Heather's demand for labour. Also, if Heather purchases some faster hat-making machines, this will increase the marginal product of the workers and there will be an increase in Heather's demand for labour. However, if there is an increase in technology so that lower-cost robots can begin to make hats, this change in technology will reduce Heather's demand for labour. Figures 12.2 and 12.3 show an increase in Heather's demand for labour and a decrease in her demand for labour, respectively.

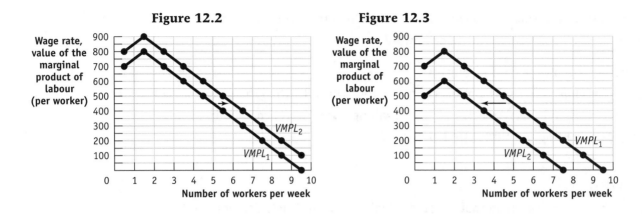

TIP #3: According to the marginal productivity theory of income distribution, every worker is paid an amount equal to the value of the marginal product of the last worker.

Most workers are not paid the value of their marginal product of labour; only the last worker is. For Heather's Hat Emporium's workers (Figure 12.1), if they are paid $350 per week, Heather will hire 6 workers. The value of the marginal product of the first worker is $700; the value of the marginal product of the second worker is $800; the values of the marginal product of the third, fourth, and fifth workers are $700, $600, and $500, respectively. (Remember: we plot the marginal product of the second worker midway between 1 and 2 on the horizontal axis.) At a wage of $350, Heather hires 6 workers because the sixth worker adds $400 to total revenue but only adds $350 to costs. However, the seventh worker adds only $300 to total revenue but adds $350 to costs. Heather will not hire the seventh worker. If Heather had many employees, the value of the marginal product would only fall slightly when an additional worker is hired. With many employees, the firm maximizes profit by choosing the level of employment at which the value of the marginal product of the last worker hired equals the wage rate.

TIP #4: As wage rate increases, the quantity of labour supplied increases (along a given labour supply curve) when the substitution effect dominates the income effect (with leisure as a normal good).

When wage increases, an individual works more hours (less leisure) due to the substitution effect, because leisure is relatively more expensive now (in terms of forgone income for having leisure). However, as wage increases, income increases and we must now consider the income effect. If leisure is a normal good, an individual will have more leisure (less work); in this case, income effect moves in the opposite direction to that of the substitution effect in terms of work-hours (labour supply). If the substitution effect dominates the income effect (with leisure as normal good), then the labour supply curve will still slope upward. However, if the income effect (with leisure as normal good) dominates the substitution effect, then the labour supply curve will slope downward; that means, as wage rate increases, an individual will work less. With leisure as an inferior good, no complications arise, because substitution effect and income effect move in the same direction when wage rate increases and as a result, the labour supply curve must slope upward.

Multiple-Choice Questions

1. An important factor of production in the modern economy is _____,
   the improvement in labour created by _____.
   a. physical capital; technology
   b. human capital; education and knowledge
   c. human capital; physical capital
   d. none of the above

2. Most Canadians receive most of their income in the form of
   a. wages and salaries.
   b. interest.
   c. rent.
   d. benefits.

3. Which of the following is an input at Gwen's Great Gyros?
   a. lamb
   b. bread
   c. the cook
   d. both a and b

4. The true share of labour in the factor distribution of income in Canada is larger
   than compensation of employees because that doesn't reflect the proprietors'
   income, also known as the
   a. return to human capital.
   b. earnings of people who own their own businesses.
   c. benefits that labour gets through working.
   d. increased productivity due to physical capital.

*Answer the following four questions based on the short-run production function for
homemade fudge at Sally's Sweet Shop, shown in the following table.*

# of Workers	Fudge per day (in pounds)
0	0
1	10
2	22
3	32
4	40
5	46
6	50

5. If Sally sells her fudge for $10 per pound, what is the value of the marginal product
   of the fourth worker?
   a. $10
   b. $80
   c. $100
   d. $400

6. Sally sells her fudge for $10 per pound and currently has 3 employees but is
   considering hiring a fourth worker. As long as her workers do not earn more than
   $_____ per day, Sally should hire the fourth worker.
   a. 30
   b. 50
   c. 60
   d. 80

7. Sally sells her fudge for $10 per pound and pays her workers $50 per day to produce fudge. How many workers should Sally hire to maximize profits?
   a. 2
   b. 3
   c. 4
   d. 5

8. Sally is able to expand her business by leasing more cooking space and buying more fudge-making machines. She still sells her fudge for $10 per pound. The value of the marginal product of the fourth worker will be _____ than _____ .
   a. less; $40
   b. greater; $50
   c. less; $65
   d. greater; $80

9. The demand curve for labour will slope downward if a firm is a price taker in the product market because
   a. the firm will pay each worker less than the previous worker.
   b. total product declines as the firm hires more workers.
   c. each worker will add less to total product than the previous worker.
   d. the demand for the good is downward sloping.

10. There will be an increase in the demand for strawberry pickers if there is
    a. increase in the demand for strawberries.
    b. decrease in the price of strawberries.
    c. decrease in the land available for strawberry production.
    d. both a and c.

11. Technological progress may decrease the demand for a factor if the progress
    a. increases the productivity of a factor.
    b. provides a cheaper substitute to a factor.
    c. encourages an increase in the demand for the good that the factor produces.
    d. all of the above.

12. Gwen's Great Gyros pays its workers $50 per day and sells gyros for $5 each. If the market wage for a worker rises to $60, what happens to Gwen's labour demand?
    a. the demand for labour increases
    b. the demand for labour decreases
    c. the quantity demanded of labour increases
    d. the quantity demanded of labour decreases

13. The marginal productivity theory of income distribution is based on the assumption that
    a. factor markets are perfectly competitive.
    b. product markets are perfectly competitive.
    c. the firm does not own any land or physical capital.
    d. none of the above.

14. A police officer in a high-crime inner city earns more than a police officer in the suburbs because of
    a. discrimination.
    b. market power.
    c. compensating differentials.
    d. efficiency wages.

15. A rookie police officer often makes less than a police officer with 20 years' experience because of
   a. discrimination.
   b. differences in human capital.
   c. efficiency wages.
   d. all of the above.

16. Unions may make it possible for discrimination to persist in labour markets because
   a. laws allow unions to discriminate on the basis of gender and ethnicity.
   b. unions bargain for better working conditions at the cost of lower wages.
   c. unions create a surplus of labour by bargaining for wages that are greater than the value of the marginal product of labour.
   d. none of the above.

17. An efficiency wage is one that
   a. is equal to the value of the marginal product.
   b. is less than the value of the marginal product.
   c. is greater than the value of the marginal product.
   d. is unrelated to the value of the marginal product.

18. As Tom's wage increases, why does he work less?
   a. Leisure is an inferior good for Tom, so as his wage goes up, he works less.
   b. Leisure is an inferior good for Tom, so as his wage goes up, he substitutes labour for leisure.
   c. Leisure is a normal good for Tom, so as his wage goes up, he works less.
   d. Leisure is a normal good for Tom, so as his wage goes up, he substitutes labour for leisure.

19. Canadians work less today and earn more even when adjusted for inflation than they did at the end of the nineteenth century. This may be evidence that
   a. the substitution effect dominates the income effect in the supply of labour.
   b. the income effect dominates the substitution effect in the supply of labour.
   c. the market labour supply curve is upward sloping.
   d. both b and c are true.

20. Mary Moneybags's stock portfolio has decreased in value due to a big stock market decline. Consequently,
   a. she will increase the quantity supplied of her labour.
   b. she will decrease the quantity supplied of her labour.
   c. she will increase her supply of labour.
   d. she will decrease her supply of labour.

21. If workers work with more tools and equipment, it will lead to all of the following **except**
   a. leftward shift of labour demand curve.
   b. rightward shift of labour demand curve.
   c. higher market wage rate.
   d. more output.

22. Even though wage rate has doubled, yet Andrew Carpenter works fewer hours because
   a. leisure is a normal good for Andrew, and his substitution effect dominates the income effect.
   b. leisure is a normal good for Andrew, and his income effect dominates the substitution effect.
   c. leisure is an inferior good for Andrew.
   d. his income effect on leisure is zero.

23. Which of the following statements is **false?**
   a. The demand curve for labour will be a horizontal line, if we assume constant marginal productivity of labour.
   b. The demand curve for labour will be a downward-sloping line, if we assume diminishing marginal productivity of labour.
   c. The labour supply curve will always slope upward, if we assume that leisure is a normal good.
   d. The labour supply curve will always slope upward, if we assume that leisure is an inferior good.

Answer questions 24–25 based on the following information:

Koli's Indian Cuisine in Charlottetown sells as many or as little somusa at a price of $1 per somusa. The Cuisine hires workers at the market wage rate of $7 per worker. The production function is represented by the following table.

Quantity of labour (workers)	Quantity of somusa
0	0
1	10
2	19
3	27
4	34
5	40
6	45
7	49
8	52

24. The Cuisine should employ
   a. 7 workers.
   b. 6 workers.
   c. 5 workers.
   d. 4 workers.

25. If the price of somusa doubles to $2 per somusa, while the wage rate increases to $10, the Cuisine should employ
   a. 7 workers.
   b. 6 workers.
   c. 5 workers.
   d. 4 workers.

Problems and Exercises

Read each question carefully and then write your answers in the space provided or on a separate sheet of paper.

1. Sam's Sandwich Shoppe sells Sam's special sandwiches for $2.50 each; its daily production function is shown in the following table. Sam pays each of his workers $50 per day.

Number of workers	Total product	Marginal product	Value of the marginal product
0	0		
1	95	_____	_____
2	180	_____	_____
3	255	_____	_____
4	320	_____	_____
5	375	_____	_____
6	420	_____	_____
7	455	_____	_____
8	480	_____	_____
9	495	_____	_____
10	500	_____	_____

a. Calculate the marginal product and the value of the marginal product of labour at Sam's Sandwich Shoppe.

b. Graph the value of the marginal product of labour curve in the figure above.

c. How many workers will Sam hire?

d. If the price of a sandwich rises to $5, how many workers will Sam hire?

e. What would happen if the price (*p*) of a sandwich was still $2.50 but Sam doubled his workers' daily pay?

2. Sam's Sandwich Shoppe gets new machinery that helps his workers make sandwiches faster. This makes his workers twice as productive as they were before.
  a. Calculate the new marginal product of labour and the new value of the marginal product of labour.

Number of Workers	Total product	Marginal product	Value of the marginal product (when *p* = $2.50 per sandwich)
0	0		
1	190	_____	_____
2	360	_____	_____
3	510	_____	_____
4	640	_____	_____
5	750	_____	_____
6	840	_____	_____
7	910	_____	_____
8	960	_____	_____
9	990	_____	_____
10	1000	_____	_____

b. Graph the value of the marginal product of labour curve in the following figure.

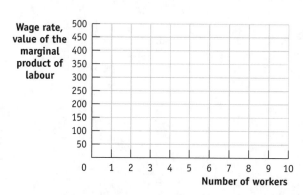

c. How many workers will Sam now hire if the workers earn $50 per day?

d. What would happen if the price of a sandwich was still $2.50 but Sam doubled his workers' daily pay?

3. Given each of the following wage disparities, explain what might be the source of the disparity.
   a. A firefighter in Chicago earns more than a firefighter in rural Maine.

   b. Bill Gates earns more than your economics professor.

   c. A unionized construction worker earns more than her nonunionized counterpart.

4. The following figure shows Ian's supply curve of labour for mowing lawns per day.

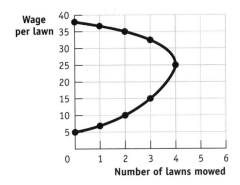

a. How would you explain the shape of Ian's supply curve? Why does the curve slope upward at low wage rates and downward at high wage rates?

b. Until recently, Ian was paid $25 per lawn and mowed 4 lawns per day. Now he is offered $35 per lawn. How will Ian react to this higher wage?

c. If Ian is one of 100 lawn mowers in the market, all of whom have the same labour supply curve as Ian, show the market supply curve in accompanying figure.

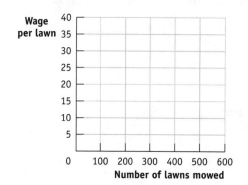

5. Vera was working 40 hours a week and earned $2,000 a week. Her wage rate has doubled. According to the substitution-effect, Vera should work 4 more hours per week and according to income-effect, Vera should take 10 extra hours of leisure per week.

a. How many hours of work per week are performed by Vera now?

b. What was her hourly wage rate before? What is her hourly wage rate now?

c. Is leisure a normal good or an inferior good?

d. Draw Vera's labour supply curve with wage rate as the vertical axis and labour hours as the horizontal axis.

6. The Cavendish Farm in PEI can sell potatoes in a competitive market at $2 per kg. It has the following production function:

Quantity of labour (workers)	Quantity of potato in kg	Marginal product
1	100	
2	190	
3	280	
4	350	
5	410	
6	460	
7	500	
8	530	
9	550	
10	560	

a. Fill in the column of marginal product.

b. If wage rate is $80, how many workers should be employed?

c. If wage rate doubles, how many workers will be employed?

*7. Suppose the output function of a price-taking firm is the following one:

$Q = 100L - L^2$, where Q is the quantity of total output and L is the quantity of labour.

The marginal product function is given next:

$MP_L = 100 - 2L$, where MP_L is the marginal product of capital and L is the quantity of labour.

a. If the wage rate is $40 for each labour and if the product price is $2 per unit of output, how many labourers (L) will be employed by the profit-maximizing firm? Find total output (Q), total revenue and total labour costs.

b. If the wage rate is $60 for each labour (the product price remains at $2 per unit of output), how many labour (L) will be employed by the profit-maximizing firm? What will be total output (Q)? What will be total revenue and total costs?

c. If the wage rate remains at $60 for each labour while the product price increases to $5 per unit of output, how many labour (L) will be employed by the profit-maximizing firm? What will be total output (Q)? What will be total revenue and total costs?

Answers to How Well Do You Understand the Chapter

1. resource, factor markets, physical capital, human capital, inputs

2. derived, income, compensation, proprietor's income

3. income, good, market price, marginal cost, marginal product, decrease, equals, demand, horizontal

4. supply, technology, labour, increase, decrease, increase, decrease, demand, increase

5. equals, marginal product, equals, distribution, last

6. disparities, wrongly, moral, gender, market power, compensating differentials, market power, efficiency wage, efficiency wage model

7. discrimination, profits, above, discriminate, increase, improve

8. time-allocation, leisure, benefit, marginal benefit

9. income effect, more, increases, normal, increases, labour supply, upward, upward, labour supply

10. horizontal, wealth

Answers to Multiple-Choice Questions

1. In the modern economy, human capital—the improvement in labour created by education and knowledge—is an important factor of production. Its importance has increased with technology. **Answer: B.**

2. Most Canadians earn most of their income in the form of wages and salaries. In the United States, compensation of employees accounts for slightly more than 70% of income. **Answer: A.**

3. An input is something that is used up in the production process, while a factor of production is an enduring source of income for its owner. For Gwen, both the lamb and bread are inputs; the cook is a factor of production. **Answer: D.**

4. Earnings of people who own their own businesses are included in "proprietors' income" in the factor distribution of income in Canada. Since part of this income can be considered a salary to the owner, the true share of labour in the factor distribution of income is larger than just compensation of employees.
Answer: B.

5. The marginal product of the fourth worker is 8 pounds of fudge; output increased from 32 pounds to 40 pounds as the fourth worker is hired. Since each pound of fudge sells for $10 per pound, the value of the marginal product of the fourth worker is $80. **Answer: B.**

6. Sally will hire the fourth worker as long as the wage is less than or equal to the value of the marginal product, $80. She will not hire the fourth worker if he or she makes more than $80. **Answer: D.**

7. If Sally pays her workers $50 per day to produce fudge, she will hire 5 workers, as shown in the following figure. The fifth worker adds $60 to total revenue and only adds $50 to cost. Sally will not hire the sixth worker because that worker adds only $40 to total revenue but $50 to costs. **Answer: D.**

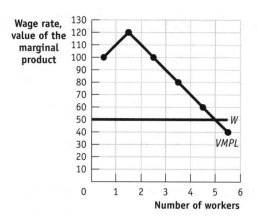

8. If Sally is able to expand her business by adding more cooking space and machinery, each worker will become more productive. The marginal product and the value of the marginal product of each worker will be higher. Therefore, the value of the marginal product of the fourth worker will be greater than $80. **Answer: D.**

9. The demand curve for labour is the value of the marginal product curve, which is the price of the good labour is producing multiplied by the marginal product of the worker. If the firm is a price taker, as the firm hires more labour and produces more output, the price of the output does not change. Therefore, the only reason the demand curve for labour slopes downward is because of diminishing marginal product. **Answer: C.**

10. The demand for strawberry pickers is a derived demand. It is derived from the market for strawberries. If there is an increase in the demand for strawberries, the price of strawberries will rise, as will the value of the marginal product of strawberry pickers, and there will be an increase in the demand for strawberry pickers. **Answer: A.**

11. It is impossible to say whether technological progress will increase the demand for a factor of production without knowing the nature of the technological progress. If the increase in technology increases the productivity of a factor or encourages an increase in the demand for the good that the factor produces, then the demand for the factor will increase. However, if it provides a cheaper substitute to a factor of production or decreases the demand for the good that the factor produces, demand for the factor will fall. **Answer: B.**

12. When the market wage rises, Gwen will hire fewer workers; it is a decrease in quantity demanded, not a decrease in demand. Gwen is moving along the labour demand curve. **Answer: D.**

13. An important assumption of the marginal productivity theory of income distribution is that factor markets are perfectly competitive. **Answer: A.**

14. The job of a police officer in the inner city is much more dangerous than that of one in the suburbs. The differential in pay is a compensating differential. **Answer: C.**

15. A rookie police officer may make less than a police officer with 20 years' experience because with experience comes additional human capital. **Answer: B.**

16. Unions replace one-on-one wage deals with collective bargaining and may succeed in raising wages above the value of the marginal product of the last worker. If they do raise wages above the value of the marginal product, there will be an excess supply of labour at that wage rate. The excess supply will allow firms to discriminate among the willing workers without any reduction in profit. **Answer: C.**

17. Firms pay an efficiency wage to motivate workers to work hard and to reduce worker turnover. This wage is higher than the value of the marginal product of labour. **Answer: C.**

18. Tom works less when the wage increases because Tom sees leisure as a normal good and the income effect of the increase in his wage outweighs the substitution effect. **Answer: C.**

19. Today Canadians are working less and earning wages higher than at the end of the nineteenth century even after adjusting for changes in inflation. This may indicate that the income effect of the increased wage has dominated the substitution effect. **Answer: B.**

20. As Mary Moneybags's stock portfolio declines, she will choose less leisure (leisure is a normal good) and work more at all wage rates. Her supply of labour has increased. **Answer: C.**

21. If workers work with more tools and equipment, the marginal product will increase and the labour demand curve will shift to the right. Given the up-sloping market supply of labour, a rightward shift of market demand will increase equilibrium workers, equilibrium wage rate, and output. **Answer: A.**

22. Leisure is a normal good for Andrew, and his income effect dominates the substitution effect. As a result, Andrew works fewer hours. **Answer: B.**

23. When leisure is a normal good, income effect works in the opposite direction to that of substitution effect. However, if income effect dominates the substitution effect, the labour supply curve will not slope upward; labour supply curve will be downward sloping. **Answer: C.**

24. The marginal revenue product of the 4th worker is $7 and the going wage rate is $7. The Cuisine will employ 4 workers. **Answer: D.**

25. The marginal revenue product of the 6th worker is $10 and the going wage rate is $10. The Cuisine will employ 6 workers. **Answer: B.**

Answers to Problems and Exercises

1. a. The following table shows the marginal product and the value of the marginal product of labour at Sam's Sandwich Shoppe.

Number of Workers	Total Product	Marginal Product	Value of the Marginal Product
0	0		
		95	$237.50
1	95		
		85	212.50
2	180		
		75	187.50
3	255		
		65	162.50
4	320		
		55	137.50
5	375		
		45	112.50
6	420		
		35	87.50
7	455		
		25	62.50
8	480		
		15	37.50
9	495		
		5	12.50
10	500		

b. The value of the marginal product of labour curve is shown in the following figure.

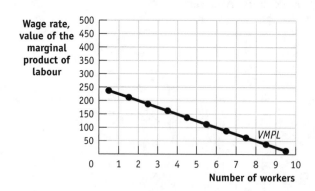

c. Sam will hire 8 workers. The value of the marginal product of the eighth worker is $62.50, while the cost of the worker is $50. Sam will not hire the ninth worker because that worker will only add $37.50 to total revenue but will cost $50 to hire.

d. If the price of a sandwich rises to $5, Sam will hire 9 workers. The value of the marginal product of the ninth worker is now $75 and the cost of that worker is $50. Sam will not hire the tenth worker because the value of the marginal product of that labourer is $25 and the cost would be $50.

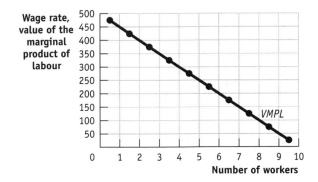

e. Referring back to the figure in part b, if the marginal cost of a worker is $100, Sam will only hire 6 workers.

2. a. The following table shows the new marginal product of labour and the new value of the marginal product of labour when Sam's workers are twice as productive as they were before.

Number of workers	Total product	Marginal product	Value of the marginal product (when p = $2.50 per sandwich)
0	0		
		190	$475.00
1	190		
		170	425.00
2	360		
		150	375.00
3	510		
		130	325.00
4	640		
		110	275.00
5	750		
		90	225.00
6	840		
		70	175.00
7	910		
		50	125.00
8	960		
		30	75.00
9	990		
		10	25.00
10	1000		

b. The accompanying figure shows the value of the marginal product of labour at Sam's Sandwich Shoppe.

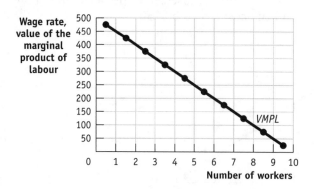

c. Sam will hire 9 workers if the workers earn $50 per day.
d. If Sam's employees earn $100 per day, Sam will only hire 8 workers. See the figure in part b.

3. a. A firefighter in Chicago would earn more than a firefighter in rural Maine because in Chicago there would be many more fires and those fires would be more dangerous than in rural Maine. The disparity would be a compensating differential.
b. Bill Gates probably earns more than your economics professor because of a difference in talent. He also has a lot more market power than your economics professor; Microsoft is not a perfect competitor. Although Bill Gates did not complete college, while your economics professor probably spent several years earning a graduate degree, Bill Gates's talents are such that he earns much more than your economics professor.
c. A unionized construction worker earns more than her nonunionized counterpart because through collective bargaining a union exerts market power to raise wages above the value of the marginal product of labour for its members.

4 a. As Ian's wage per lawn rises, he is likely to substitute labour for leisure (the substitution effect) because leisure has become more expensive—he loses a higher amount for each lawn not mowed. At the same time, as the wage per lawn rises, Ian's income increases, and given that leisure is a normal good, Ian wants to work less and have more leisure (the income effect). At wage rates below $25 per lawn, the substitution effect dominates the income effect, and as the wage rises, Ian works more. However, at wage rates above $25 per lawn, the income effect dominates the substitution effect, and Ian works less as the wage rises.
b. If Ian's pay for mowing lawns rises from $25 to $35, Ian will reduce the number of lawns mowed from 4 to 2.
c. The following figure shows the market supply curve of lawn mowers if the market consists of 100 lawn mowers with the same labour supply curve as Ian.

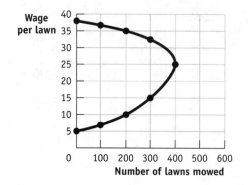

5. a. Total hours work = 40 hours + 4 hours − 10 hours = 34 hours.
  b. Hourly wage before = $2,000/40 = $50.

  Hourly wage now = $100.
  c. Leisure is a normal good, because, as income increases, leisure increases.
  d.

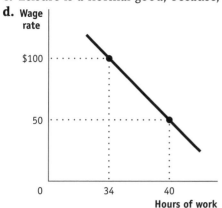

6. a.

Quantity of labour (workers)	Quantity of potato in kg	Marginal product
0	0	
1	100	100
2	190	90
3	280	80
4	350	70
5	410	60
6	460	50
7	500	40
8	530	30
9	550	20
10	560	10

  b. The profit-maximizing condition is: W = (price)(marginal product).
   When the wage rate is $80, the Cavendish Farm should employ 7 workers.
   The marginal revenue product of the 7th worker is (40)($2) = $80.
  c. If wage rate is $160, the Cavendish Farm should employ only 3 workers.

7. a. The profit-maximizing rule is: $(MP_L) \times$ (price) = wage rate.
   $(100 − 2L)(2) = 40$.
   $4L = 160$. Therefore, $L = 40$ and $Q = 2,400$.
   Total revenue = $4,800.
   Total labour costs = $1,600.
  b. The profit-maximizing rule is: $(MP_L) \times$ (price) = wage rate.
   $(100 − 2L)(2) = 60$.
   $4L = 140$. Therefore, $L = 35$ and $Q = 2,275$.
   Total revenue = $4,550.
   Total labour costs = $2,100.
  c. The profit-maximizing rule is: $(MP_L) \times$ (price) = wage rate.
   $(100 − 2L)(5) = 60$.
   $10L = 440$. Therefore, $L = 44$ and $Q = 2,464$.
   Total revenue = $12,320.
   Total labour costs = $2,640.

chapter **12** appendix

Indifference Curve Analysis of Labour Supply

Multiple-Choice Questions

Answer the following three questions based on Sophie's time allocation budget line per week in the following figure.

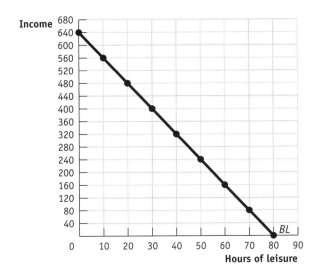

1. Sophie's hourly wage is

   a. $6.40.
   b. $8.
   c. $9.
   d. $10.

2. If Sophie's hourly wage rises to $15, the vertical intercept of Sophie's time allocation budget line will be _____ and the horizontal intercept will be

   _____.
   a. $1,200; 80 hours
   b. $1,200; 150 hours
   c. $720; 50 hours
   d. $720; 150 hours

3. If initially Sophie chose to work 45 hours but after her wage rose to $15 she chose to work 40 hours, Sophie must see
   a. labour as a normal good—the income effect of the wage increase dominates the substitution effect.
   b. labour as an inferior good—the substitution effect of the wage increase dominates the income effect.
   c. leisure as a normal good—the income effect of the wage increase dominates the substitution effect.
   d. leisure as an inferior good—the substitution effect of the wage increase dominates the income effect.

4. When an individual allocates his or her time according to the optimal time allocation rule,
   a. the marginal rate of substitution between income and leisure is greater than the wage rate.
   b. the marginal utility from an additional hour spent working equals the marginal utility from an additional hour of leisure.
   c. the marginal utility from an additional hour spent working exceeds the marginal utility from an additional hour of leisure.
   d. none of the above.

5. If an individual has a backward-bending supply curve, we know that he or she
   a. sees income and leisure as perfect substitutes.
   b. has a supply curve that slopes downward at low wage rates and upward at high wage rates.
   c. has a supply curve that slopes upward at low wage rates and downward at high wage rates.
   d. both a and b.

6. If we knew Sophie's indifference curve map for leisure and income, we could find Sophie's optimal time allocation between labour and leisure by finding the point at which
   a. she maximizes her utility while still on her time allocation budget line.
   b. she reaches the highest possible indifference curve while still on her time allocation budget line.
   c. her time allocation budget line is just tangent to an indifference curve.
   d. all of the above.

7. In the labour/leisure choice, the income effect is significant because
   a. most people get the majority of their income from wages.
   b. an increase in the wage rate can generate a significant increase in income.
   c. leisure is a normal good.
   d. all of the above.

Problems and Exercises

1. The following figure shows Max's indifference curve map for income and leisure per week.

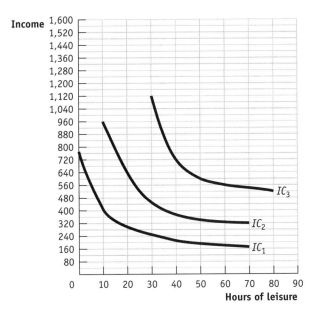

a. Show Max's time allocation budget line if he has 80 hours to allocate each week and earns $9 per hour.

b. What is his optimal time allocation?

c. If Max's wage rises to $18 per hour, show his new time allocation line. What is his new optimal time allocation?

d. Show the income and substitution effects of the wage increase.

Answers to Multiple-Choice Questions

1. We can find Sophie's hourly wage by dividing the vertical intercept of the time allocation line (the amount of income that she would earn if she worked all 80 hours and had no leisure) by 80, which gives us $8 (= $640/80). **Answer: B.**

2. If Sophie's wage rises to $15, the vertical intercept of the time allocation line will be $1,200 (= $15 × 80) and the horizontal intercept will remain at 80. **Answer: A.**

3. As Sophie's wage rises, the substitution effect will make Sophie want to work more (leisure has become more expensive). However, since she works less after the wage increase, it must be that the income effect must be making her work less. Sophie must see leisure as a normal good and the income effect must dominate the substitution effect. **Answer: C.**

4. The optimal time allocation rule says that when an individual is maximizing utility given his or her indifference curve map, the ratio of the marginal utility from an additional hour spent working equals the marginal utility from an additional hour of leisure. **Answer: B.**

5. The following figure shows a backward-bending supply curve of labour. At any wage below W_1, as the wage rate increases the quantity supplied of labour increases, while at any wage rate above W_1, the quantity supplied of labour decreases as the wage rate rises. **Answer: C.**

6. At Sophie's optimal time allocation, she will be maximizing her utility (reaching the highest possible indifference curve) given her time allocation budget line where the budget line is just tangent to an indifference curve. **Answer: D.**

7. The income effect is significant in the labour/leisure choice because wages are an important source of income, and therefore an increase in the wage rate can generate a large income effect, and leisure is a normal good. **Answer: D.**

Answers to Problems and Exercises

1. a. The following figure shows Max's time allocation budget line with his indifference curve map.

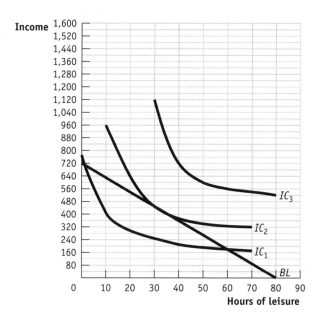

b. His optimal time allocation is to work 50 hours per week (income of $450) and have 30 hours of leisure. When Max allocates his time in this way, he is able to maximize his utility given his time allocation budget line.
c. The following figure shows Max's time allocation budget line after his wage rises to $18 per hour. His new optimal time allocation is 40 hours of labour (income of $720) and 40 hours of leisure.

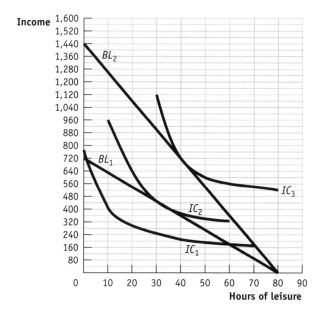

d. To show the substitution and income effects of a change in the wage rate, we need to look at the change in Max's time allocation, because leisure is now relatively more expensive (substitution effect) and because his income is higher (income effect). We can isolate the substitution effect by taking the new time allocation budget line that reflects the higher wage and shifting it back until it is just tangent to the original indifference curve on which Max was allocating his time. The dashed line in the following figure shows this hypothetical time allocation budget line (it shows how Max would allocate his time if income remained constant but he received $18 per hour for working). The movement from 30 hours of leisure (50 hours of labour) to 25 hours of leisure (55 hours of labour) is the substitution effect of the wage increase. The movement from 25 hours of leisure to 40 hours of leisure is the income effect. Leisure is definitely a normal good for Max, and the income effect dominates the substitution effect. As the wage rate rose from $9 to $18, Max reduced the quantity supplied of his labour.

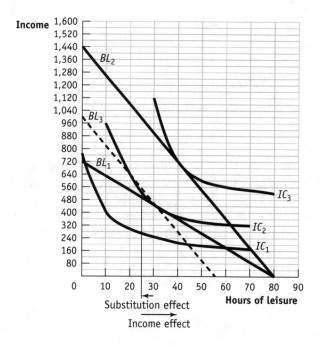

chapter **13**

Efficiency and Equity

The concepts of efficiency and equity are explained in this chapter. Using the concepts of consumer and producer surplus, we analyze efficiency in consumption, efficiency in production, and efficiency in output mix. We see how competitive markets can achieve efficiency. We also see why competitive markets may not be efficient and why markets may fail. The authors discuss the notion of equity and show that there is a trade-off between efficiency and equity. It is often (but not always) better to trade with less efficiency for more equity.

How Well Do You Understand the Chapter?

Fill in the blanks using the terms below to complete the following statements. Terms may be used more than once. If you find yourself having difficulties, please refer back to the appropriate section in the text.

beneficial	equilibrium	less	producer(s)
cannot	equitable	lower	production
competitive	equity	many	property rights
consumption	externalities	market	recording industry
cost	factor	market failure	redistribute
decrease	fewer	maximize	resources
download	general	more	signals
efficient	greater than	output	sum
efficiency	increase	owners	utility
equal to	inefficient	prices	willing

1. The competitive market economy is _____ because it is effective in producing goods and services that people want to consume. In Chapter 6, we learned that we measure consumer surplus as the difference between what buyers are _____ to pay for a good and the price. It is the gain to consumers from participating in the market. Producer surplus is the difference between price and the _____ to the sellers. It is the gain to producers from participating in the market. Total surplus is the _____ of consumer and producer surplus. In equilibrium, perfectly competitive markets (markets in which both buyers and sellers are price takers) are usually efficient, which means they _____ total surplus. Any attempt to reallocate the goods to different consumers, reallocate production to different producers, or change the level of production will _____ total surplus.

2. Markets work well because of a system of _____ and the role of prices as economic (market) _____. Property rights give the _____ of resources or goods the right to dispose of them as they choose. They make mutually beneficial transactions possible. Prices act as economic (market) _____. They provide information about consumers' willingness to pay and producers' costs to everyone in the market.

3. Markets can fail to _____ total surplus if one party attempts to prevent mutually beneficial transactions (e.g., unions in labour markets), when _____ exist (e.g., pollution), and if a good is not suited to efficient management by markets (e.g., information about the good is not available to everyone).

4. A competitive market economy is one in which both the goods markets and the factor markets are perfectly _____ and where prices are determined by supply and demand. The economy is in _____ equilibrium when all individual goods and factor markets are in equilibrium. We say an economy is _____ if it does not pass up any opportunities to make people better off without making other people worse off. An economy is efficient when there is simultaneous _____ in consumption, production, and output levels.

   • An economy is efficient in consumption if there is no way to _____ goods among consumers that makes some consumers better off without making others worse off.

   • An economy is efficient in _____ if there is no way to produce more of some goods without producing less of other goods. This means that the economy must be on its production possibility frontier, the economic model that helps economists think about the trade-offs every economy faces. When the economy is efficient in production, it will also be efficient in the allocation of _____; there is no way to reallocate factors of production among producers to produce more of some goods without producing less of others.

5. An economy is efficient in _____ levels if there isn't a different mix of output that would make some people better off without making others worse off. _____ play an important role in signaling when more or less of a good should be produced.

   • For example, if consumers would prefer more apples and fewer oranges than are currently produced, the price of apples will _____ and the price of oranges will _____; consequently, the value of the marginal product of labour working in apple orchards will _____ and the value of the marginal product of labour working in orange groves will decrease.

- From Chapter 12, we know that when labour markets are competitive, firms will hire labour to the point where the value of the marginal product of labour is _____ wage rate. Assuming that workers in apple orchards and orange groves have the same wage, then after the price of apples rises, the value of the marginal product of apple workers is _____ the value of the marginal product of orange workers. As a result of the changes in the prices of apples and oranges, apple orchards will hire _____ workers and orange groves will hire _____ until the values of the marginal product of workers are the same. Labour will be reallocated from orange production to apple production, and the economy will be back at _____. Markets for goods and services are linked through _____ markets.

6. However, as with equilibrium in individual markets, it is possible for general equilibrium in an economy to be _____. Inefficiency may occur when prices don't act as economic (market) _____. The three reasons for inefficiency are the same reasons for _____. Inefficiency occurs whenever attempts by one party to capture more resources prevents mutually _____ transactions from occurring; when side effects of pollution, or externalities, aren't properly accounted for in existing markets; and when some goods are unsuited for efficient management by markets. If the market for one good is inefficient, the general equilibrium for an economy cannot be

   _____.

7. An economy is _____ when there is no way to make some people better off without making others worse off. An efficient equilibrium may not be desirable because it is not fair or _____. We want fairness and equity. Equity means that the distribution of _____ among individuals is fair. But it is difficult to define "fair."

8. A _____ possibility frontier shows how well-off one individual or group could be for each given utility level of another group or individual. The utility possibility frontier is shaped like a production possibility frontier, it is _____ sloping and bowed out. Any point on the utility possibility frontier is efficient, while any point inside the frontier is _____. Yet, it may be that we prefer an inefficient solution because we put a high priority on _____. It is often, but not always, better to trade _____ efficiency for _____ equity.

Learning Tips

TIP #1: Markets maximize total surplus.

As we saw in Chapter 6, a market maximizes total surplus by maximizing the difference between what buyers are willing to pay for a good and the price they pay for it (consumer surplus), and by maximizing the difference between the price of the good and the sellers' cost (producer surplus). Figure 13.1 shows the total surplus in the market for apples (the shaded triangle). The demand curve shows the willingness to pay of the buyers, while the supply curve shows the costs of the producers. Every buyer who wants to buy apples at a price of $3 or more per pound can buy apples at $3 per pound. Every seller who wants to sell apples at $3 or less per pound can sell them at $3 per pound. Any reallocation to different buyers and different sellers would just lower the total surplus. Equilibrium in the apple market at a price of $3 per pound and 500 pounds of apples maximizes total surplus.

Figure 13.1

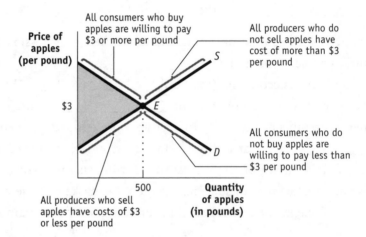

TIP #2: An economy is efficient when there is simultaneously efficiency in consumption, production, and output levels.

The definitions of the three types of efficiency are very similar.

- Efficiency in CONSUMPTION: There is no way for an economy to redistribute goods among CONSUMERS that makes *some consumers better off* without making *others worse off*.

- Efficiency in PRODUCTION: There is no way for an economy to PRODUCE *more of some goods* without producing *less of other goods*. (When there is efficiency in production, there also is efficiency in resource allocation.)

- Efficiency in OUTPUT levels: There isn't a different mix of OUTPUT for the economy that would make *some people better off* without making *others worse off*.

However, efficiency is not a goal in itself; it is just a way to achieve our goals more effectively.

TIP #3: In equilibrium, the values of the marginal product of the last worker in each industry are equal, and every worker will earn the same wage, only if there is one labour market.

If all labour is the same (i.e., has the same skill set) and workers move easily from producing one good to another, producers will hire workers until the value of the output produced by the last worker equals the current market wage rate. For example, let's assume that the same workers can produce either apples or oranges. If the value of the marginal product of labour is greater in apple production than in orange production, apple producers would be willing to pay a higher wage to these workers than orange producers. The higher wage will encourage workers to move from orange production to apple production. As they move, the marginal product, and consequently the value of the marginal product, of labour will fall in apple production and rise in orange production. Workers will continue to move from orange production to apple production until the values of the marginal product of labour in the two industries are the same. At that point, the wages earned in apple and orange production will be equal, eliminating the incentive for workers to move from producing one type of fruit to another. We need to remember that this result depends on the assumption of one labour market. If there are different skills needed in apple production and orange production, it may be difficult or impossible for a worker to leave the lower-paying orange job to take the higher-paying apple job. Consequently, the values of the marginal product of the last worker hired in different industries may not be equal and workers in different industries will not earn the same wage.

TIP #4: An economy may choose to sacrifice some efficiency for more equity.

Figure 13.2 shows the utility possibility frontier for children and senior citizens in a particular economy. Points A, B, and C are efficient; at those points, there is no way to increase the utility of senior citizens without decreasing the utility of children, or vice versa. Point D is inefficient because at that point it is possible to make one group better off without making the other worse off, or you could make both groups better off simultaneously. However, the economy may be limited to choosing between policies that will result in either the utility distribution described by point A or the utility distribution described by point D. Although point A is efficient, individuals in the economy may see the level of utility going to senior citizens at that point as being unfairly low. They may choose the inefficient point D over the efficient point A because they believe point D is the more equitable of the two points. Clearly, the economy would prefer to choose a point such as point B that gives as much utility to the senior citizens as point D but more utility to children. However, if for some reason the choice is limited to points A or D, an economy might choose less efficiency for more equity.

Figure 13.2

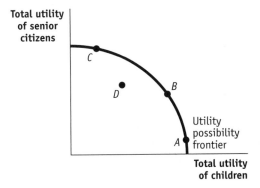

Multiple-Choice Questions

1. In equilibrium in a competitive market, it is possible to
   a. increase total surplus by reallocating the good to consumers who did not buy one.
   b. increase total surplus by reallocating production of the good to firms who did not produce any.
   c. increase total surplus by increasing output.
   d. none of the above.

2. In equilibrium in a competitive market, total surplus can be measured as
   a. the area below the demand curve and above the supply curve.
   b. the area above the demand curve and below the supply curve.
   c. the area below the consumers' willingness to pay and above the market price.
   d. the area below the market price and above the producers' cost.

3. Prices are economic signals in that when the market price is rising,
   a. it may indicate that there has been an increase in buyers' willingness to pay.
   b. it may indicate that there has been a decrease in sellers' cost.
   c. it may indicate that there has been a decrease in buyers' willingness to pay.
   d. it may indicate that many individuals will want to sell the good, putting upward pressure on the price.

4. In equilibrium in a market, total surplus is maximized because the market will allocate
   a. consumption to individuals who have the lowest willingness to pay.
   b. production to individuals who have the lowest cost.
   c. consumption to individuals who have the highest willingness to pay.
   d. both b and c.

5. Economists say that markets may fail when
   a. consumers are unable to purchase goods they would like to because the price is too high.
   b. producers are unable to sell goods they would like to because the price is too low.
   c. there are side effects that aren't properly taken into consideration by the market.
   d. there is no resale market available.

6. When the airlines changed their strategy for dealing with overbooking of flights from bumping passengers randomly to offering monetary and flight incentives for people to willingly give up their seats,
   a. this hurt travelers who paid more for their tickets more than it hurt those who paid less.
   b. this hurt travelers who really needed to get on the flight.
   c. the airlines' satisfaction ratings fell.
   d. it aided efficiency by offering everyone something they wanted.

7. The head resident assistant needs to decide how to allocate the 50 single rooms in her dorm. She is considering the following allocation mechanisms. Which is inefficient?
   a. Allocate the 50 rooms to the first 50 students to request single rooms.
   b. Allocate the rooms to the students who have a 3.8 or above grade point average even though this leaves the last 2 single rooms empty.
   c. Allocate the 50 single rooms to the first 50 students who appear on an alphabetical listing of the residents of the dorm.
   d. Allocate the 50 single rooms to the students who are the 50 tallest.

The following figure shows the value of the marginal product of labour in brownie production (VMPL_b) *and the value of the marginal product of labour in cookie production* (VMPL_c) *in the economy of Dessertland. Assume there is one labour market. Use the figure to answer the next three questions.*

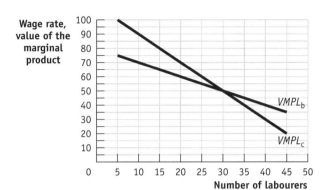

8. If the wage rate of workers in the cookie market and in the brownie market is $70, the efficient allocation of labour is to employ _____ workers in cookie production and _____ workers in brownie production.
  a. 10; 20
  b. 20; 10
  c. 25; 10
  d. 30; 30

9. If the wage rate of workers in the cookie market and the brownie market is $50, the efficient allocation of labour is to employ _____ workers in cookie production and _____ workers in brownie production.
  a. 10; 20
  b. 20; 10
  c. 25; 10
  d. 30; 30

10. If 15 workers are employed in the brownie market and 45 workers are employed in the cookie market, and workers can move easily between brownie and cookie production, how can the economy move to efficiency in output levels?
  a. It can increase labour in both brownie and cookie production.
  b. It can reduce labour in both brownie and cookie production.
  c. It can increase labour in brownie production and reduce labour in cookie production.
  d. It can increase labour in cookie production and reduce labour in brownie production.

11. An economy is efficient in consumption if
  a. there is no way to make some consumers better off without making others worse off.
  b. consumers in equilibrium have the highest willingness to pay.
  c. prices in goods market ensure that you can't increase total surplus by taking something away from someone and giving it to someone else.
  d. all of the above.

12. An economy is efficient in production if
    a. all resources are employed.
    b. there are no shortages in any markets.
    c. it is not possible to produce more of some goods without producing less of others.
    d. it is producing below the production possibility frontier.

13. An economy has an efficient allocation of resources if
    a. there is no way to reallocate factors of production among producers to produce more of some goods without producing less of others.
    b. it is efficient in production.
    c. all resources are employed.
    d. both a and b.

14. An economy is efficient in output levels if
    a. it is not possible to produce more of some goods without producing less of others.
    b. all resources are employed.
    c. there is not a different mix of output that would make some people better off without making others worse off.
    d. there is an efficient allocation of resources.

15. Dessertland is operating on its production possibility frontier but the value of the marginal product of labour producing cookies is greater than the value of the marginal product of labour producing brownies. There is just one labour market for labour producing both cookies and brownies. Dessertland's economy is
    a. efficient in production but inefficient in resource allocation and output level.
    b. efficient in production and resource allocation but inefficient in output level.
    c. efficient in production, resource allocation, and output level.
    d. inefficient in production, resource allocation, and output level.

16. The economy of Fruitland has two types of goods markets, an apple market and an orange market, and the only resource that can be shifted between the two industries is labour. If consumers begin to demand more apples and fewer oranges than are currently being produced, as Fruitland moves to general equilibrium,
    a. the prices of apples and oranges will rise.
    b. the price of apples will fall and the price of oranges will rise.
    c. the marginal product of apple workers and orange workers will rise.
    d. the marginal product of apple workers will fall and the marginal product of orange workers will rise.

17. According to John Rawls, if we are concerned about economic justice (equity), we should pursue policies that
    a. provide the greatest good for the greatest number of people.
    b. encourage individuals to produce as much as they are able but consume only what they need.
    c. place a high weight on the utility of the worse-off members of society.
    d. divide the output of the economy equally among its residents.

18. The following figure shows the utility possibility frontier for an economy. Which of the following statements about the economy is correct?
    a. Points A and B are efficient; point C is inefficient.
    b. Point A may be preferred to B if society places a higher weight on the utility of men.
    c. Point C may be preferred to A if society places a higher weight on the utility of women.
    d. All of the above.

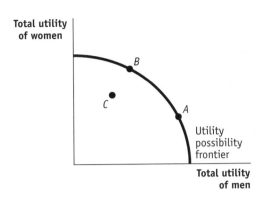

19. Economists argue that
    a. you should always choose an efficient level of utility rather than an inefficient level.
    b. you should never choose an inefficient level of utility.
    c. it may be worth trading less efficiency for more equity.
    d. it may be worth trading less equity for more efficiency.

Answer questions 20–21 on the basis of the following information:

$Q^D = 30 - 2P$ [Demand function]
$Q^S = -10 + 2P$ [Supply function]
P is the dollar price per unit of output and Q is the quantity.

20. The equilibrium price and quantity are, respectively,
    a. $10 and 10.
    b. $5 and 20.
    c. $10 and 20.
    d. $5 and 10.

21. The total surplus (sum of producer and consumer surplus) is
    a. $25.
    b. $50.
    c. $100.
    d. none of the above.

22. Consider the markets for red wine and white wine. A recent medical report has indicated that drinking a glass of red wine a day reduces heart attacks. As a result, all of the following results will occur **except**
    a. the value of the marginal product of labour in red wine industry will increase initially.
    b. more workers will be employed in red wine industry.
    c. the price of red wine will increase.
    d. the price of white wine will increase.

23. Consider a community with two types of persons, A and B. The (marginal) opportunity cost of one hour work is $20 for type A persons and $10 for type B persons. If the community council decides that everyone should work 4 hours a week for tree-planting and gardening, it will lead to
    a. inefficiency, because there exists opportunities of gain if type A persons offer more than $10 wages to type B persons to work extra hours.
    b. efficiency and equity.
    c. a situation in which type B people should do all the community work.
    d. a situation in which type A people should do all the community work.

24. Suppose good *X* generates pollution damages which are not accounted for in the supply function of good *X*. In this situation, the market equilibrium will be
a. inefficient, because the there will be more than efficient level of output in the market.
b. inefficient, because the there will be less than efficient level of output in the market.
c. efficient, because market demand will be market supply.
d. efficient and a tax on polluters will not be necessary.

Problems and Exercises

Read each question carefully and then write your answers in the space provided or on a separate sheet of paper.

1. Explain the type of market failure (e.g., market power, externality, or good not suited for efficient management by markets), if any, that the following situations describe.
   a. An electric utility has to be very large to achieve economies of scale (i.e., produce with low average total costs). It has to be so large that in many instances it will be the only producer of electricity in an area. Once it's the only producer, the utility can set a price much higher than marginal cost.

   b. Many low-income families cannot afford the $25 cost of the flu vaccine. Consequently, any flu outbreak will be larger than it would be if these families could afford the vaccine.

   c. There is a common room on each floor of a dorm and it's no one's responsibility to clean this room. Many students hold their parties in this room and dump their garbage there.

   d. Caleb would really like to own a 1964 Mustang convertible. Although he has tried saving for the car, other expenses, such as tuition, books, and food, have made it impossible to get enough money to buy the car.

2. At a particular college, the students are responsible for general cleaning (sweeping, vacuuming, and cleaning the bathrooms) of their dormitories. Based on the experiences of past years, the head resident assistant has announced that this year each student must work three hours each week to keep the dorm clean. Is this the most fair or efficient way to achieve the goal of a clean dorm?

3. On the island of Fruitland, there are two goods markets, the apple market and the orange market, and one labour market for both apple workers and orange workers. There are 130 labourers available for work and each worker is equally productive in both markets. The following table shows the total products of apple workers and orange workers.

Number of workers in apple production per day	Total apple production per day in pounds	Number of workers in orange production per day	Total orange production per day in pounds
0	0	0	0
10	26	10	35
20	48	20	66
30	66	30	93
40	80	40	116
50	90	50	135
60	96	60	150
70	98	70	161
80	98	80	168
90	96	90	171
100	90	100	170

a. Suppose that the price of apples is $2.50 per pound, the price of oranges is $4.00 per pound, and the wage rate in the labour market is $60 per day. How many workers will be employed in the apple orchards and in the orange groves? Is this economy efficient in consumption, production, and output levels? What, if anything, would we expect to change in the economy?

b. Suppose that the price of apples is $2.50 per pound, the price of oranges is $4.00 per pound, and the wage rate is $20 per day. How many workers will be employed in the apple orchards and in the orange groves? Is this economy efficient in consumption, production, and output levels? What, if anything, would we expect to change in the economy?

c. Suppose that the price of apples is $5.00 per pound, the price of oranges is $2.00 per pound, and the wage rate is $30 per day. How many workers will be employed in the apple orchards and in the orange groves? Is this economy efficient in consumption, production, and output levels? What, if anything, would we expect to change in the economy?

4. The Land of Milk and Honey produces only two goods: milk and honey. Labour is the only variable factor of production and it is subject to diminishing returns. All labour is employed in the Land of Milk and Honey, markets are perfectly competitive, and the economy is in general equilibrium. For some reason, many people who live in the Land of Milk and Honey become lactose intolerant (ill from drinking milk). What will happen to demand and price in the markets for milk and honey? How will the value of the marginal product of labour in the milk and honey markets change? How will employment of labour in the milk and honey markets change? How will the change in employment affect the marginal product of labour in milk and honey production? Will the economy return to general equilibrium?

5. Consider an economy is producing two goods, X and Y. At the current allocation of labour (L) between X and Y, the marginal product of labour in industry X is greater than the marginal product of labour in industry Y. Is current allocation an efficient allocation? What can you predict about re-allocation of labour that will lead to efficient allocation?

6. Consider a good that generates pollution damages of $2 per unit of output (market price does not reflect this per unit damage cost). The demand and supply schedules at various prices are shown in the following table:

Price	Quantity demanded	Quantity supplied
$5	500	100
6	400	200
7	300	300
8	200	400
9	100	500

a. What is the market equilibrium price and quantity?

b. If the final market price includes $2 damage costs at every unit of output, what will be the efficient level of output?

*7. Consider the following equations for good X (pulp and paper industry in St. John, New Brunswick):

$P^D = 100 - 3Q$.

$P^S = 2Q$.

a. Find the equilibrium quantity (Q) and price (P).

b. Suppose, the production of good X causes air pollution and the damage cost associated with air pollution is $20 per unit of output. Find the efficient level of output. If market continues to produce the output (as solved in part a), what will be the total surplus? What will be the total surplus if good X is produced at the efficient level?

c. Show the results of part **b** in a diagram.

Answers to How Well Do You Understand the Chapter

1. efficient, willing, cost, sum, maximize, lower

2. property rights, signals, owners, signals

3. maximize, externalities

4. competitive, general, efficient, efficiency, redistribute, production, resources

5. output, prices, increase, decrease, increase, equal to, greater than, more, less, equilibrium, factor

6. inefficient, signals, market failure, beneficial, efficient

7. efficient, equitable, utility

8. utility, downward, inefficient, equity, less, more

Answers to Multiple-Choice Questions

1. When a competitive market is in equilibrium, there is no way to increase total surplus. **Answer: D.**

2. Total surplus is the sum of consumer and producer surplus. Consumer surplus is the area below the demand curve (the consumers' willingness to pay) and above the market price. Producer surplus is the area below the market price and above the producers' cost. Therefore, total surplus is the area below the demand curve and above the supply curve. The following figure shows the total surplus in the market for apples. **Answer: A.**

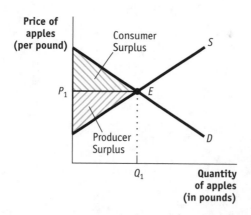

3. The market price will rise whenever there is either an increase in the buyers' willingness to pay (increase in demand) or increase in the sellers' costs (decrease in supply). A decrease in the buyers' willingness to pay or a decrease in the sellers' cost will result in a fall in the market price. **Answer: A.**

4. A competitive market will allocate goods to the buyers with the highest willingness to pay and the sellers with the lowest cost. It is for this reason that competitive markets maximize total surplus. **Answer: D.**

5. Markets may fail in that they may not maximize total surplus. This may happen when one party prevents mutually beneficial trades from occurring, when markets have side effects on others that aren't considered, and with goods that are not suited for efficient management by markets. **Answer: C.**

6. When airlines changed their strategy for dealing with overbooking of flights it aided efficiency in that those travelers who had the highest need to fly are able to fly, while those who can be compensated for willingly giving up their seats also benefit. **Answer: D.**

7. If the head resident assistant allocates single rooms based on a "first come, first served" mechanism, an alphabetical listing, or to the tallest, the allocation will be efficient, although not everyone will agree that it's equitable. However, allocating only 48 of the 50 single rooms to the students with a 3.8 grade point average or above leaves two single rooms empty, and this is not efficient. She could make two more students better off and no one worse off by moving students into the two empty rooms. **Answer: B.**

8. The economy will hire labour up to the point where the wage equals the value of the marginal product of labour. The value of the marginal product of labour in cookie production equals $70 when 20 workers are employed making cookies; the value of the marginal product of labour in brownie production equals $70 when 10 workers are employed making brownies. See the following figure. **Answer: B.**

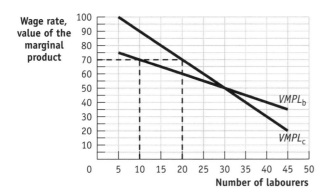

9. The economy will hire labour up to the point where the wage equals the value of the marginal product of labour. The value of the marginal product of labour in cookie production equals $50 when 30 workers are employed making cookies, and the value of the marginal product of labour in brownie production equals $50 when 30 workers are employed making brownies. See the following figure. **Answer: D.**

10. The value of the market product of the fifteenth worker employed in the brownie market is $65. The value of the marginal product of the forty-fifth worker in the cookie market is $20. Since the value of the marginal product of labour in brownie production is greater than the value of the marginal product of labour in cookies, this economy is not efficient in the allocation of resources. Because employers will pay a wage equal to the value of the marginal product of labour, brownie makers will hire workers away from cookie makers by offering higher wages than the cookie workers are currently earning. Workers will move from cookie production to brownie production until the values of the marginal product of labour in the two goods are the same. **Answer: C.**

11. An economy is efficient in consumption when you cannot make anyone better off without making someone else worse off. In a market economy, total surplus is maximized by allocating the good to the consumer with the highest willingness to pay. Any redistribution of a good will only reduce total surplus. **Answer: D.**

12. An economy is efficient when it is not possible to produce more of some goods without producing less of others. All resources may be employed, but unless they are allocated in an efficient manner the economy may be inefficient. **Answer: C.**

13. An economy has an efficient allocation of resources if there is no way to reallocate factors of production among producers to produce more of some goods without producing less of others. If the economy has an efficient allocation of resources then it must be efficient in production as well. All resources may be employed, but unless they are allocated in an efficient manner the economy may be inefficient. **Answer: D.**

14. An economy is efficient in output levels if there does not exist a different mix of output that would make some people better off without making others worse off. If it is not possible to produce more of some goods without producing less of others then the economy is efficient in production, and there must be an efficient allocation of resources. All resources may be employed, but unless they are allocated in an efficient manner the economy may be inefficient. **Answer: C.**

15. Since Dessertland is operating on its production possibility frontier, it must be efficient in production and efficient in resource allocation. However, since the value of the marginal product of labour producing cookies is greater than the value of the marginal product of labour producing brownies, the economy is not efficient in output levels. If the economy produced more cookies and fewer brownies until the values of the marginal product of labour were equal in the two markets while staying on the production possibility curve, the economy would be efficient in production, in allocation of resources, and output levels. **Answer: B.**

16. As consumers in Fruitland demand more apples and fewer oranges, the price of apples (and the value of the marginal product of labour in apple production) will rise and the price of oranges (and the value of the marginal product of labour in orange production) will fall. Firms will offer higher wages in the apple market than in the orange market, and labour will move from orange production to apple production until the value of the marginal product of labour is the same in both markets. As more labour is employed in the apple market, the marginal product of apple workers will fall and, as fewer labourers are employed in the orange market, the marginal product of orange workers will rise. **Answer: D.**

17. John Rawls in his *A Theory of Justice* argued for social and economic policies that individuals would choose if they did not know what their place in society would be. If we made policy choices behind a "veil of ignorance," we would choose policies that placed a high weight on the utility of the worse-off members of society. Jeremy Bentham offered "the greatest good for the greatest number" as a definition of efficiency, while Karl Marx believed efficiency was defined by "from each according to his ability, to each according to need." **Answer: C.**

18. All of the choices are correct. Points *A* and *B* are efficient in that they are on the utility possibility frontier, while *C* is not. However, efficiency is not equity. It may be that *A* is preferred to *B* because society places a high value on the utility of men, or that society may prefer *C* (an inefficient point) to *A* because it places a high value on the utility of women. **Answer: D.**

19. Economists argue that efficiency is not a goal in itself but a way to achieve goals. It may be that an inefficient outcome is preferred to an efficient one because it is fair. **Answer: C.**

20. Set $Q^D = Q^S$ and solve $P = 10$ and $Q = 10$. **Answer: A.**

21. Consumer surplus = $25 and producers surplus = $25. Therefore, total surplus = $50. **Answer: B.**

22. If consumers switch to red wine from white wine, the demand for white wine will decrease and price of white wine will fall. **Answer: D.**

23. Equal hours of work is inefficient, because both types of individuals will gain if type *A* people work more hours and get paid more than $10 dollars from type *B* people. **Answer: A.**

24. There will be over-production and inefficient output at the market equilibrium. **Answer: A.**

Answers to Problems and Exercises

1. a. An electric utility is an example of market failure because of market power; economies of scale are such that to be efficient you must be very large. If the firm is very large, it can exert market power that may prevent mutually beneficial trades from occurring.

   b. Flu vaccines have benefits to society other than to those who get the vaccination. If an individual receives a flu vaccine, he or she will benefit from not getting the flu. Society also benefits because that individual will not get sick and expose others to the flu. The economy's benefit from the flu vaccine is greater than just the individual's benefit. Society would be better off if more vaccinations were given. The market fails because an externality is not properly taken into consideration.

   c. The common room in the dorm is no one person's responsibility; it is everyone's responsibility. Without a system for allocating space and responsibility for cleaning up (property rights), most students will just wait and hope that someone else will do it for them. The common room will just get dirtier and dirtier. This is an example of the market failing because the common room is not suited for efficient management by markets.

   d. This is not an example of a market failure. Although Caleb would like to own a 1964 Mustang convertible, he is either not willing or not able to forgo school and food for the car. He is only willing to pay something less than the market price for the car. Other Mustang devotees are willing to pay more. The market will allocate the 1964 Mustang convertibles up to the point where the willingness to pay of the last consumer equals the cost of the last seller. At that point, the market has maximized consumer surplus.

2. There are two goals for the dorm: cleaning and studying. Everyone sharing equally in the cleaning of the dorm is not necessarily an efficient manner to achieve these two goals. Some students will be able to clean more in three hours than others will. In particular, the marginal cleaning ability of some students will be higher than others. It may be more efficient to have the better cleaners work more (their marginal cleaning product will fall) and the mediocre cleaners work less (their marginal cleaning product will rise) until the marginal product of all students is the same. Also, the opportunity cost of cleaning the dorm in terms of hours not studying will be higher for some students than for others. It may be more efficient (the dorm will have a higher average grade point average and more students will still be students next semester) if the students with the lower opportunity cost for time do more cleaning. It may be hard, however, to convince the students who clean well and have higher grade point averages that their reward for their abilities is to clean more!

3. a. To determine how many workers will be employed in the apple orchards and the orange groves, we need to find when the value of the marginal product of labour will equal the wage rate, $60. The following table and figures show the value of the marginal product of labour in the two markets. Apple orchards will employ 10 workers and the orange groves will employ 55. Since total employment (65) is far less than the labour force (130), this economy cannot be efficient in consumption, production, or output levels. We would expect the wage rate to fall in both markets and for more workers to be hired in the apple and orange markets.

Number of workers in apple production per day	Total apple production per day in pounds	Marginal product of labour in apples	Value of the marginal product of labour in apples	Number of workers in orange production per day	Total orange production per day in pounds	Marginal product of labour in oranges	Value of the marginal product of labour in oranges
0	0			0	0		
		26	65			35	140
10	26			10	35		
		22	55			31	124
20	48			20	66		
		18	45			27	108
30	66			30	93		
		14	35			23	92
40	80			40	116		
		10	25			19	76
50	90			50	135		
		6	15			15	60
60	96			60	150		
		2	5			11	44
70	98			70	161		
		0	0			7	28
80	98			80	168		
		-2	-5			3	12
90	96			90	171		
		-6	-15			-1	-4
100	90			100	170		

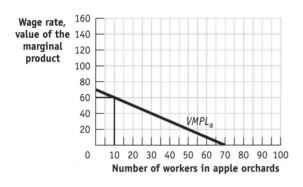

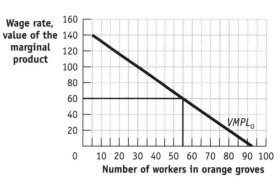

b. If the wage rate for workers is $20 per day, 50 workers will be employed in the apple orchards and 80 workers will be employed in the orange groves. Since all labour is employed and the value of the marginal product in the apple market, the value of the marginal product in the orange market, and the wage are all equal, the economy must be efficient in production and output levels. As long as there is no tendency for apple or orange prices to change, the economy is also efficient in consumption.

c. If the price of apples is $5.00 per pound and the price of oranges is $2.00 per pound, the values of the marginal product of labour in apple orchards and orange groves are as shown in the following table and figures. Apple orchards will employ 55 workers and the orange groves will employ 55. Since total employment (110) is less than the labour force (130), this economy cannot be efficient in consumption, production, or output levels. We would expect the wage rate to fall in both markets and for more workers to be hired in the apple and orange markets.

Number of workers in apple production per day	Total apple production per day in pounds	Marginal product of labour in apples	Value of the marginal product of labour in apples	Number of workers in orange production per day	Total orange production per day in pounds	Marginal product of labour in oranges	Value of the marginal product of labour in oranges
0	0			0	0		
		26	130			35	70
10	26			10	35		
		22	110			31	62
20	48			20	66		
		18	90			27	54
30	66			30	93		
		14	70			23	46
40	80			40	116		
		10	50			19	38
50	90			50	135		
		6	30			15	30
60	96			60	150		
		2	10			11	22
70	98			70	161		
		0	0			7	14
80	98			80	168		
		-2	-10			3	6
90	96			90	171		
		-6	-30			-1	-2
100	90			100	170		

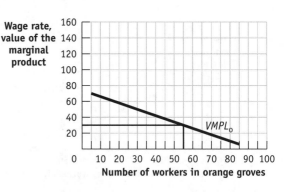

4. Starting from general equilibrium in the Land of Milk and Honey, there is a decrease in the demand for milk and an increase in the demand for honey. Consequently, the price of milk will fall, reducing the value of the marginal product of labour in the milk market, and the price of honey will rise, increasing the value of the marginal product of labour in the honey market. Since the value of the marginal product of labour is higher in the honey market, and so wages are higher in the honey market, workers will be attracted into the honey market and employment will fall in the milk market. As workers flow from milk production to honey production, the marginal product of labour making honey will fall and the marginal product of labour making milk will rise. The changes in the marginal product of labour along with the changes in the prices of the goods will once again equate the value of the marginal products of the two. The Land of Milk and Honey will return to general equilibrium.

5. Since MP^X_L is *greater than* MP^Y_L, the allocation of labour is inefficient. If more labour is allocated to X and less to Y (assuming that the diminishing marginal returns), the total output will increase. This re-allocation will continue until MP^X_L is equal to MP^Y_L.

6. **a.** The market equilibrium price is $7, where the quantity demanded and supplied is equal to 300 units.
   b. At the final price of $8 (supply-price of $6 plus damage of $2), the demand is 200 units and supply is 200 units. The efficient level of output is 200 units.

7. **a.** From the equilibrium condition that the supply-price (P^S) is equal to the demand-price (P^D), we get

   $2Q = 100 - 3Q$.

   $5Q = 100$.

   $Q = 20$.

   Price is 40.
   b. Use the condition that the supply-price plus damage cost equals the demand-price.

   $2Q + 20 = 100 - 3Q$.

   $5Q = 80$.

   $Q = 16$.

   Price is 52.

   At $Q = 20$:

The total surplus = Consumer surplus + Producer surplus – Damage costs.

$$= [(60 \times 20)(1/2)] + [(40 \times 20)(1/2)] - 20 \times 20$$

$$= 600.$$

At Q = 16,

The total surplus = Consumer surplus + Producer surplus

$$= [(48 \times 16)(1/2)] + [(32 \times 16)(1/2)]$$

$$= 640.$$

c.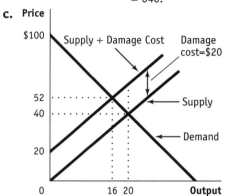

chapter 14

Monopoly

Monopoly is a market structure with only one firm. We explain the reasons for why monopolies exist. Monopoly is a price maker; price is always greater than the marginal revenue. The profit-maximizing monopolist's output is determined where *MR* equals *MC*. The monopolist always sets the price where the demand is elastic. In this chapter, we compare monopoly with perfectly competitive markets with respect to price, output, and economic welfare. How to regulate monopoly with price control is explained in this chapter. The chapter ends with a discussion of price discrimination by monopolists.

How Well Do You Understand the Chapter?

Fill in the blanks using the terms below to complete the following statements. Terms may be used more than once. If you find yourself having difficulties, please refer back to the appropriate section in the text.

all	greater than	number	price taker
antitrust policy	identical	oligopoly	quantity effect
barrier(s) to entry	illegal	one	regulation
below	increase(s)	opposite	resource
break(s) even	less	optimal output rule	single-price
deadweight loss	long run	perfect	sole
decrease(s)	low	prevent	sole right
differentiated	many	price ceiling	technical
down	market	price discrimination	two-part
earn	market power	price effect	wedge
economies of scale	natural monopoly	price elasticities	
equal(s)	network externalities	price regulation	

1. Economists identify four types of market structures: perfect competition, monopoly, _____, and monopolistic competition. In monopoly, there is only _____ producer of a good and the good is undifferentiated.

2. Unlike a perfect competitor, a monopolist is not a(n) _____. It is a firm that is the _____ producer of a good that has no close substitutes. Monopolists exert _____ to increase profit. Market power is the ability of a firm to _____ prices. Also, unlike a perfect competitor, a monopolist may earn monopoly profits in the _____.

3. Monopolies exist because there are _____ for other firms. Barriers to entry are things that _____ other firms from entering the industry. There are four different types of barriers:

- It may be that the monopolist controls a(n) _____ crucial to an industry, such as De Beers's control of the diamond mines that produced a large proportion of the world's diamonds.

- A monopoly may exist because of _____ which provide a cost advantage that is the result of having all of an industry's output produced by a single firm. We call this type of monopoly a(n) _____. Local utilities that supply water, gas, and electricity are often considered natural monopolies.

- Although usually a short-run barrier and not a long-run barrier, technological superiority often creates _____. Intel was a monopolist in the design and production of microprocessors from the 1970s through the 1990s because of technological superiority.

- However, it's important to note that in certain high-tech industries, _____ superiority is not a guarantee of success. Some high-tech industries are characterized by _____, a condition that arises when the value to the consumer of a good rises as the number of people who use the good rises.

- The Government can also create barriers to entry through patents and copyrights, the _____ to produce a product. To encourage innovation, the government ensures that the innovator will receive monopoly profits.

4. We learned in Chapter 9 that the firm will maximize profit when marginal revenue equals marginal cost. This rule is true for firms in _____ market structures. However, a monopolist is not a price taker and its demand curve is the _____ demand curve. Since the demand curve slopes downward, there is a(n) _____ between the price a monopolist receives for each unit of its product and the marginal revenue associated with that unit. The marginal revenue curve always lies _____ the demand curve.

5. A monopolist will always produce _____ and charge more for the good than a perfect competitor would have charged if the market had been perfectly competitive. While a perfect competitor will produce where price _____ marginal cost, the monopolist produces where marginal revenue _____ marginal cost. Since price is always greater than marginal revenue, the monopolist will produce where price is _____ marginal cost. While a perfect competitor will _____ in the long run (price will equal average total cost), a monopolist may earn positive profits even in the long run.

6. Since the monopolist does not produce where price equals marginal cost, there is a(n) _____ associated with a monopoly. Comparing consumer and producer surplus in a monopoly and in a perfectly competitive market, we see that the gain in producer surplus to the monopolist is _____ than the loss of consumer surplus. This leads to _____.

7. The government tries to prevent a monopoly from forming or attempts to break it up through antitrust policy. However, this only works if the industry is not a(n) _____.

If the industry is a natural monopoly, there are two ways the government can minimize the deadweight loss: public ownership and _____.
Rather than allowing a private monopoly to exist, the government can establish a public organization to provide the good and minimize the _____.
Canada Post and the New Brunswick Power Commission are two examples of public ownership of natural monopolies. Disadvantages of public ownership are that the firms have no incentive to keep costs _____ or to offer high-quality products, and they may also serve political interests.

8. _____ limits the price that a monopolist is allowed to charge. The government can impose a price ceiling on a monopoly so the firm just _____. Consumers will benefit because the firm will produce _____ and charge less with government regulation, and overall welfare increases. However, it is hard for the government to determine the optimal _____, and the firm has little incentive to report costs accurately or to provide high-quality products.

9. A(n) _____ monopolist offers its product for all consumers at the same price. Many monopolists find that they can _____ their profits by selling the same good to different customers for different prices. Not unique to monopolists, this practice is called _____. Monopolists are able to profit from price discrimination when they can identify two or more groups of consumers who differ in their _____ of demand. Although selling the same good or service to different people at different prices may be _____, many firms are able to impose restrictions (the airlines have lower fares if you stay over a Saturday night) that reveal a consumer's price elasticity of demand. Monopolists charge higher prices to consumers with _____ price elasticities of demand and lower prices to those with _____ price elasticities of demand.

10. We say that a firm practices _____ price discrimination when it is able to charge each consumer the maximum that he or she is willing to pay. If a firm is able to practice perfect price discrimination, price _____ marginal revenue and the deadweight loss associated with a monopolist is completely eliminated. Price discrimination techniques include advance purchase restrictions, volume discounts, and _____ tariffs. Government policies regarding monopolists focus more on minimizing the deadweight loss than on preventing price discrimination because price discrimination can _____ efficiency.

Learning Tips

TIP #1: Marginal revenue is always less than the price for a monopolist.

A monopolist faces a downward-sloping market demand curve, and to increase output the monopolist must lower prices. Table 14.1 shows a monthly demand curve for AlwaysTV's basic service; AlwaysTV is the only cable television provider in Collegetown. (AlwaysTV has one price per household.) To increase sales, AlwaysTV must lower prices for all households. For example, if AlwaysTV charges $100 per month, it can sell basic service to 2,000 households. If it wants to sell basic service to an additional 1,000 households, it will have to lower the price of basic service to $90 per month for all households. The quantity effect of the lower price is that AlwaysTV sells basic service to 1,000 additional households for $90 per month, or an increase in total revenue of $90,000; the price effect is that AlwaysTV reduces the price of basic service by $10 to the original 2,000 customers, so total revenue goes down by $20,000. The marginal revenue of selling basic service to 3,000 customers is $70 (= [$90,000 − $20,000]/1,000). Marginal revenue is less than the price. Figure 14.1 shows AlwaysTV's demand curve and marginal revenue curve.

Table 14.1

Price of basic service	Quantity demanded of basic service (in thousands)
120	0
110	1
100	2
90	3
80	4
70	5
60	6
50	7
40	8
30	9
20	10

Figure 14.1

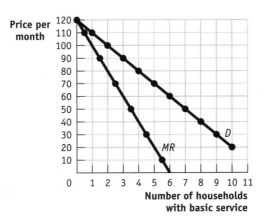

TIP #2: Facing identical cost and demand conditions in a market, a monopoly will charge a higher price and produce a lower level of output than if the market were perfectly competitive.

Let's assume we are considering a market in which there is no fixed cost of production and the marginal cost of production is constant. If this were true, then marginal cost equals average total cost and marginal cost would be constant, as shown in Figures 14.2 and Figure 14.3. Those figures also show a downward-sloping demand curve, and Figure 14.3 shows the monopolist's marginal revenue curve. (The marginal revenue curve for the perfect competitor is constant at the market price.) In Figure 14.2, we show that in a perfectly competitive market, the profit-maximizing point is where marginal cost intersects the demand curve; the price in the market is P_C and output is Q_C. In Figure 14.3, we show that a monopolist will produce where marginal cost intersects the marginal revenue curve; it will charge a price of P_M and sell an output of Q_M. Clearly, the monopoly charges a higher price ($P_M > P_C$) for a lower level of output ($Q_M < Q_C$) than if the market were perfectly competitive. We can also see the deadweight loss associated with the monopoly. When the market is perfectly competitive, consumer surplus is the large triangle under the demand curve and above the marginal cost curve in Figure 14.2. When the market is a monopoly, consumer surplus falls dramatically, with some of the loss of consumer surplus transferred to producer surplus; but some of the loss of consumer surplus is lost to the economy. See Figure 14.3.

Figure 14.2

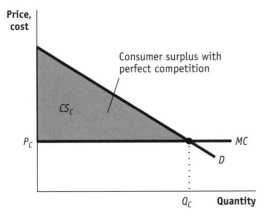

Figure 14.3

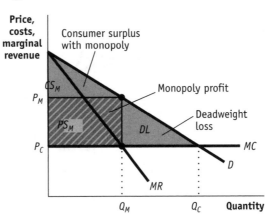

TIP #3: Network externalities may create a barrier to entry, especially in high-tech industries.

In high-tech industries the value to the consumer of a good rises as the number of people who also use the good rises. Consequently, the firm that has the largest number of consumers—the largest network—has an advantage over its competitors that may allow it to be a monopolist. Some argue that Microsoft has become a monopolist through network externalities.

TIP #4: When a natural monopoly exists, the government can try to minimize the deadweight loss by imposing a price ceiling at the price where the monopolist breaks even.

A natural monopoly exists whenever economies of scale provide an advantage to having one firm produce for the entire market. Figure 14.4 shows the average total cost curve for a natural monopoly; it continuously falls over the relevant range of output. The unregulated monopolist will want to produce where marginal revenue equals marginal cost, as shown in Figure 14.4, charging a price of P_M and selling Q_M.

Figure 14.4

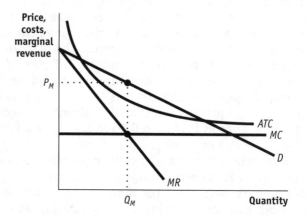

The government might want to try to completely eliminate the deadweight loss associated with the monopoly by imposing a price ceiling at a price equal to P_C in Figure 14.5. At that point, the firm would earn a loss (equal to $[ATC_C - P_C] \times Q_C$), and in the long run it would exit the industry.

Figure 14.5

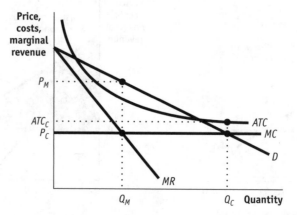

The government can minimize the deadweight loss associated with the unregulated monopolist and the firm will stay in business if the government sets the price ceiling at the price at which the average total cost curve intersects the demand curve. Figure 14.6 shows that if the government imposes a price ceiling of P_R, the monopolist will produce Q_R. The deadweight loss will be substantially smaller than for the unregulated monopoly.

Figure 14.6

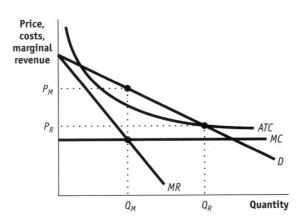

Multiple-Choice Questions

1. A market that is characterized by a large number of sellers and a differentiated product is a
   a. perfectly competitive market.
   b. monopoly.
   c. oligopoly.
   d. monopolistic competitor.

2. A monopolist is able to raise its price above the perfectly competitive level because
   a. it is a price taker.
   b. of market power.
   c. economic profits do not exist.
   d. of price elastic demand.

3. For a monopoly or oligopoly to exist, there must be barriers to entry, such as
   a. control of necessary resource or input.
   b. government regulations.
   c. economies of scale in production.
   d. all of the above.

4. Electric utilities are frequently natural monopolies because
   a. they own a natural resource, such as a waterfall, that is essential to producing electricity.
   b. the government grants them the monopoly with an exclusive license.
   c. economies of scale exist that provide a large advantage to having all electricity generated by one firm.
   d. the demand for electricity intersects the average total cost curve when the average total cost curve is increasing.

Answer the following two questions based on the following figure.

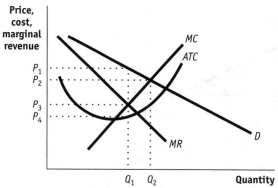

5. To maximize profit, a monopolist will produce _____ units of output and set a price of _____.
   a. Q_1; P_1
   b. Q_2; P_2
   c. Q_1; P_3
   d. Q_2; P_4

6. If the previous figure showed a perfectly competitive market, equilibrium output would be _____ and equilibrium price would be _____.
   a. Q_1; P_1
   b. Q_2; P_2
   c. Q_1; P_3
   d. Q_2; P_4

7. The marginal revenue curve for a monopolist always lies
   a. above the demand curve.
   b. on the demand curve.
   c. below the demand curve.
   d. none of the above.

Answer the next two questions using the following information: AlwaysTV is the only cable television provider in Collegetown. When AlwaysTV raises its price for basic service from $40 to $50 per month, the number of subscribers falls from 100,000 to 80,000.

8. The price elasticity of demand is
   a. 0.40.
   b. 0.80.
   c. 1.00.
   d. 1.25.

9. Marginal revenue is
   a. $0.
   b. $10.
   c. $40.
   d. $50.

10. As the price of basic service rises, the price effect tends to _____ total revenue and the quantity effect tends to _____ it.
   a. raise; raise
   b. lower; lower
   c. raise; lower
   d. lower; raise

11. The wedge between price and marginal revenue exists because as the price of a good falls and more is sold,
   a. the price effect dominates the quantity effect.
   b. the quantity effect dominates the price effect.
   c. each unit adds more to total revenue than the price at which it is sold.
   d. each unit adds less to total revenue than the price at which it is sold.

12. Which of the following statements comparing a perfectly competitive market and a monopoly is correct?
   a. Price is greater than marginal cost in a monopoly and price equals marginal cost in a perfectly competitive market.
   b. When a monopoly exists, producer surplus is less than in a perfectly competitive market.
   c. Monopoly output will be greater than the output of a comparable perfectly competitive industry.
   d. In the long run, economic profits are driven to zero in both a monopoly and a perfectly competitive market.

13. Which of the following is *not* a way for the government to try to reduce some of the inefficiency of a monopoly?
   a. Instead of allowing a private monopolist to control an industry, the government establishes a public agency to provide the good and protect consumers' interests.
   b. The government imposes a price ceiling that allows the monopolist to only break even.
   c. The government gives firms the sole right to produce a good or service with patents or copyrights.
   d. All of the above.

Answer the following three questions based on the following figure.

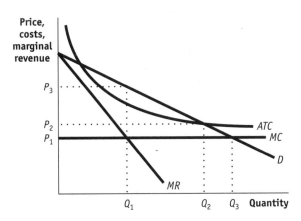

14. An unregulated monopolist will produce _____ units of output and charge a price of _____.
   a. Q_1; P_1
   b. Q_1; P_3
   c. Q_2; P_2
   d. Q_3; P_1

15. Compared with the unregulated monopolist, if the government set a price ceiling of P_1, the deadweight loss would be _____ and the monopolist would
_____.
   a. smaller; earn a smaller economic profit
   b. zero; earn an economic loss
   c. smaller; break even
   d. zero; earn a smaller economic profit

16. Compared with the unregulated monopolist, if the government set a price ceiling of P_2, the deadweight loss would be _____ and the monopolist would
_____.
   a. smaller; earn a smaller economic profit
   b. zero; earn an economic loss
   c. smaller; break even
   d. zero; earn a smaller economic profit

17. If barriers other than economies of scale exist that may create a monopoly, the government should institute
   a. price ceilings to minimize the deadweight loss.
   b. price floors to minimize the deadweight loss.
   c. policies that protect companies from firms that will imitate the product of the monopolist.
   d. policies that prevent the monopoly from arising.

18. AlwaysTV, Collegetown's only cable television provider, can identify two types of consumers: college students and permanent Collegetown residents. College students have a higher price elasticity of demand for basic cable service than do the permanent residents. If AlwaysTV charges college students a _____ price than the permanent residents, the deadweight loss will be _____.
   a. lower; smaller
   b. lower; bigger
   c. higher; smaller
   d. higher; bigger

19. Price discrimination _____ the efficiency of the market by reducing
_____.
   a. increases; producer surplus
   b. increases; the deadweight loss
   c. decreases; the deadweight loss
   d. decreases; producer surplus

20. Compared with a monopolist that charges one price to all customers, if a monopolist practices perfect price discrimination, consumer surplus is _____ and the deadweight loss is _____.
   a. zero; zero
   b. smaller; larger
   c. larger; smaller
   d. impossible to determine; impossible to determine

21. Which of the following is not an example of price discrimination?
   a. a cellular phone company that charges different rates for weekday and weekend service
   b. an amusement park that charges higher prices for adults than for senior citizens and children
   c. a college that charges different tuitions (when financial aid and scholarships are included) to different students
   d. different movie theaters charging different ticket prices to the same movie

22. Consider a monopoly equilibrium output where $MR = MC = \$6$. At the equilibrium price-point on the demand, the demand is
a. inelastic.
b. elastic.
c. unit-elastic.
d. perfectly elastic.

23. At the current output, the marginal revenue is $5, marginal cost is $4, and average total cost is also $4 (which happens to be the minimum ATC). Therefore, we can conclude that the
a. monopolist is maximizing its profit.
b. monopolist should not change output.
c. monopolist should increase output.
d. monopolist should decrease output.

Answer questions 24–26 on the basis of a monopolist's demand and cost schedules:

Units of output	Price	Total costs
0	_____	$10
1	$40.00	14
2	37.50	22
3	35.00	34
4	32.50	50
5	30.00	70
6	27.50	94
7	25.00	122

24. If the monopolist follows the optimal rule of marginal revenue being equal to marginal cost, the equilibrium output will be
a. 4.
b. 5.
c. 6.
d 7.

25. If the monopolist follows the optimal rule of marginal revenue being equal to marginal cost, the equilibrium price and marginal cost will be, respectively,
a. $30 and $20.
b. $30 and $24.
c. $25 and $20.
d. $25 and $24.

26. The price at $25 is *not* an equilibrium price, because the monopolist can increase

its profit; the monopolist should _____ price and

_____ output.
a. increase; increase
b. increase; decrease
c. decrease; increase
d. decrease; decrease

27. Consider a natural monopoly with a downward sloping average total cost curve. If regulating authority imposes a price where $P = MC$, it will lead to
a. fair price.
b. zero profit.
c. losses.
d. inefficient output.

Answer optional questions 28–30 on the basis of the following information:

$P = 100 - Q.$ [Inverse demand function]

$MR = 100 - 2Q.$

$ATC = MC = 40.$

*28. In monopoly, the consumer surplus is
   a. 1,350.
   b. 900.
   c. 600.
   d. 450.

*29. The deadweight loss under monopoly is
   a. $1,350.
   b. $900.
   c. $600.
   d. $450.

*30. With complete (perfect price discrimination), the monopolist earn an economic profit of
   a. $1,800.
   b. $1,350.
   c. $900.
   d. $600.

Problems and Exercises

Read each question carefully and then write your answers in the space provided or on a separate sheet of paper.

1. The Island Waters Company has a monopoly on selling bottled water from a special spring in Island thought to have medicinal benefits. The following table shows the demand curve for gallons of Island Waters per month. The company has no fixed costs and its marginal cost is constant at $4 per gallon.

Price per gallon	Gallons of water (in thousands)	Total revenue (in thousands)	Marginal revenue
$10	0		
9	10		
8	20		
7	30		
6	40		
5	50		
4	60		
3	70		
2	80		
1	90		
0	100		

a. Complete the table by calculating the total revenue and marginal revenue associated with different prices of a gallon of water. (Hint: remember that marginal revenue is the change in total revenue divided by the change in output.)

b. Graph the demand curve, marginal revenue curve, marginal cost curve, and the average total cost curve for Island Waters in the following figure.

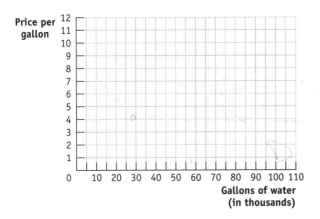

c. At what price and output will Island Waters maximize profit? How much profit will it earn at that price and output? What is the price elasticity of demand between $8 and $6? Does the monopolist produce along the price inelastic portion of the demand curve?

d. If this were a competitive market rather than a monopoly, what would be the equilibrium price and output?

e. On the graph, show the deadweight loss associated with the monopolist.

2. There is a monopoly that is very similar to the Island Waters Company in Sarnia except that the water from the Sarnia spring has different medicinal properties. The Sarnia Waters Company has the same demand as the Island Waters Company, but it has fixed costs of production; the marginal cost and average total cost curves are shown in the following figure.

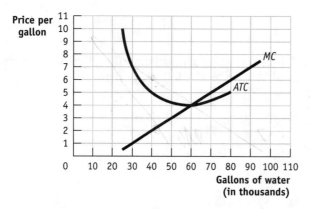

a. Graph the demand curve and marginal revenue curve in the previous figure.

b. At what price and output will Sarnia Waters maximize profit? How much profit will it earn at that price and output? What is the price elasticity of demand between $7 and $5? Does the monopolist produce along the price inelastic portion of the demand curve?

c. If this were a competitive market rather than a monopoly, what would be the equilibrium price and output?

d. On the graph, show the deadweight loss associated with the monopolist.

3. Mayfield Electric Company is the sole provider of electricity to the city of Mayfield. The following figure shows the demand and marginal revenue curves for electricity in Mayfield, as well as the marginal and average total cost curves.

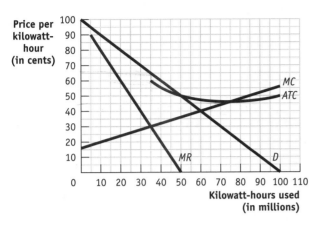

a. What will be the equilibrium price and output in the market if Mayfield Electric is not regulated? How much profit will Mayfield Electric earn?

b. The newly elected mayor of Mayfield wants to regulate the monopoly so that price and output will be the same as if the market were perfectly competitive. As the mayor's economic advisor, explain why this will not work. What other options exist for regulating Mayfield Electric?

4. The city of Mayfield runs a monopoly bus service and can identify two different types of riders: senior citizens (1,000 individuals) and people under age 65 (2,000 individuals). Senior citizens are willing to pay $1.00 for an all-day ticket, while everyone else is willing to pay $2.50 for an all-day ticket. The marginal cost of an all-day ticket is constant at $0.50, and there is no fixed cost.

a. If the bus company cannot discriminate on the basis of price and charges everyone $1, who will buy tickets? How much profit will the bus company earn? What is the total surplus in the market? How is it divided between consumers and producers?

b. If the bus company cannot discriminate on the basis of price and charges everyone $2, who will buy tickets? How much profit will the bus company earn? What is the total surplus in the market? How is it divided between consumers and producers?

c. If the bus company cannot discriminate on the basis of price and charges everyone $2.50, who will buy tickets? How much profit will the bus company earn? What is the total surplus in the market? How is it divided between consumers and producers?

d. If the bus company cannot discriminate on the basis of price and charges everyone $3.00, who will buy tickets? How much profit will the bus company earn? What is the total surplus in the market?

e. If the bus company charges $1.00 to senior citizens and $2.50 to everyone else, who will buy tickets? How much profit will the bus company earn? What is the total surplus in the market? How is it divided between consumers and producers?

5. The monopolist's cost and revenue schedules are given in the following table.

Units of output (Q)	Price (P)	Total revenue	Marginal revenue (MR)	Total cost	Marginal cost (MC)
0	_____	_____	_____	$10	_____
1	$40.00	$40.00	$40.00	14	$4
2	37.50	22		22	
3	35.00	34		34	
4	32.50	50		50	
5	30.00	70		70	
6	27.50	94		94	
7	25.00	122		122	

a. Fill in the columns of *MR* and *MC*.

b. What is monopolist's total fixed cost?

c. What are the equilibrium output and price if the monopolist follows the optimal rule of $MR = MC$?

d. What is the economic profit at equilibrium?

6. Consider the following statements and explain why the statement is true or false.
   a. The monopolist always makes economic profit.

   b. With perfect price discrimination, the consumer surplus is zero.

*7. Consider a monopoly with the following information:
   $P = 100 - Q.$ [Inverse demand function]
   $MR = 100 - 2Q.$
   $ATC = MC = 40.$
   a. Use the previous information and draw a diagram to show the equilibrium price and quantity in monopoly.

   b. What will be the equilibrium price and quantity in a perfectly competitive market? Show the above combination in the above graph.

c. Find consumer surplus in monopoly and consumer surplus in perfect competition.

d. Find monopoly profit and deadweight loss.

e. If the monopolist is able to practice perfect price discrimination, what will be the monopoly output and the monopoly profit?

Answers to How Well Do You Understand the Chapter

1. oligopoly, one

2. price taker, sole, market power, increase, long run

3. barriers to entry, prevent, resource, economies of scale, natural monopoly, barriers to entry, technical, network externalities, sole right

4. all, market, wedge, below

5. less, equals, equals, greater than, break even

6. deadweight loss, less, deadweight loss

7. natural monopoly, price regulation, deadweight loss, down

8. price regulation, breaks even, more, price ceiling

9. single, increase, price discrimination, price elasticities, illegal, lower, higher

10. perfect, equals, two-part, increase

Answers to the Multiple-Choice Questions

1. A monopolistically competitive market is one where there are many sellers of a differentiated product. A perfectly competitive market also has many sellers, but they produce a standardized product. An oligopoly has few sellers of either a standardized or differentiated product; a monopoly is a market with one seller of a standardized product. **Answer: D.**

2. Unlike a perfect competitor, a monopolistic competitor is not a price taker; it can raise its price above the perfectly competitive level because it can exert market power. **Answer: B.**

3. Barriers to entry, such as control of a necessary resource or input, government regulations, economies of scale in production, and technological superiority, prevent firms from entering oligopolies or monopolies. **Answer: D.**

4. Electric utilities have large fixed costs of production. They are so large that their average total cost curve slopes downward for the range of output relevant for market demand. Since the firm can gain economies of scale by producing larger amounts of output, ultimately one firm will produce for the whole market. When economies of scale are such that only one firm can exist in the market, that market is a natural monopoly. **Answer: C.**

5. A monopolist will produce the level of output where marginal revenue equals marginal cost; from the figure provided, the monopolist will produce Q_1 units of output. The monopolist will charge P_1 because it is the highest price at which it can sell Q_1 units of output. **Answer: A.**

6. If the market were perfectly competitive, the equilibrium output would be where marginal cost equals demand, or Q_2 units of output. The price would equal P_2. **Answer: B.**

7. Marginal revenue is the change in total revenue due to a change in output. To increase output by one unit, the monopolist must lower the price of the good. The quantity effect increases total revenue by the additional unit sold times the price of the good. However, the price effect decreases total revenue because the monopolist had to lower the price on all units of the good that it had sold previously. Therefore, the marginal revenue associated with the last unit sold is less than the price. The marginal revenue curve lies below the demand curve. **Answer: C.**

8. The price elasticity of demand is the percent change in quantity demanded divided by the percent change in price:

$$\text{Price elasticity of demand} = \frac{\% \text{ change in quantity demanded}}{\% \text{ change in price}}$$

$$= \frac{\text{Change in Quantity}/\text{Quantity}_{average}}{\text{Change in Price}/\text{Price}_{average}}$$

$$= \frac{20{,}000/(100{,}000 + 80{,}000)/2}{10/(50 + 40)/2} = \frac{20{,}000/90{,}000}{10/45}$$

$$= \frac{22.2\%}{22.2\%} = 1.0$$

Answer: C.

9. When the price is $40 per month, AlwaysTV had 100,000 subscribers and total revenue of $4,000,000. After the price increased to $50 per month, the number of subscribers fell to 80,000, but total revenue remained constant at $4,000,000. Marginal revenue is zero. **Answer: A.**

10. As the price of basic service rises, AlwaysTV will have fewer customers. The price effect is tending to increase total revenue (they sell basic service at a higher price), but they have fewer customers because of the quantity effect. **Answer: C.**

11. Whether the price effect dominates the quantity effect or vice versa tells us whether marginal revenue is negative or positive, not that marginal revenue is less than price. The wedge between price and marginal revenue exists because as the price of a good falls, the monopolist sells more, but the addition to total revenue is something less than the price at which the additional output is sold. **Answer: D.**

12. In equilibrium in a perfectly competitive market, price equals marginal cost because perfect competitors produce where marginal revenue equals marginal cost, and marginal revenue equals price in that market. A monopolist also produces where marginal revenue equals marginal cost, but price is always greater than marginal revenue for a monopolist. **Answer: A.**

13. Two ways to reduce the inefficiency associated with a monopolist are to regulate it so that it will only break even or establish a public agency to provide the good. When the government issues a patent or license to a firm, it is erecting a barrier to entry that leads to inefficiency. **Answer: C.**

14. An unregulated monopolist will produce the level of output where marginal revenue equals marginal cost. This occurs at Q_1 units of output; the monopolist will charge P_3 for that level of output. **Answer: B.**

15. At P_1, the monopolist would produce Q_3 units of output; this is also the price and output that would exist if this market were perfectly competitive. There is no deadweight loss, but since average total cost is greater than P_1 at Q_3, the firm will earn an economic loss. **Answer: B.**

16. At a price ceiling of P_2, the monopolist would produce Q_2 units of output. There would be a smaller deadweight loss in comparison to the unregulated monopoly market, and since P_2 equals average total cost at Q_2 units of output, the monopolist will break even. **Answer: C.**

17. When barriers to entry exist for reasons other than economies of scale, the government should prevent the monopoly from organizing or should break the monopolist up using antitrust policies. **Answer: D.**

18. If AlwaysTV charges different prices to different consumers, it should charge a higher price to those customers with a lower price elasticity of demand (the permanent residents) and a lower price to those with a higher price elasticity of demand (the college students). When AlwaysTV practices price discrimination, the deadweight loss will be smaller than it would be under a one-price policy. **Answer: A.**

19. Price discrimination encourages monopolists to produce more, thereby increasing the efficiency of the market by reducing the deadweight loss. **Answer: B.**

20. If a monopolist practices perfect price discrimination, it will make each customer pay the highest price that they are willing to pay, eliminating any consumer surplus. Since price will equal marginal cost for the last unit produced, there will be no deadweight loss. **Answer: A.**

21. The only example that is not price discrimination is when different movie theaters charge different ticket prices to see the same movie. Different movie theaters offer different experiences to moviegoers. For example, some theaters have more comfortable chairs, better sound systems, and convenient parking, while others do not. The difference in ticket prices may reflect the difference in the services provided, not price discrimination. **Answer: D.**

22. Since $MR > 0$, the demand is elastic. **Answer: B.**

23. At the current output, $MR > MC$. Therefore, the firm is not maximizing profit. The monopolist should produce more and as a result will earn more profit until $MR = MC$. **Answer: C.**

24. At output 5, the $MR = \$20$ and the $MC = \$20$. Therefore, the equilibrium output is 5. **Answer: B.**

25. At the output where $MR = MC$, the price is $30 and the marginal revenue is $20. **Answer: A.**

26. At an output of 7, where price is $25, the MR is less than the MC. The firm should increase price and reduce output until the firm reaches the point where $MR = MC$. **Answer: B.**

27. With natural monopoly, the $P < ATC$ at the point where $P = MC$. Therefore, the firm will incur losses. **Answer: C.**

28. The equilibrium price under monopoly is $70. The consumer surplus is $450. **Answer: D.**

29. With monopolization (as compared to competitive equilibrium), the loss of consumer surplus is $1,350. The monopoly profit is $900. Therefore, the deadweight loss is ($1,350 − $900) = $450. **Answer: D.**

30. With perfect price discrimination, the equilibrium output is 60 and economic profit is $1,800 (with zero consumer surplus). **Answer: A.**

Answers to Problems and Exercises

1. a. The following table shows the total revenue and marginal revenue for the Island Waters Company.

Price per gallon	Gallons of water (in thousands)	Total revenue (in thousands)	Marginal revenue
$10	0	$0	
			$9
9	10	90	
			7
8	20	160	
			5
7	30	210	
			3
6	40	240	
			1
5	50	250	
			−1
4	60	240	
			−3
3	70	210	
			−5
2	80	160	
			−7
1	90	90	
			−9
0	100	0	

b. The following figure shows the demand curve, marginal revenue curve, marginal cost curve, and the average total cost curve for Island Waters.

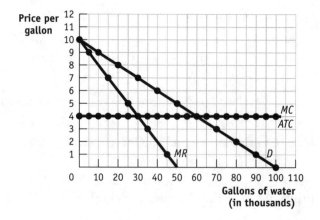

c. Following the optimal output rule, Island Waters will produce where marginal revenue equals marginal cost, 30,000 gallons of water, and charge a price of $7 per gallon. Profit will equal $90,000 (= [$7 – $4] × 30,000). The price elasticity of demand between prices of $8 and $6 is 2.33:

$$\text{Price elasticity of demand} = \frac{\text{\% change in quantity demanded}}{\text{\% change in price}}$$

$$= \frac{\text{Change in Quantity/Quantity}_{\text{average}}}{\text{Change in Price/Price}_{\text{average}}}$$

$$= \frac{20{,}000/(40{,}000 + 20{,}000)/2}{2/(8 + 6)/2} = \frac{20{,}000/30{,}000}{2/7}$$

$$= \frac{66.7\%}{28.6\%} = 2.33$$

The price elasticity of demand is greater than one; therefore, demand is price elastic.

d. If this were a competitive market, equilibrium market output would be 60,000 gallons of water and the equilibrium price would be $4.

e. The deadweight loss is shown as the shaded triangle in the following figure.

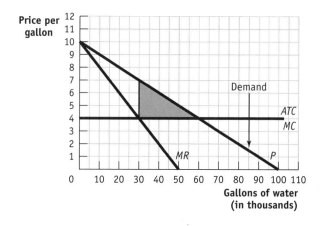

2. a. The following figure shows the demand and marginal revenue curves for the Sarnia Waters Company.

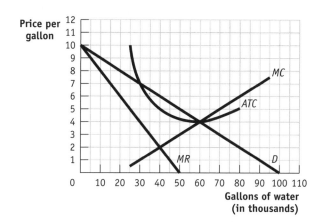

b. Following the optimal output rule, Sarnia Waters will maximize profit by producing where marginal revenue equals marginal cost, an output level of 40,000 gallons of water, and charging a price of $6 per gallon. The average total cost of producing 40,000 gallons is $5. The firm will earn a profit of $40,000 (= $[P - ATC] \times Q = [\$6 - \$5] \times 40,000$). The price elasticity of demand between prices of $7 and $5 is

$$\text{Price elasticity of demand} = \frac{\%\ \text{change in quantity demanded}}{\%\ \text{change in price}}$$

$$= \frac{\text{Change in Quantity/Quantity}_{average}}{\text{Change in Price/Price}_{average}}$$

$$= \frac{20,000/(50,000 + 30,000)/2}{2/(7 + 5)/2} = \frac{20,000/40,000}{2/6}$$

$$= \frac{50.0\%}{33.3\%} = 1.5$$

The monopolist does not produce along the price inelastic portion of the demand curve. The price elasticity of demand is greater than one; demand is price elastic between prices of $7 and $5 per gallon.

c. If the market were perfectly competitive, equilibrium output would equal 60,000 gallons and the price would be $4 per gallon.

d. The deadweight loss is shown as the shaded triangle in the following figure.

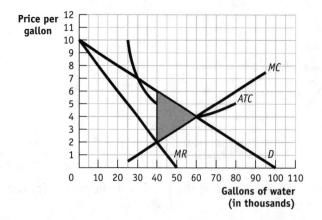

3. a. The unregulated monopolist will produce the optimal level of output, 35 million kilowatt-hours of electricity, and charge a price of $65. Profit will equal $1.75 million (= $[P - ATC] \times Q = [\$65 - \$60] \times 35$).

b. A perfectly competitive firm would produce where price equals marginal cost. The perfectly competitive market would provide 60 million kilowatt-hours at a price of 40¢ per kilowatt-hour. If the city of Mayfield set a price ceiling of 40¢ per kilowatt-hour, the monopolist's optimal output rule would have it produce 60 million kilowatt-hours, but at that price average total cost would exceed price; the monopolist would earn a loss and shut down in the long run. Since Mayfield needs electricity, this would hurt the city.

A better option would be to regulate the monopolist so that it would only break even. The government could do this by imposing a price ceiling of 50¢ per kilowatt-hour. With this price ceiling, Mayfield Electric will produce 50 million kilowatt-hours of electricity and the firm will stay in business, but the deadweight loss will be smaller than it would be if the government did not regulate it.

4. a. At a price of $1, all 3,000 residents of Mayfield will ride the bus each day, and the bus company will earn a profit of $1,500 per day (= [P − ATC] × Q = [$1.00 − $0.50] × 3,000). Total surplus is $4,500. Each of the 2,000 non-seniors was willing to pay $2.50 but only pays $1.00, so consumer surplus is $3,000 (= [$2.50 − $1.00] × 2,000). The cost of providing the 3,000 all-day tickets is $0.50 each, but the bus company receives $1.00 each, so producer surplus is $1,500 (= [$1.00 − $0.50] × 3,000.)
   b. At a price of $2, only the 2,000 non-senior residents of Mayfield will ride the bus each day, and the bus company will earn a profit of $3,000 (= [P − ATC] × Q = [$2.00 − $0.50] × 2,000) per day. Total surplus is $4,000. Each of the 2,000 non-seniors was willing to pay $2.50 but only pays $2.00, so consumer surplus is $1,000 (= [$2.50 − $2.00] × 2,000). The cost of providing the 2,000 all-day tickets is $0.50 each, but the bus company receives $2.00 each, so producer surplus is $3,000 (= [$2.00 − $0.50] × 2,000).
   c. At a price of $2.50, only the 2,000 non-senior residents of Mayfield will ride the bus each day, and the bus company will earn a profit of $4,000 (= [P − ATC] × Q = [$2.50 − $0.50] × 2,000) per day. Total surplus is $4,000, all of which goes to the producer. The price equals the consumers' willingness to pay.
   d. At a price of $3.00, no one will ride the bus. There is no profit and no surplus.
   e. If the bus company charges $1.00 to senior citizens and $2.50 to everyone else, it will be practicing perfect price discrimination. The price to all consumers equals their willingness to pay so there is no consumer surplus. Profit will equal $4,500 (= [$0.50 × 1,000] + [$2.00 × 2,000]). Total surplus is $4,500, all of which goes to the producer.

5. a.

Units of output (Q)	Price (P)	Total revenue	Marginal revenue (MR)	Total cost	Marginal cost (MC)
0	___	___	___	$10	___
1	$40.00	$40	$40	14	$4
2	37.50	75	35	22	8
3	35.00	105	30	34	12
4	32.50	130	25	50	16
5	30.00	150	20	70	20
6	27.50	165	15	94	24
7	25.00	175	10	122	28

b. Total fixed cost is $10, even though output is zero.
c. Output = 5 and price = $30.
d. $80.

6. a. *False.* Profit depends on average cost and price at the equilibrium output. It is possible that at the equilibrium output, the price is less than average total cost.

   b. *True.* With perfect price discrimination, the consumer surplus (that can be obtained, had there been competitive market) becomes monopolist's profit. Therefore, consumer surplus is zero.

7. a.

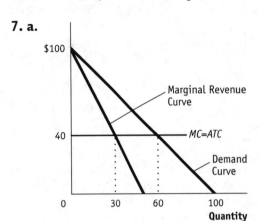

   b. In monopoly, $MR = MC$. From $100 - 2Q = 40$, we can solve $Q = 30$ and $P = \$70$.
   In perfect competition, $P = MC$.
   From $100 - Q = 40$, we can solve $Q = 60$ and $P = \$40$.

   c. Consumer surplus in monopoly = $(100-70)(30)1/2$
   $\qquad\qquad\qquad\qquad\qquad\qquad = \$450.$
   Consumer surplus in perfect competition = $(100 - 40)(60)1/2$
   $\qquad\qquad\qquad\qquad\qquad\qquad\qquad\qquad = \$1,800.$

   d. The monopoly profit = \$900.
   Deadweight loss = (\$1,800 − \$450) − \$900 = \$450.

   e. Output = 60 and the total profit = \$1,800.

chapter 15

Oligopoly

This chapter explores various types of collusive and non-collusive oligopoly models. We introduce prisoner's dilemma in this chapter. Using game theory, we also describe the strategic behaviours of oligopoly firms.

How Well Do You Understand the Chapter?

Fill in the blanks using the terms below to complete the following statements. Terms may be used more than once. If you find yourself having difficulties, please refer back to the appropriate section in the text.

above	excess	monopolist	railroads
agree	expand	monopoly	repeat
benefit	flatter	monopoly profits	retaliate
Bertrand	formal	more	revenue
cartel	game theory	Nash equilibrium	rewards
collude	greater	non-cooperative	Sherman Antitrust
collusion	illegal	non-price	steeper
concentration ratio	imperfect	competition	strategic
cooperative	competition	oligopoly	tacit collusion
cost	interdependence	outcomes	tit for tat
differentiated	kinked demand	payoff	trusts
differentiating	long time	payoff matrix	two
dominant	marginal cost	price leadership	will
duopolist	marginal revenue	price war	will not
equals	market power	producer(s)	

1. A(n) _____ is a market with only a few sellers. A firm (or
_____) in such an industry is known as an oligopolist. Each of the
sellers has some _____ in that its decision about how much to produce would affect the market price. When no one firm has a monopoly, but each
recognizes that it can affect market prices, the market is characterized by
_____. Oligopoly is a form of imperfect competition. Economies of
scale are an important source of oligopoly; bigger producers have a(n)
_____ advantage over smaller producers.

2. We cannot determine whether a market is an oligopoly by merely looking at the
number of _____ in the industry. Some oligopolistic markets have
many firms, but only a few of them have _____.
Economists use the four-firm _____, the share

of industry sales by the top four firms in the market, as an indication of how much _____ individual firms have.

3. We have learned that all firms produce the level of output at which marginal revenue _____ marginal costs. However, when looking at an oligopoly, it is sometimes puzzling to determine marginal _____. In oligopolistic markets, firms frequently _____ to increase their combined profits. A(n) _____ is an agreement by several producers that increases their combined profits by telling each one how much to produce. Collusion and cartels are _____ in Canada.

4. A duopoly is an oligopoly with just _____ firms, each firm is known as a(n) _____. If the firms act as competitors, they will drive the price in the market down to the level of _____. However, if they collude and agree to set a particular price and produce a particular level of output, they can enjoy _____. The downfall of collusion is that each firm may cheat and make _____ profits by producing more than the agreed-upon amount. When firms ignore the effects of their actions on each other's profits, they are engaging in _____ behaviour. Collusion is more profitable than non-cooperative behaviour, yet it is difficult to get firms to _____ to collusive behaviour. Even though illegal in Canada, oligopolies often try to achieve collusion without a(n) _____ agreement.

5. Industries that face constraints on their ability to produce output (those industries that require big investments in fixed costs) are much more amenable to _____. Because it is difficult for them to produce more when they undercut their rival's price, it is easier for them to agree to share the market and maintain a price _____ marginal cost. This is known as quantity competition, or the Cournot model of oligopoly.

However, if oligopolists are not constrained in production, either because it is easy to _____ their production capability or because of _____ capacity, each firm will find that it can increase sales by cutting prices. In these cases, firms will continue to cut prices until the price is _____ to marginal cost, the same outcome as in the perfectly competitive market. This is known as price competition, or the _____ model.

6. Firms in an oligopoly recognize their _____; each firm's profit depends on the actions of its rivals, and its rivals' profits depend on what it does. It is similar to playing a game, and we use _____ to help us understand oligopolies. Game theory helps us understand behaviour when the _____ to one player depend not only on his or her actions but on those of the other players as well.

7. The rewards received by a player in a game, such as the profits earned by an oligopolist, are that player's _____. In its simplest version of a duopoly, game theory helps us to understand each firm's decision regarding whether to collude or not to collude through _____ matrix. The payoff matrix (with two firms) contains four boxes that show the results from four possible _____ for the firms. The payoff matrix can explain why each firm has an opportunity to _____ at the expense of the rival firm, they will both act this way and will be worse off than if they had chosen to collude; this is a version of the classic prisoner's dilemma. To cheat on a collusive agreement is the _____ strategy; it's the firm's best action regardless of the action taken by the other firm. We also call this non-cooperative equilibrium a(n) _____ , after the mathematician John Nash.

8. The prisoner's dilemma explains games that are only played once. However, oligopolists expect to be in business for years and expect to make decisions repeatedly about whether to collude or not; they _____ their games. A firm will engage in _____ behaviour, considering the reactions of its rivals to today's decisions. Firms know that their rivals will engage in a strategy of _____, playing cooperatively at first and then doing whatever the other player did in the previous period. Tit for tat rewards _____ behaviour and punishes cheating. When oligopolists expect to continue in business for a(n) _____ , they will often behave in a way that is helpful to the other firms in the industry. Even without a formal agreement, oligopolies will engage in _____ and limit production and raise prices in a way that raises each other's profits.

9. Once _____ exists in an oligopoly, it is in the individual firm's best interest to behave carefully. No one firm wants its rivals to interpret any action as _____. If a firm tries to increase its output by lowering prices, the firm will expect its rivals to _____ by lowering their prices. However, if the firm reduces output by raising prices, the firm will expect its rivals to ignore the price change and gain _____ market share. This leads to a(n) _____ curve for an oligopolist. The demand curve is kinked at the tacit collusion equilibrium, with a _____ demand curve for prices above the kink and a _____ demand curve for prices below the kink. The kink in the demand curve generates a break in the _____ curve, where the break in the _____ is just below the kink. According to the optimal output rule, the firm maximizes profits by producing the level of output where marginal revenue _____ marginal cost. Since there is a break in the marginal revenue curve, any marginal _____ curve that falls within the break gap will generate the same optimal level of output. A change in an individual oligopolist's marginal cost within the break in marginal revenue _____ change price and output.

10. Tacit collusion rarely results in prices at the monopoly level because various factors, such as the number of firms in the industry, _____ products, different interests, and bargaining power of buyers, limit the ability to coordinate behaviour in oligopolies. Tacit collusion often breaks down into a(n) _____ and prices sometimes fall to competitive levels. Oligopolists try to avoid price wars by _____ their products in an attempts to distinguish them from their rivals' products. Oligopolists sometimes follow a pattern of behaviour called _____ where the big firm (leader) sets its price and the others (small firms) follow. There is also often a tacit understanding that although they will not compete on price, they will engage in _____ such as advertising, to increase sales.

Learning Tips

TIP #1: Although the oligopolist faces a downward-sloping demand curve and has market power to set prices above the perfectly competitive level, its marginal revenue is higher than a monopolist's because the monopolist faces a less elastic demand curve than the one faced by the oligopolist.

Figure 15.1 shows the demand curve for fugglenuts. Suppose a monopoly will sell 2,000 pounds of fugglenuts at a price of $8 and have revenue of $16,000 per year. If the monopolist lowers the price to $7, they will sell 3,000 pounds of fugglenuts and earn revenue of $21,000 per year. Total revenue rose because the quantity effect (selling an additional thousand pounds of fugglenuts at a price of $7, or $7,000) exceeds the price effect (lowering the price by $1 on the 2,000 units the firm had sold at a price of $8, or –$2,000). Marginal revenue of the 3,000th unit is $5 ($5,000/1,000).

Figure 15.1

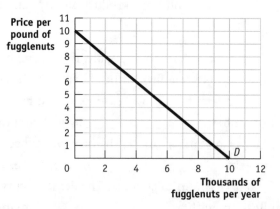

Thousands of
fugglenuts per year

If the fugglenut market were an oligopoly, no one firm would sell 2,000 pounds of fugglenuts at a price of $8; they would sell less than 2,000 pounds. For example, let's say that the fugglenut industry had two firms (it was a duopoly) and they colluded to share the market: each firm agreed to produce 1,000 units at a price of $8. If one of the firms cheated on the agreement and lowered their price to $7 but the other firm maintained its price at $8, marginal revenue would be greater than $5 (the marginal revenue for the same price change when the market is a monopoly). As the firm lowers its price from $8 to $7, it will sell an additional thousand pounds of fugglenuts and total revenue will rise $7,000 because of the quantity effect. The firm will also have to lower the price by $1 per pound on the original 1,000 units sold, for a price effect of –$1,000. The marginal revenue associated with the firm lowering its price by $1 per pound is $6 per pound ($6,000/1,000).

TIP #2: It is easier for firms to agree to set price and share the market when they face constraints on how much either can produce.

When oligopolists agree to share a market to maximize joint profits, individual firms recognize that if they cheat on that agreement and charge a slightly lower price and sell more, their individual profit will increase. This will only work if the oligopolist can increase production. In some industries, especially ones with large capital requirements, firms cannot easily expand output. Therefore, the incentive to cheat is much less than in an industry where it is relatively easy to expand production. Collusive agreements work better when firms cannot easily expand output. We call this quantity competition, or Cournot behavior. In industries that have low capital requirements or that have excess capacity, the incentive to cheat is much greater and it is more difficult to get firms to abide by a collusive agreement. These markets have a lot of price competition and firms are likely to engage in Bertrand behavior, undercutting their rivals' price, until the price is at the perfectly competitive level.

TIP #3: In game theory, a firm has a dominant strategy whenever it would choose the same course of action regardless of what policy its rival chooses.

Table 15.1 shows the payoff matrix for the only two coffeehouses, Javamania and BeanCrazy, in Mayville. The payoff matrix assumes that each firm chooses between a high-price strategy and a low-price strategy each year and that its earnings depend on its rival's actions.

Table 15.1

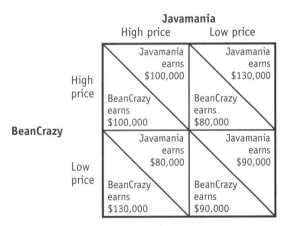

When Javamania is trying to decide whether to pursue a high-price or low-price strategy, it wants to consider each strategy under the two possible price strategies of BeanCrazy.

- If BeanCrazy sets a high price, Javamania can choose to set a high price or a low price. If Javamania sets a high price, Javamania earns $100,000 per year, but if it sets a low price, Javamania would earn even more, $130,000. So if Javamania knew that BeanCrazy was going to set a high price, Javamania would definitely set a low price.

- On the other hand, if BeanCrazy sets a low price, Javamania can again choose to set a high price or a low price. If Javamania sets a high price, Javamania will earn $80,000 per year, while if Javamania sets a low price, it will earn $90,000. If Javamania knew that BeanCrazy was going to set a low price, Javamania would set a low price.

Regardless of whether BeanCrazy sets a high price or a low price, Javamania would set a low price. The low-price strategy is Javamania's dominant strategy.

If the payoff matrix for Javamania and BeanCrazy were as shown in Table 15.2, Javamania would not have a dominant strategy.

Table 15.2

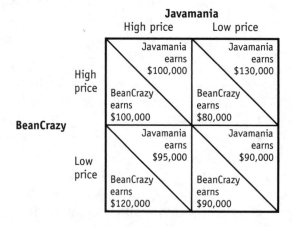

If BeanCrazy has a high-price policy, Javamania will earn more by following a low-price policy; however, if BeanCrazy follows a low-price policy, Javamania will earn more by following a high-price policy. Without knowing BeanCrazy's strategy, Javamania does not know whether the high-price or the low-price policy will maximize its earnings.

Multiple-Choice Questions

1. Oligopolies are market structures in which there are
a. few firms.
b. barriers to entry.
c. incentives for collusion with other firms.
d. all of the above.

2. The following table shows the percentage of sales in the newspaper market in Collegetown. What is the four-firm concentration ratio for that market?

Newspaper	Percent of industry sales
The Student Daily	10
Collegetown Journal	4
The University Press	10
The Profile	5
The Town Record	25
Collegetown News	40
The College Caller	6

a. 29%
b. 40%
c. 65%
d. 85%

3. Which of the following statements about oligopolies are correct?
   a. Oligopolists always collude with their competitors to maximize joint profits.
   b. It is easier for oligopolists to agree to a pricing strategy when there are output constraints.
   c. It is easier for oligopolists to collude when their goods are differentiated.
   d. In equilibrium, oligopolists maximize total surplus.

4. The fugglenut market has only two firms, the Best Fugglenut Co. and Fugglenuts-R-Us. They form a cartel to increase the price of fugglenuts. They will maximize their joint profits when they both _____, and the Best Fugglenut Co. will maximize its profits when it _____ the agreement.
   a. abide by the agreement; abides by
   b. cheat on the agreement; cheats on
   c. cheat on the agreement, abides by
   d. abide by the agreement; cheats on

5. The fugglenut market has only two firms, the Best Fugglenut Co. and Fugglenuts-R-Us. They form a cartel to increase the price of fugglenuts. If they compete on the basis of price, they will eventually
   a. enjoy monopoly profits.
   b. break even.
   c. price at the perfectly competitive level.
   d. go out of business.

6. Game theory is very useful for studying how firms behave when there is
   a. a kinked demand curve.
   b. a price effect but no quantity effect.
   c. interdependence in payoffs.
   d. a cartel.

7. In game theory, the prisoner's dilemma occurs when
   a. each firm has an incentive to cheat but both firms are worse off if they do.
   b. there is a cartel and the penalty for cheating is expulsion from the cartel.
   c. the firms follow a tit-for-tat strategy.
   d. none of the above.

8. In repeated prisoner's dilemma games,
   a. the firms will often revert to competing with prices until the price is at the perfectly competitive level.
   b. the firms will often revert to competing with prices until they just break even.
   c. the firms will often follow a tit-for-tat strategy and, without explicit collusion, eventually maximize joint profits.
   d. the firms will often follow a tit-for-tat strategy and, without explicit collusion, eventually minimize joint profits.

Use the following figure to answer the next two questions.

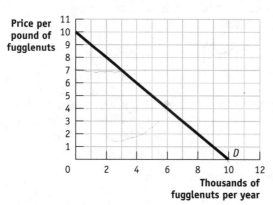

9. The fugglenut market has only two firms, the Best Fugglenut Co. and Fugglenuts-R-Us. The preceding figure shows the market demand curve for fugglenuts. If the two firms have marginal costs equal to $4 per pound and agree to share the market equally, the price in the market will be _____ and each will sell _____ pounds of fugglenuts.
   a. $4; 3,000
   b. $0; 1,000
   c. $7; 1,500
   d. $5; 2,500

10. The fugglenut market has only two firms, the Best Fugglenut Co. and Fugglenuts-R-Us. The preceding figure shows the market demand curve for fugglenuts. If the two firms have marginal costs equal to $4 per pound and engage in price competition, the price in the market will be _____ and each will sell _____ pounds of fugglenuts.
   a. $4; 3,000
   b. $0; 10,000
   c. $7; 6,000
   d. $5; 5,000

Use the following table to answer the next four questions. The table shows the payoff matrix each month for the two bookstores in Pelmar when each is considering its pricing strategy.

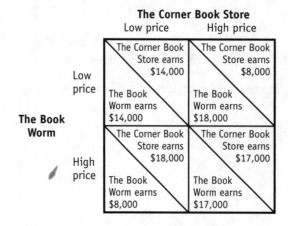

11. The dominant strategy for The Corner Book Store
   a. is to charge a high price.
   b. is to charge a low price.
   c. is to charge what The Book Worm does.
   d. does not exist.

12. The Nash equilibrium in the Pelmar book market is when
   a. both firms set a low price and each earns $14,000 per month.
   b. both firms set a high price and each earns $17,000 per month.
   c. The Book Worm sets a high price and earns $8,000 per month, while The Corner Book Store sets a low price and earns $18,000 per month.
   d. The Book Worm sets a low price and earns $18,000 per month, while The Corner Book Store sets a high price and earns $8,000 per month.

13. If The Book Worm followed a high-price strategy one month, just to find it earned only $8,000 because The Corner Book Store followed a low-price strategy, and The Book Worm then decided to lower prices for the next month, we would say that they are following
   a. a kinked demand model.
   b. a dominant strategy.
   c. a tit-for-tat strategy.
   d. none of the above.

14. Month after month, the bookstores follow a tit-for-tat strategy. Eventually they will achieve a tacit collusive equilibrium where
   a. both firms set a low price and each earns $14,000 per month.
   b. both firms set a high price and each earns $17,000 per month.
   c. The Book Worm sets a high price and earns $8,000 per month, while The Corner Book Store sets a low price and earns $18,000 per month.
   d. The Book Worm sets a low price and earns $18,000 per month, while The Corner Book Store sets a high price and earns $8,000 per month.

15. In the following table, the dominant strategy for The Corner Book Store
   a. is to advertise.
   b. is to not advertise.
   c. is to do whatever The Book Worm does.
   d. does not exist.

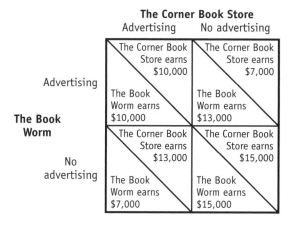

16. The fugglenut market has only two firms, the Best Fugglenut Co. and Fugglenuts-R-Us. Through tacit collusion the Best Fugglenut Co. and Fugglenuts-R-Us each arrive at an equilibrium price and quantity and see their demand curve as kinked. This means that the Best Fugglenut Co. expects Fugglenuts-R-Us to _____ any price increase and _____ any price decrease.
    a. ignore; follow
    b. follow; ignore
    c. ignore; ignore
    d. follow; follow

17. The fugglenut market has only two firms, the Best Fugglenut Co. and Fugglenuts-R-Us. Through tacit collusion they each arrive at an equilibrium price and quantity and see their demand curve as kinked. Fugglenuts-R-Us will be reluctant to raise its price because it sees that portion of the demand curve as _____, and if it raised price, total revenue would _____.
    a. price elastic; fall
    b. price inelastic; fall
    c. price elastic; rise
    d. price inelastic, rise

18. Competition Act in Canada made which of the following actions illegal?
    a. companies meeting and agreeing to charge a particular price
    b. companies meeting and agreeing to produce a certain amount
    c. oligopolies merging to form a monopoly
    d. all of the above.

19. Tacit collusion is more difficult to achieve
    a. the smaller the number of firms in the industry.
    b. the more standardized the product exchanged in the industry.
    c. the greater the differences in costs in the industry.
    d. when oligopolists face many small buyers of their good.

20. In an oligopoly that tacitly sets prices through a pattern of price leadership, you will often find
    a. cheating.
    b. nonprice competition.
    c. less advertising.
    d. different firms functioning as price leaders over time.

21. Which of the following statements is true?
    a. The total profit earned by firms in Cournot's duopoly model is greater than the monopoly profit.
    b. In Bertrand's duopoly model, where each firm has identical average total cost (which is also equal to marginal cost), the total economic profit is zero.
    c. In the kinked demand curve model, the demand curve beyond the kink is more elastic in comparison to the demand curve before the kink.
    d. A cartel is an example of non-collusive oligopoly behaviours.

    *Answer optional questions 22–24 on the basis of the following information:
    The inverse market demand function is: $P = 100 - Q$, where P is the dollar price per unit of output (Q).
    The monopolist's marginal revenue function is: $MR = 100 - 2Q$.
    The firm's cost function is such that each firm's average total cost (ATC) is $40 and the marginal cost (MC) is equal to ATC.

*22. In a collusive oligopoly model with two firms, the market price will be _____ and each firm will earn an economic profit of _____.
   a. $70; $900
   b. $70; $450
   c. $40; $450
   d. $40; $900

*23. In Bertrand's duopoly model, the market price will be
   a. $70.
   b. $40.
   c. below $40.
   d. above $40.

*24. In Cournot's duopoly model,
   a. the price will be $70 and each firm will earn an economic profit of $450.
   b. the price will be higher than $70 and each firm will earn an economic profit higher than $450.
   c. the price will be lower than $70 and each firm will earn an economic profit lower than $450.
   d. there will be price war and price will fall to $40.

25. The kinked demand curve model explains
   a. price wars amongst oligopoly firms.
   b. price rigidity.
   c. why firms do not need to bring costs down to make more profits.
   d. why the demand curve faced by an oligopoly firm is inelastic.

Problems and Exercises

Read each question carefully and then write your answers in the space provided or on a separate sheet of paper.

1. The following table shows the number of firms and the percentage of sales going to each firm for various industries in an economy. Calculate the four-firm concentration ratio for each industry. What industries appear oligopolistic?

Industry	Firm 1	Firm 2	Firm 3	Firm 4	Firm 5	Firm 6	Firm 7	Firm 8	Firm 9	Firm 10	Firm 11	Firm 12	Firm 13	Firm 14	Firm 15	Firm 16	Firm 17	Firm 18	Firm 19	Firm 20
Film production	40	5	2	2	1	4	2	1	40	3										
Aircraft manufacturing	60	40																		
Software	10	5	4	6	8	9	50	2	6											
Health care	35	10	25	3	4	6	2	4	8	3										
Candy manufacturing	2	2	6	8	10	12	4	2	1	6	7	4	3	7	6	11	5	1	2	1
Legal services	2	2	20	2	2	3	5	2	5	1	3	3	38	3	2	2	2	1	1	1
Fugglenut production	10	10	10	10	10	10	10	10	10	10										

2. On the island economy of Bookland, there are two colleges, North Bookland College (NBC) and South Bookland College (SBC). The following table shows the market demand schedule for one year of full-time college each year in Bookland. Both NBC and SBC have no fixed costs and marginal cost and average costs equal to $4,000.

Number of students	Tuition
0	$20,000
1,000	18,000
2,000	16,000
3,000	14,000
4,000	12,000
5,000	10,000
6,000	8,000
7,000	6,000
8,000	4,000
9,000	2,000
10,000	0

a. Draw the market demand, marginal revenue, marginal cost, and average total cost curves in the market for one-year of full-time college each year in Bookland in the preceding figure. If the market for college education in Bookland was perfectly competitive, what would be the optimal level of output and equilibrium tuition in Bookland? What would be the economic profit in a perfectly competitive market?

b. If the market for college education in Bookland was a monopoly, what would be the optimal level of output and equilibrium tuition in Bookland? What would be the economic profit in the monopoly?

c. If NBC and SBC agree to share the market equally, at each tuition level, each school would have half the market demand. Graph their demand and marginal revenue, marginal cost, and average total cost curves in the following figures. What would be the optimal level of output and equilibrium tuition in Bookland? What does each college earn in economic profit? How does this outcome differ from part b?

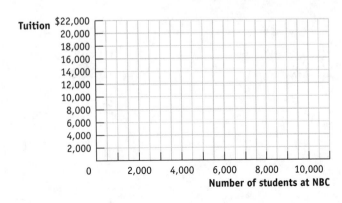

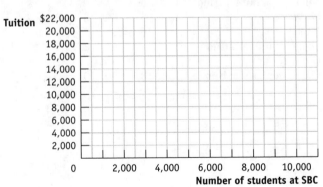

d. What would happen if SBC continues to honor its agreement to share the market but NBC lowers tuition by $2,000? How will SBC react?

3. The agreement to share the college education market in Bookland breaks down and NBC and SBC begin to behave in a noncooperative manner. Each college sees itself as having one of two options for tuition: it can charge $12,000 per year or $8,000 per year. The payoff matrix in the following table shows the profit earned each year by the two colleges under each tuition option.

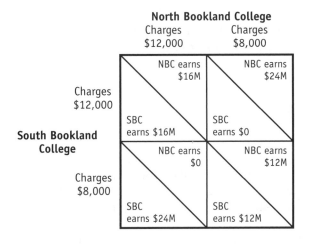

a. What is the noncooperative Nash equilibrium?

b. What would happen if NBC considered charging $8,000 while SBC charged $12,000? If NBC did charge $8,000 and SBC stayed in business, what tuition do you expect SBC would charge next year? Is this tit-for-tat behavior? How would NBC react? What would happen over time? Why do oligopolists who expect to participate for many years in an industry engage in tacit collusion?

4. The newspaper industry has four large daily newspapers that dominate the market. *The Daily Economy* is one of those newspapers. After years of competing with one another, the market has found a tacit collusive equilibrium at a price of $1.00. At that price, *The Daily Economy* sells 50,000 papers each day.

   a. If *The Daily Economy* believes that if they lowered prices their rival newspapers would also cut their prices, and if they raised prices their rival newspapers would not change theirs and gain market share, what does the demand curve facing *The Daily Economy* look like? What does their marginal revenue curve look like? Where will the marginal cost curve be located? (Assume that the marginal cost curve is upward sloping.)

   b. Does the kinked demand model of an oligopoly explain why, in the absence of large changes in costs, tacit collusion keeps price and output constant in oligopolistic markets?

5. Consider two duopoly firms (firm *A* and firm *B)* with identical costs of *ATC* = *MC* = $2. If both firms collude and maintain the high price of $6 per unit of output, they will sell 2.5 million units. If one firm keeps the high price of $6 and the other firm cheats and keeps the low price of $4, the low-price firm will sell 6 million units and the high-price firm will sell 1 million units. If both firms keep the low price of $4, each firm will sell 3 million units.

   a. Find the payoff matrix in the following table.

		Firm *A*	
		High price	Low price
Firm *B*	High price	Profit of firm *A* = Profit of firm *B* =	Profit of firm *A* = Profit of firm *B* =
	Low price	Profit of firm *A* = Profit of firm *B* =	Profit of firm *A* = Profit of firm *B* =

   b. If firm *A* keeps the high price, firm *B* should keep the _____ price. Why?

c. If firm *A* keeps the low price, firm *B* should keep the _____ price. Why?

d. What is the dominant strategy of firm *A*?

e. What is the dominant strategy of firm *B*?

6. Consider two duopoly firms (firm *A* and firm *B*) with identical costs of $ATC = MC = \$2$. If both firms collude and maintain the high price of $6 per unit of output, they will sell 2.5 million units. If one firm keeps the high price of $6 but the other firm cheats and keeps the low price of $4, the low-price firm will sell 4 million units and the high-price firm will sell 2 million units. If both firms keep the low price of $4, each firm will sell 3 million units.

a. Find the payoff matrix in the following table.

		Firm *A*	
		High price	Low price
Firm *B*	High price	Profit of firm *A* = Profit of firm *B* =	Profit of firm *A* = Profit of firm *B* =
	Low price	Profit of firm *A* = Profit of firm *B* =	Profit of firm *A* = Profit of firm *B* =

b. If firm *A* keeps the high price, firm *B* should keep the _____ price. Why?

c. If firm *A* keeps the low price, firm *B* should keep the _____ price. Why?

d. What is the dominant strategy of firm *A*?

e. What is the dominant strategy of firm *B*?

*7. Consider the following inverse market demand function:

$P = 100 - Q.$

If the market demand belongs to a monopoly firm, the monopolist's marginal revenue is:

$MR = 100 - 2Q.$

Each firm's $ATC = MC = \$40$.

a. What will be the output and market price in a competitive market?

b. What will be the equilibrium output and price in monopoly? What will be the monopoly profit?

c. Suppose that there are two identical firms in an oligopolistic market, where the equilibrium output of each firm is 20.
What will be the market price and profit of each firm?

d. If two firms collude and form a cartel, what will be the market price and profit for each firm?

Answers to How Well Do You Understand the Chapter

1. oligopoly, producer, market power, imperfect competition, cost

2. producers, market power, concentration ratio, market power

3. equals, revenue, collude, cartel, illegal

4. two, duopolist, marginal cost, monopoly profits, greater, non-cooperative, agree, formal

5. collusion, above, expand, excess, equal, Bertrand

6. interdependence, game theory, rewards

7. payoff, payoff, outcomes, benefit, dominant, Nash equilibrium

8. repeat, strategic, tit for tat, cooperative, long time, tacit collusion

9. tacit collusion, non-cooperative, retaliate, greater, kinked demand, flatter, steeper, marginal revenue, marginal revenue, equals, cost, will not

10. differentiated, price war, differentiating, price leadership, non-price competition

Answers to Multiple-Choice Questions

1. Oligopolies are industries that have few firms and barriers to entry, and the firms recognize the incentive to collude. **Answer: D.**

2. To calculate the four-firm concentration ratio for the newspaper market, you need to add up the percent of industry sales going to the largest four firms. In the table provided, the largest firms are *Collegetown News*, *The Town Record*, *The Student Daily*, and *The University Press*. Those four firms account for 85% of industry sales. **Answer: D.**

3. Of the four statements, the correct one is that "it is easier for oligopolists to agree to a pricing strategy when there are output constraints." Firms that cannot expand output will have little incentive to lower prices since they will not be able to increase output; they will be much more willing to agree on an industry price and keep to the agreement. **Answer: B.**

4. Oligopolists can maximize joint profits temporarily when they abide by a collusive agreement, but one of them can maximize its own profits by cheating on the agreement while its rival abides by it. **Answer: D.**

5. If oligopolists compete on the basis of price they will drive the price down to marginal cost, the same price that would exist in a perfectly competitive market. **Answer: C.**

6. Game theory explains how oligopolists behave because it provides a framework for comparing the success of different policies by considering how a rival will react and how that will influence a firm's profit. Game theory is useful for studying behavior when there is interdependence in payoffs. **Answer: C.**

7. The prisoner's dilemma is a game in which each firm has an incentive to choose a policy that benefits itself at its rival's expense, but that when both firms act in this way they are worse off than if they had chosen a different policy. **Answer: A.**

8. In repeated prisoner's dilemma games, through tit for tat firms will recognize that they benefit by cooperating and are hurt by cheating. The firms will eventually achieve an equilibrium that maximizes joint profits. **Answer: C.**

9. If the two firms agree to share the market equally, they will try to maximize joint profit by producing where marginal revenue corresponding to the market demand curve equals marginal cost. As the following figure shows, this occurs at output equal to 3,000 pounds of fugglenuts each year. Each firm will produce half, or 1,500 pounds, and charge a price of $7 per pound. **Answer: C.**

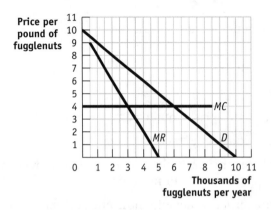

10. If the two firms engaged in price competition, price would fall to the perfectly competitive level where price equals marginal cost. From the preceding figure, we see that with price competition, price would equal $4 and each firm would produce 3,000 pounds of fugglenuts each year. **Answer: A.**

11. If The Book Worm chooses a low-price strategy, The Corner Book Store will earn $14,000 per month if it follows the same low-price strategy or $8,000 if it follows a high-price strategy. The Corner Book Store will choose to follow the low-price strategy. However, if The Book Worm chooses a high-price strategy, The Corner Book Store will earn $18,000 by following a low-price strategy or $17,000 if it follows a high-price strategy. Again the better strategy for The Corner Book Store is to follow a low-price strategy. Since The Corner Book Store should follow a low-price strategy regardless of the strategy chosen by The Book Worm, it is the dominant strategy. **Answer: B.**

12. The Nash equilibrium, also known as a noncooperative equilibrium, occurs when each player follows the strategy that maximizes its own profit. In the table provided, the Nash equilibrium is when each firm follows a low-price strategy and each earns $14,000 per month. **Answer: A.**

13. When one firm chooses to do whatever the other firm did in the previous period, we say it is following a tit-for-tat strategy. **Answer: C.**

14. If firms follow a tit-for-tat strategy over time, they begin to realize that they are rewarded for cooperative behavior and hurt by noncooperative behavior. Soon the firms will achieve tacit collusion, where each firm follows a high-price strategy and each earns $17,000 per month. **Answer: B.**

15. There is no dominant strategy. If The Book Worm advertises, The Corner Book Store will maximize its earnings by advertising. However, if The Book Worm does not advertise, The Corner Book Store will maximize its profits by not advertising. There is no strategy that The Corner Book Store can choose to maximize its earnings without knowing the strategy of The Book Worm. **Answer: D.**

16. If the Best Fugglenut Co. sees its demand curve as kinked, it expects that if it lowered its price its rival, Fugglenuts-R-Us, will retaliate (follow) by lowering its price. On the other hand, if the Best Fugglenut Co. raises its price, Fugglenuts-R-Us would gain market share at Best Fugglenut's expense, and therefore the Best Fugglenut Co. expects that they would not match (ignore) the price change. **Answer: A.**

17. If Fugglenuts-R-Us sees its demand curve as kinked, it will be reluctant to raise price because Best Fugglenut Co. will not follow the price increase and Fugglenuts-R-Us will find its sales drop dramatically. If it raised its price, Fugglenuts-R-Us's total revenue would fall because the demand curve above the kink is price elastic. **Answer: A.**

18. Illegal antitrust actions in the United States include companies meeting and agreeing to charge a particular price or to produce a certain amount. Antitrust policy also does not allow oligopolies to merge and form monopolies. **Answer: D.**

19. Tacit collusion is difficult to achieve when there are a large number of firms, the firms have differentiated products and complex pricing schemes, the firms differ in what they view as an equitable distribution of the market (differing costs for firms in the industry), and large buyers are in a position to bargain for lower prices. **Answer: C.**

20. If firms do not compete on price, they will often try to compete by differentiating their products and advertising the superiority of their products. **Answer: B.**

21. In Cournot's duopoly, the combined profit is less than the monopoly profit. In the kinked demand curve, the demand is more elastic above the kink and the demand is less elastic below the kink. A cartel is an example of collusive oligopoly. In the Bertrand model, the price is driven down to average total cost and there exists no economic profit at the end. **Answer: B.**

22. The collusive oligopoly equilibrium is the same as the monopoly equilibrium. With the $MC = MR$ rule, we can solve output as 30 and price at \$70. The economic profit is \$900, which is shared by each firm; each firm earns an economic profit of \$450. **Answer: B.**

23. In Bertrand's model, the price is driven down to \$40. **Answer: B.**

24. In Cournot's model, the price will be less than \$70, but more than \$40. Each firm will earn less profit compared to the profit each firm would have earned under a collusive oligopoly. **Answer: C.**

25. In the kinked demand curve model, the price stays at the kink and the price remains stable and rigid. **Answer: B.**

Answers to Problems and Exercises

1. The following table shows the four-firm concentration ratios for the various industries.

Industry	Four-firm concentration ratio
Film production	89
Aircraft manufacturing	100
Software	77
Health care	78
Candy manufacturing	41
Legal services	68
Fugglenut production	40

The industries that appear oligopolistic are aircraft manufacturing, film production, health care, and software. In particular, it is interesting that in the film production industry 89% of the market is concentrated in four firms, while there are 10 firms in the market. The candy manufacturing industry is the least oligopolistic.

2. a. The following figure shows the market demand, marginal revenue, marginal cost, and average total cost curves for one year of full-time college each year in Bookland. If the market were perfectly competitive, equilibrium output would be where marginal cost intersects the demand curve at 8,000 students at an equilibrium tuition of $4,000. Since price equals average total cost, there would be no economic profit if the market were perfectly competitive.

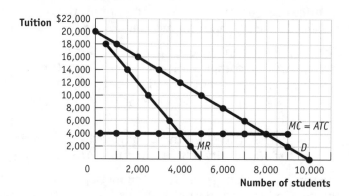

b. If the market for college education in Bookland was a monopoly, then the firm would produce where marginal revenue intersects marginal cost in the preceding figure, or at a level of enrollment of 4,000 students and tuition of $12,000. The monopolist would earn $32,000,000 (= [$12,000 − $4,000] × 4,000) in economic profit.

c. If NBC and SBC agree to share the market equally, the following figures show the demand and marginal revenue, marginal cost, and average total cost curves at each college. Following the optimal output rule, they will each enroll 2,000 students and charge tuition of $12,000. Each college will earn $16,000,000 in economic profit. Price, output, and economic profit are the same as they would be if the market were a monopoly; the colleges are enjoying monopoly profits.

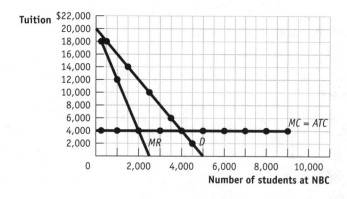

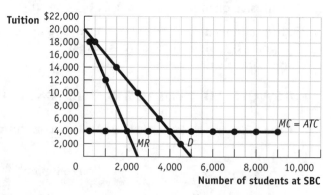

d. If SBC honors its agreement but NBC lowers tuition by $2,000, assuming the education is the same at both colleges and that NBC does not have a constraint on the number of students it can enroll, all students willing to pay $10,000 in tuition will attend NBC. NBC will enroll 5,000 students and earn a profit of $30,000,000. The following year, SBC will lower its tuition and the two colleges will be in a price war. Without tacit collusion, tuition will fall to $4,000, the competitive level.

3. a. When NBC is considering tuition, it considers it under two assumptions: (i) that SBC will charge $12,000, and (ii) that SBC will charge $8,000:

    i. If SBC charges $12,000 and NBC charges $12,000, NBC will earn $16M. However, if SBC charges $12,000 and NBC charges $8,000, NBC will earn $24M. So, NBC will want to charge $8,000 if SBC charges $12,000.

    ii. If SBC charges $8,000 and NBC charges $12,000, NBC will earn nothing, while if NBC charges $8,000, NBC will earn $12M. NBC will want to charge $8,000 if SBC charges $8,000.

NBC will opt to charge $8,000 regardless of the tuition SBC charges. The same is true for SBC. This is a noncooperative Nash equilibrium: each will charge tuition of $8,000 and earn $12M per year when they would have maximized joint profits if they had charged $12,000.

b. If NBC charged $8,000 while SBC charged $12,000, NBC would earn $24M while SBC earned nothing. SBC would not sit by and watch NBC earn $24M in profit while SBC earns nothing. In response, SBC would lower its tuition to at least $8,000. This is tit-for-tat behaviour. Knowing that SBC will react this way if it reduces tuition encourages NBC to keep the tuition at $12,000, even without a formal agreement. Oligopolists who expect to participate for many years in an industry recognize that it is in their best interest to engage in tacit collusion; that is how they will maximize their profit.

4. a. The following figure shows that the demand curve facing *The Daily Economy* is kinked. Since the demand curve is kinked, the marginal revenue curve is broken, with the break in the marginal revenue curve directly under the kink in the demand curve. The marginal cost curve can be drawn a number of places (the figure shows two), but it must be drawn so that the marginal cost curve goes through the break in the marginal revenue curve.

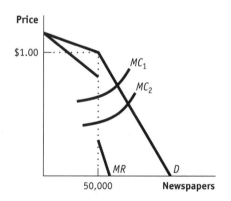

b. Unless there are large changes in marginal cost—unless, in the preceding figure, the marginal cost of producing the 50,000th newspaper no longer falls within the break in the marginal revenue curve—the profit-maximizing level of output remains 50,000 newspapers and price remains $1.00 per newspaper.

5. a. All figures in the payoff matrix in the following table are in million dollars.

		Firm B	
		High price	Low price
Firm A	High price	Profit of firm A = $10 Profit of firm B = $10	Profit of firm A = $4 Profit of firm B = $12
	Low price	Profit of firm A = $12 Profit of firm B = $4	Profit of firm A = $6 Profit of firm B = $6

b. If firm A keeps the high price, firm B should keep the *low* price. If firm A keeps the high price, firm B has two options; it can keep the high price and earn $10 million, or it can keep the low price and earn $12 million. Since $12 million is greater than $10 million, the optimal strategy for firm B is to keep the low price.

c. If firm A keeps the low price, firm B should keep the *low* price. If firm A keeps the low price, firm B has two options; it can keep the high price and earn $4 million, or it can keep the low price and earn $6 million. Since $6 million is greater than $4 million, the optimal strategy for firm B is to keep the low price.

d. The dominant strategy of firm A is the low price.

e. The dominant strategy of firm B is the low price.

6. a. All figures in the payoff matrix in the following table are in million dollars.

		Firm B	
		High price	Low price
Firm A	High price	Profit of firm A = $10 Profit of firm B = $10	Profit of firm A = $8 Profit of firm B = $8
	Low price	Profit of firm A = $8 Profit of firm B = $8	Profit of firm A = $6 Profit of firm B = $6

b. If firm A keeps the high price, firm B should keep the *high* price. If firm A keeps the high price, firm B has two options; it can keep the high price and earn $10 million or it can keep the low price and earn $8 million. Since $10 million is greater than $8 million, the optimal strategy for firm B is to keep the high price.

c. If firm A keeps the low price, firm B should keep the *high* price. If firm A keeps the low price, firm B has two options; it can keep the high price and earn $8 million or it can keep the low price and earn $6 million. Since $8 million is greater than $6 million, the optimal strategy for firm B is to keep the high price.

d. The dominant strategy of firm A is the high price.

e. The dominant strategy of firm B is the high price.

7. a. In a competitive market, the output will be 60 (based on the $MC = P$ rule) and the market price is $40.

b. By setting $MR = MC$, we can solve the equilibrium output in monopoly as 30 and equilibrium price at $70. The monopoly profit is $900.

c. Since each firm produces 20 units, the total output is 40 and the market price is $60. Each firm will earn $400.

d. If two firms collude and form a cartel, the market price will be same as the monopoly price and profit for each firm will be $400.

## chapter 16

Monopolistic Competition and Product Differentiation

Monopolistic competition is a market structure with many firms, each producing a differentiated product (brand name). Each firm has some market power and its price is greater than its marginal revenue. When firms make economic profit in the short run, new firms enter the market in the long run until each firm earns zero economic profit. Unlike perfect competition in the long run, the monopolistic firm has excess capacity. Advertisement expenses are very high in this market.

How Well Do You Understand the Chapter?

Fill in the blanks using the terms below to complete the following statements. Terms may be used more than once. If you find yourself having difficulties, please refer back to the appropriate section in the text.

advertise	diversity	leave	optimal output
advertising	downward-sloping	left	perfect competitors
asset(s)	economic profits	limited	quality
average total cost	equals	less	right
benefit(s)	excess capacity	location	service
brand name	exit out	marginal revenue	signal
break even	gains	market power	too many
closest	greater than	minimum	type
competition	information	move	value in diversity
differentiate(d)	large	mutually beneficial	waste

1. Monopolistic competition describes a market in which there are _____ numbers of competing firms selling _____ products. The market also has relatively free entry into and _____ of the industry. Monopolistic competition is common in _____ industries and also some manufacturing industries. Each monopolistic competitor recognizes that the firm faces competitions from its rivals, but there are _____ rivals to have tacit collusion. Monopolistic competitors are not price takers; each firm has some _____. However, the firm's power to set high prices is limited by the _____ it faces from other firms in the industry.

2. There are three ways in which monopolistic competitors attempt to differentiate their firms from their rivals: by style or by type, by _____, and by quality. For example, competitors in the fast-food industry often differentiate in terms of the ____type____ of cuisine they offer. Service industries frequently try to differentiate by location; consumers tend to choose the _____closest_____ seller rather than the cheapest. Other firms diversify by cheaper, low-quality goods and others offer pricier, high-quality goods. Some monopolistic competitors, such as automobile dealerships, try to differentiate themselves in all three ways.

3. Product differentiation can take several forms, but there are two important features of industries with differentiated products: competition among sellers and _____. Competition among sellers means that even though sellers of products are not offering identical goods, they are to some extent competing for a(n) _____ market. Value in diversity refers to the _____ to consumers from the proliferation of differentiated products catering to diverse tastes.

4. Because monopolistic competitors offer a distinct product, each firm faces a(n) _____ demand curve and a downward-sloping _____ curve. Like monopolies and firms in perfectly competitive markets, monopolistic competitors will choose to produce according to the _____ rule, where marginal revenue equals marginal cost.

5. In the short run, a monopolistic competitor can face any of three situations: (1) earn an economic profit, (2) _____, or (3) earn an economic loss. If at the optimal level of output, price is _____ than the average total cost, the firm will earn an economic profit. If at the optimal level of output price equals average total cost, the firm will _____. However, if price is less than the ____AVC____ at the optimal level of output, the firm will earn a loss.

6. If firms are earning _____ in the short run, in the long run other firms will be attracted into the industry. As more firms enter the industry, the demand curve facing individual monopolistic competitors will shift to the _____ until the economic profits are eliminated. If firms are earning economic losses in the short run, in the long run firms will _____ the industry and the demand curve facing the remaining monopolistic competitors will shift to the _____ until the losses are eliminated.

7. In the long run, all monopolistic competitors will _____. In long-run equilibrium, monopolistic competitors are similar to _____ in that they both produce the level of output at which price equals average total cost. However, a monopolistic competitor will not produce where average total costs are at a _____ or where price _____ marginal cost, as

does occur in perfect competition. Monopolistic competitors produce along the downward-sloping portion of the average total cost curve; we say that they produce with _____, they produce less than the output at which average total cost is minimized. Since price is _____ marginal cost in long-run equilibrium, we know that some _____ trades do not take place and a deadweight loss exists, as it does with a monopoly.

8. Two crucial aspects of product-differentiation are _____ and brand names. Advertising plays an important role in allowing firms to _____ their products in monopolistically competitive markets. Unlike a perfect competitor, which can sell as much as they want at the going price, monopolistic competitors _____ to get people to buy more of their products. Most advertising provides _____ to buyers about the good or service; however, some advertisements, such as celebrity endorsements, don't seem to provide much information, except that the advertisement may pro-vide a(n) _____ to consumers that the firm is large and stable enough to pay for such an endorsement. In as much as advertising may work by influencing consumers to switch from one good to another that is virtually the same, advertising may be an economic _____.

9. A(n) _____, owned by a particular firm, distinguishes a firm's prod-ucts from those of its competitors. Brand name and goodwill are important _____ to many firms. Like advertising, it is not clear whether society _____ from brand names. The brand name does convey information but it may also create unjustified _____.

Learning Tips

TIP #1: We can determine if a monopolistic competitor earns a profit or loss in the short run by comparing price and average total cost.

For all firms, total profit is total revenue minus total cost, or

$$\text{Profit} = TR - TC.$$

If we divide through the equation by quantity, we can see that average profit equals aver-age revenue minus average total cost, and average revenue is the market price:

$$\text{Profit}/Q = TR/Q - TC/Q = P - ATC$$

or

$$\text{Profit} = (P - ATC) \times Q.$$

Although average revenue is always equal to the price, a monopolistic competitor differs from a perfect competitor in that to sell more, a monopolistic competitor has to lower the price of the good. If the price is greater than average total cost, the firm will earn an economic profit. If the price equals average total cost, the firm will just break even. However, if the price falls short of average total cost, the firm will earn a loss.

Figure 16.1 shows a monopolistic competitor earning an economic profit in the short run. A monopolistic competitor will produce where marginal revenue equals marginal cost. In Figure 16.1, we see that the monopolistic competitor will produce Q_1 units of output and charge a price of P_1. We can see that at a price of P_1, the firm will earn a profit of $(P_1 - ATC_1) \times Q_1$ (the shaded rectangle).

Figure 16.1

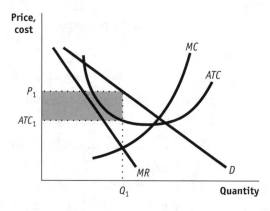

In Figure 16.2, the firm will only break even. The monopolistic competitor will maximize profit at Q_2 and charge a price P_2; at this level of output price equals average total cost $(P_2 = ATC_2)$.

Figure 16.2

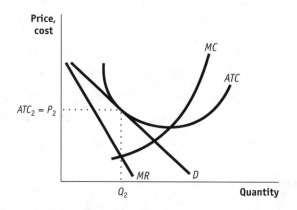

In Figure 16.3, the firm will earn an economic loss. At the level of output where marginal revenue equals marginal cost, Q_3, average total cost, ATC_3, exceeds the price, P_3, and the firm earns a loss equal to $(ATC_3 - P_3) \times Q_3$ (the shaded rectangle).

Figure 16.3

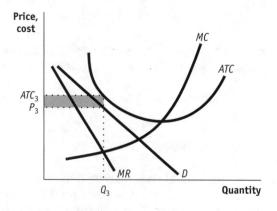

TIP #2: The long-run adjustment in a monopolistically competitive market will always result in all firms breaking even.

Since there are few if any barriers to entry or exit, monopolistic competitors will break even in the long run. If monopolistic competitors are earning economic profits in the short run, as shown in Figure 16.1, other firms will be attracted into the industry in the long run. As firms enter the industry, the demand curves facing the existing firms will shift to the left and they will respond by producing less and charging lower prices. This will continue until all firms in the industry just break even. If monopolistic competitors were earning a loss but continuing to produce in the short run, they will leave the industry in the long run. As firms leave the industry, the existing firms will find that their demand curves will shift to the right and they will respond by increasing price and output. This process will continue until all firms in the industry break even.

TIP #3: In long-run equilibrium, a monopolistic competitor will produce a level of output where price equals average total cost, price exceeds marginal cost, and average total cost is not at a minimum.

Figure 16.4 shows a monopolistic competitor in long-run equilibrium. Since there are few if any barriers to entry, all monopolistic competitors will just break even; price equals average total cost. This is the same as in a perfectly competitive market. We also know that a monopolistic competitor faces a downward-sloping demand curve, so that price exceeds marginal revenue; at the same time, marginal revenue equals marginal cost (the optimal output rule), so price must exceed marginal cost. Unlike perfect competitors, who produce where price equals marginal cost, monopolistic competitors produce with a deadweight loss because some mutually beneficial trades do not take place. Finally, monopolistic competitors produce with excess capacity; they produce along the downward-sloping portion of the average total cost curve. Again, if we compare them to perfect competitors, who produce where price equals minimum average total cost, monopolistic competitors produce where average total cost is greater than marginal cost and average total cost is declining.

Figure 16.4

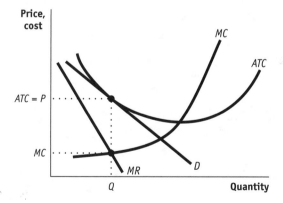

Multiple-Choice Questions

1. A market that is characterized by monopolistic competition is like a monopoly in that _____, and like a perfectly competitive market in that _____.
   a. firms face a downward-sloping demand curve; there are no barriers to entry
   b. firms face a perfectly price elastic demand curve; it has no supply curve
   c. firms may earn economic profits in the long run; there is no deadweight loss
   d. firms break even; firms produce with excess capacity

2. Which of the following industries is monopolistically competitive in Canada?
   a. soft drink industry
   b. diamond industry
   c. wheat industry
   d. clothing industry

3. If a restaurant tries to cater to the low-price end of a monopolistically competitive market by only offering counter service (customers must order and take their meals from a counter) and skimping on ingredients, we could say that it is trying to differentiate itself on the basis of
   a. location.
   b. quality.
   c. style or type.
   d. both b and c.

4. In monopolistically competitive markets, there is product differentiation because
   a. each firm is a price taker.
   b. there is competition among sellers.
   c. there is value in diversity.
   d. both b and c.

Use the following figure to answer the next two questions. It shows the monthly demand, average total cost, marginal revenue, and marginal cost curves for Silkee Scarves, a monopolistically competitive firm.

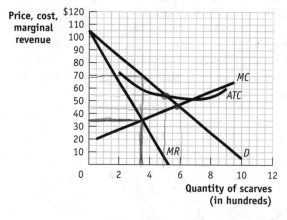

5. In the short run, Silkee Scarves will produce _____ hundred scarves, charge a price of _____, and earn a profit of _____.
   a. 8; $25; $0
   b. 3.5; $35; $3,500
   c. 3.5; $70; $3,500
   d. 5; $55; $0

6. In the long run,
   a. Silkee Scarves will experience a decrease in demand.
   b. Silkee Scarves will experience an increase in demand.
   c. Silkee Scarves will not experience a change in demand.
   d. it is impossible to determine what will happen to Silkee Scarves' demand.

The accompanying figure shows different profit positions for a monopolistic competitor in the short run. Use this figure to answer the next five questions.

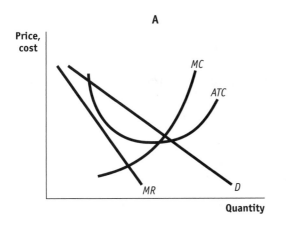

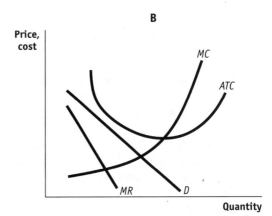

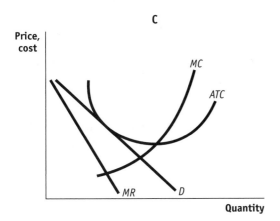

7. Which of the panels in the figure shows a monopolistic competitor in long-run equilibrium?
   a. A
   b. B
   c. C
   d. None of the above.

8. Which of the panels in the figure shows a monopolistic competitor earning an economic profit?
   a. A
   b. B
   c. C
   d. Both A and B.

9. Which of the panels in the figure shows a monopolistic competitor earning an economic loss in the short run?
   a. A
   b. B
   c. C
   d. None of the above.

10. Which of the panels in the figure show a monopolistic competitor producing with excess capacity?
  a. only A and B
  b. only B and C
  c. only A and C
  d. A, B, and C

11. If monopolistic competitors find themselves in a position similar to panel B in the figure, in the long run the _____ curves facing firms in the industry will _____.
  a. demand and marginal revenue; shift to the right
  b. demand and marginal revenue; shift to the left
  c. average total cost and marginal cost; shift to the right
  d. average total cost and marginal cost; shift to the left

12. In zero-profit equilibrium, the demand curve must be tangent to the average total cost curve because
  a. if any part of the demand curve lies above the average total cost curve, the firm will earn positive profits.
  b. if the demand curve lies everywhere below the average total cost curve, the firm will earn negative profits.
  c. firms will enter or leave the industry if there are either positive profits or negative profits in the industry.
  d. of all of the above.

13. In long-run equilibrium, a perfectly competitive firm and a monopolistically competitive firm are similar in that they both produce a level of output at which
  a. price equals marginal cost.
  b. price equals average total cost.
  c. marginal cost equals average total cost.
  d. there is excess capacity.

14. In long-run equilibrium in a monopolistically competitive industry, we know that some mutually beneficial trades do not take place because price is
  a. less than average total cost.
  b. less than marginal revenue.
  c. greater than marginal cost.
  d. greater than average total cost.

15. In long-run equilibrium in a monopolistically competitive industry, there is excess capacity because marginal cost is
  a. less than average total cost.
  b. less than the price.
  c. greater than marginal revenue.
  d. greater than average total cost.

16. Unlike perfect competitors, monopolistic competitors often advertise because
  a. they are price takers.
  b. they sell standardized products.
  c. they produce with excess capacity.
  d. they want to produce where price equals marginal cost.

17. Some argue that even though monopolistic competitors produce where price exceeds marginal cost, this inefficiency may be beneficial because it is offset by
    a. the economic profit earned by the firms.
    b. the value of the diversity of products.
    c. the market power wielded by firms.
    d. all of the above.

18. A monopolistic competitor engages in advertising to
    a. provide information about its good or product.
    b. differentiate its product from those of its rivals.
    c. increase the demand for its good or service.
    d. all of the above.

19. Which of the following advertisements provides information to the consumer?
    a. "CarbChips have half the carbohydrates of regular potato chips."
    b. "The Taj Mahal restaurant is like a trip to India."
    c. "Brainpower Books—just think it!"
    d. "Avion Airlines wants to take you higher."

20. One of the drawbacks of advertising and brand names is that
    a. they increase profits for firms in the industry.
    b. they may create product differentiation and market power where there is no real difference in the product.
    c. they encourage competition.
    d. they minimize the difference between price and marginal cost.

21. In monopolistic competition, each firm is a _____ and each firm makes _____ economic profit in the long run.
    a. price-taker; zero
    b. price-maker; positive
    c. price-maker; zero
    d. price-taker; positive

22. Unlike perfect competition, the long run equilibrium output for a firm under monopolistic competition is at a point where
    a. the average total cost is minimum.
    b. the average total cost is upward sloping, and the firm produces more than the capacity output.
    c. the average total cost is downward sloping, and the firm produces less than the capacity output.
    d. $P = MC$.

Consider the following data for a firm in a monopolistically competitive market structure in the short run and answer questions 23–25. The average total cost in the short run is U-shaped, and it is the lowest possible average-total cost curve when we consider the long-run situation.

Output = 25.

$P = \$10$.

$MC = \$7$.

$MR = \$7$.

$ATC = \$6$.

23. Given the previous data, the firm should
   a. produce more.
   b. produce less.
   c. not change output.
   d. should charge a higher price.

24. Given the previous data, the firm in the long run
   a. should make as much profit as it makes in the short run.
   b. should produce less than 25 units.
   c. will face the same price of $10 as it faced in the short run.
   d. will make a positive but much less economic profit.

25. Given the previous data, new firms will enter the market in the long run, and we will see each of the following outcomes, **except**
   a. the firm will face a lower market price.
   b. the firm will produce output at the minimum possible *ATC*.
   c. the firm will produce output at a point which lies below the point with minimum average total cost.
   d. the firm will earn zero economic profit in the long run.

26. Which of the following statements is true?
   a. The firm under monopolistic competition can produce capacity output where *ATC* is the minimum in the short run.
   b. The firm under monopolistic competition can produce capacity output in the long run.
   c. The firm under monopolistic competition cannot have economic losses in the short run.
   d. The firm under monopolistic competition can have economic losses in the long run.

Problems and Exercises

Read each question carefully and then write your answers in the space provided or on a separate sheet of paper.

1. Tango's Tamales is a small restaurant on a busy street known as Restaurant Row. The following table shows the firm's demand schedule and the following figure shows the restaurant's marginal cost and average total cost curves.

Number of tamales (in hundreds)	Price of a tamale
0	$11.00
1	9.50
2	8.00
3	6.50
4	5.00
5	3.50
6	2.00
7	0.50

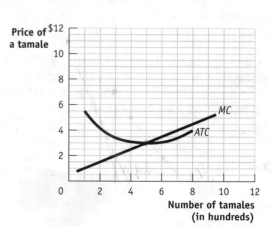

a. Graph the demand and marginal revenue curves facing Tango's Tamales in the preceding figure.

b. What are the optimal level of production and the profit-maximizing price of tamales? How much profit is Tango's Tamales earning? What do you expect to happen in the long run?

c. More stores open on Restaurant Row and the demand for Tango's Tamales falls. The following table shows the new demand schedule. Graph the new demand and marginal revenue curves in the following figure. What are the optimal level of production and the profit-maximizing price of tamales? How much profit is Tango's Tamales earning? What do you expect to happen in the long run?

Number of tamales (in hundreds)	Price of a tamale
0	$5.00
1	4.50
2	4.00
3	3.50
4	3.00
5	2.50
6	2.00
7	1.50
8	1.00
9	0.50
10	0.00

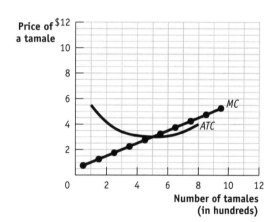

2. The accompanying figures show the marginal and average total cost curves for a perfect competitor and a monopolistic competitor in the long run. Assume both are operating in the long run and draw the demand and marginal revenue curves for each. Compare the two long-run equilibriums by focusing on the relationships between price and marginal cost, price and average total cost, and marginal cost and average total cost.

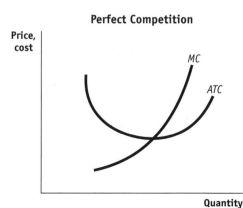

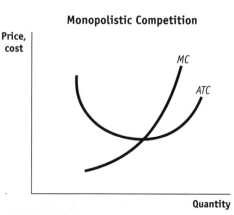

3. In your ethics class, a discussion about advertising has focused on how it wastes resources by persuading consumers to buy things they do not need. How would you defend advertising and the importance/impact of establishing a brand name?

4. a. What are the similarities and dissimilarities between monopoly and monopolistic competition?

b. What are the similarities and dissimilarities between perfect competition and monopolistic competition?

5. Consider the following data for a firm in a monopolistic market structure in the short run. The average total cost in the short run is u-shaped, and it is the lowest possible average-total cost curve when we consider the long-run situation.

Output = 25.

$P = \$12$.

$MC = \$6$.

$MR = \$7$.

$ATC = \$10$.

a. What is the amount of economic profit? Is this firm maximizing profit? Explain.

b. Is there an excess capacity at the current output? Explain.

c. Should the firm increase or decrease output? Explain.

d. What will be the long-run outcomes?

6. The following graph represents a firm in a monopolistic market in the short run.

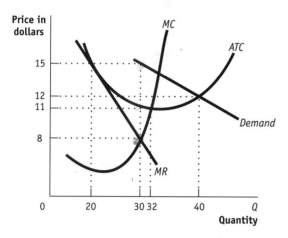

a. What is the equilibrium output?

b. What is the equilibrium price?

c. What are *MR* and *MC* at the equilibrium output?

d. What is the total revenue at the equilibrium?

e. What is the total cost at the equilibrium?

f. What is the total profit at the equilibrium?

g. What will the firm's profit be in the long run? Why?

Answers to How Well Do You Understand the Chapter

1. large, differentiated, exit out, service, too many, market power, competition

2. location, type, closest

3. value in diversity, limited, gains

4. downward-sloping, marginal revenue, optimal output

5. break even, greater than, break even, average total cost

6. economic profits, left, leave, right

7. break even, perfect competitors, minimum, equals, excess capacity, greater than, mutually beneficial

8. advertising, differentiate, advertise, information, signal, waste

9. brand name, assets, benefits, market power

Answers to Multiple-Choice Questions

1. A monopolistic competitor is like a monopoly in that the firm faces a downward-sloping demand curve and has market power to set a price above marginal cost. It is like a perfect competitor in that there are no barriers to entry and all firms break even in the long run. **Answer: A.**

2. The soft drink industry is oligopolistic, the diamond industry is a monopoly, the wheat industry is perfectly competitive, and the clothing industry is monopolistically competitive. **Answer: D.**

3. The restaurant is differentiating itself both in terms of quality, because it is a low-price restaurant, and of style or type, because counter service does not appeal to all diners. **Answer: D.**

4. Monopolistic competitors differentiate their products because they want to attract buyers from their rivals and consumers will pay for diversity. **Answer: D.**

5. Silkee Scarves will produce 3.5 hundred (350) scarves because that is where marginal revenue equals marginal cost (the optimal output rule), and it will charge a price of $70. The average total cost of producing the 3.5 hundred scarves is $60; average profit is $10, and total profit is $3,500. **Answer: C.**

6. In the long run, firms will be attracted to the scarf industry by the short-run profits and the demand for Silkee Scarves will fall. **Answer: A.**

7. In long-run equilibrium, a monopolistic competitor will just break even. Panel C shows a monopolistic competitor breaking even. At the level of output where marginal revenue equals marginal cost, price equals average total cost. **Answer: C.**

8. Panel A shows a monopolistic competitor earning an economic profit. In panel A, at the level of output at which marginal revenue equals marginal cost, price is greater than average total cost. **Answer: A.**

9. Panel B shows a monopolistic competitor earning a loss in the short run. At the level of output at which marginal revenue equals marginal cost, average total cost is greater than price (the firm earns a loss). **Answer: B.**

10. A firm is producing with excess capacity if it is producing a level of output for which average total cost is decreasing. If average total cost is decreasing, marginal revenue must be less than average total cost. In all three panels, at the level of output at which marginal revenue equals marginal cost, the firm is producing with excess capacity. **Answer: D.**

11. Panel B shows a monopolistic competitor earning a loss but continuing in business in the short run. In the long run, firms will leave the industry and the demand and marginal revenue curves facing the remaining firms in the industry will shift to the right. **Answer: A.**

12. If the demand curve at any point lies above the average total cost curve in the short run, a monopolistic competitor will earn a positive profit, other firms will enter the industry in the long run, and the demand curve facing the original firm will fall until it is just tangent to the demand curve and all firms break even. If a firm's demand curve lies everywhere below the average total cost curve in the short run, a monopolistic competitor will earn a loss and leave the industry in the long run. The demand curves facing the remaining firms will rise until they are just tangent to the demand curves and all firms break even. **Answer: D.**

13. Because there are no barriers to entry or exit, perfect competitors and monopolistic competitors will break even in the long run; price equals average total cost. **Answer: B.**

14. We know that in long-run equilibrium in a monopolistically competitive industry, some mutually beneficial trades do not take place because price is greater than marginal cost. Society would be better off with more produced. **Answer: C.**

15. A monopolistic competitor always produces where marginal revenue equals marginal cost and price is greater than marginal revenue; it produces where marginal revenue is less than price. In long-run equilibrium, a monopolistic competitor will produce where price equals average total cost. Therefore, in the long run, a monopolistic competitor will produce where marginal revenue is less than average total cost and average total cost must be declining. A monopolistic competitor in the long run will produce with excess capacity. **Answer: A.**

16. Unlike perfect competitors, who can sell as much as they want at the market price, monopolistic competitors produce with excess capacity and would like to sell more at the market price. Monopolistic competitors advertise to increase sales. **Answer: C.**

17. Since consumers value the diversity of products in monopolistically competitive markets, it may be worth paying a price that is greater than marginal cost. **Answer: B.**

18. The goal of advertising is to provide information and differentiate the product to increase the demand for the good or service. **Answer: D.**

19. The only advertising slogan to provide information is "CarbChips have half the carbohydrates of regular potato chips." The other slogans tell little about the monopolistic competitors' products as distinct from their competitors. **Answer: A.**

20. Advertising and brand names do not necessarily increase profits or minimize the difference between price and marginal cost. They do increase competition among firms, which is an advantage of advertising. The disadvantage is that they may create product differentiation and market power where there is no real difference in their product. **Answer: B.**

21. Each firm is a price-maker ($P > MR$) in monopolistic competition. Firms enter or exit until each firm makes zero economic profit. **Answer: C.**

22. Capacity output is located at a point where the *ATC* is at a minimum. Since the downward-sloping *ATC* is tangent with the demand curve faced by the firm, the equilibrium output takes place at a point below the capacity output. **Answer: C.**

23. Since *MR* = *MC*, the firm is maximizing its profit; therefore, the firm should not change output. **Answer: C.**

24. Due to the existence of economic profit in the short run, new firms will enter in the long run and each firm's demand curve will shift in (each firm will have a smaller market share), and as a result, the firm will produce less than 25 units of output. **Answer: B.**

25. Since the *ATC* is U-shaped and since the *ATC* is tangent with the downward-sloping firm's demand curve in the long-run equilibrium, the firm cannot produce at the point where the *ATC* is at a minimum. **Answer: B.**

26. All the statements are false except the one stating that the firm can produce at the capacity output where *ATC* is a minimum and earn economic profit in the short run. **Answer: A.**

Answers to Problems and Exercises

1. a. The following figure shows the demand, marginal revenue, marginal cost, and average total cost curves for Tango's Tamales.

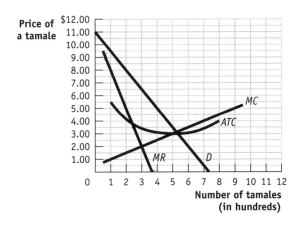

b. The optimal level of production is 300 tamales and the profit-maximizing price is $6.50. Since average total cost is $3.50, the firm is earning average profit of $3, or a total profit of $900. In the long run, firms will be attracted to the industry by the profit, and demand for Tango's Tamales will decrease.

c. The accompanying figure shows new demand and marginal revenue curves for Tango's Tamales after more stores open on Restaurant Row. The optimal level of production is still 300 tamales, but the profit-maximizing price is $3.50. Since average total cost is $3.50, average profit and total profit are zero. The firm is in long-run equilibrium.

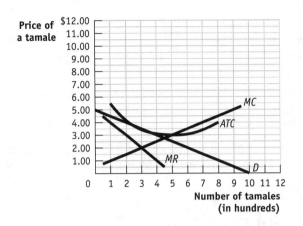

2. The following figures show a perfect competitor and a monopolistic competitor in long-run equilibrium. They are similar in that both the monopolistic competitor and the perfect competitor break even—price equals average total cost—in the long run. They are earning just what's necessary to keep them in business in the long run.

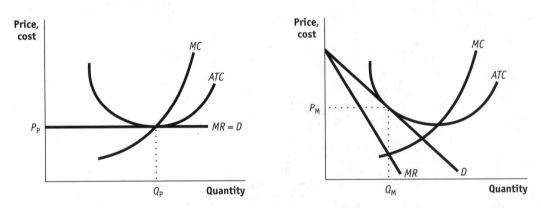

However, the perfect competitor will produce where price equals marginal cost and where the average total cost curve is minimized, while the monopolistic competitor produces where price exceeds marginal cost and where the average total cost curve is declining (excess capacity). When price equals marginal cost, we know that all mutually beneficial trades take place. In a monopolistically competitive market, not all mutually beneficial trades take place. Also, unlike a perfect competitor, a monopolistic competitor does not produce where the average total cost curve is minimized; it produces with excess capacity.

3. While the primary purpose of advertising is to get people to buy more of a seller's product, advertisements and brand names also provide information to potential buyers about what a firm or product has to offer. They can provide information about how the good or service is produced and how it compares to others in the market. They may also provide an incentive to a firm to improve its product. Finally, advertising can be entertaining. Many people who are not football fans watch the Super Bowl merely to enjoy the entertaining (and expensive) commercials. Even advertising that does not seem to provide information about a good, such as celebrity endorsements or advertisements during the Super Bowl, may provide a signal to potential consumers about the financial security of a firm.

4. a. The similarities are:

Both monopoly and firms under monopolist competition are price-makers $(P > MR)$ and both are inefficient, because $P > MC$.

The dissimilarities are:

Monopoly has one firm, while monopolistic competition has many firms.

Products are differentiated in monopolistic competition.

New firms cannot enter the market in monopoly, while new firms can enter the market in monopolistic competition.

Monopoly firm can make economic profit in the long run, but in monopolistic competition, all firms make zero economic profit in the long run.

b. The similarities are:

New firms can enter the market in both perfect competition and in monopolistic competition.

Firms make zero profit in both perfect competition and in monopolistic competition.

The dissimilarities are:

Firms are price-takers in perfect competition $(P = MR)$, while firms are price-takers $(P > MR)$ in monopolistic competition.

5. a. Profit $= TR - TC = \$50$.

The firm is not maximizing profit, because $MR > MC$.

b. There is an excess capacity, because at the current output, marginal cost (MC) is less than average total cost (ATC). The MC is less than the ATC when the output is below the point where the ATC is at a minimum (the capacity output point).

c. The firm should increase output, because $MR > MC$.

d. New firms will enter the market; the demand curve faced by each firm will shift to the left; and eventually each firm will make zero economic profit.

6. a. 30.

  b. $15.

  c. $8.

  d. $450.

  e. $330.

  f. $120.

  g. Zero; because new firms will keep on entering the market until each firm makes no economic profit.

chapter 17

International Trade

The basis for mutually beneficial international trade is the theory of comparative advantage. A country has comparative advantage in producing a good for which the country has relatively lower opportunity cost. The main sources of comparative advantage are: factor endowments, differences in climate and technology. Why a country has a comparative advantage (lower opportunity costs) in a given good is explained by the Heckscher-Ohlin model, which states that a country has a comparative advantage in a good that uses factors that are relatively more abundant. Gains from trade are explained with the two-country Ricardian constant-cost model. We study trade protection, tariff, and quota, and see the deadweight loss. The arguments for and against trade protection are highlighted in this chapter. We end the chapter with discussions on trade agreements, NAFTA and WTO.

How Well Do You Understand the Chapter?

Fill in the blanks using the terms below to complete the following statements. Terms may be used more than once. If you find yourself having difficulties, please refer back to the appropriate section in the text.

abundant	economic policies	income gap	quota rents
advantage	economies of scale	increase	ratio
agreements	encourage	increasing returns	rise
autark	export	infant industry	scarce
capital	factor endoments	intensive	straight line
capital-intensive	fall	international	tariff
climate	foreign	labour-intensive	technology
comparative	free trade	licenses	temporary
constant	gains	lower	total surplus
deadweight	higher	lowered	trade
decrease	highly educated	new jobs	trade agreements
discourage	import-competing	physical	trade protection
differs	imported	price takers	world
domestic	import quotas	quantity	

1. Most nations engage in _____; their residents produce goods that are sold (exported) to residents of other nations, and they import goods and services that were produced in other nations. Exports and imports have grown tremendously over the last few decades. Nations trade because there are _____ from trade, and these gains arise from _____. A country has a comparative advantage in producing a good if the opportunity cost of producing the good is _____ for that country than for other

countries. As long as the opportunity cost of producing goods _____ among countries, there is a basis for trade.

2. The Ricardian model of international trade analyzes international trade under the assumption that the opportunity costs are _____ and the production possibility frontier is a(n) _____. From it, we can see that total consumption in countries will be _____ with trade than in autarky (when a nation does not engage in any trade).

3. There are three main sources of comparative advantage: international differences in climate, international differences in _____, and international differences in technology.

   • Differences in _____ explain why many tropical nations export products such as coffee, sugar, and bananas, while countries in temperate zones export goods such as wheat and corn.

   • The Heckscher-Ohlin model of international trade focuses on differences in _____ to explain trade. According to this model, a nation has comparative advantage in a good whose production is _____ _____ in the factors of production that are _____ in that nation. Factor intensity of production compares the _____ of factors used to produce a good; clothing production is labour-intensive, while oil production is _____ _____ intensive.

   • Japan's success in exporting cars during the 1970s and 1980s seems to be the result of differences in _____. Improvements in technology in Japan _____ the opportunity cost of producing cars, giving the Japanese a comparative advantage in automobile production.

4. Another reason for international trade lies in the role of increasing returns. The production of a good is characterized by _____ if the productivity of labour and other resources rises with the level of production. Increasing returns are known as _____, and they also can give rise to monopolies because they give large firms an advantage over small ones.

5. Leontief found that contrary to the Heckscher-Ohlin model, the United States imported more _____ goods than it exported, something known as the Leontief paradox. The paradox was resolved by understanding that Leontief measured capital as just _____ capital. When human capital was included in the definition of capital, the United States did export capital-intensive goods and imported _____ goods.

6. We can also look at trade using the supply and demand model. In autarky, _____ demand (quantity demanded by domestic consumers) and _____ supply (quantity supplied by domestic producers) determine equilibrium price and output. Once we open the economy to trade, we assume that domestic consumers and domestic producers can buy or sell as much of the good on the world market as they want without affecting the _____ price, the price at which that good can be bought or sold on the world market. Domestic consumers and domestic producers are _____ in the world market.

7. If the world price is lower than the domestic _____ price when the economy opens to trade, the price in the domestic market will _____ to the level of the world price and domestic consumers will begin to purchase foreign-produced goods (imports). Domestic producers will sell _____ and earn smaller _____, while domestic consumers will buy _____ and earn a larger _____. With trade, the _____ in the market increase. The gain of consumer surplus to domestic consumers is _____ than loss of producer surplus to domestic producers.

8. If the world price is higher than the domestic autarky price when the economy opens to trade, the price in the domestic market will _____ to that of the world price and domestic producers will begin to _____ the good. Domestic producers will sell _____ and earn a _____ producer surplus, while domestic consumers will buy _____ and earn a _____ consumer surplus. With trade, the total surplus in the market will increase; the gain of producer surplus to domestic producers is _____ than the loss of consumer surplus to domestic consumers.

9. According to the Heckscher-Ohlin model, a nation has a comparative advantage in producing the good that is _____ in the factor that is abundant in that country. As a nation specializes in the good that is intensive in the factor that is _____, the demand for that factor increases and the price of that factor will _____; as the nation reduces the production of the good that is intensive in the factor that is _____, the demand for that factor will _____ along with the price of the scarce factor. This may explain some of the widening of the _____ between Canada and developing countries. Canada and other developed countries have a comparative advantage in goods and services that require a(n) _____ workforce; those workers already have higher wages than less-educated workers, and the effect of trade tends to increase the disparity of wages.

10. An economy engages in _____ when the government does not attempt either to reduce or to increase the levels of exports and imports that occur as a result of supply and demand. Although most economists advocate free trade, many governments have instituted policies that limit imports, known as _____, Common protectionist measures are tariffs and _____.

11. A(n) _____ is an excise tax levied on imports. Although at one time tariffs were imposed because they were an easy source of government revenue, they are used today to _____ imports and protect import-competing domestic producers. The tariff will increase the market price, domestic producers will produce _____. Imports will fall, producer surplus will _____, consumer surplus will _____, and the government will raise revenue from the tariff. However, the gain to domestic producers and the government is _____ than the loss of consumer surplus. The tariff generates a(n) _____ loss for society.

12. An import quota is a legal limit on the _____ of a good that can be imported and is usually administered through _____ that can give the license holder the right to import a limited quantity each year. We saw in Chapter 4 that the import quota has the same effect as a(n) _____, with the exception of the quota rent. An import quota can limit imports of the good to the same level as a tariff; the difference is that rather than raising revenue for the government, the import quota provides _____ to the holders of the import licenses. The government could charge for the licenses and raise the same revenue as does an import tariff, but in Canada the economic rent goes to the license holder.

13. Three arguments put forth to justify trade protection are national security, job creation, and the _____ argument. The national security argument asserts that we need to protect the industries producing goods that may be vulnerable to disruption in time of _____ conflict. Others argue that by protecting some industries we can create _____ in import-competing industries. The infant-industry argument holds that new industries require a _____ period of trade protection to get established.

14. The primary reason for trade protection seems to be the political power of _____ producers. Tariffs and import quotas _____ producer surplus and _____ consumer surplus. Domestic producers of a good are usually fewer in number, easier to organize, and wield _____ political influence than do the domestic consumers.

15. Nations have attempted to pursue the goal and benefits of free trade through international trade _____. Through them, a nation agrees to engage in

_____ trade protection against the exports of other countries in return for a promise by other countries to do the same for its own exports. Some agreements are between just two or three nations, such as the North American Free Trade Agreement (NAFTA), while others cover most nations of the world. The World Trade Organization (WTO) oversees global trade agreements. It provides the framework for the negotiations involved in major international _____, and it resolves _____ disputes between member nations of WTO.

Learning Tips

TIP #1: In the two-good, two-nation Ricardian model, we can identify which nation has a comparative advantage in a good by comparing the slopes of the production possibility frontiers.

The Ricardian model of international trade assumes that the opportunity costs are constant and not increasing, as we discussed in Chapter 2. The nation whose production possibility frontier has the flatter slope has a comparative advantage in the good measured on the horizontal axis. We see the gains from trade because nations can consume outside their production possibility frontier. Let's look at a hypothetical example of the trade of airplanes and oil between Mexico and Canada. Figures 17.1 and 17.2 show the annual production possibility frontiers for airplanes and oil in Mexico and in Canada.

Figure 17.1

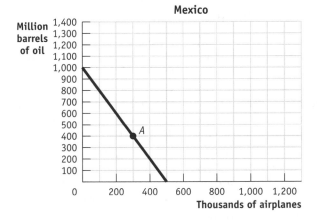

Figure 17.2

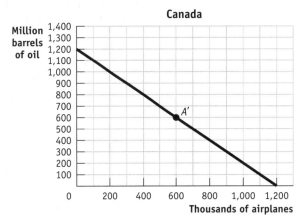

In autarky, Mexico would produce and consume 300 thousand airplanes and 400 million barrels of oil (point A in Figure 17.1) and Canada would produce 600 thousand airplanes and 600 million barrels of oil (point A' in Figure 17.2). The opportunity cost of producing 500 thousand airplanes in Mexico is 1,000 million barrels of oil, or 2 million barrels of oil for each 1 thousand airplanes. In Canada, the opportunity cost of producing 1,200 thousand airplanes is 1,200 million barrels of oil, or 1 million barrels of oil for 1 thousand airplanes. The opportunity cost of producing airplanes in Canada is lower than in Mexico; Canada has a comparative advantage in airplanes and Mexico has a comparative advantage in oil. The opportunity cost of airplanes (how much oil do we have to give up to get 1 thousand airplanes) is the slope of the production possibility frontier. Since the production possibility frontier is flatter for Canada, Canada must have a comparative advantage in airplanes.

If each nation specializes in the good in which it has a comparative advantage, Canada specializes in producing airplanes and Mexico specializes in producing oil; Canada will produce 1,200 thousand airplanes (point B' in Figure 17.4) and Mexico will produce 1,000 million barrels of oil (point B in Figure 17.3). If each nation agreed to trade 600 million barrels of oil for 400 thousand airplanes (a rate of trade of 3 million barrels of oil for 2 thousand airplanes), Mexico could consume at point C and Canada at C' in Figures 17.3 and 17.4. Each nation gains from trade because points C and C' lie outside each nation's production possibility frontier.

Figure 17.3

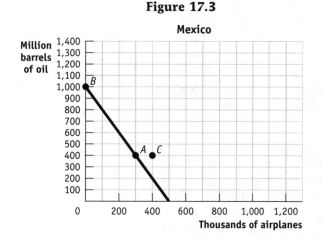

Mexico

Figure 17.4

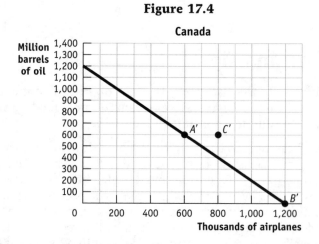

Canada

TIP #2: When looking at a domestic market, the increase in total surplus that results when the good is imported (the domestic price in autarky is higher than the world price) or exported (the domestic price in autarky is higher than the world price) represents the gains from trade.

Figure 17.5 shows the domestic demand and domestic supply of peaches. If there were no trade in peaches, the price in the market would be P_A, and Q_A would be exchanged. Consumer surplus would be F and producer surplus would be $G + H$. If the market is opened to trade and the world price of peaches is P_W, the price in the domestic market will fall to P_W. Domestic producers will sell Q_1 units of peaches, domestic consumers will purchase C_1, and the difference between C_1 and Q_1 represents the volume of imported peaches. At P_W, consumers will enjoy a surplus of $F + G + J + K$; domestic producer surplus will fall to just H. Consumers still get their original surplus (F), plus part of producer surplus in autarky is transferred to the consumer (G), and in addition they receive $J + K$. Total surplus has increased by $J + K$. Producers are hurt by the imports, but the gain to consumers more than makes up for the producers' loss. Table 17.1 summarizes the gains and losses of consumer, producer, and total surplus.

Figure 17.5

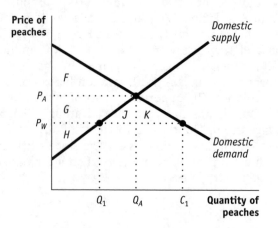

Table 17.1

	At $P = P_A$	At $P = P_W$	Net gain/loss
Consumer surplus	F	$F + G + J + K$	$+ (G + J + K)$
Producer surplus	$G + H$	H	$- G$
Total surplus	$F + G + H$	$F + G + H + J + K$	$+ (J + K)$

Figure 17.6 shows the domestic demand and domestic supply of coffee beans. If there were no trade in coffee beans, the price in the market would be P_A and Q_A would be exchanged. Consumer surplus would be $R + S + T$ and producer surplus would be $U + V$. If the market is opened to trade and the world price of coffee beans is P_W, the price in the domestic market will rise to P_W. Domestic producers will sell Q_1 units of coffee beans, domestic consumers will purchase C_1, and the difference between C_1 and Q_1 will be the volume of exported coffee beans. At P_W, consumers will only have a surplus of R; producer surplus will increase to $S + T + U + V + W$. Producers still get their original surplus $(U + V)$, plus part of consumer surplus in autarky is transferred to the producers $(S + T)$, and in addition they receive W. Total surplus has increased by W. Consumers are hurt by the exports, but the gain to producers more than makes up for the consumers' loss. Table 17.2 summarizes the gains and losses to consumer, producer, and total surplus.

Figure 17.6

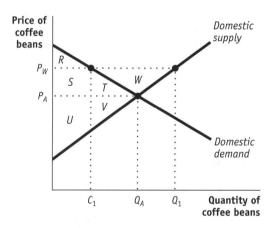

Table 17.2

	At $P = P_A$	At $P = P_W$	Net gain/loss
Consumer surplus	$R + S + T$	R	$- (S + T)$
Producer surplus	$U + V$	$S + T + U + V + W$	$+ (S + T + W)$
Total surplus	$R + S + T + U + V$	$R + S + T + U + V + W$	$+ W$

TIP #3: When the government levies a tariff on an import, there is a deadweight loss.

The tariff, like an excise tax, discourages some mutually beneficial trades, and this creates an excess burden for society. Figure 17.7 shows the market for peaches again. Starting from a position of free trade, we want to analyze the effects of an import tariff. A tariff will increase the price of the good received by the producers and paid by the consumers while decreasing imports. When the government levies the tariff, the price of peaches rises to P_T from P_W; before the tariff, imports equaled $C_1 - Q_1$, and after the tariff imports fell to $C_2 - Q_2$. Table 17.3 shows the gains and losses to consumer surplus, producer surplus, total surplus, and government revenue due to the tariff.

Figure 17.7

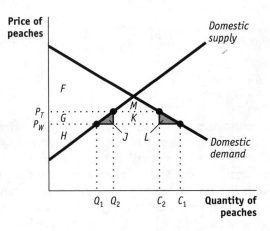

Table 17.3

	At $P = P_W$	At $P = P_T$	Net gain/loss
Consumer surplus	$F + G + J + K + L + M$	$F + M$	$-(G + J + K + L)$
Producer surplus	H	$G + H$	$+ G$
Government		K	$+ K$
Society	$F + G + H + J + K + L + M$	$F + G + H + K + M$	$-(J + L)$

Consumers are worse off because of the tariff; consumer surplus falls by $G + J + K + L$. Producers are better off; producer surplus rises by part of the loss in consumer surplus, G. The government raises K in revenue from the tariff. However, the loss of $J + L$ from consumer surplus is not gained by anyone. This is the deadweight loss associated with the tariff.

TIP #4: An import quota can achieve the same reduction in imports as a tariff but the loss to society may be much larger.

An import quota is a legal limit on the quantity of a good that can be imported. The government usually administers a quota by issuing licenses that give the holders a right to import a particular quantity of a good each year. By limiting the quantity that can be imported, the government creates a quota rent for the license holders. Figure 17.8 shows the effect of a quota in the market for peaches that limits total imports to $Q_2 - C_2$. The price in the domestic market will rise to P_T. Table 17.4 summarizes the gains and losses to consumer, producer, and total surplus due to the quota.

Figure 17.8

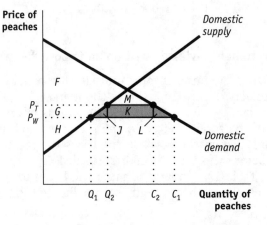

Table 17.4

	At $P = P_W$	At $P = P_T$	Net gain/loss
Consumer surplus	$F + G + J + K + L + M$	$F + M$	$- (G + J + K + L)$
Producer surplus	H	$G + H$	$+ G$
Society	$F + G + H + J + K + L + M$	$F + G + H + M$	$- (J + K + L)$

The loss to the domestic economy from the quota is larger than the loss from the import tariff. The government can attempt to minimize the loss by selling the import licenses for a total amount equal to K.

Multiple-Choice Questions

1. The economy of Westlandia can produce 100 units of cotton if it produces no tractors, or 25 tractors and no cotton; the economy of Eastlandia can produce 80 units of cotton if it produces no tractors, or 10 tractors and no cotton. There would be gains from trade if
   a. Westlandia specialized in the production of tractors and Eastlandia specialized in cotton.
   b. Westlandia specialized in the production of cotton and Eastlandia specialized in tractors.
   c. Westlandia specialized in the production of both tractors and cotton.
   d. Eastlandia specialized in the production of both tractors and cotton.

2. In the Ricardian model of international trade, the production possibility frontiers
   a. are convex to the origin.
   b. are straight lines.
   c. show increasing opportunity costs of production.
   d. show decreasing opportunity costs of production.

Use the following figures to answer the next two questions. The figures show the production possibility frontiers for Finland and Germany. Assume that in autarky, Finland produces 500 thousand phones and 175 thousand cars and Germany produces 600 thousand phones and 200 thousand cars.

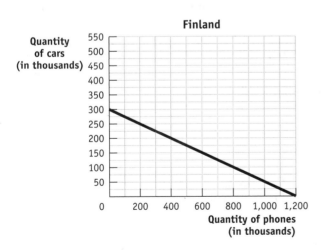

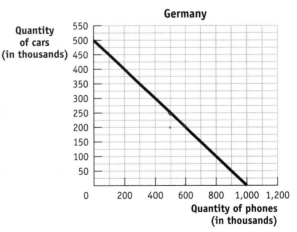

3. Refer to the figures on page 413. The opportunity cost of a phone in Finland is _____ of a car, while the opportunity cost of a phone in Germany is _____.
   a. $1/2$; 2
   b. 4; $1/2$
   c. $1/4$; $1/2$
   d. 4; $1/4$

4. Refer to the figures on page 413. When the two countries specialize in the production of the good in which they have a comparative advantage, total production of phones will increase by _____ thousand and total production of cars will increase by _____ thousand.
   a. 100; 100
   b. 100; 125
   c. 1,200; 500
   d. 1,200; 1,000

5. The primary source of Saudi Arabia's comparative advantage in oil production is
   a. climate.
   b. factor endowments.
   c. technology.
   d. increasing returns.

6. Trade in manufactured goods between advanced countries probably is based on
   a. differences in climate.
   b. differences in factor endowments.
   c. differences in technology.
   d. increasing returns.

7. According to the Heckscher-Ohlin model of international trade, nations that are abundant in _____ will have a comparative advantage in producing goods that are intensive in the use of _____ in the production process.
   a. capital; labor
   b. labor; capital
   c. capital; capital
   d. None of the above.

8. The Leontief paradox is that in 1951 the United States exported mostly _____ goods and imported _____ goods, in conflict with the Heckscher-Ohlin model. The solution to the paradox was to include _____ in the definition of capital.
   a. labor-intensive; capital-intensive; oil
   b. capital-intensive; labor-intensive; oil
   c. capital-intensive; labor-intensive; human capital
   d. labor-intensive; capital-intensive; human capital

9. As nations specialize in the good in which they have a comparative advantage and trade, we expect the wages of the abundant factor to _____ and of the scarce factor to _____.
   a. increase; increase
   b. decrease; decrease
   c. increase; decrease
   d. decrease; increase

Use the accompanying figure to answer the next two questions. The figure shows the domestic market for soybeans in Westlandia.

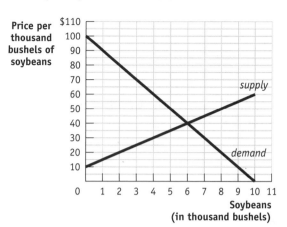

10. If the world price of soybeans is $50 per thousand bushels, domestic producers in Westlandia will produce _____ thousand bushels of soybeans, domestic consumers will buy _____ thousand bushels of them, and the difference between quantity demanded and quantity supplied represents Westlandia's

_____.

    a. 6; 3; exports
    b. 4; 3; imports
    c. 2; 8; imports
    d. 8; 5; exports

11. If the world price of soybeans is $20 per thousand bushels, domestic producers in Westlandia will produce _____ thousand bushels of soybeans, domestic consumers will buy _____ thousand bushels of them, and the difference between quantity demanded and quantity supplied represents Westlandia's

_____.

    a. 6; 3; exports
    b. 4; 3; imports
    c. 2; 8; imports
    d. 8; 5; exports

Use the following figure to answer the next three questions. The figure shows the domestic market for soybeans in Eastlandia.

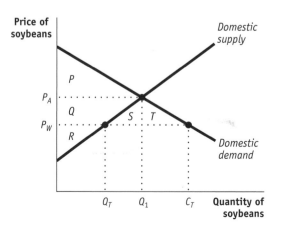

12. In autarky the price of soybeans in Eastlandia is P_A, and the world price is P_W. If Eastlandia opens to trade, consumer surplus will _____ to _____.

 a. decrease; P
 b. increase; $P + Q$
 c. decrease; $P + Q + S$
 d. increase; $P + Q + S + T$

13. In autarky the price of soybeans in Eastlandia is P_A, and the world price is P_W. If Eastlandia opens to trade, producer surplus will _____ to _____.

 a. decrease; R
 b. increase; $R + Q$
 c. decrease; $R + Q + S$
 d. increase; $R + Q + S + T$

14. When Eastlandia opens its soybean market to trade, the net gain to total surplus is represented by
 a. $S + T$.
 b. $Q + S + T$.
 c. $Q + R + S + T$.
 d. $P + Q + R + S + T$.

15. International trade may be a factor in the increased wage inequality in Canada because this nation is abundant in _____ and specializes in goods that are intensive in this factor. In this way, the wages of _____ workers, who have relatively high wages, rise, and the wages of _____ workers fall.
 a. land; farm; nonfarm
 b. human capital; highly educated; less-educated
 c. physical capital; manufacturing; service
 d. physical capital; unionized; nonunionized

Answer the next four questions using the accompanying figure. The figure shows the domestic market for soybeans in Eastlandia with a world price of P_W when the government has imposed a tariff that increased the price of soybeans to P_T.

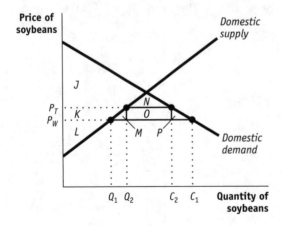

16. When Eastlandia imposes a tariff that raises the price of soybeans to P_T, imports of soybeans will fall from
   a. C_1 to C_2.
   b. Q_2 to Q_1.
   c. $C_1 - Q_1$ to $C_2 - Q_2$.
   d. $C_2 - Q_2$ to $C_1 - Q_1$.

17. When Eastlandia imposes a tariff that raises the price of soybeans to P_T, the net loss to total surplus is
   a. N.
   b. $M + P$.
   c. $M + N + P$.
   d. $M + N + O + P$.

18. Eastlandia could have reduced imports to the same level with an import quota as it did with a tariff. Eastlandia could have issued licenses to import _____ units of imports.
   a. C_2
   b. Q_2
   c. $C_1 - Q_1$
   d. $C_2 - Q_2$

19. Assuming that the quota rents from the tariff go to foreigners, the net loss to total surplus of the quota will be
   a. N.
   b. $M + P$.
   c. $M + O + P$.
   d. $M + N + O + P$.

20. Which of the following arguments to protect an industry from trade do economists find lacking validity?
   a. During wartime, a particular industry is essential for economic stability.
   b. If we limit imports, we can increase the number of jobs in our country.
   c. Industries need some time to establish themselves before competing on world markets.
   d. Both a and b lack validity.

21. Which of the following international organizations rules on disputes concerning global trade agreements?
   a. North American Free Trade Agreement
   b. The European Union
   c. The World Trade Organization
   d. none of the above

22. Importing Bangladeshi cotton shirts will cause all of the following benefits **except**
   a. Canadian consumers will benefit due to lower prices.
   b. the opportunity cost of shirts will be relatively less in Canada.
   c. the average productivity of Canadian workers will increase.
   d. the standard of living in Canada will increase.

Use the accompanying table to answer questions 23–25.

Assume constant cost.

One hour of labour can produce the following goods in Canada and Mexico.

Country	Wine	Beer
Canada	10 bottles	10 bottles
Mexico	2 bottles	4 bottles

23. Which of the following statements is true?
    a. The opportunity cost of 1 bottle of wine in Canada is 10 bottles of beer.
    b. The opportunity cost of 1 bottle of wine in Mexico is 4 bottles of beer.
    c. The opportunity cost of 1 bottle of beer in Mexico is 0.5 bottles of wine.
    d. The opportunity of 1 bottle of beer in Canada is –1 bottle of wine.

24. Canada has comparative advantage in
    a. both wine and beer.
    b. wine.
    c. beer.
    d. neither good.

25. Mexico has comparative advantage in
    a. both wine and beer.
    b. wine.
    c. beer.
    d. neither good.

26. According to the Heckscher-Ohlin model, Canada
    a. imports more labour-intensive goods.
    b. imports more capital-intensive goods.
    c. exports more labour-intensive goods.
    d. has comparative advantages in all goods that Canada produces.

27. If Ontario imposes a tariff on Chilean wine, the price of Chilean wine in Ontario
    will _____ and the production of wine in the Niagra Region will

    _____.
    a. increase; increase
    b. increase; decrease
    c. decrease; decrease
    d. decrease; increase

28. If Canada is a price-taker in the world-market and if the world price increases,
    a. the total surplus in Canada will increase.
    b. the total surplus in Canada will decrease.
    c. the total surplus in Canada may increase or decrease.
    d. the quantity of output in Canada will not change.

29. One of the arguments for trade protection is that
    a. we need to protect the industries producing goods that may be vulnerable to disruption in time of international conflict.
    b. trade protection increases the economic welfare of a nation.
    c. trade protection increases competition in the domestic market.
    d. trade protection benefits consumers.

30. NAFTA has failed in all the following **except**
    a. it reduced economic welfare and reduced productivity.
    b. it led to some employment losses in Canada.
    c. it failed to exclude Canada's water resources.
    d. it failed to protect publicly-provided Medicare in Canada.

Problems and Exercises

Read each question carefully and then write your answers in the space provided or on a separate sheet of paper.

1. Assume that Canada and China face the production possibility frontiers shown in the following tables for lumber and toys.

Canada

Toys (in millions)	Lumber (in millions of board feet)
0	300
1	250
2	200
3	150
4	100
5	50
6	0

China

Toys (in millions)	Lumber (in millions of board feet)
0	200
2	160
4	120
6	80
8	40
9	20
10	0

a. What is the opportunity cost of producing toys in Canada? What is the opportunity cost of producing toys in China? Which nation has a comparative advantage in producing toys? Which nation has a comparative advantage in producing lumber?

b. Plot the production possibility frontiers for Canada and China in the following figures. What are the slopes of the production possibility frontiers? Which nation has the flatter slope? Does that nation have a comparative advantage in toys (the good measured on the horizontal axis)? How does this answer compare with your answer to part a above?

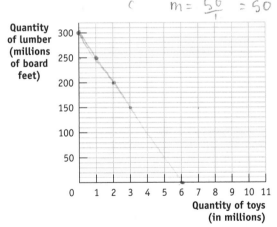

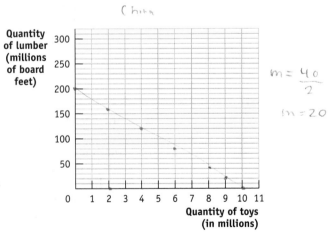

c. Suppose in autarky Canada produces 3 million toys and 150 million board feet of lumber, while China produces 3 million toys and 140 million board feet of lumber. Show how, if each nation specializes in the good of its comparative advantage, total production of toys and lumber for the two nations together can increase.

d. Is it possible with trade for Canada to consume 5 million toys and 120 million board feet of lumber and China to consume 5 million toys and 180 million board feet of lumber? How do we know that both Canada and China gain from trade?

2. The accompanying table shows Canada's domestic demand and Canada's domestic supply schedules for peanuts. Plot the domestic demand and supply curves in the following figure.

Price per ton of peanuts	Quantity of peanuts demanded (in million tons)	Quantity of peanuts supplied (in million tons)
$0	4.5	0.0
100	4.0	1.0
200	3.5	2.0
300	3.0	3.0
400	2.5	4.0
500	2.0	5.0
600	1.5	6.0
700	1.0	7.0
800	0.5	8.0
900	0.0	9.0

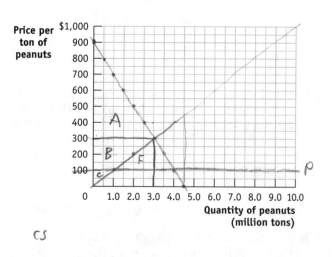

a. What would be the equilibrium price and quantity of peanuts in autarky?

$E^P = 300/ton$

$E_Q = 3.0$ tons (million)

b. If the world price of peanuts is $100 per ton and Canada opens the peanut market to trade, will Canada import or export peanuts? How many peanuts will Canadian producers sell? How many peanuts will Canadian consumers buy? What will be the volume of trade in peanuts? Label the preceding figure and complete the accompanying table to show the gains and losses to consumer, producer, and total surplus.

	In autarky	With trade	Net gain/loss
Consumer surplus	A	A+B+F	+(B+F)
Producer surplus	B+C	C	−B
Total surplus	A+B+C	A+B+C+F	+F

$CS = A$

$PS = B+C$

$MS = A+B+C$

c. If the world price of peanuts is $600 per ton, will Canada import or export peanuts? How many peanuts will Canadian producers sell? How many peanuts will Canadian consumers buy? What will be the volume of trade in peanuts? Redraw domestic demand and supply curves in the following figure and label your figure to complete the following table to show the gains and losses to consumer, producer, and total surplus.

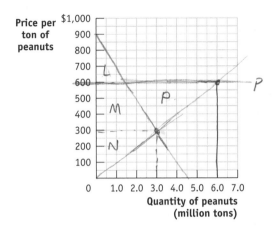

PS below price above supply curve.

CS below demand above price.

	In autarky	With trade	Net gain/loss
Consumer surplus	L + M	L	−M
Producer surplus	N	P + M + N	+(m + P)
Total surplus	L + M + N	P + M + N + L	+P

change between 2

3. Continuing the peanut example in problem 2, suppose the world price of peanuts is $100 per ton. Fearful that many domestic peanut farmers will go out of business, the government imposes a tariff of an additional $100 per ton on peanuts. Once again draw the domestic demand and supply curves, and show the new price of peanuts in Canada's market.

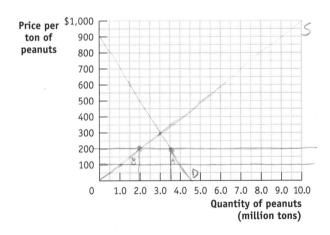

a. How much will domestic producers sell and domestic consumers buy?

b. What will be the volume of trade?

c. How much revenue from the tariff will the government receive?

d. Label your graph to show the deadweight loss from the tariff.

e. Could the government reduce imports to the same level using an import quota? What volume of imports should the government allow? How will consumer, producer, and total surplus with an import quota compare to that of a tariff?

4. The production possibility curves with two goods, *X and Y,* for Canada and Mexico are shown in the accompanying figure.

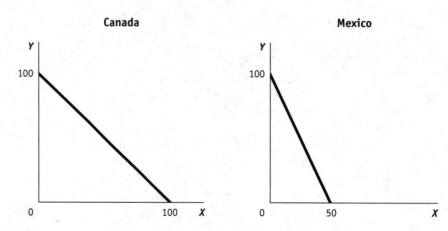

a. What is the opportunity cost of 100 units of good X in Canada? The opportunity cost of 1 unit of X?

b. What is the opportunity cost of 100 units of good Y in Canada? The opportunity cost of 1 unit of Y?

c. What is the opportunity cost of 50 units of good X in Mexico? The opportunity cost 1 unit of X?

d. What is the opportunity cost of 100 units of good Y in Mexico? The opportunity cost 1 unit of Y?

e. Which country has comparative advantage in which product? Why?

*5. Consider a price-taking economy with the following demand-supply functions.

$Q^D = 100 - P.$

$Q^S = P.$

a. What is the equilibrium price in autarky?

b. If the world-price is $20, what is the amount of import into this economy? What is consumer surplus in this economy?

c. Suppose the import quota is 30 units. What will be the equilibrium price in this economy? What will be domestic supply?

6. Evaluate the need for trade protection for the textile industry in Canada based on three arguments presented in this chapter.

7. Consider the following demand-supply curves of a small price-taking economy in the world trade market.

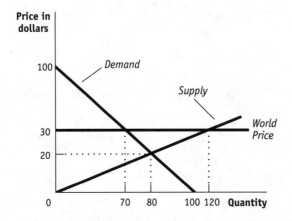

a. What is the equilibrium price in autarky? Find the value of consumer surplus, producer surplus, and total surplus.

b. If the world price is $30, what will be total export? Find the value of consumer surplus, producer surplus, and total surplus in this situation.

Answers to How Well Do You Understand the Chapter

1. trade, gains, comparative advantage, lower, differs

2. constant, straight line, higher

3. factor endowments, climate, factor endowments, intensive, abundant, ratio, capital, technology, lowered

4. increasing returns, economies of scale

5. capital-intensive, physical, labour-intensive

6. domestic, domestic, world, price-takers

7. autarky, fall, less, profit, more, consumer surplus, total surplus, larger

8. rise, export, more, greater, less, smaller, greater

9. intensive, abundant, rise, scarce, decrease, income-gap, highly educated

10. free trade, trade protection, import quotas

11. tariff, discourage, more, increase, decrease, less, deadweight

12. quantity, licenses, tariff, quota rent

13. infant industry, international, new jobs, temporary

14. import-competing, increase, decrease, more

15. agreements, less, trade agreements, trade

Answers to Multiple-Choice Questions

1. The opportunity cost of a tractor in Westlandia is 100 units of cotton for 25 tractors, or 4 units of cotton for 1 tractor. The opportunity cost of a tractor in Eastlandia is 80 units of cotton for 10 tractors, or 8 units of cotton for 1 tractor. It is cheaper to produce tractors in Westlandia. Westlandia has a comparative advantage in tractors, and Eastlandia has a comparative advantage in cotton. There will be gains from trade if Westlandia specialized in the production of tractors and Eastlandia specialized in cotton. **Answer: A.**

2. The Ricardian model of international trade assumes that the production possibility frontiers are straight lines. When this is true, the opportunity costs of production are constant. **Answer: B.**

3. Finland can produce 300 thousand cars and no phones, or 1,200 thousand phones and no cars; the opportunity cost of 300 thousand cars is 1,200 thousand phones, or $\frac{1}{4}$ of a car for 1 phone. Germany can produce 500 thousand cars and no phones, or 1,000 thousand phones and no cars; the opportunity cost of 500 thousand cars is 1,000 thousand phones, or $\frac{1}{2}$ of a car for 1 phone. **Answer: C.**

4. In autarky, Finland and Germany produced 1,100 thousand phones and 375 thousand cars combined. With specialization in production, they will produce 1,200 thousand phones and 500 thousand cars. Phone production increases by 100 thousand and car production increases by 125 thousand. **Answer: B.**

5. The primary source of Saudi Arabia's comparative advantage in oil production is its factor endowment. Saudi Arabia has one-fourth of the world's known oil reserves. **Answer: B.**

6. Trade in developed countries can be explained by increasing returns. In the auto industry, both the United States and Canada produce automobiles and their components, but each tends to specialize in one model or component. **Answer: D.**

7. The Heckscher-Ohlin model states that a country has a comparative advantage in a good whose production is intensive in the factors that are abundantly available in that country. If a nation is abundant in capital, it will have a comparative advantage in producing capital-intensive goods. **Answer: C.**

8. The Leontief paradox is that the United States, a capital-abundant nation, appeared to export labor-intensive goods in 1951 while importing capital-intensive goods. Leontief, however, only considered physical capital in his definition of capital. When you include human capital with physical capital, the paradox no longer exists. **Answer: D.**

9. As nations specialize in the good in which they have a comparative advantage, they will demand more of the abundant factor, increasing its price, and less of the scarce factor, decreasing its price. **Answer: C.**

10. The following figure shows that at the world price of soybeans of $50 per thousand bushels, domestic producers will produce 8 thousand bushels of soybeans, domestic consumers will buy 5 thousand bushels, and 3 thousand bushels will be exported. **Answer: D.**

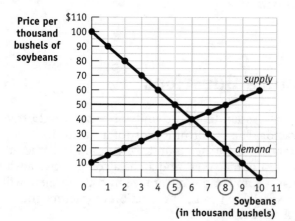

11. The accompanying figure shows that if soybeans are at a world price of $20 per thousand bushels, domestic producers will produce 2 thousand bushels of soybeans, domestic consumers will buy 8 thousand bushels, and 6 thousand bushels will be imported. **Answer: C.**

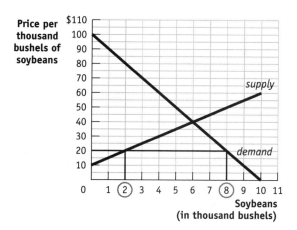

12. The following table summarizes the gains and losses to consumer, producer, and total surplus when the nation begins to trade. Consumer surplus increases to $P + Q + S + T$. **Answer: D.**

	In autarky	With trade	Net gain/loss
Consumer surplus	P	$P + Q + S + T$	$+ (Q + S + T)$
Producer surplus	$Q + R$	R	$- Q$
Total surplus	$P + Q + R$	$P + Q + R + S + T$	$+ (S + T)$

13. Again, the preceding table summarizes the gains and losses to consumer, producer, and total surplus when the nation begins to trade. Producer surplus decreases to R. **Answer: A.**

14. The preceding table shows the net gain to total surplus is $S + T$. **Answer: A.**

15. Increased wage inequality may be the result of Canada having a lot of human capital and specializing in goods that are human-capital-intensive. Wages of highly educated workers (workers with large investments in human capital) rise and wages of less-educated workers fall. **Answer: B.**

16. When Eastlandia imposes a tariff and the price of soybeans rises to P_T, imports will fall from $C_1 - Q_1$ to $C_2 - Q_2$. **Answer: C.**

17. The following table summarizes the gains and losses to consumer surplus, producer surplus, government revenue, and total surplus from the tariff. The net loss to total surplus is $M + P$. **Answer: B.**

	At $P = P_W$	At $P = P_T$	Net gain/loss
Consumer surplus	$J + K + M + N + O + P$	$J + N$	$- (K + M + O + P)$
Producer surplus	L	$K + L$	$+ K$
Government		O	$+ O$
Society	$J + K + L + M + N + O + P$	$J + K + L + N + O$	$- (M + P)$

18. If Eastlandia issued licenses to import $C_2 - Q_2$ units of imports, it would have reduced imports to the same level as did the tariff. **Answer: D.**

19. The accompanying table summarizes the gains and losses to consumer surplus, producer surplus, government revenue, and total surplus from the import quota. **Answer: C.**

	At $P = P_W$	At $P = P_T$	Net gain/loss
Consumer surplus	$J + K + M + N + O + P$	$J + N$	$-(K + M + O + P)$
Producer surplus	L	$K + L$	$+ K$
Government			
Society	$J + K + L + M + N + O + P$	$J + K + L + N + O$	$-(M + O + P)$

20. Economists believe that if job creation is the goal of trade protection, it will not achieve that goal. When a nation imposes a barrier to imports (a tariff or import quota), its trading partners will respond by doing the same. Although we may gain jobs in import-competing industries, we will lose jobs in the export industries. **Answer: B.**

21. The World Trade Organization rules on disputes between countries concerning global trade agreements. **Answer: C.**

22. The opportunity cost of producing shirts in Canada is relatively high and, as a result, Canada imports Bangladeshi shirts, leading to more consumers' benefits, economic welfare, and higher productivity. **Answer: B.**

23. Costs cannot be negative. The opportunity cost of 1 bottle of beer in Mexico is 0.5 bottles of wine. **Answer: C.**

24. The opportunity cost of 1 bottle of wine is 1 beer in Canada, and the opportunity cost of 1 bottle of wine is 2 bottles of beer in Mexico. Therefore, Canada has a comparative advantage in wine. **Answer: B.**

25. The opportunity cost of 1 bottle of beer is 1 bottle of wine in Canada, and the opportunity cost of 1 bottle of beer is 0.5 bottle of wine in Mexico. Therefore, Mexico has a comparative advantage in beer. **Answer: C.**

26. Canada imports labour-intensive goods. **Answer: A.**

27. A tariff will increase the wine price in Ontario, and there will more wine production in Ontario. **Answer: A.**

28. Even though a higher price will reduce consumer surplus, the gain in producer surplus will be greater than the loss of consumer surplus and as a result, the total surplus in Canada will increase. **Answer: A.**

29. Trade protection reduces competition, consumer surplus, and economic welfare. Protecting national security is one of the arguments for trade protection. **Answer: A.**

30. NAFTA has led to some employment losses, and it has failed to protect water resources and Medicare. However, NAFTA has led to more net economic welfare and more productivity. **Answer: A.**

Answers to Problems and Exercises

1. a. Canada can produce either 6 million toys and no lumber, or 300 million board feet of lumber and no toys. The opportunity cost of producing toys in Canada is 300 million board feet of lumber for 6 million toys, or 50 board feet of lumber for 1 toy. China can produce either 10 million toys and no lumber, or 200 million board feet of lumber and no toys. The opportunity cost of producing toys in China is 200 million board feet of lumber for 10 million toys, or 20 board feet of lumber for 1 toy. It is cheaper to produce toys in China; China has a comparative advantage in producing toys. Canada has a comparative advantage in producing lumber.

   b. The following figures show the production possibility frontiers for Canada and China.

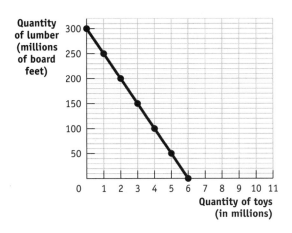
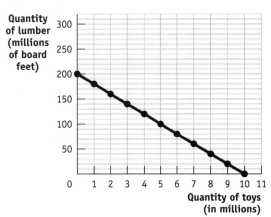

The slope of Canada's production possibility frontier is –50 and the slope of China's production possibility frontier is –20. The slopes are the opportunity costs of producing a toy in each country. China has the flatter slope and has a comparative advantage in toys, which is the good measured on the horizontal axis. Looking at the slopes gives us the same answers about opportunity costs as we found in part a.

   c. In autarky, Canada and China jointly produce 6 million toys and 290 million board feet of lumber. If Canada specializes completely in the production of lumber, it can produce 300 million board feet of lumber, while China can produce 10 million toys if it just produces toys. If Canada and China specialize in the good of each's comparative advantage, total production of toys can increase by 4 million and production of lumber will increase by 10 million board feet.

   d. If Canada produces 300 million board feet of lumber and trades 180 million to China for 5 million toys (exchanging 36 board feet of lumber for 1 toy), Canada will consume 5 million toys and 120 million board feet of lumber, while China will consume 5 million toys and 180 million board feet of lumber. Since each nation is able to consume outside its production possibility frontier, they both gain from trade.

2. The following figure shows Canada's domestic demand and supply curves for peanuts.

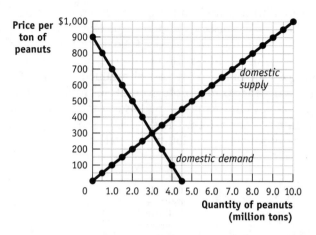

a. In autarky, the equilibrium price is $300 per ton and the equilibrium quantity is 3 million tons of peanuts.

b. If the world price is $100 per ton, Canada will import peanuts (domestic consumers will be attracted by the lower world price and buy peanuts on the world, rather than the domestic, market). Domestic producers will only sell 1 million tons of peanuts, consumers will buy 4 million tons, and 3 million tons will be imported. The following figure and table show the gains and losses to consumer, producer, and total surplus. (Your areas may be labeled differently.)

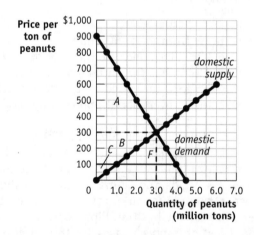

	In autarky	With trade	Net gain/loss
Consumer surplus	A	A + B + F	+ (B + F)
Producer surplus	B + C	C	− B
Total surplus	A + B + C	A + B + C + F	+ F

c. If the world price is $600 per ton, Canada will export peanuts (domestic producers will be attracted by the higher world price and sell peanuts on the world, rather than the domestic, market). Domestic producers will sell 6 million tons of peanuts, consumers will buy 1.5 million tons, and 4.5 million tons will be exported. The following figure and table show the gains and losses to consumer, producer, and total surplus. (Your areas may be labeled differently.)

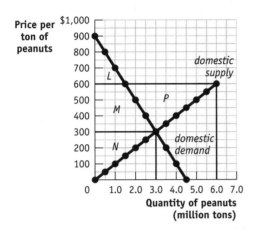

	In autarky	**With trade**	**Net gain/loss**
Consumer surplus	$L + M$	L	$-M$
Producer surplus	N	$M + N + P$	$+(M + P)$
Total surplus	$L + M + N$	$L + M + N + P$	$+P$

3. The accompanying figure shows the domestic market for peanuts with a world price of $100 and a tariff price of $100.

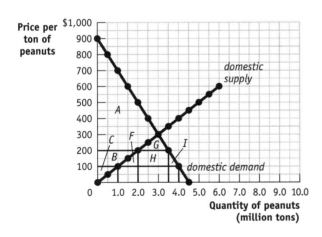

a. With the tariff, domestic producers will sell 2 million tons of peanuts and domestic consumers will buy 3.5 million tons of peanuts.

b. Imports will be 1.5 million tons of peanuts.

c. The government will receive $100 per ton for 1.5 million tons, or $150 million.

d. The deadweight loss from the tariff is $F + I$.

e. The government could reduce imports of peanuts to 1.5 million tons by only granting licenses to import 1.5 million. Consumer and producer surplus will be the same under a tariff or an import quota. However, the deadweight loss will be larger because there is no revenue to the government. The deadweight loss will be $F + H + I$.

4. a. The opportunity cost of 100 units of X is 100 units of Y. The opportunity cost of 1 unit of X is 1 unit of Y.

   b. The opportunity cost of 100 units of Y is 100 units of X. The opportunity cost of 1 unit of Y is 1 unit of X.

   c. The opportunity cost of 50 units of X is 100 units of Y. The opportunity cost of 1 unit of X is 2 units of Y.

   d. The opportunity cost of 100 units of Y is 50 units of X. The opportunity cost of 1 unit of Y is 0.5 units of X.

   e. Canada has comparative advantage in X, because the opportunity cost of 1 unit of X is lower. Mexico has comparative advantage in Y, because the opportunity cost of 1 unit of Y is lower.

5. a. Set $Q^D = Q^S$ and solve price in autarky as $50.

   b. At the world price of $20, $Q^D = 80$ and $Q^S = 20$. Therefore, the amount of import is $(80 - 20) = 60$.

   c. With import quota, the available supply in this economy is domestic supply plus 30 units. Therefore, set $100 - P = 30 + P$ and solve P as $35. At $35, the domestic supply is 35 units.

6. The three arguments for trade protection are: national defense, job creation, and the infant-industry argument. The national defense argument is not a valid reason to protect the textile industry in Canada. If we have trade protection for the textile industry, as in the job creation argument, we are supporting inefficient uses of labour in Canada, because the same goods can be produced elsewhere with cheaper costs. Efficient allocation of resources will result in Canada if we don't have trade protection. The infant-industry argument is inapplicable by virtue of the fact that the textile industry is not a new industry.

7. a. The equilibrium price in autarky is $20. The consumer surplus = $3,200 = (80)(80)/2.

   The producer surplus = $800. Total surplus = $4,000.

   b. At the world price of $30, $Q^S = 120$, $Q^D = 70$ and export = $120 - 70 = 50$. Consumer surplus = $2,450, producer surplus = $1,800, and total surplus = $4,250.

chapter 18

Uncertainty, Risk, and Private Information

Risks and information are important in economic decisions. We start with the notion of expected return. We describe risk-averse behaviours using the principle of diminishing marginal utility of income. We explore why people are willing to pay others to assume some risks and how markets for insurance can minimize or eliminate risks. We also discuss asymmetric information, adverse selection, and moral hazard.

How Well Do You Understand the Chapter?

Fill in the blanks using the terms below to complete the following statements. Terms may be used more than once. If you find yourself having difficulties, please refer back to the appropriate section in the text.

asymmetric	financial risk	mutual	selection
aversion	franchises	mutually beneficial	shares
capital	greater	payoff	signal
certainty	high	personal stake	signaling
cost	higher	pooling	small
decrease(s)	income	predictability	state
deductible	increases(s)	premium	supply
demand	independent	private information	themselves
differs	insurance	probability	uncertainty
diminishing	large	random	utility
diversification	less	right	warranties
efficient allocation	low	risk aversion	warranty
eliminate	moral hazard	risk-tolerant	weather
expected	more	screen	weighted
fair	multiplied	screening	

1. Most people don't like risk because risk involves the _____ of future outcomes, so people are willing to pay to reduce it. In this chapter, we focus on the uncertainty of monetary outcomes, also known as _____. A(n) _____ variable is a variable with an uncertain future. We can calculate the _____ value of a random variable by measuring the _____ average of all possible values for the variable, where the weights on each possible value correspond to the _____ of that value occurring. The different outcomes for the random variable depend upon the

future _____ of the world, which we don't know with _____ but to which we can assign probabilities.

2. Risk-averse people don't like risk and are willing to pay to avoid it. We assume that individuals attempt to maximize their _____ total utility (the expected value of an individual's total utility, given uncertainty about the future) and that there is a(n) _____ marginal utility of income. A(n) _____ insurance policy is an insurance policy in which the premium equals the expected value of the claims. A fair insurance policy will _____ expected utility as long as an individual faces _____ marginal utility of income. However, even if the _____ is higher than the expected value of the claim, an individual may still want to buy the policy if the expected utility with the policy is _____ than the expected utility without the policy.

3. People differ in terms of their degree of _____. We assume that each individual has a diminishing marginal utility of _____, but some may value an increase in income less than others do. The reason is that a dollar gained when income is low adds _____ to utility than a dollar gained when income is high. Risk aversion _____ among individuals because of differences in preferences (people differ in how their marginal _____ is affected by income), and differences in wealth or income (people with _____ incomes tend to be more risk-averse than those with high incomes). The more risk-averse an individual is, the _____ the premium he or she will be willing to pay to avoid risk.

4. Expensive consumer goods, such as cars and television, frequently come with a(n) _____, guarantee that they will be repaired or replaced if something goes wrong with them during a specified time period. The warranty serves as a _____ that the good is of high quality, but it is also a form of consumer insurance. If the warranty increases expected utility, a consumer may be willing to buy an expensive good with a warranty at a(n) _____ price than a good without a warranty, even if the additional _____ is greater than the expected future claims paid by the manufacturer.

5. Insurance is based on two principles: (1) trade in risk can produce _____ gains from trade, and (2) some risk can be made to disappear through _____. The market for insurance transfers risk from people who most want to get rid of it (the most risk-averse) to people who are more _____. The _____ of insurance is the amount of insurance provided at all possible premiums during a specified time period, holding everything else constant. As the premium increases, the quantity of insurance supplied also _____. The _____ for insurance is the amount of insurance demanded at all possible premiums during a specified time

period, holding everything else constant. As the premium _____, quantity demanded of insurance decreases.

6. The market for insurance produces a(n) _____ of risk. Those who are most willing to bear risk are those who end up bearing it. _____ at risk refers to the funds that an insurer puts at risk when agreeing to provide insurance. The premium received by insurers is usually _____ than the expected loss.

7. _____ reduces and possibly eliminates risk. In its simplest form, diversification is not putting all your eggs in one basket. It refers to investing in several different things, where the possible losses are _____ events. One can _____ risk by combining events that are independent. Two events are _____ if each of them is neither more nor less likely to happen if the other one happens. The probability that two independent events will both happen equals the probability of one even occurring _____ by the probability that the other will occur.

8. Today many investors diversify by holding _____ in different companies, which makes the chance of losing everything very _____.

_____ is a strong form of diversification in which an individual takes a _____ share in many independent events. It produces a(n) _____ with very little uncertainty. By taking advantage of the _____ that comes from looking at large numbers of independent events, _____ companies are pooling their risks. The opportunity to engage in pooling shifts the _____ curve of insurance to the _____; insurance companies will take on _____ risk and charge a(n) _____ premium than they do without pooling.

9. If events are positively correlated (one event is more likely to occur if some other event occurs), risk cannot be eliminated. Losses due to severe _____ that may affect a large region of the country, political events that may affect a group of nations, or business cycles (fluctuations in the output of the economy as a whole) are positively correlated financial risks that investors cannot avoid through _____.

10. Markets do two things well; they allow investors to _____ any risk that can be diversified away, and they allocate the remaining risk to those who are most willing to bear it. But markets don't do well with dealing in risk when there is _____, situations where some people know things that other people don't know. Private information is also known as _____ _____ information. There are two distinct types of private information problems: adverse selection and _____. Private information can distort economic decisions and sometimes prevent _____ transactions from occurring. An important source of private information is that people generally know more about _____ than other people do.

11. Adverse _____ occurs when an individual knows more about the way things are than other people do. Private information leads buyers to expect hidden problems in items offered for sale, leading to low prices, and to the best items being kept off the market. It also affects insurance companies in that people know _____ about their behaviour and their risk of an adverse outcome than do the insurance companies.

12. Adverse selection can be reduced through _____ which involves using observable information to make inferences about an individual's private information. Adverse selection can also be diminished by _____ private information through actions that credibly reveal what individuals know. Used car dealers may offer _____ on cars or advertise how long they've been in business as signs of their long-term reputation.

13. _____ occurs when an individual knows more about his or her own actions than do other people. To avoid the problem of moral hazard, it is important that individuals have a(n) _____ in what happens. This is why insurance companies will not insure for 100% of losses, why salespeople often work on commission, and why fast-food chains are often _____.
Insurance companies use a(n) _____, a sum the individual must pay before being compensated following a loss, to reduce moral hazard. By offering a menu of policies with different premiums and deductibles, insurance companies can _____ their customers. For example, a low-risk customer will often buy insurance with a lower _____ but a higher _____ than a high-risk customer.

Learning Tips

TIP #1: Expected value (*EV*) of a random variable is a weighted average of all possible values (*S$_i$*), where the weights on each possible value equal the probability (*P$_i$*) of that value occurring:

$$EV = (P_i \times S_i) + (P_2 \times S_2) + \dots + (P_N \times S_N).$$

We use expected value whenever there is uncertainty about future outcomes. It's easiest to see how to use the formula in an example. A family is trying to estimate their daughter's tuition but they don't know which of three colleges she will attend. There are three possibilities for tuition, depending on the college she attends: $10,000, $14,000, and $18,000. They assess there is a 20% probability that the daughter will attend the college with $10,000 tuition, a 40% probability that she will attend the $14,000 college, and a 40% probability that she will attend the $18,000 college. The expected value of tuition is

$$EV = (0.20 \times \$10,000) + (0.40 \times \$14,000) + (0.40 \times \$18,000) = \$14,800$$

Although the expected value of tuition is $14,800, the family never expects actual tuition to equal $14,800; tuition will be $10,000, $14,000, or $18,000.

TIP #2: Individuals desire to reduce risk because of diminishing marginal utility of income.

Let's assume in the example above that the family knows that it will pay the daughter's tuition from an income of $100,000. Therefore, it expects that there is a 20% chance that income after tuition will be $90,000, a 40% chance that it will be $86,000, and a 40% chance that it will be $82,000. Table 18.1 and Figure 18.1 show the utility schedule and curve for income after tuition for this family.

Table 18.1

Income after Tuition	Utility
$80,000	1,800
82,000	2,800
84,000	3,500
85,200	3,800
86,000	3,950
88,000	4,200
90,000	4,350
92,000	4,450
94,000	4,500

Figure 18.1

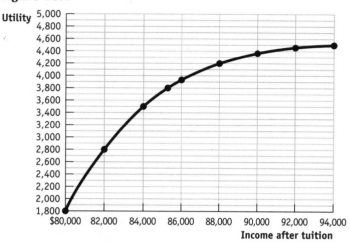

The expected utility is the weighted average for the three possibilities of utility from income after tuition, where the weights are the probabilities that the particular tuitions will occur:

$$EV = (0.20 \times 4,350) + (0.40 \times 3,950) + (0.40 \times 2,800) = 3,570.$$

The utility associated with income after expected tuition ($85,200 = $100,000 − $14,800) is 3,800. The family would be willing to pay $14,800 for an insurance policy that would pay the daughter's tuition. (This would be a fair-value insurance policy because the cost of insurance is the expected value of the payoff.) With insurance, the utility of income after tuition of $85,200 is 3,800 utils, while the expected utility without insurance is only 3,570. Even though there is a 60% probability that without insurance the family's income after tuition will be higher than $85,200, the family prefers to eliminate the uncertainty about its income after tuition. Their preference is due to the diminishing marginal utility associated with income after tuition. If only we could find such tuition insurance!

TIP #3: It is possible to reduce or completely eliminate risk through diversification when events are not positively correlated.

As long as events are not positively correlated (one event is more likely to happen if some other event happens), you can reduce risk, and it may be possible to eliminate it completely.

Two enterprising college students, Kalila and Deshawn, form their own companies to make money during the summer at a vacation site. Kalila forms a company to sell sunglasses, thinking that she can make money selling them to tourists who forget them, and Deshawn forms one to sell rain ponchos, thinking the optimistic travelers will find themselves all wet on rainy days. A third student, Ramona, doesn't plan to work this summer but will instead invest a $2,000 gift from her grandmother in either or both of her friends' companies. All three students expect that there is a 50% probability of a sunny summer and a 50% probability of a rainy summer.

Investing in one of the two companies leaves Ramona with a great deal of uncertainty. If Ramona invests only in Kalila's company and it's a sunny summer, she will earn $5,000, but if it's a rainy summer she will lose $2,000. If Ramona invests only in Deshawn's company and it's a rainy summer, she will earn $5,000, but if it's a sunny summer she will lose $2,000.

However, if Ramona invests half her money in Kalila's company and half in Deshawn's, she can completely eliminate risk. Her expected earnings during a sunny summer are 50% of the $5,000 she will earn from Kalila's company ($2,500), less 50% of the $2,000 loss from Deshawn's company ($1,000), or $1,500. Her expected earnings during a rainy summer are 50% of the $5,000 she will earn from Deshawn's company ($2,500), less 50% of the $2,000 loss from Kalila's company ($1,000), or $1,500. By investing equally in Kalila's and Deshawn's companies, Ramona eliminates all risk and will earn $3,000 whether it is a rainy or sunny summer. The reason Ramona can completely eliminate risk is that a sunny summer and a rainy summer cannot be positively correlated—one cannot happen if the other happens.

TIP #4: If private information is not available to some market participants, economic decisions may be distorted and some mutually beneficial transactions may not take place.

Like markets for goods, risk markets allocate risk efficiently when all participants have full information. When all participants don't have access to all information, adverse selection and moral hazard lead to some mutually beneficial transactions not taking place.

Adverse selection describes the problem when buyers expect that sellers do not disclose all relevant information, and so buyers assume some hidden problems exist; consequently, buyers are willing to pay a lower price than if they were sure they had all information. Given that buyers expect some undisclosed problems, sellers of goods without such problems will be reluctant to offer goods for sale at the lower price and some mutually beneficial transactions do not take place. Adverse selection can be minimized with screening (buyers using available information to infer something about sellers' private information) and signaling (sellers revealing some private information to buyers).

Moral hazard occurs when an individual knows more about his or her likely behavior, especially when insurance is involved. If you had insured your car completely against theft (the company would pay you 100% replacement if your car is stolen), what incentive would you have to park in safe places and lock your car? The insurance company doesn't know your likely behavior, but it tries to provide an incentive for you to take all reasonable precautions by making sure that you too would have to pay if your car is stolen. This is usually done through a deductible. Again, it may be that even with deductibles some mutually beneficial transactions will not take place.

Multiple-Choice Questions

1. Natasha knows that there is a 40% probability that next year her income will be $40,000 and a 60% probability that her income will be $50,000. Her expected income is
   a. $42,000.
   b. $45,000.
   c. $46,000.
   d. $48,000.

2. The total utility of income curve for a risk-averse person
   a. is upward sloping.
   b. gets flatter as income increases.
   c. shows increasing marginal utility.
   d. both a and b.

Use the following table to answer the following three questions. The table shows the utility schedule for the Johnson family. The Johnsons have a car but live in an area with a lot of car thefts. The probability of a car like the Johnsons' car being stolen is 25%. The Johnsons expect to have $56,000 to spend on other goods and services next year if they don't have their car stolen, and $40,000 if their car is stolen and they have to replace it (the cost of the replacement is $16,000).

Income available after car expenses (in thousands)	Utility (utils)
$40	950
42	1,100
44	1,210
46	1,313
48	1,380
50	1,430
52	1,480
54	1,520
56	1,550
58	1,565
60	1,575

3. Without insurance, the Johnsons' expected income available for spending on goods and services is _____ and their expected utility is _____.
   a. $40,000; 950 utils
   b. $50,000; 1,250 utils
   c. $52,000; 1,400 utils
   d. $56,000; 1,550 utils

4. If the Johnsons can buy insurance for theft on their car for a premium of _____, they will maximize their expected utility by buying the insurance.
   a. $6,000
   b. $8,000
   c. $10,000
   d. none of the above

5. The premium on a fair insurance policy for the Johnsons' car would be
   a. $4,000.
   b. $6,000.
   c. $8,000.
   d. $10,000.

6. A risk-averse person will choose to purchase insurance to reduce risk
   a. at any premium.
   b. when the reduction in risk leaves the expected value of his or her income available for other goods and services unchanged.
   c. up to but not exceeding the point at which the premium is that of a fair insurance policy.
   d. both b and c.

Use the accompanying figure to answer the next question. The figure shows the utility curves for Ellen and Sally and how their utility will be affected by an increase or decrease of $100 in income.

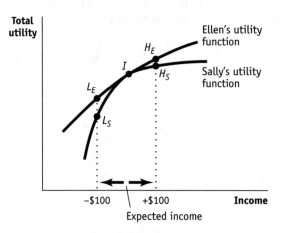

7. Which of the following statements about the preceding figure is correct?
   a. Ellen is more risk-averse than Sally.
   b. Ellen will gain more from insurance than will Sally.
   c. Sally will gain very little from a gain in income compared with Ellen, but she will lose a lot of utility from a fall in income.
   d. All of the above.

8. An important reason why Ellen and Sally may differ in their aversion to risk is that they may differ in
   a. how their marginal utility is affected by income.
   b. their initial wealth holding or initial income level.
   c. their understanding of risk.
   d. both a and b.

9. When faced with an "unfair" insurance policy, one with a premium larger than the expected claims,
   a. no one will buy it.
   b. only risk-tolerant individuals will buy it.
   c. risk-averse individuals will buy it as long as the utility associated with the insurance is greater than expected utility without the insurance.
   d. risk-averse individuals will buy it as long as the utility associated with the insurance is less than expected utility without the insurance.

10. Capital at risk refers to
   a. the total premium received by an insurance company.
   b. the funds that potentially could be paid out by an insurance company.
   c. the expected loss an individual may sustain without insurance.
   d. the risk that the insurance company may go bankrupt.

11. The insurance market is efficient in that
   a. premiums are always kept to the level of a fair insurance policy.
   b. deductibles eliminate moral hazard.
   c. society as a whole engages in less risky behavior.
   d. it transfers risk from those who most want to get rid of it to those least bothered by the risk.

12. Which of the following are *not* independent events?
   a. forgetting your umbrella; it rains
   b. a hurricane hits Miami; Miami experiences a shortage of bottled water
   c. a tornado hits the headquarters of a corporation; the CEO is indicted for fraud
   d. you receive an A on your economics test; you win the lottery

13. On any particular day, the probability that your car will be stolen is 5% and the probability that you will be sick is 2%. The probability that both happen on the same day is
   a. 0.1%.
   b. 1%.
   c. 3%.
   d. 7%.

14. When an insurance company insures 100,000 households across the state against fire destroying their home, it will
   a. be fairly certain of the number of fires that will occur.
   b. be engaging in a strategy known as pooling of risks.
   c. know with a fair amount of certainty the expected payoff on the insurance policies.
   d. all of the above.

15. Pooling _____ premiums and _____ the number of people insured.
   a. increases; increases
   b. increases; decreases
   c. decreases; increases
   d. decreases; decreases

16. Suppose the wealth of the sellers in the insurance market falls. We would expect insurance premiums to _____ as the _____.
   a. rise; supply curve shifts left
   b. fall; supply curve shifts right
   c. fall; demand curve shifts left
   d. rise; demand curves shifts right

17. Which of the following is *not* a limit to diversification?
   a. events that are not positively correlated
   b. losses due to bad weather
   c. war that limits access to a key raw-material area
   d. business cycles

18. Sellers of some goods may have private information to which buyers are not privy. This leads to
   a. higher prices for the goods.
   b. a surplus of goods on the market.
   c. many mutually beneficial transactions not taking place.
   d. all of the above.

19. Bill is considering purchasing an alarm system or theft insurance for his car. Although the cost of the two is the same, he buys the insurance because he knows that he rarely remembers to lock the car doors and thinks he will forget to put the alarm on as well. This is a situation involving
   a. moral hazard.
   b. adverse selection.
   c. signaling.
   d. screening.

20. The premium on insurance is often _____ to the deductible; this allows insurance companies to _____ their customers.
    a. inversely related; screen
    b. equal; pool
    c. directly related; signal
    d. equal; charge a fair premium to

Samantha is graduating with a B.A. in Economics. Samantha's earnings and associated probabilities in the coming year are given in the accompanying table.

Earnings	Probability
$60,000	10%
$50,000	30%
$40,000	40%
$20,000	20%

21. Samantha's expected income is
    a. $60,000.
    b. $50,000.
    c. $40,000.
    d. none of the above.

22. Suppose you are buying a lottery ticket. There is a probability of 95% that you will win nothing, a 1% probability that you will win $100, and a 4% probability that you will win $10. The expected value of your winnings is
    a. $100.00.
    b. $14.00.
    c. $1.40.
    d. none of the above.

23. To build a reputation of yourself as a very caring owner of a clothing manufacturing factory, you offer 20% more sick-leave days with pay than other businesses in your country. As a result, you end up getting less healthy workers, because healthy workers in other companies are happy in their present jobs. This is an example of
    a. moral hazard.
    b. adverse selection.
    c. symmetric information.
    d. both moral hazard and adverse selection in a world, with symmetric information.

24. Suppose $U = N^{0.5}$, where U is the total utility and N is income. The probability that your monthly income is $1,200 is 50%, and the probability that your monthly income is $2,000 is 50%. Your expected utility is
    a. 1,600.
    b. 400.
    c. 40.
    d. none of the above.

25. Suppose $U = N^{0.5}$, where U is the total utility and N is income. You are in a TV game show. The game show host offers you a choice: $1,500 outright cash or to flip a coin whereby heads will give you $2,000 and tails will give you $1,200. You should
    a. flip the coin.
    b. take the $1,500.
    c. be equally happy with both choices.
    d. not gamble in this case.

Problems and Exercises

Read each question carefully and then write your answers in the space provided or on a separate sheet of paper.

1. Mary Moneybags is considering investing in four different companies and the stock price of each is $10 per share. She recognizes that the price of the stock of each of the companies is affected by the overall strength of the Canadian economy. There are three possibilities for the Canadian economy for the next year: weak, average, strong. The following table shows her expectations for each stock's end-of-year price under the three possibilities for the Canadian economy.

States of the Economy

	Weak	Average	Strong
Plum Computers	$5.00	$13.00	$30.00
Nile.com	15.00	14.00	9.00
Gaggle	17.00	10.00	3.00
Untel	8.00	15.00	25.00

   a. If the probability that the economy will be weak is 10%, average is 80%, and strong is 10%, which stock should Ms. Moneybags buy if she wants the stock with the highest expected value at the end of the year? What will be her expected gain if she invests in that stock?

   b. If the probability that the economy will be weak is 70%, average is 10%, and strong is 20%, which stock should Ms. Moneybags buy if she wants the stock with the highest expected value at the end of the year? What will be her expected gain if she invests in that stock?

   c. If the probability that the economy will be weak is 40%, average is 20%, and strong is 40%, which stock should Ms. Moneybags buy if she wants the stock with the highest expected value at the end of the year? What will be her expected gain if she invests in that stock?

2. Ira Bookton works as a librarian at the university and earns $50,000 per year. He is considering a job at the local bookstore, where his pay will be based on the store's profits. If profits are greater than $100,000 per year, Ira will earn $65,000; if profits are less than $100,000 but greater than or equal to $50,000, he will earn $50,000; and if profits are less than $50,000, Ira will earn $40,000. Ira's utility schedule for income is shown in the accompanying table.

a. Draw his utility curve in the following figure. How would you describe Ira's marginal utility for income?

Income (in thousands)	Utility
$30	1,500
35	1,900
40	2,250
45	2,550
50	2,800
55	3,000
60	3,150
65	3,250
70	3,300

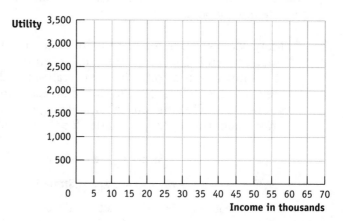

b. Ira believes there is a 20% probability that the store will earn more than $100,000 in profits, a 50% probability that it will earn greater than or equal to $50,000, and a 30% probability that it will earn less than $50,000. What is Ira's expected income if he takes the job at the local bookstore? If Ira wants to maximize expected utility, should he take the job at the local bookstore or continue as a university librarian?

c. Ira believes that there is a 25% probability that the store will earn more than $100,000 in profits, a 50% probability that it will earn greater than or equal to $50,000, and a 25% probability that it will earn less than $50,000. What is Ira's expected income if he takes the job at the local bookstore? If Ira wants to maximize expected utility, should he take the job at the local bookstore or continue as a university librarian?

d. Ira believes that there is a 30% probability that the store will earn more than $100,000 in profits, a 50% probability that it will earn greater than or equal to $50,000, and a 20% probability that it will earn less than $50,000. What is Ira's expected income if he takes the job at the local bookstore? If Ira wants to maximize expected utility, should he take the job at the local bookstore or continue as a university librarian?

3. You are considering investing in an indoor water park or outdoor amusement park in a summer resort town. Here are the possibilities for earning on the two investments:

- If the weather is good, you will earn $50,000 on your investment in the outdoor amusement park, and there is a probability of 75% that the weather will be good. However, if the weather is bad, you will lose $25,000, and there is a 25% probability that the weather will be bad.

- If the weather is good, you will lose $25,000 on your investment in the indoor water park, and there is a probability of 75% that the weather will be good. However, if the weather is bad, you will earn $200,000, and there is a 25% probability that the weather will be bad.

a. What are your expected earnings if you invest only in the outdoor amusement park?

b. What are your expected earnings if you invest only in the indoor water park?

c. What are your expected earnings if you invest half in the outdoor amusement park and half in the indoor water park? (Assume that your gains and losses will be half of what they were stated as being above.)

d. Would you diversify your investment? Why?

4. Identify the following scenarios as adverse selection or moral hazard and propose a solution.
   a. You insure your bicycle against theft. You ride your bicycle to the library just before closing to get a book needed for a term paper and don't stop to lock your bike to the bike stand.

   b. Your throat tickles and you're concerned that you may be developing a sore throat. You stop by the free clinic to have your throat looked at by one of the campus physicians.

c. Rashim would like to sell his existing computer to upgrade to a more powerful one by advertising on the bulletin board in the student center. He decides against it because the used computers listed on the board are underpriced.

5. Rob's total utility function is $U = N^{0.5}$ and the marginal utility function is $MU = 1/2N^{0.5}$, where U is total utility, MU is marginal utility, and N is income. If $N = \$400$, what are U and MU? If N is $\$1,600$, what are U and MU?

6. Rob's total utility function is $U = N^{0.5}$ and the marginal utility function is $MU = 1/2N^{0.5}$, where U is total utility, MU is marginal utility, and N is income. Is Rob risk-averse? Why? If not, why not?

7. Suppose you have bought a new car for $25,000. The car dealer offered you a warranty (at a price of $1,000) that you will be given full reimbursement if your car runs into a major accident in your first year of ownership. The probability of a major accident is 20%. Should you buy the one-year warranty?

Answers to How Well Do You Understand the Chapter

1. uncertainty, financial risk, random, expected, weighted, probability, states, certainty

2. expected, decreasing, fair, increase, decreasing, premium, greater

3. risk aversion, income, more, differs, utility, low, larger

4. warranty, signal, higher, cost

5. mutual, diversification, risk-tolerant, supply, increases, demand, increases

6. efficient allocation, capital, larger (greater)

7. diversification, independent, decrease, independent, multiplied

8. shares, small, pooling, small, payoff, predictability, insurance, supply, right, more, lower

9. weather, diversification

10. eliminate, private information, asymmetric, moral hazard, mutually beneficial, themselves

11. selection, more

12. screening, signaling, warranties

13. moral hazard, personal stake, franchises, deductible, screen, premium, deductible

Answers to Multiple-Choice Questions

1. Natasha's expected income is a weighted average of her possible incomes, where the weight on each income is the probability that income will occur:

   expected income = (0.40 × $40,000) + (0.60 × $50,000) = $46,000.

   Her expected income is $46,000. **Answer: C.**

2. If a person is risk-averse, his or her total utility curve will be upward sloping, but its slope will be diminishing (the curve will get flatter as income increases). **Answer: D.**

3. The Johnsons' expected income available for spending on goods and services other than the car is a weighted average of their possible incomes, where the weight on each income is the probability that income will occur:

   expected income = (0.75 × $56,000) + (0.25 × $40,000) = $52,000.

   Their expected utility is a weighted average of their possible utilities, where the weight on each utility is the probability that utility will occur:

   expected utility = (0.75 × 1,550) + (0.25 × 950) = 1,400.

   Answer: C.

4. If the Johnsons pay $6,000 for car insurance, the expected utility of income after the premium is paid will be 1,430, which is higher than expected utility without insurance. The Johnsons will buy the insurance at that premium. However, if the premium were $8,000 or $10,000, utility would be either 1,380 or 1,313; at those premiums expected utility without insurance is higher than utility with insurance and the Johnsons would not buy the insurance. **Answer: A.**

5. The fair insurance premium is that at which the premium equals the expected value of the claim. In this case, there is a 75% probability of no claim and a 25% probability of a $16,000 claim:

$$\text{expected claim} = (0.75 \times \$0) + (0.25 \times \$16,000) = \$4,000.$$

Answer: A.

6. A risk-averse person will choose to purchase insurance to reduce risk if the expected utility associated with income available for spending on other goods and services after paying the premium is greater than or equal to expected utility without insurance. **Answer: B.**

7. Starting from expected income, if income falls by $100, Sally will lose more utility than will Ellen. If income rises by $100 from expected income, Ellen will gain more utility than Sally. Sally is more risk-averse than Ellen. **Answer: C.**

8. Individuals differ in risk aversion for two main reasons: differences in how income affects marginal utility and difference in initial wealth or income. **Answer: D.**

9. Individuals may still buy an "unfair" insurance policy as long as the expected utility after paying the premium is greater than expected utility without insurance. **Answer: C.**

10. The funds that potentially could be paid out by an insurance company are capital at risk. **Answer: B.**

11. Economists believe that insurance markets are efficient in that they transfer risk from the most risk-averse individuals to those who are more risk-tolerant. **Answer: D.**

12. All of the events are independent with the exception of a hurricane hitting Miami and a shortage of bottled water in Miami. When a hurricane is expected, people try to stock up on bottled water, anticipating that after a hurricane there may be a problem with tap water, resulting in an excess demand for bottled water. **Answer: B.**

13. Having your car stolen and being sick are independent events. The probability of two independent events occurring is equal to the probability that one occurs multiplied by the probability the other occurs. The probability of having your car stolen and being sick on the same day is 0.1% ($= 0.05 \times 0.02$). **Answer: A.**

14. By insuring 100,000 households across the state, an insurance company is pooling its risks. When it does this, it knows with some certainty the number of fires that will occur and the expected payoff on its policies. **Answer: D.**

15. The opportunity to engage in pooling encourages a greater supply of insurance, reducing premiums and increasing the number of people insured. **Answer: C.**

16. If sellers of insurance experience a decrease in wealth, there will be a decrease in the supply of insurance and insurance premiums will rise. **Answer: A.**

17. Diversification is limited by losses due to bad weather, war that limits access to a key raw-material area, and business cycles. However, if events are not positively correlated or independent, diversification can reduce risk. **Answer: A.**

18. When some sellers know more about hidden problems than do the buyers of a good, this will lead to lower prices. As buyers expect problems even when none exist, some goods will be kept off the market due to the lower prices, and some mutually beneficial transactions will not take place. **Answer: C.**

19. Bill knows more about his own behavior than does the insurance company. Even though the cost of the alarm system equals the premium for the insurance, he knows that his forgetfulness requires that he buy the insurance. This is a problem of moral hazard. **Answer: A.**

20. To screen customers, insurance companies offer lower premiums to those willing to commit to higher deductibles. A low-risk individual will prefer a low-premium and high-deductible policy because they do not expect to submit a claim. This is a way in which insurance companies can screen their policy holders. **Answer: A.**

21. Samantha's expected income

= $60,000(0.1) + $50,000(0.3) + $40,000(0.4) + $20,000(.2) = $41,000.

Answer: D.

22. Expected value

= 0(0.95) + $100(0.01) + $10(0.04) = $1.40. **Answer: C.**

23. Unhealthy workers self-select their jobs in your factory, but you have a case of adverse selection because you don't know the medical conditions of prospective workers. **Answer: B.**

24. Expected income = $1,200(.5) + $2,000(.5) = $1,600.

Expected utility = $1,600^{0.5} = 40$.

Answer: C.

25. Expected win with coin-flip = $2,000(.5) + $1,200(.5) = $1,600.

Since $1,600 > $1,500, you should flip the coin. **Answer A.**

Answers to Problems and Exercises

1. a. The following table shows the expected value of the four stocks given that there is a 10% probability that the economy will be weak, 80% that it will be average, and 10% that it will be strong. The expected value of each stock was calculated using the following equation:

$$EV = (0.10 \times Price_{weak}) + (0.80 \times Price_{average}) + (0.10 \times Price_{strong}).$$

Under this scenario, Ms. Moneybags should choose to invest in Untel; her expected gain is $5.30 per share.

State of the Economy

	Weak	Average	Strong	EV
Probability	0.1	0.8	0.1	
Plum Computers	$5.00	$13.00	$30.00	$13.90
Nile.com	15.00	14.00	9.00	13.60
Gaggle	17.00	10.00	3.00	10.00
Untel	8.00	15.00	25.00	15.30

b. The following table shows the expected value of the four stocks given that there is a 70% probability that the economy will be weak, 10% that it will be average, and 20% that it will be strong. The expected value of each stock was calculated using the following equation:

$$EV = (0.70 \times Price_{weak}) + (0.10 \times Price_{average}) + (0.20 \times Price_{strong}).$$

Under this scenario, Ms. Moneybags should choose to invest in Nile.com; her expected gain is $3.70.

State of the Economy

	Weak	Average	Strong	EV
Probability	0.7	0.1	0.2	
Plum Computers	$5.00	$13.00	$30.00	$10.80
Nile.com	15.00	14.00	9.00	13.70
Gaggle	17.00	10.00	3.00	13.50
Untel	8.00	15.00	25.00	12.10

c. The following table shows the expected value of the four stocks given that there is a 40% probability that the economy will be weak, 20% that it will be average, and 40% that it will be strong. The expected value of each stock was calculated using the following equation:

$$EV = (0.40 \times Price_{weak}) + (0.20 \times Price_{average}) + (0.40 \times Price_{strong}).$$

Under this scenario, Ms. Moneybags should choose to invest in Plum Computers; her expected gain is $6.60.

State of the Economy

	Weak	Average	Strong	EV
Probability	0.4	0.2	0.4	
Plum Computers	$5.00	$13.00	$30.00	$16.60
Nile.com	15.00	14.00	9.00	12.40
Gaggle	17.00	10.00	3.00	10.00
Untel	8.00	15.00	25.00	16.20

2. a. Ira's total utility curve is shown below; since the total utility curve is increasing at a diminishing rate (is positively sloped by getting flatter), Ira has a diminishing marginal utility for income.

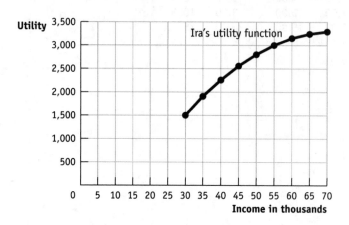

b. Ira's expected income from the bookstore is a weighted average of his possible incomes, where the weight on each income is the probability that income will occur:

expected income = (0.20 × $65,000) + (0.50 × $50,000) + (0.30 × $40,000) = $50,000.

His expected utility from the job at the bookstore is a weighted average of his possible utilities, where the weight on each utility is the probability that utility will occur:

expected utility = (0.20 × 3,250) + (0.50 × 2,800) + (0.30 × 2,250) = 2,725.

If Ira takes the job at the bookstore, his expected income is the same as at the library, but his expected utility is lower; his expected utility at the bookstore is 2,725, compared with 2,800 at the university library. Ira should continue to work at the university library.

c. Ira's expected income from the bookstore is a weighted average of his possible incomes, where the weight on each income is the probability that income will occur:

expected income = (0.25 × $65,000) + (0.50 × $50,000) + (0.25 × $40,000) = $51,250.

His expected utility from the job at the bookstore is a weighted average of his possible utilities, where the weight on each utility is the probability that utility will occur:

expected utility = (0.25 × 3,250) + (0.50 × 2,800) + (0.25 x 2,250) = 2,775.

If Ira takes the job at the bookstore, his expected income is $51,250 (higher than the $50,000 at the library), but his expected utility is still lower (2,775) than at the library (2,800). Ira should continue to work at the university library.

d. Ira's expected income from the bookstore is a weighted average of his possible incomes, where the weight on each income is the probability that income will occur:

expected income = (0.30 × $65,000) + (0.50 × $50,000) + (0.20 × $40,000) = $52,500.

His expected utility from the job at the bookstore is a weighted average of his possible utilities, where the weight on each utility is the probability that utility will occur:

expected utility = (0.30 × 3,250) + (0.50 × 2,800) + (0.20 × 2,250) = 2,825.

If Ira takes the job at the bookstore, his expected income is $52,500 (higher than the $50,000 at the library), and his expected utility is higher (2,825) than at the library (2,800). Ira should take the job at the bookstore.

3. The following table summarizes the earnings on the two investments under the two states, good weather and bad weather.

	Good weather	**Bad weather**
	Earnings	
Probability	0.75	0.25
Outdoor amusement park	+$50,000	−$25,000
Indoor water park	−25,000	+200,000

a. If you invest only in the outdoor amusement park, your expected earning will be $31,250.

Expected earnings = (0.75 × [+$50,000]) + (0.25 × [−$25,000]) = $31,250.

b. If you invest only in the indoor water park, your expected earnings will be $31,250.

Expected earnings = (0.75 × [−$25,000]) + (0.25 × [+$200,000]) = $31,250.

c. If you invest half in the outdoor amusement park and half in the indoor, in good weather you would earn $12,500 and in bad weather $87,500. Your expected earnings will be $31,250.

Expected earnings = (0.75 × [+$12,500]) + (.25 × [+$87,500]) = $31,250.

d. Although your expected earnings are the same whether you invest completely in the outdoor amusement park, completely in the indoor water park, or diversify your investment by investing half in each park, when you diversify you have eliminated the possibility of losing money. When you diversify you also reduce the risk associated with your return. You will either earn $12,500 or $87,500, with expected earnings of $31,250.

4. a. This is a problem of moral hazard. You know more about your behavior (the likelihood of making a last-minute trip to the library and of leaving the bike unlocked) than does the insurance company. The insurance company can minimize the moral hazard problem by requiring a higher deductible. To avoid paying the deductible, you will take the extra minutes to lock your bike.

b. This is a problem of adverse selection. You know whether you're likely to run to the free clinic for every little ache or pain or not. The free clinic can try to make sure they see only people who believe themselves ill enough to need a doctor by requiring a fee to see a campus physician. But then, of course, the clinic will no longer be free.

c. This is a problem of adverse selection. Some students sell their computers because they have decided to upgrade to more powerful computers, but others sell theirs because their computers don't work well. Not knowing the reason why any one student is offering to sell his or her computer, students will only buy if the price reflects hidden problems. To minimize the adverse selection problem, Rashim could offer a 30-day money-back guarantee on his computer in exchange for a higher sale price.

5. When income = $400, $U = 20$ and $MU = 1/40$.

When income = $1,600, $U = 40$ and $MU = 1/80$.

6. Rob is risk-averse, because as income increases, marginal utility diminishes.

7. Expected return = $25,000(.2) + 0(.98) = $500.

Since the price of warranty is greater than $500, you may decide not to have the warranty. But if you perceive that the differential between the warranty price and the expected return is less than the utility you will derive for having a warranty, you should buy the warranty.

chapter 19

Externalities

Externalities, pollution, and market failures are discussed in this chapter. The socially optimal level of pollution is found at a point where the marginal benefit curve of pollution intersects the marginal cost curve of pollution. We also see how government intervention may reduce inefficiencies associated with externalities. The Coase theorem shows the circumstances where the efficient amount of pollution can be achieved without government intervention. We also show the role of taxes and tradable emission permits in achieving efficient levels of emissions.

How Well Do You Understand the Chapter?

Fill in the blanks using the terms below to complete the following statements. Terms may be used more than once. If you find yourself having difficulties, please refer back to the appropriate section in the text.

above	equal(s)	marginal benefit	social
benefit(s)	external benefit	marginal external	social benefit
better off	externalities	market price	socially optimal
cheaply	firms	markets	society
Coase	good government	minimum	tax
cost(s)	intervention	more	too many
creation of	high	negative	too much
knowledge	incentives	optimal	tradable
decreases	increases	pay	tradable emissions
desirable	inefficient	Pigouvian	tradable permits
education	internalize(d)	Pigouvian subsidy	transaction costs
efficient	less	Pigouvian taxes	willingness to pay
environmental	less polluting	pollution	zero
environmental standards	low	positive	
	marginal	scarce	

1. Externalities exist when individuals impose _____ on others or provide _____ to others who are not participating in the market. Pollution is an example of a(n) _____ externality (an uncompensated cost imposed on others), while education creates _____ externalities (benefits conferred to others who have not paid for the good).

2. We do not want to completely eliminate pollution, because avoiding pollution uses _____ resources that could be used to produce other goods and services. This chapter develops a framework to determine the _____ level of an externality, such as pollution.

3. The _____ social cost of pollution is the additional cost imposed on society as a whole by an additional unit of pollution. The marginal social cost of pollution _____ with the amount of pollution produced. The marginal social _____ of pollution is the additional gain to society from an additional unit of pollution, and we measure it as the highest _____ for the right to emit a unit of pollution across all producers. The marginal social benefit of pollution _____ with extra pollution emitted. The socially _____ quantity of pollution is the amount of pollution society would choose if all benefits and costs were considered; it is the level of pollution at which the marginal social benefit _____ the marginal social cost of pollution.

4. The market cannot achieve the optimal level of pollution because the only benefits of pollution accrue to _____, while the costs of pollution are imposed on _____. Without _____, firms will have no incentive to consider the costs of pollution they impose on others. As long as the marginal benefit is greater than _____, the firm will continue to emit pollution; only when the marginal benefit is _____ will the firm stop polluting. However, at that level of pollution, the marginal social cost of pollution will be very _____ and will be greater than the marginal _____.

5. When the government does not intervene to correct negative _____ such as pollution, there is a(n) _____ outcome. Some people could be made _____ without making others worse off. Society would be better off if _____ pollution were produced.

6. The _____ theorem states that even in the presence of externalities, an economy can reach an efficient solution as long as transaction costs are sufficiently _____. When one person's action—such as playing loud music—creates a negative externality for someone else—such as disturbing his or her peace and quiet—the two people can make a deal. The Coase theorem says that the one person can _____ the other, and both will be content. When individuals consider externalities in this way (with zero transaction costs of negotiations), they _____ the externality and achieve _____ outcomes without government intervention.

7. Individuals may not be able to internalize externalities if the costs of communication are _____ (for example, many people may be involved), the costs of a binding agreement are _____ (it may require hiring an expensive lawyer), or there are delays as both sides hold out for more favourable terms.

8. The governments of all advanced nations play an active role in protecting the environment, primarily by specifying _____ (rules to protect the environment by specifying actions by producers and consumers). In Canada, the Clean Air Act is the principal enforcer of environmental policies at the national level. Economists believe that the inflexibility of environmental standards does not allow _____ in pollution at a(n)_____ cost. They believe that we could have an efficient outcome if pollution were directly controlled using taxes and _____.

9. An emission _____ is a tax that depends on the amount of pollution a firm produces. If the government imposes a tax equal to the marginal _____ at the socially optimal quantity of pollution, the firm will only emit pollution up to the point where the firm's marginal _____ equals the tax (or the optimal social marginal cost). Through the tax, the government induces the polluters to consider the true _____ to society of their actions; the polluters will _____ the externality. An emissions tax is a more _____ way to reduce pollution than an environmental standard because the tax ensures that the marginal social benefit of pollution is _____ for all sources of pollution, while an environmental standard does not. When the marginal _____ of pollution is the same for all plants, there is no way to rearrange pollution reduction among the various plants that will achieve the _____ level of pollution at a lower total _____. An "emissions" tax is a misnomer in that such a tax can be a solution to other activities that generate _____ _____ externalities, such as driving during rush hour. Taxes that reduce external costs are also called _____. The main problem with emissions or Pigouvian taxes is that it is difficult for the government to estimate the tax that will bring about the _____ quantity.

10. _____ are licenses to emit limited quantities of emissions that can be bought and sold by polluters. The permits are _____ in that firms are allowed to buy the right to emit extra pollution from other firms that are willing to cut pollution _____ than the quantity specified in the permits they receive. The tradable permits create _____ in the rights to pollute. The market price of the permit determines the _____ _____ of emissions: a firm that pollutes at a point where the marginal social benefit of pollution is _____ than the market price of the permit will sell the permit to a firm for which the marginal benefit of pollution exceeds the _____. All firms will produce where the marginal benefit of pollution is _____ to the market price of a permit. Similar to emissions taxes, the tradable permit system ensures that those who can reduce pollution _____ are the ones who do so. The main problem in administering a tradable permit system is determining the optimal quantity of pollution. Government may issue _____ permits (not reduce pollution enough) or too few permits (reduce pollution too much).

Emissions taxes and tradable permits also provide _____ to create and use less-polluting technology.

11. Pollution is usually a side effect of an activity that is _____.
Sometimes it is not possible to control the pollution directly, and it is necessary to control the original activity. This approach allows us to understand how the original activity is influenced by policies designed to manage the _____ externality. It also allows us to evaluate the positions of those who argue against _____ policy because it impedes the desirable activities. Finally, it gives us a way to think about the related problem of _____ externalities, or external benefits.

12. When production of a good or service generates a negative externality, we need to distinguish between the marginal _____ cost and the marginal private cost of production. The marginal social cost of a good or activity is the marginal cost of production plus its _____ cost. Without government intervention, the market will produce _____ of a good with a negative externality. In the example in the chapter of livestock and pollution, the market will produce a quantity of livestock that exceeds the _____ quantity if the government does not intervene in the market.

13. When pollution itself cannot be targeted, the government can still use _____ or permits to reduce pollution. In these cases, the government may tax the original activity or require a license to engage in the activity. With government intervention, external costs will be completely _____ in the private decisions of producers. Emission taxes and _____ encourage the creation and adoption of _____ production methods. Directly addressing pollution with pollution (emissions standard) is carried out in units of _____, while the alternative is carried out in units of _____ produced that yield pollution. Regulators who set emissions standard generally prefer to adopt policies that target pollution directly.

14. We can analyze the production of goods that produce _____ externalities in a similar way to those that have negative externalities. The _____ is the most important source of external benefits in the modern economy. When there are external benefits, the marginal social benefit is greater than marginal private _____. The marginal social benefit of a good or activity is equal to the marginal benefit that accrues to consumers plus its marginal _____. If a positive externality exists, the marginal social

benefit of a good or activity lies _____ the demand curve. If the government does not intervene, the market will produce a quantity that is inefficiently _____. The government can encourage a(n) _____ in production of the good or activity by granting a(n) _____, a payment designed to encourage the production of goods and activities that yield external benefits.

15. Economists are generally _____ enthusiastic about industrial policies to promote positive externalities than they are about taxes and permits to discourage negative externalities, because positive externalities are harder to identify and measure. One activity with external benefits that receives considerable subsidies is _____.

Learning Tips

TIP #1: The socially optimal quantity of pollution is the quantity of pollution that society would choose if all costs and benefits were considered.

When a firm pollutes the environment while producing a good for a market, the costs of pollution are borne not by the producers but by individuals who have no say in the market, while the benefits of polluting—such as the savings from not purchasing and using pollution-reducing machinery—accrue only to the firm. From the firm's perspective, the marginal cost of pollution is zero. In Figure 19.1, the firm continues to produce until the marginal social benefit is zero at Q_{MKT}.

However, the marginal social costs of pollution increase as more pollution is produced. Since firms will continue to pollute until the marginal benefit of pollution is zero, the pollution market is inefficient. From Figure 19.2 we can see that when the marginal social benefit of pollution is zero at Q_{MKT}, the marginal social cost of pollution is much greater than zero. This is an inefficient outcome because we could make some people better off without making others worse off; reducing pollution would increase total surplus. The socially optimal quantity of pollution is where marginal social benefit equals marginal social cost; that occurs at Q_{OPT} in Figure 19.2, and the marginal social benefit equals marginal social cost at P_{OPT}.

Figure 19.1

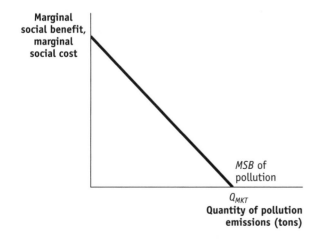

Figure 19.2

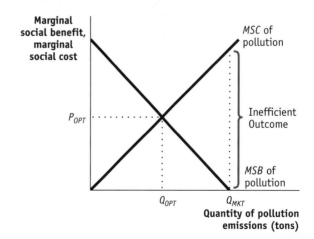

TIP #2: An emissions tax and tradable emission permits are more efficient ways to reduce pollution than are environmental standards.

An environmental standard reduces the level of pollution that any activity can produce without considering differing costs associated with reducing pollution. Let's look at an industry with two firms that use different technology; it is more costly for the first firm (Firm I) to reduce pollution than it is for the second (Firm II). Consequently, the firm with higher costs of reducing pollution, Firm I, has a greater marginal benefit of pollution. Figure 19.3 shows the marginal benefit of pollution for the two firms.

Figure 19.3

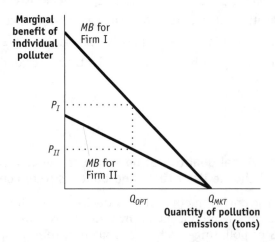

Without government intervention, the two firms will produce pollution equal to $2 \times Q_{MKT}$. If the socially optimal quantity of pollution is $2 \times Q_{OPT}$, the government may try to limit each firm to produce Q_{OPT} units of pollution. When both firms reduce their emission to Q_{OPT}, Firm I does so at a higher cost (P_I) than does Firm II. This is inefficient because the same quantity of pollution could be achieved at a lower cost by allowing Firm I to pollute more than Q_{OPT} and requiring Firm II to pollute less than Q_{OPT}, until the marginal benefit of pollution to the two firms is equal. When each firm values a unit of pollution equally, there is no way to achieve the desired level of pollution at a lower total cost.

There are two efficient ways for the government to reduce pollution to the socially optimal quantity. The first is by imposing an emissions tax on each unit of pollution. This will raise the marginal cost of pollution from zero to the per-unit tax. In Figure 19.4, Firm I will produce a higher quantity of pollution (Q_I) than Firm II, but the marginal benefit of pollution to both plants is the same and equal to the per-unit emissions tax. By adjusting the tax, the government can reduce the total amount of pollution ($Q_I + Q_{II}$) to the socially optimal level of production ($2 \times Q_{OPT}$). The government has reduced pollution to the socially optimal quantity at minimum cost; it is an efficient outcome.

Figure 19.4

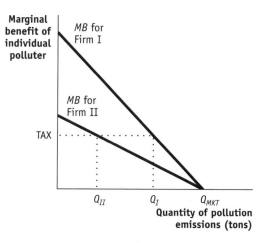

An alternative to an emissions tax is for the government to issue tradable permits or licenses to emit limited amounts of pollution. If in the example above the government issues tradable permits that allow a quantity of pollution equal to $Q_I + Q_{II}$, the firms will buy and sell the permits until the price of a permit equals P_{PER}. At that price, the marginal benefit of pollution to the two firms is the same. Figure 19.5 shows that the equilibrium price of the permit, P_{PER}, equals the per-unit tax in the preceding figure.

Figure 19.5

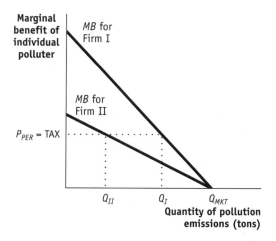

TIP #3: When the external cost cannot be directly controlled, the government can move the market to the socially optimal level by imposing a Pigouvian tax or granting a license to produce the good or service with the external cost.

Let's explore this tip by looking at the market for cigarettes. Although the market for cigarettes is oligopolistic, we will assume it is perfectly competitive to simplify our analysis. Smoking cigarettes creates many external costs to society, including health problems for those who do not smoke. The marginal social benefit of smoking accrues only to individual smokers, while the marginal social cost of smoking includes the cost to the cigarette manufacturer plus the health costs to society. In Figure 19.6, the market demand curve shows the marginal benefit of smoking (the highest willingness to pay for an additional unit of smoking), and the market supply curve reflects the marginal costs to the cigarette manufacturers. In a competitive market with no government intervention, the equilibrium price would be P_{MKT} and the equilibrium quantity would be Q_{MKT}. However, when we add the external costs of smoking to the supply curve, we get the marginal social cost curve of cigarettes as shown in Figure 19.7. From that figure we see that the socially optimal quantity and price of cigarettes is Q_{OPT} and P_{OPT}.

Figure 19.6

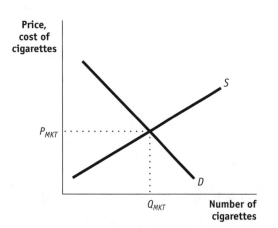

Figure 19.7

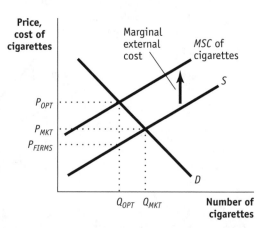

The government can bring about the socially optimal quantity of cigarettes by imposing a Pigouvian tax in the market equal to $P_{OPT} - P_{FIRMS}$, or by issuing tradable permits to buy or sell a maximum quantity of cigarettes equal to Q_{OPT}.

TIP #4: The government may choose to subsidize the good or service to encourage a good or service that has an external benefit.

We can explore this tip with the example of flu shots. When a person gets a flu shot, not only has he or she substantially lowered the risk of contracting the flu (private benefit), but the person has also reduced the probability that others will contract the flu from them (social benefit). Figure 19.8 shows a hypothetical market for flu shots. Without any government intervention, the market will be in equilibrium at a price of P_{MKT} and a quantity of Q_{MKT}. If we consider the marginal social benefits of flu shots, Figure 19.9, we can see that the socially optimal level is Q_{OPT} (higher than Q_{MKT}) and the socially optimal price is P_{OPT} (higher than P_{MKT}).

Figure 19.8

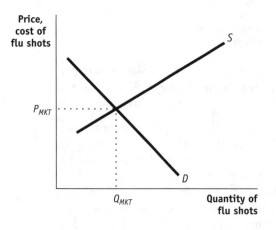

Figure 19.9

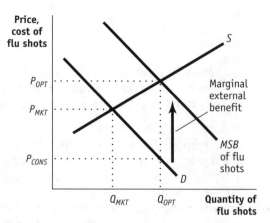

The government can bring about the socially optimal quantity of flu shots by granting a Pigouvian subsidy in the market equal to $P_{OPT} - P_{CONS}$. Note that the subsidy is greater than the difference between the market price and the optimal price.

Multiple-Choice Questions

1. Negative externalities may cause markets to be inefficient if they
   a. impose costs on individuals who are not market participants, but the market participants don't consider those costs.
   b. lead to a market equilibrium in which the marginal social cost exceeds the marginal social benefit.
   c. lead to a market equilibrium in which some people can be made better off without making others worse off.
   d. do all of the above.

2. Which of the following is an example of a negative externality?
   a. A late-season hurricane destroys the grapefruit crop in Florida.
   b. The government imposes a tax in the market for grapefruit.
   c. Fertilizers used in the production of grapefruits are believed to be adversely affecting wildlife in Florida.
   d. Many Florida grapefruit growers go bankrupt because of an increase in imported grapefruits.

3. Economists measure the marginal social cost of pollution as the
   a. highest willingness to pay among all members of society to avoid an additional unit of pollution.
   b. minimum cost of cleaning up an additional unit of pollution.
   c. marginal social benefit less the marginal cost of production.
   d. marginal cost of production less marginal social benefit.

4. Economists measure the marginal social benefit of pollution as
   a. zero.
   b. the additional gain to society as a whole from an additional unit of pollution.
   c. marginal social cost less the marginal cost of production.
   d. marginal cost of production less marginal social cost.

5. According to the Coase theorem, it is possible to achieve an efficient solution in the presence of externalities without government intervention as long as
   a. a legal contract is signed.
   b. transaction costs are low.
   c. many parties are involved.
   d. none of the above.

6. If a private solution is reached that achieves the socially optimal quantity of a good or service in the presence of externalities, then
   a. the externality has been internalized.
   b. any negative externality has been eliminated.
   c. the marginal social benefit is zero.
   d. both a and b.

Use the following figure to answer the next five questions.

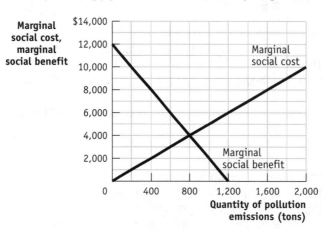

7. If the government does not intervene in the pollution market, equilibrium will occur where the marginal social benefit is _____ and the marginal social cost is _____.
   a. $0; $6,000
   b. $0; $10,000
   c. $4,000; $4,000
   d. $8,000; $8,000

8. The socially optimal quantity of pollution is
   a. zero.
   b. 800 tons of pollution.
   c. 1,200 tons of pollution.
   d. 2,000 tons of pollution.

9. If the government imposed an environmental standard that did not allow total pollution emitted to exceed 600 tons,
   a. there would still be too much pollution because any pollution is too much pollution from an economist's perspective.
   b. there would still be too much pollution because the marginal social cost of pollution would still exceed the marginal social benefit of pollution.
   c. there would be too little pollution because the marginal social benefit of pollution would exceed the marginal social cost of pollution.
   d. that would achieve the socially optimal level of pollution.

10. The Pigouvian tax that would bring about the socially optimal level of pollution equals _____ per ton.
   a. $2,000
   b. $4,000
   c. $6,000
   d. $10,000

11. The government could bring about the socially optimal level of pollution by issuing tradable emissions permits that allow a maximum of _____ tons of pollution.
   a. 0
   b. 400
   c. 800
   d. 1,200

12. In an industry of various firms with plants that pollute the environment to different extents, the government requires that each plant reduce its emissions to a certain level to reach a certain environmental standard. This environmental standard is
a. better than a tax because it reduces pollution without any cost to the firm.
b. fair because it treats all firms the same.
c. inefficient because the reduction in pollution could have been achieved at a lower cost.
d. none of the above.

13. Economists prefer for governments to use emissions taxes and tradable permits rather than environmental standards to reduce pollution because emissions taxes and tradable permits ensure that
a. pollution will be reduced to the socially optimal quantity in an efficient manner.
b. those who can reduce pollution most cheaply are the ones to do so.
c. the marginal benefit of pollution is the same for all plants.
d. all of the above.

The following figure shows the market for cattle in a small economy. Use the figure to answer the next three questions.

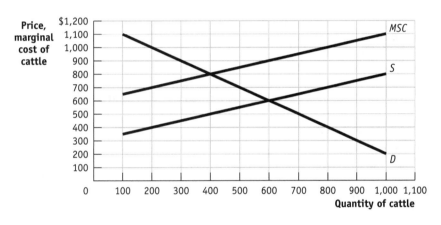

14. The socially optimal price of cattle is _____ and the socially optimal quantity is _____.
a. $600; 600
b. $900; 600
c. $500; 400
d. $800; 400

15. In the market for livestock, the marginal external cost of cattle is
a. $300.
b. $500.
c. $600.
d. $800.

16. The government can reduce the quantity of cattle to the socially optimal quantity either by imposing a Pigouvian tax equal to _____ per unit of cattle or issue tradable permits that restrict the quantity of cattle to _____ units.
a. $300; 400
b. $800; 400
c. $300; 600
d. $900; 600

17. If the government is choosing between policies that target pollution directly or target production of the original good, it
    a. doesn't matter because the outcome will be the same regardless of the policy undertaken.
    b. should choose to target production of the original good because firms will reduce production of the good with the negative externality.
    c. should choose to target pollution directly because it encourages the creation and adoption of less-polluting production methods.
    d. should choose whichever method raises the largest revenue.

18. When a positive externality exists and the government does not correct it, the equilibrium market price is _____ than the socially optimal price and the equilibrium market quantity is _____ than the socially optimal quantity.
    a. lower; lower
    b. higher; higher
    c. lower; higher
    d. higher; lower

19. The distance between the demand curve and the marginal social benefit curve equals the
    a. marginal social cost.
    b. average social cost.
    c. marginal external cost.
    d. marginal external benefit.

20. Which of the following is usually associated with a positive externality?
    a. sale of a sports car
    b. purchase of a new stereo system
    c. innovation in the semiconductor industry
    d. All of the above.

21. A Pigouvian subsidy is a form of
    a. industrial policy.
    b. externality.
    c. technology spillover.
    d. none of the above.

22. At the socially optimal level of pollution,
    a. pollution is zero.
    b. the marginal social benefit of pollution is zero.
    c. the marginal cost of pollution is zero.
    d. the difference between the marginal social benefit of pollution and the marginal social cost of pollution is zero.

23. An emission tax on polluters will
    a. externalize the internal costs of pollution.
    b. encourage less-polluting production methods.
    c. reduce the tax revenues from emission taxes.
    d. eliminate pollution.

24. Once the polluting firm (producing a private good) is subjected to the Pigouvian tax, it internalizes the negative externality and as a result,
    a. the market price will increase and output will increase.
    b. the market price will increase and output will decrease.
    c. the market price will decrease and output will increase.
    d. the market price will decrease and output will decrease.

25. The Coase theorem states that
   a. if there are negative externalities, the government must intervene to ensure the efficient solution.
   b. with significant negotiation costs, private parties can arrive at the efficient solution without government intervention.
   c. with zero negotiation costs, private parties can arrive at the efficient solution without government intervention.
   d. market fails and as a result, we require optimal governmental intervention.

26. Which of the following conditions must be satisfied when we apply the Coase theorem?
   a. There should be a small number of participants.
   b. There should be zero transaction costs.
   c. The basic property rights must be clearly specified.
   d. All of the above conditions must be satisfied.
   e. None of the above conditions must be satisfied.

27. If the marginal social cost curve shifts to the left (due to new medical reports of health hazards of pollution), the optimal level of pollution
   a. will decrease.
   b. will increase.
   c. will remain the same.
   d. may increase or decrease, depending on the emission standards set by the government.

Answer questions 28–30 on the basis of the following graph.

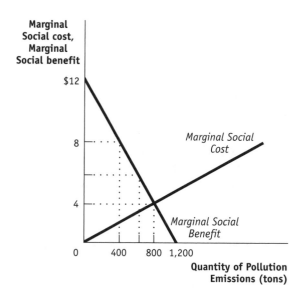

28. If the pollution tax is $4 per unit of emissions, the polluters will pay all of the following except
   a. zero taxes if pollution emissions are zero.
   b. $1,600 in total taxes if pollution emissions are 400 units.
   c. $3,200 in total taxes if pollution emissions are 800 units.
   d. $4,800 in total taxes if pollution emissions are 1,200 units.
   e. zero taxes if pollution emissions are 1,200 units.

29. Refer to the previous graph. Which of the following statements is false?
  a. If pollution emissions are zero, polluters pay zero taxes, but will lose $7,200 in terms of forgone earnings.
  b. If pollution emissions are 400 units, polluters pay $1,600 in total taxes, but will lose $3,200 in terms of foregone earnings.
  c. If pollution emissions are 800 units, polluters pay $3,200 in total taxes, but will lose $800 in terms of foregone earnings.
  d. If pollution emissions are 1,200 units, polluters pay $4,800 in total taxes, but lose nothing in terms of foregone earnings.
  e. If pollution emissions are zero, polluters pay zero taxes, but will lose $14,400 in terms of forgone earnings.

30. Refer to the previous graph. If the emission tax is $4 per unit of pollution emissions, the total costs to the polluters (at the optimal level) will be
  a. $7,200.
  b. $4,800.
  c. $4,000.
  d. $3,200.

31. When negative externality occurs in the production of a good, then
  a. the marginal social cost is less than the marginal private cost.
  b. the marginal social cost is greater than the marginal private cost.
  c. the marginal social cost is equal to the marginal private cost.
  d. too few resources are used in the production.

32. Which of the following policies has the **least** effect on the uses of technology that generates less pollution emissions?
  a. emission taxes
  b. corrective Pigouvian taxes
  c. emission standards
  d. tradable emission permits

33. Which of the following statements is true?
  a. The Coase theorem assumes equal distribution of benefits.
  b. According to the Coase theorem, the polluters will be paid by the victims of pollution if the property-rights to pollute belong to the polluters.
  c. The trading of pollution permits is an example of an emission's standard.
  d. The Coase theorem assumes many participants and substantial transaction costs of negotiations.

34. The Coase theorem
  a. applies in situations where the negative externalities as well as negotiation costs are substantial.
  b. assumes that the emission standards are set by governments.
  c. assumes that the government intervention is not needed, and market by itself can resolve externality problems.
  d. assumes that the property right determines the optimal level of pollution.

35. The creation of markets for tradable emission permits will provide
  a. an incentive not to pollute and encourage the use of pollution-abatement technology.
  b. an incentive not to pollute, but would not encourage pollution-abatement.
  c. neither an incentive not to pollute nor encourage pollution-abatement.
  d. encourage pollution-abatement, but will not provide incentives to reduce pollution.

Problems and Exercises

Read each question carefully and then write your answers in the space provided or on a separate sheet of paper.

1. Identify what type of externality (positive or negative) is described below.
   a. Your next-door neighbor installs a Mosquito Magnet (a machine that eliminates mosquitoes) near the property line dividing your property from hers.

   b. Your next-door neighbor begins to provide shelter to all homeless animals in the community.

   c. The city-owned vacant lot across from your home becomes a community garden.

   d. The city-owned vacant lot across from your home becomes a sewer-treatment plant.

2. The town of Pelmar has two offset printing shops, The Printed Page and Prints-R-Us. Each print shop releases volatile organic compounds (VOCs) into the air that contribute to the formation of smog. The following figure shows the marginal social benefit of the VOCs to each firm.

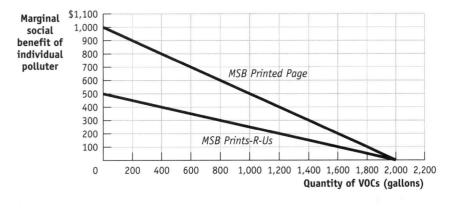

   a. Without any government intervention, what level of VOCs will be emitted each year by the two print shops?

   b. Pelmar decides to reduce VOC emissions by the printers to a total of 1,600 gallons. If Pelmar required that each firm produce a maximum of 800 gallons of VOCs per year, what would be the marginal social benefit of VOCs to each firm? Is this an efficient way to reduce VOCs in the town?

  c. How large a Pigouvian tax would be needed to reduce Pelmar's emissions to 1,600 gallons of VOCs per year? How many gallons of VOCs would each firm emit? Is this an efficient way to reduce VOCs in the town?

  d. Are there any other methods that Pelmar could use to reduce the VOCs to 1,600 gallons per year?

3. A local nightclub regularly brings various bands to town and several times a year brings the very popular Unthankful Living. The Unthankful Living always draws a large crowd but they also bring some very grubby groupies with them. These groupies often sleep in the park, wash in the public restrooms, and have loud parties lasting to the early hours of the morning. The following figure shows the market for tickets for a typical Unthankful Living concert and the marginal social cost of the tickets.

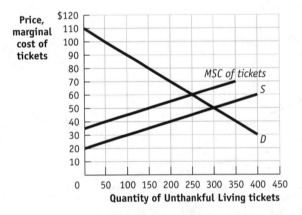

  a. What is the market equilibrium price and quantity of Unthankful Living concert tickets? What is the marginal external cost of a ticket? What is the socially optimal price and quantity of Unthankful Living concert tickets?

  b. What are the possibilities for internalizing the externality without government intervention?

c. How can a tax help the town's government ensure that those attending the Unthankful Living concert internalize the externality?

d. If the town's government limited ticket sales to Unthankful Living concerts to 200 tickets, would this be an efficient way to correct for the negative externality?

4. In the past few years Vacationtown has been plagued by mosquitoes. The town council is worried that if they don't do something about the mosquitoes the town's tourism will suffer, but they are reluctant to use any chemical means to get rid of them for the same reason. An environmentally conscious resident argues that if they could increase the number of bat houses in the town, the bats would eat the mosquitoes and the town would eliminate the problem without spraying pesticides. The market for bat houses in Vacationtown is shown in the following figure.

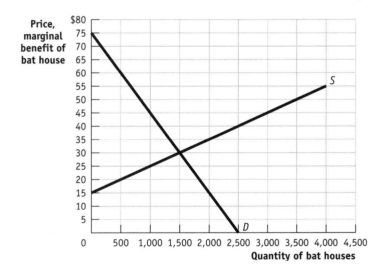

a. What is the market equilibrium price and quantity of bat houses?

b. If the marginal external benefit of bat houses is estimated at $20, draw the marginal social benefit curve of bat houses in the preceding figure. What is the socially optimal quantity and price of bat houses?

c. How can Vacationtown bring about the socially optimal quantity and price of bat houses?

5. Consider the following graph.

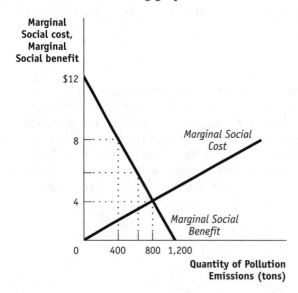

a. With maximum emissions, the total benefit to the polluters (income earned) will be _____.

b. With 800 units of emissions, the total benefit to the polluters (income earned) will be _____, and income foregone will be _____.

c. With 400 units of emissions, the total benefit to the polluters (income earned) will be _____, and income foregone will be _____.

d. With zero emissions, the total benefit to the polluters (income earned) will be

_____, and income foregone will be _____.

e. The optimal tax-rate of pollution is _____. Why?

g. Should the polluters comply with the tax and pollute the optimal amount? Why?

6. Tom likes loud music. Tom's marginal benefit curve of loud music is given in the accompanying figure. His neighbours suffer from noise pollution; the neighbours' marginal cost curve is also given in the accompanying figure.

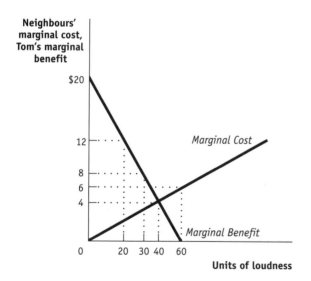

a. According to the Coase theorem, what is the optimal loudness? Why?

b. If the property-right (in terms of playing loud music) belongs to Tom, his neighbours will be willing to pay Tom a price of $_____ per unit of loudness. What will be the net gain to the neighbours after the payments are made to Tom? What will be the net gain to Tom?

c. If the property-right (no noise pollution) belongs to his neighbours, Tom will be willing to pay them a price of $_____per unit of loudness. What will be the net gain to Tom after the payments were made to his neighbours? What will be the net gain to Tom?

*7. This question deals with tradable emission permits. Assume that there are two polluting firms, A and B.

Marginal benefit function of firm A is:

$MB_A = 120 - 3E_A$, where E_A represents units of emissions by firm A.

Marginal benefit function of firm B is:

$MB_B = 400 - 5E_B$, where E_B represents units of emissions by firm B.

See the accompanying graphs, where the vertical line represents marginal benefit and the horizontal line represents units of emissions.

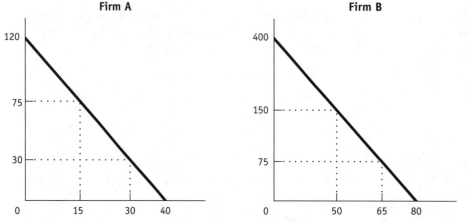

Assume that the firm A is given 30 permits and the firm B is given 50 permits. Each permit allows 1 unit of emission.

Suppose firm A sells 15 permits to firm B at a price of $75 per permit.

What is the net gain to firm A? What is the net gain to firm B? Explain.

Answers to How Well Do You Understand the Chapter

1. costs, benefits, negative, positive

2. scarce, optimal

3. marginal, increases, benefit, willingness to pay, decreases, optimal, equals

4. firms, society, government intervention, zero, zero, high, social cost

5. externalities, inefficient, better off, less

6. Coase, low, pay, internalize, efficient

7. high, high

8. environmental standards, reduction, minimum, tradable permits

9. tax, social cost, social benefit, cost, internalize, efficient, equal, social benefit, optimal, cost, negative, Pigouvian taxes, socially optimal

10. tradable permits, tradable, more, markets, marginal benefit, less, market price, equal, cheaply, too many, incentives

11. desirable, negative, environmental policy, positive

12. social, marginal external, too much, socially optimal

13. Pigouvian taxes, internalized, tradable permits, less-polluting, pollution, goods

14. positive, creation of knowledge, benefits, external benefit, above, low, increase, Pigouvian subsidy

15. less, education

Answers to Multiple-Choice Questions

1. Negative externalities impose costs on individuals who do not participate in the market, and market participants do not consider these costs. Negative externalities lead to markets that produce a quantity greater than the socially optimal quantity, where marginal social cost exceeds marginal social benefit. When negative externalities exist, it is possible to make some people better off without making others worse off. **Answer: D.**

2. Although a hurricane and a tax may adversely affect the grapefruit market and the increase in imports may reduce sales among domestic producers, they are not costs imposed on individuals who are not in the grapefruit market and that the participants ignore. However, if fertilizers used in the grapefruit market are adversely affecting wildlife, that is a negative externality. **Answer: C.**

3. The marginal social cost of pollution is the highest willingness to pay to avoid an additional unit of pollution. **Answer: A.**

4. The marginal social benefit of pollution is not zero. It is the gain to society from an additional unit of pollution. It takes scarce resources to avoid pollution, resources that could be used to produce other goods and services. The marginal social benefit is the savings that firms would enjoy by emitting an additional unit of pollution. **Answer: B.**

5. The Coase theorem states that even in the presence of externalities, markets can reach an efficient solution as long as transaction costs are low. For example, the costs of communication are low because few individuals are involved, legal fees are low, and there are no delays caused by some sides holding out for a better deal. **Answer: B.**

6. When a private solution is reached that corrects a negative externality so that the socially optimal quantity of a good is achieved, we say that the externality has been internalized or that it has been eliminated. It is eliminated in that the costs borne by non-market participants are now considered. **Answer: D.**

7. If the government does not intervene, firms will produce up until the point where the marginal social benefit is zero; that occurs at a quantity of pollution of 1,200 tons. At that quantity, the marginal social cost equals $6,000. **Answer: A.**

8. The socially optimal quantity of pollution occurs where the marginal social benefit of pollution equals the marginal social cost. In the figure, it occurs at a level of pollution of 800 tons. **Answer: B.**

9. An environmental standard that limited pollution to 600 tons would be inefficient because the marginal social benefit of pollution would exceed the marginal social cost. Some individuals could be made better off without making others worse off. There would be too little pollution. **Answer: C.**

10. A Pigouvian tax of $4,000 per ton would raise the marginal cost to polluters from zero to $4,000, and they would emit pollution up to the point where the marginal social benefit equals $4,000 per ton. This coincides with the socially optimal quantity of pollution of 800 tons. **Answer: B.**

11. If the government issues tradable permits equal to the socially optimal quantity of pollution, it will also achieve an efficient solution. Based on the figure provided, the government should provide permits to emit 800 units of pollution. **Answer: C.**

12. When the government imposes an environmental standard requiring firms to keep emissions at or under a certain level, the marginal social benefit of pollution differs among plants. This is an inefficient solution because the same reduction in pollution could be achieved at a lower cost. **Answer: C.**

13. Taxes and tradable permits are preferred over environmental standards because they have the potential to reduce pollution to the socially optimal quantity and keep the marginal social benefit of pollution to all firms equal (there is no cheaper way to reduce pollution). Those who can reduce pollution most cheaply are the ones to do so. These are efficient means to achieve the socially optimal quantity of pollution. **Answer: D.**

14. The socially optimal price and quantity of cattle occur where the marginal social cost curve intersects the demand curve. In the figure provided, the socially optimal price is $800 and the socially optimal quantity is 400 units of cattle. **Answer: D.**

15. The marginal external cost of cattle is the difference between the marginal social cost of cattle and the supply curve. In this example, the external cost of cattle is $300. **Answer: A.**

16. With no government intervention, the equilibrium market price will be $600 per unit of cattle and the equilibrium quantity will be 600 units of cattle. To achieve the socially optimal quantity, the government can either impose a tax equal to the marginal external cost, $300, or issue permits that restrict the units of cattle to 400. **Answer: A.**

17. A government regulator will always choose to target pollution directly if the pollution can be measured. Targeting pollution directly provides incentives for firms to invest in less-polluting production methods and also reduces the disincentive to produce goods that people value. **Answer: C.**

18. When a positive externality exists, the marginal social benefit curve lies above the demand curve. Therefore, the market equilibrium price and quantity are lower than the socially optimal price and quantity. **Answer: A.**

19. The distance between the demand curve and the marginal social benefit curve equals the marginal external benefit. **Answer: D.**

20. The sale of a sports car only yields benefits to the owner; it may have a negative externality in that usually cautious drivers tend to drive faster in sports cars. Similarly, the purchase of a new stereo benefits the owner; it may have a negative externality to those living around the owner if he or she plays the music too loud. On the other hand, innovation in the semiconductor industry usually has technology spillovers that provide an external benefit as knowledge spreads among individuals and firms. **Answer: C.**

21. A Pigouvian subsidy is granted to encourage activities that yield external benefits and is a form of industrial policy. An industrial policy is a policy that supports industries expected to yield positive externalities. **Answer: A.**

22. At the optimal level, the marginal social benefit equals the marginal social cost. **Answer: D.**

23. An emission tax will internalize the external costs of pollution, and it will encourage less-polluting production methods to reduce the tax-costs incurred by the firms. **Answer: B.**

24. Per-unit tax will shift the supply curve. As a result, the market price will increase and output will decrease in the market. **Answer: B.**

25. The Coase theorem favours decentralized market solutions. With zero negotiation costs, the market can arrive at the efficient level of pollution. **Answer: C.**

26. All the conditions stated in the question are conditions of the Coase theorem. **Answer: D.**

27. The intersection of the new marginal social cost curve with the marginal social benefit curve will take place at a lower level of emissions. Therefore, the new level of optimal pollution will be smaller. **Answer: A.**

28. Zero emissions mean zero taxes, but that means maximum loss of total benefits. The higher emissions are, the greater are total tax payments. **Answer: E.**

29. The optimal level of emissions is 800 units. The total tax payments equal $3,200 and the foregone income is $800. **Answer: E.**

30. The optimal level of emissions is 800 units and the total costs are equal to $4,000 ($3,200 as tax-costs plus $800 as foregone income). **Answer: C.**

31. With negative externality, the marginal social cost is greater than the marginal private cost. **Answer: B.**

32. Emission standards don't encourage pollution abatements. **Answer: C.**

33. The optimal level of pollution emissions does not depend on the property-rights, but the direction of payments depend on the property-rights. If the property right belongs to the polluters, the victims will pay polluters, and these payments will be less than the total social costs incurred by the victims. **Answer: B.**

34. The Coase theorem suggests market solutions as opposed to governmental intervention. **Answer: C.**

35. The tradable emission permits encourage reductions in pollution. **Answer: A.**

Answers to Problems and Exercises

1. a. When your neighbor installs a Mosquito Magnet near the property line dividing your property from hers, it will also eliminate mosquitoes on your property. This is a positive externality for you.

   b. When your neighbor turns his or her home into a shelter for all homeless animals in the community, there may be an external benefit for the community as a whole, but it will be a negative externality for you. Presumably the animals will spend at least some time outside, uh, doing what animals do, and this could be quite noisy and smelly.

   c. If the city-owned vacant lot across from your home becomes a community garden, there will be a positive externality. Rather than looking out onto a lot with some weeds and garbage, you will now see vegetables and pretty flowers.

   d. If the city-owned vacant lot becomes a sewer-treatment plant, it will definitely be a negative externality. The smells and big trucks will impose an external cost on you.

2. a. Without government intervention, both The Printed Page and Prints-R-Us will produce VOCs up to the point at which the marginal social benefit of the VOCs equals zero. This occurs when both firms produce 2,000 gallons of VOCs.

   b. If Pelmar imposed an environmental standard that limited each firm to produce a maximum of 800 gallons of VOCs, the marginal social benefit of VOCs to The Printed Page would be $600, while the marginal social benefit to Prints-R-Us is $300. See the following figure. It would be more costly for The Printed Page to reduce its emissions to 800 gallons of VOCs than it would be for Prints-R-Us. The same reduction in pollution would occur at a cheaper cost if Prints-R-Us reduces pollution to a greater extent than does The Printed Page.

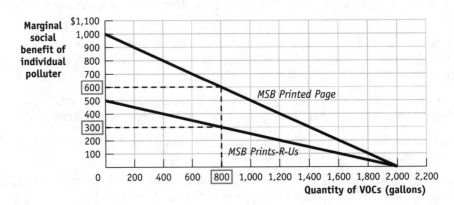

c. The following figure shows that if the government of Pelmar imposed a Pigouvian tax equal to $400, it would reduce VOC emissions to a total of 1,600 gallons and the marginal social benefit of pollution in the two printing firms would be equal. The Printed Page would emit 1,200 gallons of VOCs, while Prints-R-Us would emit 400 gallons of VOCs. This is an efficient way to reduce pollution of VOCs to 1,600 gallons because it could not be done in a cheaper manner.

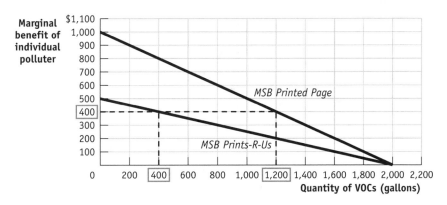

d. Pelmar could also use a tradable permit scheme to reduce emissions to 1,600 gallons of VOCs. If they issued permits that allowed maximum emissions of 1,600 gallons, the two firms would trade those permits until the price of the permit was $400. The Printed Page would then emit 1,200 gallons of VOCs and Prints-R-Us would emit 400 gallons.

3. a. The market will be in equilibrium where demand equals supply; the market equilibrium price is $50 per ticket and the equilibrium quantity is 300 tickets. The marginal external cost of a ticket is $15; it is the amount by which the marginal social cost curve lies above the supply curve. The socially optimal quantity is 250 tickets at a price of $60.

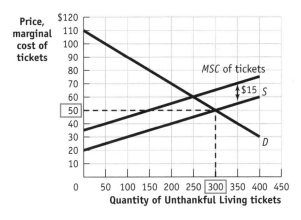

b. It would be difficult to internalize this externality without government intervention. Although the benefit of the concert goes to those who attend the concert and the owner of the nightclub may be able to represent their interests, the costs are shared by all the residents of the town who are affected by the groupies who follow the band. It will be difficult to work out a plan (the transaction costs are high) for internalizing the externality when so many parties are involved.

c. The government can represent the residents' interests by imposing a tax that covers the external cost of the concert. If the government imposed a Pigouvian tax of $15 per ticket, the price of a ticket would rise to $60 and 250 tickets would be sold. This is the socially optimal price and quantity; at this price and output, the marginal social cost of the tickets equals the marginal social benefit of the tickets.

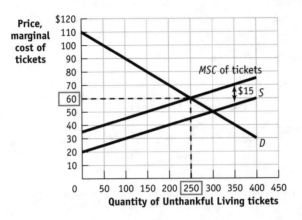

d. If the town's government limited ticket sales to 200 tickets, this would not be an efficient way to correct for the negative externality. At 200 tickets, the price, $70 per ticket, will exceed the marginal social cost of tickets, $55 per ticket; society would be better off if more tickets are available.

4. a. The market equilibrium price is $30 and the equilibrium quantity is 1,500 bat houses.

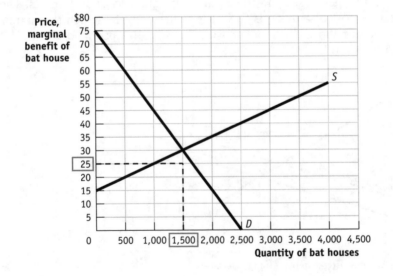

b. The marginal social benefit curve of bat houses is shown in the following figure. The socially optimal quantity and price occurs where the marginal social benefit intersects the supply curve. The socially optimal price is $35 per bat house and the socially optimal quantity is 2,000 bat houses.

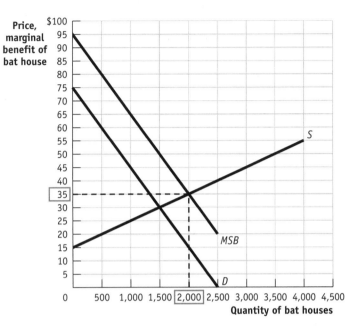

c. Vacationtown can bring about the socially optimal quantity and price of bat houses by granting a Pigouvian subsidy equal to $20, the marginal external benefit.

5. a. Estimate the value of the triangle.
($12)(1,200)(1/2) = $7,200
b. Income earned = ($12 − $4)(800)(1/2) + ($4)($800) = $6,400.
Income foregone = ($4)(400)(1/2) = $800
c. Income earned = ($12 − $8)(400)(1/2) + ($8)(400) = $4,000.
Income foregone = ($8)(800)(1/2) = $3,200
d. Income earned = 0
Income foregone = ($12)(1,200) = $7,200
e. The optimal tax rate is $4.
The optimal tax rate is determined at a point where the *MB* equals the *MC*.
g. If firm complies with the per unit tax of $4, it pays ($4)(800) = $3,200 in taxes and foregoes income of ($4)(400)(1/2) = $800. Therefore, the total cost to the firm is $4,000. The firm's net earning is ($12 − $4)(800)(1/2) = $3,200. Any other level of emission will lead to greater costs. If, for example, the firm emits 1,200 units of emissions, it will pay ($4)(1,200) = $4,800 in taxes and the firm's net earning will be $7,200 − $4,800 = $2,400, which is less than the earnings with 800 units of emissions. If, for example, the firm emits 400 units of emissions, it will pay $1,600 in taxes and it will forego an income of ($8)(800)(1/2) = $3,200. The firm's net earnings will be $7,200 − $1,600 − $3,200 = $2,400, which is less than the taxes paid at 800 units of emissions.

6. a. The optimal loudness is 40 units, where the society's total costs equal the total damage costs to neighbours ($80) plus a foregone benefit ($40) to Tom. Any other units of loudness will lead to greater costs to society.
b. Price = $4 per unit of loudness. Neighbours pay $80 to Tom. With an extra 20 units of loudness (beyond the optimal level of 40 units), the disturbance costs to the neighbours would have been $100. Therefore, the net gain to neighbours is $20. The net gain to Tom is $40.

c. Price = $4 per unit of loudness. Tom will pay $160 to his neighbours. Without music, the neighbours would have saved $80 worth of disturbance costs. Therefore, the net gain to the neighbours is $80. Without 40 units of loudness of music, Tom would have suffered a loss of $480. Therefore, the net gain to Tom after making payments to his neighbours is $320.

7. Gain to firm A = Revenue from selling permits minus loss of earning due to less pollution.

$$= (\$75)(15) - [(\$15)(30) + (\$45)(15)(1/2)] = \$337.50$$

Gain to firm B = Income earned from more pollution (more production of output) minus cost of buying permits.

$$= [(\$75)(15)(1/2) + (\$75)(15)] - (\$75)(15) = \$562.50$$

chapter 20

Public Goods and Common Resources

The criteria of non-excludability and non-rivalry are used to distinguish public goods from private goods. When goods are non-rival and non-excludable, market fails to provide a socially efficient level of those goods and government may intervene to bring about efficiency. We also see why common resources are over-used and how we can maintain efficient stock of common resources.

How Well Do You Understand the Chapter?

Fill in the blanks using the terms below to complete the following statements. Terms may be used more than once. If you find yourself having difficulties, please refer back to the appropriate section in the text.

advertisements	free-rider	more	public good
can	government	no limit	rival
cannot	greater	non-excludable	scarce
common resource	high	non-rival	sum
cost-benefit analysis	higher	non-rival in consumption	too little
efficient	how much		too much
efficiently	internalize	overused	total surplus
equals	less	prevent	unavailable
excludable	low	private	voluntary
firms	marginal benefit	property rights	zero
free ride	marginal cost	public	

1. We can characterize goods by whether they are _____ or non-excludable and whether they are rival or _____ in consumption. A good is excludable if the suppliers of the good can _____ people who do not pay from consuming it. A good is _____ if the suppliers cannot prevent consumption by people who do not pay for it. A good is rival in consumption if the same unit of the good _____ be consumed by more than one person at the same time. A good is _____ in consumption if more than one person can consume the same unit of the good at the same time.

2. We define a good that is both excludable and rival in consumption as a(n) _____ good; a book is an example of a private good. _____ goods are goods that are non-excludable and non-rival in

consumption; a police force that provides public safety is a public good. A common resource is a good that is _____ in consumption but _____; clean air is a common resource. A good that is excludable and non-rival in consumption is defined as an artificially _____ good; electronic books (e-books) are artificially scarce goods. (An e-book is a book that can be downloaded in either print or audio form from the Internet.)

3. Private goods are the only goods that markets can provide _____ in a competitive market. When a good is either _____ or non-excludable, markets will fail to achieve efficiency without government intervention. If a good is _____, rational consumers will be unwilling to pay for it. They will take a(n) _____ on anyone who does pay. Consequently, the market will fail to be efficient in that _____ of this non-excludable good will be produced. If a good is non-rival, like an e-book, then the marginal cost of letting an additional customer download an e-book is _____. If the _____ is zero, the efficient price to the consumer is also zero. Producers will be unwilling to sell an e-book, or any non-rival good, at a price of zero (how would they earn any revenue?), so again the market will suffer from inefficiently _____ consumption.

4. A public good is both non-excludable and _____ in consumption; it is the exact opposite of a private good. A local police force is a(n) _____ in that you cannot exclude anyone from benefiting from a police force (if the police are successful in deterring crime in the area, it benefits all residents, not just those who pay to support the police force), and one person's consumption of a safe community does not preclude another from benefiting from it as well. It will be difficult to get individuals to pay for a police force because of the _____ problem. Since the public safety that a police force provides is _____ in consumption, the efficient price is zero. The market will not be able to provide a(n) _____ quantity of police services.

5. There are some public goods that do not depend on _____ _____ intervention. Some goods may be provided through _____ contributions or activities (such as private donations to support education or volunteer fire departments). Others may be supplied by private individuals or _____; such as broadcast television that is supported by _____. Finally, it may be possible to take some potentially _____ goods and make them excludable; for example, the use of television detection vans to ensure that television watchers in the U.K. are those who have paid their yearly license fee for television. Most of these solutions are imperfect in some way, and so the _____ often provides public goods.

6. When the government provides a public good, it is difficult to determine _____ of the good to provide. Since a public good is _____, the marginal social benefit of a unit of a good is equal to the _____ of the individual marginal benefits that are enjoyed by all consumers of that unit. An individual's _____ is his or her willingness to pay for another unit of the public good supplied. To maximize society's welfare, the government should produce the public good up until the point where the marginal social benefit _____ the marginal social cost. However, it is difficult to measure the marginal social benefit of a public good. In practice, governments engage in _____ when they estimate the social costs and social benefits of providing a public good. Although estimating the social costs are usually easy, it is difficult to estimate social benefit.

7. A(n) _____ is non-excludable and rival in consumption: you can't stop someone from consuming the good, and more consumption by him or her means _____ of the good available for you. Fish are a common resource. There is little cost to fishing (a fishing pole), and in many streams there is _____ to the number of fish one could catch; yet every fish that one person catches is _____ to anyone else. If left to the market, common resources will be _____; individuals ignore the fact that their use depletes the amount of the resource remaining for others. For a common resource, the marginal social cost of the resource is _____ than the individual's marginal cost, and without government intervention the market solution will use _____ of the common resource than is socially optimal.

8. Similar to policies to correct for an externality, taxis and tradable licenses are two ways to induce individuals to _____ the costs they impose on others. Another alternative is to assign _____ to the common resource. Common resources are subject to overuse because nobody owns them. If the resource had an owner, he or she would have an incentive to protect the value of the good and to use it _____ .

9. Artificially scarce goods are excludable but _____ _____ in consumption. An e-book is an artificially scarce good. The marginal cost to society of another person downloading and reading or hearing the book is _____, yet an individual can only download the book for a price. Since the price of an artificially scarce good is _____ than the marginal cost, an inefficiently low quantity of the good is produced and consumed; there is a loss in _____ .

Learning Tips

TIP #1: An easy way to identify whether a good is a private good, public good, common resource, or artificially scarce good is to characterize the good as either rival or nonrival in consumption and as either excludable or nonexcludable.

Starting with a private good and rotating clockwise through the different types of goods identified in Table 20.1 (Figure 20-1 in your text) shows:

- if the good is both rival in consumption and excludable, it is a private good.

- an artificially scarce good is one that is excludable but nonrival in consumption.

- if the good is both nonrival in consumption and nonexcludable, it is a public good.

- a common resource is rival in consumption but nonexcludable.

Table 20.1

	Rival in consumption	Nonrival in consumption
Excludable	Private good	Artificially scarce good
Nonexcludable	Common resource	Public good

TIP #2: Marginal social benefit is the sum of individual marginal benefits. Assume that the marginal cost equals the marginal social cost.

When deciding how much of a public good to supply, the government compares the marginal cost of an additional unit with the marginal social benefit. As long as the marginal social benefit is greater than the marginal cost, the government should supply an additional unit. Only when the marginal cost exceeds the marginal social benefit should the government stop supplying the public good. Since a public good is nonexcludable, one individual's consumption of the good does not affect another's consumption of the good; the marginal social benefit of an additional unit is the sum of the individual marginal benefits of all consumers of the public good.

Table 20.2 and Figure 20.1 show the individual marginal benefits enjoyed by the three consumers of a public good, Bert, Ernie, and Elmo, as well as the marginal cost associated with the good. Since the marginal cost is always greater than the individual's marginal benefit, none of the three will buy the public good.

Table 20.2

Quantity of a public good	Bert's individual marginal benefit	Ernie's individual marginal benefit	Elmo's individual marginal benefit	Marginal cost
0				
	$5.00	$10.00	$4.50	$10.50
1				
	4.00	9.00	4.00	11.50
2				
	3.00	8.00	3.50	12.50
3				
	2.00	7.00	3.00	13.50
4				
	1.00	6.00	2.50	14.50
5				
	0.00	5.00	2.00	15.50
6				
		4.00	1.50	16.50
7				
		3.00	1.00	17.50
8				
		2.00	0.50	18.50
9				
		1.00	0.00	19.50
10				
		0.00		20.50

Figure 20.1

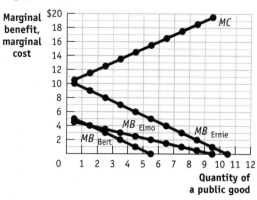

Yet, from society's perspective, they are all better off with the public good provided. Figure 20.2 shows the marginal social benefit curve and the marginal cost curve. The marginal social benefit curve is the vertical sum of the individual marginal benefits at each quantity of output. The efficient quantity of the public good (the quantity at which the marginal social benefit equals the marginal social cost) is 3 units of the public good.

Figure 20.2

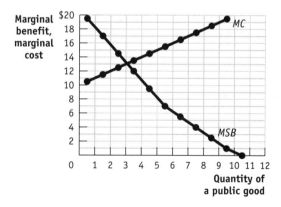

TIP #3: The loss in total surplus in equilibrium for an artificially scarce good is similar to the loss in total surplus associated with a natural monopoly.

An artificially scarce good is one in which the good is nonrival in consumption but excludable. The marginal cost of an additional unit is zero. But since the firm will only produce if price is greater than zero (the firm must earn some revenue), price will always be greater than marginal cost. Also, because the marginal cost is zero, there are no variable costs of production associated with the artificially scarce good; all costs are fixed costs. This means the average total cost curve is always declining. This is similar to a natural monopoly: average total costs for a natural monopoly are declining over the relevant range of production, and therefore marginal cost is always less than average total cost. Since in the long run any monopolist will charge a price greater than or equal to average total cost, we know that for a natural monopolist price must be greater than marginal cost. Whenever price is greater than marginal cost, there is a loss in total surplus and the market equilibrium will not be efficient. Figures 20.3 and 20.4 show the loss in total surplus (shaded triangles) in a market for an artificially scarce good and in a natural monopoly.

Figure 20.3 An Artificially Scarce Good

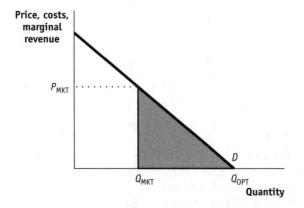

Figure 20.4 A Natural Monopoly

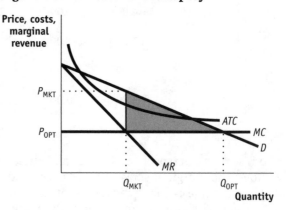

Multiple-Choice Questions

1. If a supplier of a good cannot prevent people who don't pay for the good from consuming it, we say that the good is
a. excludable.
b. nonexcludable.
c. rival in consumption.
d. nonrival in consumption.

2. If a unit of a good cannot be consumed by more than one person at the same time, we say that the good is
a. excludable.
b. nonexcludable.
c. rival in consumption.
d. nonrival in consumption.

3. A good that benefits people whether or not they have paid for it and whose benefits to any one individual do not depend on how many others also benefit is a(n)
a. private good.
b. public good.
c. common resource.
d. artificially scarce good.

4. Which of the following is an example of a public good?
   a. a homeless shelter
   b. a street light
   c. a public tennis court
   d. a city bus

5. A good that many people can consume whether or not they have paid for it but whose consumption by each person reduces the amount available to others is a(n)
   a. private good.
   b. public good.
   c. common resource.
   d. artificially scarce good.

6. Which of the following goods is an artificially scarce good?
   a. downloadable music
   b. clean water
   c. tickets to a sold-out concert
   d. very expensive perfume

7. If a good is nonexcludable, then _____ will exist and there will be _____ production.
   a. zero marginal cost; inefficiently high
   b. zero marginal cost; inefficiently low
   c. the free-rider problem; inefficiently high
   d. the free-rider problem; inefficiently low

8. If a good is nonrival in consumption, then _____ will exist and there will be _____ consumption.
   a. zero marginal cost; inefficiently high
   b. zero marginal cost; inefficiently low
   c. the free-rider problem; inefficiently high
   d. the free-rider problem; inefficiently low

9. In a competitive market, when goods are excludable and also rival in consumption, producers have _____ to produce and the price equals _____.
   a. little incentive; zero
   b. little incentive; marginal cost
   c. incentive; zero
   d. incentive; marginal cost

10. Which of the following may be a solution when a good is both nonexcludable and nonrival in consumption?
   a. voluntary contributions or activities
   b. self-interested individuals or firms
   c. government provision
   d. All of the above.

11. No individual has an incentive to provide the efficient quantity of a public good because
   a. the marginal cost of the good exceeds the individual's marginal benefit.
   b. the marginal cost of the good is less than the individual's marginal benefit.
   c. the socially optimal price of the good would be zero, and there is no chance of making a profit.
   d. both a and c.

12. When determining the optimal level of production for a public good, governments face a problem in that
    a. it is difficult to estimate individual marginal benefit.
    b. it is not possible to observe how much people are willing to pay for an additional unit of the good.
    c. people often overstate the amount of a public good they desire.
    d. all of the above.

13. For public goods, the market will produce an _____ quantity of the good because marginal social benefit _____ marginal private benefit.
    a. inefficiently high; is less than
    b. efficient; equals
    c. inefficiently low; is greater than
    d. efficient; is greater than

14. Public goods, such as national defense, should be provided to the point where the marginal cost of production equals
    a. the maximum price any individual is willing to pay for that unit.
    b. the highest marginal benefit from any individual consumer of the good.
    c. the sum of the individual marginal benefits from all consumers of that unit.
    d. zero (the marginal cost of allowing another individual to consume the good).

15. There are two individuals who will share in the consumption of a public good. Each has a marginal benefit curve identical to the one in the following figure. If the marginal cost of the good is $8, what is the efficient quantity of this good?

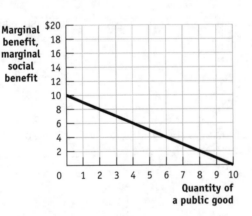

    a. 2 units
    b. 4 units
    c. 6 units
    d. 8 units

16. Common resources and public goods are similar in that both are _____, but they differ in that a common resource is _____, while a public good is not.
    a. rival in consumption; excludable
    b. nonrival in consumption; excludable
    c. excludable; rival in consumption
    d. nonexcludable; rival in consumption

17. The market does not produce a socially efficient quantity of a common resource because the marginal social
a. cost of a common resource exceeds the private marginal cost.
b. benefit of a common resource exceeds the sum of the individuals' private benefit.
c. cost of producing an additional unit is zero.
d. none of the above.

18. Which of the following is a way in which the government can intervene to achieve the socially optimal quantity of a common resource?
a. assign property rights
b. impose a tax on usage
c. grant a limited number of tradable permits to use the good
d. All of the above.

19. Producers of artificially scarce goods are similar to natural monopolists because
a. they charge a price above marginal cost and there is a loss in total surplus.
b. they produce where marginal cost equals marginal benefit and can earn a profit in the long run.
c. average total cost is less than marginal cost.
d. there are no fixed costs of production.

20. Artificially scarce goods are like public goods because they are both
_____, but they differ from public goods in that artificially scarce goods are _____.
a. rival in consumption; nonexcludable
b. nonrival in consumption; excludable
c. excludable; rival in consumption
d. nonexcludable; rival in consumption

Answer questions 21–24 on the basis of the following table which represents the total Benefits of having police officers in a community comprised of individuals *A* and *B*.

Number of police Officers	A's total benefit	B's total benefit
1	$1,000	$800
2	$1,800	$1,200
3	$2,400	$1,400

21. For the 2nd police officer, *A* is willing to pay _____ and *B* is willing to pay _____.
a. $1;800; $1,200
b. $1,400; $1,000
c. $800; $400
d. $2;400; $1,400

22. The community's marginal benefit from having the 3rd police officer is
a. $3,800.
b. $3,000.
c. $800.
d. indeterminate.

23. If the cost of each police officer is $1,100, the community should hire
a. one police officer.
b. two police officers.
c. three police officers.
d. more than three police officers.

24. Refer to the previous table. If the cost of each police officer is $1,100 and if the optimal number of police officers are hired, then the net gain to the community will be
    a. $500.
    b. $700.
    c. $800.
    d. zero.

25. Consider a community with four people. The marginal benefit of the 10th unit of public good is $10 for Vera, $15 for Andrew, $20 for Sarah and $25 for John. If 10 units of public goods are considered as efficient quantity of public goods, then the marginal cost of public good should be
    a. between $10 and $25.
    b. $25.
    c. $70.
    d. higher than $70.

26. The demand curve for a private good is found by the _____ summation of individual's demand curves; the market demand curve for a public good is found by the _____ of the individual's demand curves.
    a. horizontal; horizontal
    b. vertical; vertical
    c. vertical; horizontal
    d. horizontal; vertical

27. Due to the free-rider problem, the quantity of public good supplied will be
    a. equal to the efficient quantity.
    b. less than the efficient quantity.
    c. more than the efficient quantity.
    d. equal to the quantity of the public good demanded.

28. Since people can enjoy the benefits of clean air, whether they pay for it or not, it leads to
    a. rivalry in consumption.
    b. excludability in a market system.
    c. a free-rider problem.
    d. a beggar thy neighbour problem.

29. With common resources (assume that the market supply curve represents marginal private cost),
    a. the marginal social cost lies below the market supply curve.
    b. the marginal social cost lies above the market supply curve.
    c. the market equilibrium is an efficient equilibrium.
    d. the market price is too low.

30. The free-market equilibrium enrolment in educational institutions
    a. will be lower than the socially efficient level.
    b. will be socially efficient.
    c. will be too much.
    d. will exceed the socially optimal level.

Problems and Exercises

Read each question carefully and then write your answers in the space provided or on a separate sheet of paper.

1. For each of the goods and services that the government provides listed below, identify whether it is rival or nonrival in consumption and whether it is excludable or nonexcludable. Is the good a public good, common resource, or artificially scarce good? Without government intervention, how will the market equilibrium quantity compare to the socially efficient quantity?
   a. traffic lights

   b. computer software ready for download from the Internet

   c. fishing

   d. fire protection

2. The government of a town of 10,000 residents is considering establishing an animal control department. The following table shows the individual marginal benefit to each resident of the animal control officers (all residents have the same individual marginal benefit schedule). The marginal cost of each animal control officer is $30,000.

Number of animal control officers	Individual marginal benefit
0	
	$10.50
1	
	9.50
2	
	8.50
3	
	7.50
4	
	6.50
5	
	5.50
6	
	4.50
7	
	3.50
8	
	2.50
9	
	1.50
10	

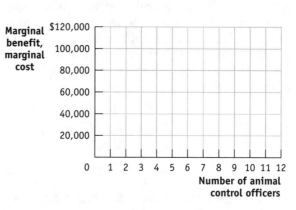

a. Why would the town's government consider the provision of animal control services to be a public good?

b. In the preceding figure, graph the marginal cost and marginal social benefit of each animal control officer. How many animal control officers will the town hire?

c. If the town loses 5,000 residents to the big city, what will be the socially optimal quantity of animal control officers? Draw the new marginal social benefit curve in the preceding figure.

3. A public beach is a common resource; it is nonexcludable but rival in consumption. Individuals have little if any incentive to consider how their actions affect others. For example, anyone can go to the beach, but once they've laid down their towel, no one else can have their spot. On a nice day, it may be crowded and noisy at the beach. Although space and quiet are at a premium, there is nothing to ensure that individuals consider the costs they impose on others by the space they occupy or noise they make. How can the government intervene to get individuals to consider the costs they impose on others?

4. LaSilva Moneymaker writes a daily investment newsletter, with bulletins as needed during the trading day. Her newsletter has one of the highest success rates in picking stocks that will outperform the market. Her subscribers receive their newsletters by e-mail, along with any needed bulletins. The primary cost of producing the newsletter is Ms. Moneymaker's time. The marginal cost of an additional subscriber is zero.

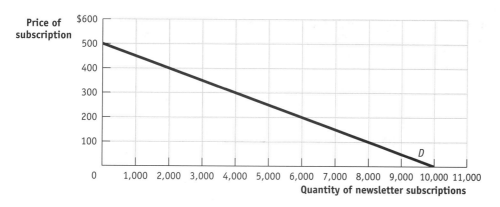

a. If the demand curve for the newsletter subscriptions is as shown in the preceding figure, what is the efficient quantity of subscriptions?

b. If Ms. Moneymaker charges $250 per subscription, shade the loss in total surplus in the preceding figure.

c. How is the market for Ms. Moneymaker's newsletter similar to a natural monopoly?

d. How could the government reduce the inefficiency in this market?

5. The accompanying table represents the total benefits of having police officers in a community comprised of individuals *A* and *B*. The price for each police officer is $1,000.

Number of police officers	*A*'s total benefit	*A*'s marginal benefit	*B*'s total benefit	*B*'s marginal benefit
1	$1,000		$800	
2	1,800		1,200	
3	2,400		1,400	
4	2,800		1,500	

a. Fill in the following columns.

Number of police	Community's total benefits	Total costs	Total net benefits
1			
2			
3			
4			

b. What is the optimal number of police officers? Why?

*6. Consider a common resource where the marginal private costs are zero.

The demand function of common resource follows:
$Q = 100 - P$, where Q stands for the quantity of common resources and P stands for the dollar price for each unit of common resources.
a. What will be the market equilibrium P and Q?

b. If the marginal social cost is constant at $20 for every unit of resources, what will be the socially optimal price and quantity?

*7. There are three individuals in a community with the following marginal benefit functions:

$MB_A = 40 - 4Q$.

$MB_B = 20 - 2Q$.

$MB_C = 5 - 0.5Q$.

Q represents the units of public goods with non-excludability and non-rival characteristics.

a. Find the community's marginal benefit function.

b. If the marginal cost (which equals average total cost in this example) is $13, what will be the optimal Q? What will be the tax-price for each individual?

Answers to How Well Do You Understand the Chapter

1. excludable, non-rival, prevent, non-excludable, cannot, non-rival

2. private, public, rival, non-excludable, scarce

3. efficiently, non-rival in consumption, non-excludable, free ride, too little, zero, marginal cost, low

4. non-rival, public good, free rider, non-rival, efficient

5. government, voluntary, firms, advertisements, public, government

6. how much, non-rival, sum, marginal benefit, equals, cost benefit analysis

7. common resource, less, no limit, unavailable, overused, higher, more

8. internalize, property rights, efficiently

9. non-rival, zero, greater, consumer surplus

Answers to Multiple-Choice Questions

1. If a supplier cannot prevent an individual who doesn't pay for a good from consuming it, we call it a nonexcludable good. **Answer: B.**

2. If the same unit of a good can only be consumed by one person it is rival in consumption. **Answer: C.**

3. If a good benefits individuals whether or not they have paid for it, the good is nonexcludable, and if their benefits do not depend on how many others also benefit, the good is nonrival in consumption. We define such a good as a public good. **Answer: B.**

4. A street light is a public good because it is nonexcludable (people who don't pay for the light still benefit from the light), and it is nonrival (one person's benefit from the light doesn't preclude anyone else from benefiting from the light). A homeless shelter, a public tennis court, and a city bus are all rival in consumption and therefore not public goods. **Answer: B.**

5. If a good benefits individuals whether or not they have paid for it, the good is nonexcludable, and if consumption by one individual precludes consumption by another, the good is rival in consumption. We define such a good as a common resource. **Answer: C.**

6. An artificially scarce good is an excludable good but nonrival in consumption. Downloadable music is the only response that fits both criteria. **Answer: A.**

7. When it is impossible to exclude those who don't pay from enjoying a good or service, no one will want to pay for the good and the free-rider problem will exist. If no one wants to pay for it, too little, if any, of the good will be produced. **Answer: D.**

8. When the consumption of a good by one individual does not preclude the consumption of it by another, the marginal cost of producing the last unit is zero and the efficient price to the consumer is also zero. However, producers will charge a positive price (higher than the efficient price) and the good will suffer from inefficiently low consumption. **Answer: B.**

9. If a good is excludable and rival in consumption, the good must be a private good. Producers in a competitive market will have an incentive to produce and the price of the good will equal the marginal cost of production. **Answer: D.**

10. When a good is both nonexcludable and nonrival in consumption, it is a public good; although it may be provided by voluntary contributions or activities or by self-interested individuals or firms, this is often difficult, so it is most often provided by the government. **Answer: D.**

11. Individuals do not purchase public goods because the marginal cost of the good usually exceeds the individual's marginal benefit. **Answer: A.**

12. When the government provides a public good, it is difficult for the government to estimate the individual marginal benefit and therefore determine the quantity of the good at which the marginal cost equals the marginal social benefit (the sum of individuals' marginal benefits). This is because the government cannot observe how much people are willing to pay for an additional unit of the good and because people often overstate the amount of the public good they desire. **Answer: D.**

13. The market produces too little of a public good because the marginal social benefit is greater than the marginal private benefit. **Answer: C.**

14. The efficient quantity of a public good is the quantity at which the marginal cost of production equals the sum of the individual marginal benefits from all consumers of that unit. Since the good is nonrival in consumption, marginal social benefit is the sum of the individual marginal benefits. **Answer: C.**

15. The efficient quantity of the public good is the point at which the marginal social benefit (the sum of the individual marginal benefits) equals marginal cost. The following figure shows the individual's marginal benefit, marginal social benefit, and marginal cost. The efficient quantity of the good is 6 units. **Answer: C.**

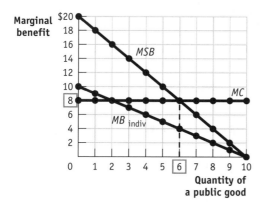

16. Public goods and common resources are nonexcludable goods, but a public good is nonrival in consumption, while a common resource is rival in consumption. **Answer: D.**

17. The market does not produce a socially efficient quantity of a common resource because individuals have no incentive to consider the cost to others of their actions. Marginal social cost exceeds private marginal cost and too much of the common resource is consumed. **Answer: A.**

18. All three (assigning property rights, imposing a tax, and granting a limited number of tradable permits) will raise the marginal cost of consuming the common resource and can reduce consumption to the socially optimal quantity. **Answer: D.**

19. The marginal cost of producing an artificially scarce good is zero; therefore, the efficient price is zero. However, firms charge a positive price, creating a loss in total surplus in the market for the artificially scarce good. This is similar to a natural monopolist that charges a price above marginal cost and also creates a loss in total surplus. **Answer: A.**

20. Artificially scarce goods and public goods are both nonrival in consumption, but artificially scarce goods are excludable, while public goods are not. **Answer: B.**

21. For the 2nd police officer, the marginal benefit for *A* is $800, and the marginal benefit for *B* is $400. The marginal benefit determines (marginal) willingness to pay. **Answer: C.**

22. The community's marginal benefit is equal to the sum of individual's marginal benefit. For the 3rd police officer, the marginal benefit for *A* is $600 and for *B*, $200. Therefore, the society's marginal benefit is $800. **Answer: C.**

23. The optimal number of police officers is found where the community's net total benefit is at a maximum. The community's total net benefit equals $800 = $1,800 + $1,200—(2)($1,100), when two police officers are hired and this is the maximum net benefit. **Answer: B.**

24. The community's total net benefit equals $800 = $1,800 + $1,200 − (2)($1,100), when two police officers are hired. This is the maximum net benefit when two police officers are hired. Any other number of police officers will not maximize the community's net benefit. **Answer: C.**

25. The efficient quantity of the public good is found where the marginal cost equals the sum of the marginal benefit of four individuals. The sum of the marginal benefits is $70. **Answer: C.**

26. The demand curve for a private good is found by the horizontal summation of an individual's demand curves; the demand curve for a public good is found by the vertical summation of an individual's demand curves. **Answer: D.**

27. With the free-rider problem, there will under-provision of public goods. **Answer: B.**

28. Free-ride problems arise when we have non-excludable and non-rival public goods. **Answer: C.**

29. With common resources, the marginal social cost is above the marginal private cost. **Answer: B.**

30. The free-market enrolment will be lower than the socially optimal enrolment. **Answer: A.**

Answers to Problems and Exercises

1. a. A traffic light is a nonexcludable good and nonrival in consumption; it is a public good. The marginal cost of a traffic light exceeds the individual marginal benefit to any one individual. Therefore, the market will provide few if any traffic lights.

b. Computer software that can be downloaded from the Internet is an artificially scarce good; it is an excludable good (downloading can be limited to those who pay) but nonrival in consumption (if one person downloads the software, it does not preclude anyone else from downloading it). The marginal cost of an additional download is zero. Since firms will only sell the software at a positive price, the price of the good will exceed the marginal cost and the equilibrium quantity will be less than the efficient quantity.

c. Fishing is nonexcludable but rival in consumption; it is a common resource. Since no one individual has to consider the costs they impose on others, they will consume to the point where individual marginal cost equals individual marginal benefit. The point at which marginal benefit equals marginal social cost, the socially efficient quantity, is at a lower quantity. Therefore, equilibrium output will be higher than the socially efficient quantity.

d. Fire protection is nonexcludable and nonrival in consumption; it is a public good. Similar to traffic lights, the marginal cost of fire protection exceeds the individual marginal benefit to any one individual. The market will provide little if any fire protection.

2. a. Animal control services are a public good in that the benefits of it are nonexcludable (even those who don't pay for it benefit from it) and nonrival in consumption (one person's benefit does not affect anyone else's benefit).

b. The following table and graph show the marginal social benefit and marginal cost of animal control officers. The marginal social benefit of each animal control officer is 10,000 times that for the individual. Given that the marginal cost per officer is $30,000, the town should employ 8 animal control officers.

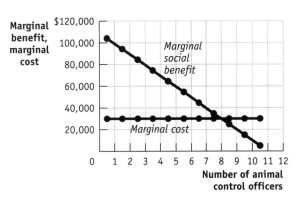

Number of animal control officers	Individual marginal benefit	Marginal social benefit
0		
	$10.50	$105,000
1		
	9.50	95,000
2		
	8.50	85,000
3		
	7.50	75,000
4		
	6.50	65,000
5		
	5.50	55,000
6		
	4.50	45,000
7		
	3.50	35,000
8		
	2.50	25,000
9		
	1.50	15,000
10		

c. If the town loses 5,000 of its residents, the marginal social benefit of each animal control officer will fall by half. The following figure shows the new marginal social benefit per worker. The town should now employ 5 workers because that is the point at which the marginal social benefit equals marginal cost.

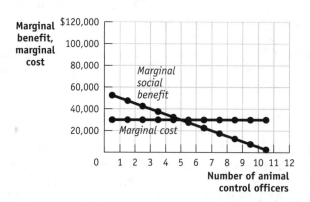

3. There are three ways in which the government can induce individuals to internalize the costs they impose on others: imposing taxes, issuing tradable permits, and assigning property rights. Some beaches attempt to tax individuals by requiring that all beachgoers pay an entry fee. They could also issue a certain number of beach passes each day that are tradable and only allow people with a beach pass to use the beach. They could also sell the beachfront property to a private firm, who will act in its best interest to maximize profit.

4. a. The efficient quantity of newsletter subscriptions is 10,000; it is the point at which the price equals the marginal cost of zero.
b. The loss in total surplus is shaded in the following figure.

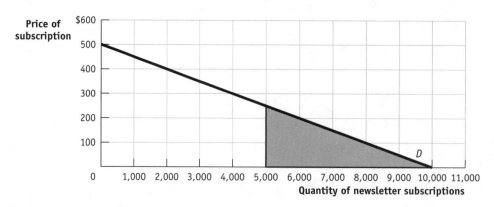

c. The market for Ms. Moneymaker's newsletter is similar to a natural monopoly because Ms. Moneymaker charges a price above marginal cost and there is a loss in total surplus.
d. The government could reduce the inefficiency in the market in the same way that it reduces the inefficiency for a natural monopoly. It could regulate the price that Ms. Moneymaker charges. Although the efficient price is zero, if the government made Ms. Moneymaker give her newsletter away for free, she would probably stop producing the newsletter. The government could, however, make Ms. Moneymaker produce at a price that just equals her average total cost. This would reduce the inefficiency but ensure that Ms. Moneymaker will stay in business.

5. a.

Number of police	Community's total benefits	Total costs	Total net
1	$1,800	$1,000	$800
2	3,000	2,000	1,000
3	3,800	3,000	800
4	4,300	4,000	300

b. The optimal number of police officers is two, where the net benefits of $1,000 are maximum.

6. a. Since the marginal cost is zero, free-market will use where price is zero. The market will use 100 units of resources.

b. With a social marginal cost of $20, we should set price at $20. The socially optimal price is $20 and the quantity is 80.

7. a. When we sum individual's marginal benefits, we get community's marginal benefit function, which is:

$\Sigma MB = 65 - 6.5Q$.

b. Set MC equal ΣMB.

$13 = 65 - 6.5Q$.

$Q = 8$.

The tax-price of each individual equals the marginal benefit.

$P_A = 40 - 4Q = 40 - 4(8) = \$8$.

$P_B = 20 - 2Q = 20 - 2(8) = \$4$.

$P_C = 5 - 0.5Q = 5 - 0.5(8) = \$1$.

chapter 21

Taxes, Social Insurance, and Income Distribution

We evaluate the government's tax policies and spending policies in terms of efficiency and equity. The benefit principle and the ability-to-pay principle are examined. We discuss issues of poverty, income inequality, and income redistribution in Canada.

How Well Do You Understand the Chapter?

Fill in the blanks using the terms below to complete the following statements. Terms may be used more than once. If you find yourself having difficulties, please refer back to the appropriate section in the text.

ability-to-pay	equal	measure	sales
administrative	equity	median voter	skilled
average	government	minimizes	smaller
barrier	greater	more	social insurance
base	higher	much	tax base
benefit(s)	hurt	negative income	taxes
cash	income	non-excludable	trade-off
collect	increasing	percentage	transfer payments
discourage	inequality	poverty line	transfers
distort(s)	in-kind transfers	price elasticities	wedge
efficiency	less	progressive	welfare payments
efficient	low	protect	
employment	marginal	regardless	
English	means	retirement income	

1. When imposing taxes, the government strives to achieve both tax _____ and tax fairness (equity). A tax is efficient when it _____ the costs to the economy of collecting taxes. There is a fundamental _____ between equity and efficiency.

2. We saw in Chapter 6 that an excise tax drives a(n) _____ between the price paid by consumers and that received by producers. Consumers are hurt by the tax in that they pay more for the good; producers are _____ by the tax in that they receive less for the good. The difference between the price paid by the consumers and the price received by the producers is the per-unit tax. How much of the tax burden will be borne by consumers and how much by producers is

503

influenced by the relative _____ of demand and supply. The party (suppliers or demanders) with the lower price elasticity will bear a(n) _____ burden of the tax.

3. Taxes cause deadweight losses because they _____ incentives. Consumers and producers make different decisions when they encounter taxes. The most _____ tax distorts incentives the least (_____ the deadweight loss). Governments also want to design a tax system that minimizes the _____ costs of the tax. The administrative costs are the resources used both to _____ the tax and pay it.

4. Is our tax system fair? Horizontal _____ means similar and identical people should face similar or identical taxes. To ensure that people pay similar or identical taxes and have the same access to public services, the federal _____ in Canada transfers tax revenues from the rich provinces to poor provinces. These _____ are known as equalization payments. Vertical _____ refers to fair tax treatment for people in different circumstances with different incomes. Vertical equity can be looked at from the perspectives of two different conflicting principles: the benefits principle and the _____ principle. The benefits principle asserts that those who _____ from public spending should beat the burden of the tax that pays for that spending. It seems reasonable to expect that individuals should pay in proportion to the _____ they receive from government spending. The ability-to-pay principle asserts that those with _____ ability to pay should pay more of a tax; high-income individuals should pay _____ than low-income individuals.

5. Canada's federal income tax system is based on the _____ principle: families pay a(n) _____ share of their income in taxes as their income rises. Even though government collects most tax revenues from income tax, we also see tax revenues from sales tax, profit tax, property tax, and payroll tax. The Employment Insurance (EI) benefits in Canada are funded by payroll taxes both on workers and employers. The EI system is self-financing, (meaning total contributions by workers and firms are equal to total _____ to unemployed workers).

6. A lump-sum tax is a tax that is _____ for everyone. It does not consider the _____ principle. Although many view a lump-sum tax as unfair, the advantage of such a tax is that it does not _____ incentives.

7. Every tax has two important features: the _____ and the tax structure. The tax base is the _____ or value, such as income or property value, that determines how much _____ an individual pays. A tax may be based on the income of an individual or family from wages and investments (_____ tax), the earnings an employer pays to an employee (payroll tax), the value of goods sold (_____ tax), a firm's profits (profits tax), the value of property (property tax), or an individual's or family's wealth (wealth tax). The tax structure specifies how the tax depends on the tax _____. A proportional tax or flat tax, where a taxpayer pays the same _____ of tax base regardless of the levels of income or wealth, is an example of a tax structure. If a tax represents a higher percentage of income for individuals with high incomes and a lower percentage for those with low incomes, we say that it is a(n) _____ tax. If the tax represents a smaller percentage of income for individuals with high incomes and a _____ percentage for those with low incomes, it is a regressive tax. Although Canada has a mix of progressive taxes (such as the personal income tax) and regressive taxes (such as the payroll tax and the sales tax), the overall system tends to be _____.

8. Most people prefer progressive taxes because they seem fairer, based on the _____ principle. However, the more progressive a tax system, the _____ efficient is the system. The _____ tax rate on income is the ratio of income taxes paid by an individual to his or her income; the _____ tax rate on income is the additional tax an individual pays if his or her income goes up by $1. For a progressive tax system, the marginal tax rate is _____ than the average tax rate at every income level, and this may _____ incentives. Higher marginal income tax rates may _____ individuals from working. Although the ability-to-pay principle supports a(n) _____ tax system, it may lead to efficiency loss.

9. Governments use taxes to raise money to fund spending. Governments spend to provide public goods, to provide _____, and to engage in redistribution.

- Public goods are goods that are _____ and non-rival in consumption, so government provision improves efficiency.

- Social insurance is government spending to _____ people against financial risks, such as expensive medical treatment or unexpected unemployment. This represents _____ of modern government spending.

- Redistribution of income occurs when the government _____ the well-off and uses the money to provide income or services, such as housing and medical care, to the poor. Redistribution of income and social insurance are similar in that they both involve _____ (payments received from the government for which no good or service is produced); but they differ in that social insurance is provided to individuals _____ of income or wealth, whereas social insurance programs that attempt to redistribute income are only available for those with sufficiently _____ income. To qualify for redistribution of income, an individual must pass a(n) _____ test to show that he or she has sufficiently low income. In 2001, the spending on social services and health care accounted for 46% of the total government spending in Canada.

10. In Canada, Statistics Canada uses low-income cut-off (LICO) to determine poverty lines. Families are poor if they live below the _____. The poverty rate is the percentage of people below the poverty line. Currently, about 17% of people in Canada live below the poverty line.

11. There is a close association between poverty and lack of adequate _____; many of the poor are working poor, workers with income at or below the poverty line. Lack of education and of proficiency in _____ can be barriers to higher income. Discrimination is also a formidable _____ to advancement.

12. _____ and in-kind transfers are two important ways to aid the poor in Canada.

- Welfare payments are _____ payments to poor families; the main welfare program in Canada is the Social Assistance Payments.

- In-kind _____ provide the poor with specific goods and services. Medicare coverage, vision care, and housing subsidies are examples of _____.

13. The distribution of income in Canada shows a considerable amount of _____: in 1997 the poorest 20% of families received just over 2% of the total earned income, while the richest 20% received just over 44%. Over the last 15 years, inequality has been _____. Rapid technological change that has increased the demand for _____ or talented workers, growing international trade that allows Canada to import labour-intensive products from countries with relatively _____ wages, and increasing immigration has contributed to the increasing inequality.

14. Those who advocate redistribution of income base it on the _____ principle. Redistribution adds _____ to the welfare of the recipients than it subtracts from the welfare of the taxpayers. There are two main arguments against redistribution. The first is a philosophical argument that redistribution is not a legitimate role of _____. The second is that redistribution discourages productive activity: a highly progressive tax system may discourage high-income families from working additional hours, because high _____

tax rates reduce the reward from working. Programs that aid families with low income may also discourage productive activity in that those families may lose some benefits with higher income.

15. Decisions about _____ and efficiency are determined by elections. Political parties try to convince workers that their policies are in the voters' best interests. In general, voters with lower incomes favour more progressive taxes while higher-income voters prefer _____ progression and less redistribution. In an election where the majority rule, the median voter theorem says that actual policies will most clearly reflect the preferences of the _____. Since we are rarely voting just on issues concerning equity and efficiency of taxes and governments spending, it may be that political parties are not advocating policies that only the _____ prefers.

Learning Tips

TIP #1: An excise tax distorts incentives and is inefficient; the price elasticities of supply and demand determine the incidence of the tax.

Figure 21.1 shows the market for cigarettes and the effect of an excise tax in that market. Without the tax, the cigarette market will be in equilibrium at a price of P_E and a quantity of Q_E. Once the government imposes a tax equal to $P_C - P_P$, the price the consumer will pay will rise to P_C, the price the producer receives will fall to P_P, and only Q_T units are exchanged. The tax distorts the market by changing the behavior of the consumers and producers. At Q_T, consumers are willing to pay more than the cost to the producers of supplying the good in the market. The economy loses the potential gain from the greater production and consumption of the good. The shaded triangle represents the deadweight loss, or excess burden, from the tax.

Figure 21.1

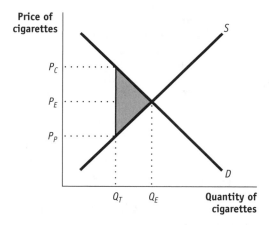

Figures 21.2 and 21.3 show how the burden from the tax varies with the relative price elasticities of demand and supply. The party with the lower price elasticity will bear the greater burden of the tax. In Figure 21.2, the supply curve is relatively more price inelastic than the demand curve. In this case, when the government imposes a tax equal to $P_C - P_P$ in the market, the price the consumer pays rises, but not by as much as the price the producers receive falls. When the supply curve is more price inelastic than the demand curve, the suppliers pay more of the tax.

Figure 21.2

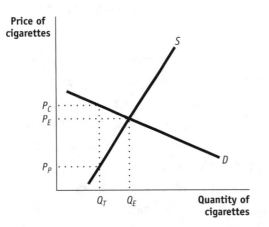

Figure 21.3

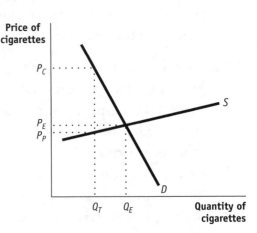

In Figure 21.3, we have the more realistic example of the demand curve being more price inelastic than the supply curve. In this case, when the government imposes an excise tax, the price the consumers pay rises much more than the fall in the price the producers receive. When the demand curve is more price inelastic than the supply curve, the demanders pay more of the tax.

TIP #2: Under a progressive income tax system, the marginal tax rate will be higher than the average tax rate.

Consider the economy of Taxland, where the personal income tax system is progressive: any income less than or equal to $10,000 is not taxed; income greater than $10,000 but less than or equal to $50,000 is taxed at 10%; and income over $50,000 is taxed at 20%. Table 21.1 shows five families with different incomes and their tax bills under this system.

Table 21.1

Family	Income	Tax on income less than or equal to $10,000	Tax on income greater than $10,000 but less than or equal to $50,000	Tax on income greater than $50,000	Tax bill	Marginal tax rate	Average tax rate
Anderson	$7,000	$0	$0	$0	$0	0%	0%
Brown	11,000	0	100	0	100	10	0.9
Chu	45,000	0	3,500	0	3,500	10	7.8
Dahwe	51,000	0	4,000	200	4,200	20	8.2
Estevez	75,000	0	4,000	5,000	9,000	20	12.0

The marginal tax rate is the rate at which any additional income is taxed. The average tax rate is the family's tax bill divided by their income. The Anderson family doesn't pay any income tax; their marginal and average tax rates are both zero. For all other families, as their income rises and their additional income is taxed at higher rates, their marginal tax rate is greater than their average tax rate. Although the Estevez family only pays 12% of its income in taxes, its marginal tax rate is 20 percent. When considering earning additional income, the family will make the decision knowing that whatever additional income they earn, they will only take home 80% of it.

TIP #3: Notches in antipoverty programs can lead to high marginal tax rates for the poor.

A notch is a situation in which earning more actually leaves an individual worse off. Again, let's consider the economy of Taxland. In addition to the progressive tax system, Taxland has policies to redistribute income to the poor: families earning $5,000 or less receive $2,000 in benefits from the government, while families earning more than $5,000 but less than or equal to $10,000 receive $1,000 in benefits from the government. Families earning more than $10,000 receive no government benefits. Table 21.2 shows three families earning less than $10,000 and the effective marginal tax rate on an additional $1,000 in income.

Table 21.2

Family	Before an additional $1,000 in income			After an additional $1,000 in income			Effective marginal tax rate
	Income	Benefits	Effective income	Income	Benefits	Effective income	
Franklin	$2,075	$2,000	$4,075	$3,075	$2,000	$5,075	0%
Garcia	4,050	2,000	6,050	5,050	1,000	6,050	100
Hu	9,500	1,000	10,500	10,500	0	10,500	100

Effective income is the family's income plus the value of benefits received. If the Franklin family has the opportunity to earn an additional $1,000 in income, they should definitely do so. The increase in income will not affect the benefits they receive from the government; the family's effective income rises by the full $1,000. The marginal tax rate on the additional $1,000 is zero. However, if the Garcia family has the opportunity to earn an additional $1,000 in income, they will lose $1,000 in benefits from the government. Earning the additional $1,000 does not change their effective income; it is as though the government taxed the $1,000 in additional income at a rate (effective marginal tax rate) of 100%. Similarly, if the Hu family earns $1,000 more in income, they will lose all supplemental benefits from the government and their effective income will not change. Although they earn $1,000 more, their effective income remains the same. The effective marginal tax rate is 100%.

Multiple-Choice Questions

1. A tax system is efficient when
   a. the "right" people actually bear the burden of taxes.
   b. it minimizes the costs to the economy of tax collection.
   c. it does not create deadweight losses.
   d. all of the above.

2. An excise tax on cigarettes will
   a. increase the price producers receive for cigarettes.
   b. decrease the price consumers pay for cigarettes.
   c. drive a wedge between the price consumers pay and producers receive for cigarettes.
   d. reduce equilibrium output with little if any effect on price.

3. The government imposes an excise tax in a particular market. The smaller the price elasticity of supply in this market,
   a. the more the burden of the tax will fall on producers.
   b. the more the burden of the tax will fall on consumers.
   c. the higher will be the price producers receive for the good.
   d. the higher will be the price consumers pay for the good.

4. According to the benefits principle, taxes should be paid
   a. by everyone since everyone benefits, directly or indirectly, from the public goods that taxes provide.
   b. by those who benefit directly from the public good.
   c. by those with the greater ability to pay.
   d. according to the value of the tax base.

5. A lump-sum tax
   a. does not distort marginal incentives.
   b. is better at promoting efficiency than a value-based tax.
   c. is a regressive tax.
   d. is all of the above.

6. If the government can make the tax system more efficient without creating greater inequity,
   a. it should do so.
   b. it means that the existing tax system is poorly designed.
   c. it indicates that there isn't a trade-off between equity and efficiency.
   d. all of the above.

7. Canada's personal income tax reflects the _____ principle of taxes, while the payroll tax reflects the _____ principle.
   a. benefits; ability-to-pay
   b. ability-to-pay; benefits
   c. ability-to-pay; ability-to-pay
   d. benefits; benefits

8. A flat tax is
   a. the same as a lump-sum tax.
   b. a progressive tax.
   c. a proportional tax.
   d. none of the above.

9. A family's income equals $40,000 and their wealth equals $50,000. If they are subject to a flat wealth tax of 10%, the family's wealth tax bill will equal
   a. $4,000.
   b. $5,000.
   c. $10,000.
   d. $14,000.

10. The government imposes a tax of $500 per household to fund a new public library. This tax is a
    a. regressive tax.
    b. proportional tax.
    c. progressive tax.
    d. flat tax.

11. In Taxland, personal income up to and including $20,000 is not taxed; income greater than $20,000 but less than or equal to $40,000 is taxed at a rate of 10%; and income over $40,000 is taxed at a rate of 25%. A family earning income equal to $64,000 in Taxland will pay _____ in personal taxes.
    a. $6,000
    b. $8,000
    c. $11,250
    d. $16,000

12. In Taxland, personal income up to and including $20,000 is not taxed; income greater than $20,000 but less than or equal to $40,000 is taxed at a rate of 10%; and income over $40,000 is taxed at a rate of 25%. A family earning income equal to $64,000 will pay a marginal tax rate of _____ and an average tax rate of

_____.
   a. 12.5%; 25%
   b. 10%; 15%
   c. 25%; 12.5%
   d. 25%; 25%

13. When a tax system is progressive, the marginal tax rate _____ the average tax rate.
   a. equals
   b. is greater than
   c. is less than
   d. There is no relationship between the marginal and average tax rates under a progressive tax system.

14. In 1998, taxpayers in the highest tax bracket (with income over $100,000) faced
   a. a marginal tax rate of 49%.
   b. a lower marginal tax rate than the marginal tax rate in the recent past.
   c. a less progressive income tax system as compared to the past tax rate.
   d. all of the above.

15. Social insurance programs and programs that attempt to redistribute income are similar in that they both _____, but they differ in that programs to redistribute income _____ and social insurance programs are not.
   a. try to reduce poverty; are means tested
   b. try to reduce poverty; are available to everyone regardless of income
   c. are means tested; are efficient
   d. are means tested; are transfer payments

16. Which of the following represents the largest percentage of federal spending in Canada?
   a. spending for public goods
   b. spending for social insurance programs
   c. spending for programs that redistribute income
   d. spending for defense

17. Which of the following statements is **false?**
   a. Government spending as a percent of GDP has now been brought down to its lowest level in over 20 years.
   b. In 2002, the government spending as a percentage of GDP is about 40.6%.
   c. When we compare government spending as a percent of GDP for the seven 7 largest economies in 2002, Canada stands at the top of the list.
   d. Since 1992, there has been a sharp declining trend in total government spending as a percentage of GDP.

18. The poverty line is adjusted over time to reflect
   a. changes in the tax code.
   b. increases in the cost of living.
   c. increases in the average standard of living.
   d. growing income inequality.

19. Which of the following are associated with living in poverty?
   a. lack of adequate employment
   b. lack of education
   c. lack of proficiency in English
   d. All of the above.

20. The median voter theorem states that in an election by majority rule between two candidates,
   a. actual policies will reflect the preferences of the median voter.
   b. candidates and parties will be reluctant to take extreme positions.
   c. candidates and parties will take similar positions.
   d. all of the above.

21. Which of the following statements is **false** regarding the poverty situation in Canada?
   a. The poverty rate is negatively related to both employment and education.
   b. Aboriginals have the highest poverty rate.
   c. Single parent families account for about 60% of the poor people.
   d. Visible minorities account for about 10% of the poor people.

22. Consider a given upward sloping supply curve. The incidence of excise tax on consumers
   a. decreases as the demand curve becomes more elastic.
   b. decreases as the demand curve becomes less elastic.
   c. is unrelated to elasticities.
   d. falls more on consumers as the demand curve becomes more elastic.

23. Equalization payments in Canada relate to
   a. payments to poverty-stricken people.
   b. transfers of funds from Federal government to have-not provinces.
   c. transfers of funds from Federal government to rich provinces.
   d. social debt service costs for provincial governments.

24. As marginal tax rate goes down,
   a. the tax system becomes less progressive.
   b. the tax system becomes more progressive.
   c. people below the taxable income level gain extra benefits.
   d. the government always collects more tax revenues.

25. With regard to poverty rates in Canada, which of the following statement is **false?**
   a. The overall poverty rate has remained around 15% during the last 20 years.
   b. The poverty rate for children rose during the 1990s.
   c. The poverty rate for the elderly fell during the 1990s.
   d. At present, the incidence of poverty among the elderly is greater than the incidence of poverty among children.

Problems and Exercises

Read each question carefully and then write your answers in the space provided or on a separate sheet of paper.

1. The governments of Wineland and Beerland impose an excise tax on alcohol products to fund some drinking-in-moderation programs and to pay for some of the social costs associated with drinking. The following figures show the supply and demand for alcohol in Wineland and Beerland.

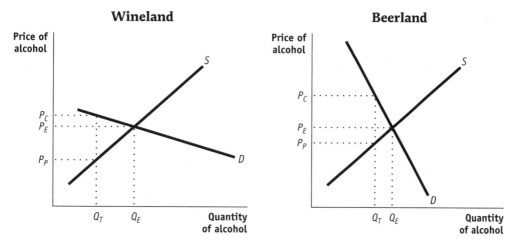

a. How do the demand and supply curves for alcohol compare in the two countries? How is the burden of the tax shared by consumers and producers of alcohol in both countries? Show the deadweight loss from the tax in both countries in the preceding figures.

b. Evaluate the tax in the two countries on the basis of what you know about the exise tax efficiency and equity.

c. Is the tax based on the benefits principle or the ability-to-pay principle?

2. For the following taxes in Ontario, identify (i) the tax base and tax structure, (ii) whether it is based on the ability-to-pay or the benefits principle, (iii) if it is a lump-sum or proportional tax, and (iv) if it is a progressive or regressive tax.

a. In 2004, owners of cars in Toronto paid a property tax of 2% each year on the assessed value of their cars. The tax revenue is used to fund motor vehicle services and to maintain the roads.

b. In 2004, owners of cars in Toronto paid $20 per year to register their cars. The tax revenue is used to fund motor vehicle services and to maintain the roads.

c. In 2004, Ontario taxes gasoline at a rate of 7.5%. The tax revenue is used to fund motor vehicle services and to maintain the roads.

d. In 2004, personal income taxes for taxpayers filing as individuals in Ontario are based on the following table.

Income greater than	Tax rate
$0	1%
750	2
2,250	3
3,750	4
5,250	5
7,000	6

3. The economy of Taxland bases its tax policy on the ability-to-pay principle and has government programs to help redistribute income. The personal income tax system is progressive: income less than or equal to $10,000 is not taxed; income greater than $10,000 but less than or equal to $50,000 is taxed at 20%; and income over $50,000 is taxed at 40%.

a. Given the five families and their incomes in the following table, calculate their marginal and average tax rates by completing the table. What is the relationship between marginal and average tax rates?

Family	Income	Tax on income less than or equal to $10,000	Tax on income greater than $10,000 but less than or equal to $50,000	Tax on income greater than $50,000	Total tax bill	Marginal tax rate	Average tax rate
Johnson	$5,000	___	___	___	___	___	___
Klein	15,000	___	___	___	___	___	___
Lee	49,000	___	___	___	___	___	___
Martinez	51,000	___	___	___	___	___	___
Norton	80,000	___	___	___	___	___	___

b. Benefits in Taxland are also based on income. Families earning $3,300 or less receive $3,000 in benefits; families earning more than $3,300 but less than or equal to $6,600 receive $2,000 in benefits; those earning more than $6,600 but less than $10,000 receive $1,000; and those earning $10,000 or more receive nothing. The following table shows five families earning less than $10,000. Calculate the effective marginal tax rate on an additional $1,500 in income for each family by completing the table. If faced with the opportunity to earn $1,500 in additional income, which families will be more likely to exploit the opportunity?

	Before an additional $1,500 in income			After an additional $1,500 in income			
Family	Income	Benefits	Effective income	Income	Benefits	Effective income	Effective marginal tax rate
Olson	$1,750	___	___	$3,250	___	___	___
Pierce	3,200	___	___	4,700	___	___	___
Quinn	3,500	___	___	5,000	___	___	___
Ruiz	6,500	___	___	8,000	___	___	___
Singh	9,600	___	___	11,100	___	___	___

4. There are ten households in Loppland; the following table shows each household's income.

Household	Income
Abbott	$45,000
Brown	15,000
Cruz	80,000
Denton	500
Ellis	22,500
Feingold	57,000
Gomez	8,000
Hong	7,000
Irwin	35,000
Johnson	120,000

   a. Look at the distribution of income in Loppland by dividing the population into quintiles based on income. How much income—both in dollars and as a share of total Loppland income—do households in the first quintile share? How much do they share in the second, third, fourth, and fifth quintiles? Is there income inequality in Loppland?

   b. Can you explain why income inequality may be less than it appears in Loppland?

5. Consider the progressive tax schedule in the accompanying graph:

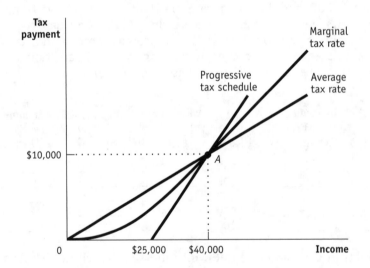

   a. Consider point A. What is the average tax rate? What is the marginal tax rate?

   b. As income tax increases, the average tax rate increases/decreases (circle the correct choice). As income tax increases, the marginal tax rate increases/decreases (circle the correct choice). The marginal tax rate remains higher/lower than the average tax rate (circle the correct choice). The marginal tax rate in Canada increased/decreased (circle the correct choice) in the 1990s as compared to the same rate in the 1970s and the 1980s.

c. The flatter the tax schedule graph, the more/less progressive the tax becomes (circle the correct choice).

6. Use the data based on the fiscal year of 2001. What are the major tax sources in Canada? Which tax source results in the most tax revenue in Canada? Is Canada's tax system progressive or regressive?

7. Describe briefly the poverty situation and the trend in the Canadian poverty rate.

8. Discuss the debate concerning taxes, transfers, and income-distribution in Canada.

Answers to How Well Do You Understand the Chapter

1. efficiency, minimizes, trade-off

2. wedge, hurt, price elasticities, greater

3. distort, efficient, minimizes, administrative, collect

4. equity, government, transfers, equity, ability-to-pay, benefit, benefits, greater, more

5. ability-to-pay, increasing, benefits

6. equal, ability-to-pay, distort

7. tax base, measure, tax, income, sales, base, percentage, progressive, higher, progressive

8. ability-to-pay, less, average, marginal, higher, distort, discourage, progressive

9. social insurance, non-excludable, protect, much, taxes, transfer payments, regardless, low, means

10. poverty line

11. employment, English, barrier

12. welfare, cash, transfers, in-kind transfers

13. inequality, increasing, skilled, low

14. ability-to-pay, more, government, marginal

15. equity, less, median voter, median voter

Answers to Multiple-Choice Questions

1. All taxes are inefficient in that they create deadweight losses. However, we want taxes to be efficient in that they minimize the costs to the economy of collecting the taxes. **Answer: B.**

2. When the government imposes an excise tax on cigarettes, the price the consumers pay for cigarettes rises, while the price the producers receive for selling cigarettes falls. The difference, or wedge, between the price the consumers pay and the price the produces receive equals the per-unit tax. **Answer: C.**

3. When the government imposes an excise tax on a good, both the consumers and producers bear some burden of the tax. The burden will fall more heavily on the party (demander or supplier) who has the smaller price elasticity. The smaller the price elasticity of supply, the more the producers will bear the burden of the tax. **Answer: A.**

4. There are two principles of tax fairness: the benefits principle and the ability-to-pay principle. The benefits principle asserts that those who benefit directly from public spending should bear the burden of the tax that pays for that spending. The ability-to-pay principle asserts that those with greater ability to pay a tax should pay more tax. **Answer: B.**

5. A lump-sum tax does not distort incentives in that everyone pays the same tax. So the tax does not lead individuals to avoid activities because they would increase their taxes; in that way, it promotes efficiency. Lump-sum taxes are regressive because it takes a larger percentage of income for low-income individuals to pay the tax than for high-income individuals. **Answer: D.**

6. If the tax system can be made more efficient without creating greater inequity, the existing system must be poorly designed. Because there isn't a trade-off between efficiency and equity, the government should aim to make the system more efficient. **Answer: D.**

7. The personal income tax reflects the ability-to-pay principle and it is progressive. The payroll tax is based on the benefit principle. **Answer: B.**

8. A flat tax is defined as a proportional tax where all taxpayers pay the same percentage. **Answer: C.**

9. The family will pay 10% of their wealth, or $5,000 in wealth taxes. **Answer: B.**

10. If the government imposes a $500 lump-sum tax to fund a new public library, the tax will represent a higher proportion of income for low-income families than for high-income families. It is a regressive tax. **Answer: A.**

11. A family earning $64,000 will pay no taxes on the first $20,000; it will pay 10% on the $20,000 it earns between $20,000 and $40,000, or $2,000; and it will pay 25% on the $24,000 over $40,000, or $6,000, for a total of $8,000. **Answer: B.**

12. In the question above, we calculated that a family earning $64,000 will pay $8,000 in taxes, for an average tax rate of 12.5 percent (= $8,000/$64,000). The marginal tax rate is the rate at which the last dollar was taxed, or 25%. **Answer: C.**

13. Whenever the tax system is progressive (you pay a higher proportion of your income in taxes as your income rises), the marginal tax rate is greater than the average tax rate. In the question above, under the progressive tax system, we found that the marginal tax rate was higher than the average tax rate. **Answer: B.**

14. All statements are correct. **Answer: D.**

15. Social insurance and redistribution programs are attempts to reduce poverty. Reducing poverty can be viewed as a public good in that most people prefer to live in a society where everyone has enough to eat, decent housing, etc. The programs differ in that social insurance programs are available for everyone, while programs to redistribute income are only available to those whose income is low enough to meet a means test. **Answer: A.**

16. Compared with spending for public goods, programs that redistribute income, and defense spending, spending for social insurance programs is the largest percentage of federal spending in Canada. **Answer: B.**

17. Canada stands somewhere in the middle among the largest economies in the world when we consider government spending as a percent of GDP. **Answer: C.**

18. The poverty line has been adjusted over time to reflect increases in the cost of living but not to reflect increases in the average standard of living. **Answer: B.**

19. Lack of adequate employment, lack of education, and the lack of proficiency in English are all associated with living in poverty. **Answer: D.**

20. The median voter theorem states that in an election by majority rule in which voters decide about policy, the actual policies will reflect the preferences of the median voter. Candidates and parties will be reluctant to take extreme views because they will lose to others with more moderate views. This will lead to candidates and parties taking similar policy positions. **Answer: D.**

21. All of the statements are true *except* the one stating that visible minorities account for 10% of the poor people in Canada; they comprise about 33% of the poor population. **Answer: C.**

22. The incidence of tax on consumers decreases as the demand curve becomes more elastic. **Answer: A.**

23. Equalization payments are transfers of funds from the Federal government to have-not provinces. **Answer: B.**

24. A lower marginal tax rate makes the tax system less progressive. Lower marginal tax rates do not benefit the people living below the level of taxable income. It benefits higher-income groups. **Answer: A.**

25. The incidence of poverty among children is greater than among the elderly. **Answer: D.**

Answers to Problems and Exercises

1. **a.** The supply curves look similar in Wineland and Beerland, but in Wineland the demand curve is relatively more price elastic than supply, and in Beerland the demand curve is relatively less price elastic than supply. In both economies, the consumers' burden is the increase in the price they pay with the tax, or $P_C - P_E$; the producers' burden is the decrease in the price they receive with the tax, or $P_E - P_P$. In Wineland, the consumers pay a smaller portion of the tax than do the producers. In Beerland, the consumers pay a larger portion of the tax than do the producers. The shaded triangles are the deadweight loss in the alcohol markets in Wineland and Beerland.

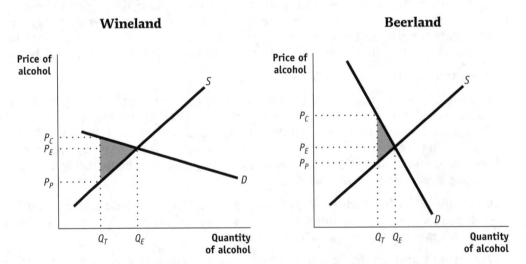

b. In both Beerland and Wineland, there is a loss of efficiency due to the tax. The loss is bigger in Wineland than in Beerland because the demand curve is more price elastic in Wineland. (See Chapter 5 for a more detailed explanation of how the elasticities of the curve affect the size of the deadweight loss.) To evaluate the tax on the basis of equity, we need to use the two principles of fairness in taxation: the benefits principle and the ability-to-pay principle. In terms of benefits, the tax does seem fair because only individuals who consume alcohol pay the tax and they will be the main beneficiary of the alcohol awareness and drinking-in-moderation programs. From the ability-to-pay perspective, the tax does not do as well in terms of equity. Since the excise tax is a per-unit tax, it is a regressive tax; low-income individuals will pay a higher percentage of their income in the tax than will high-income individuals.

c. The tax is based on the benefits principle because, again, only individuals who consume alcohol pay the tax, and they will be the main beneficiaries of the alcohol awareness and drinking-in-moderation programs.

2. a. (i) The base is the value of cars in Toronto the structure is that taxpayers pay 2% of the value of their cars. (ii) It is based on both the benefits and the ability-to-pay principles; the tax revenue helps motor vehicle services and maintains the roads, and those who have more expensive cars pay more than those with less expensive cars. (iii) It is a proportional tax; it's 2% of the value of each car. (iv) It's not easy to tell whether it is progressive or regressive. Inasmuch as the value of a car reflects the value of the owner's income, it may be neither progressive nor regressive. However, if more high-income people have cars with relatively low value, the tax may be regressive.

b. (i) The base is the number of cars in Toronto; the structure is that each car owner pays $20. (ii) It is based on the benefits principle; again because the revenue from the $20 helps fund motor vehicle services and maintain the roads. (iii) It is a lump-sum tax; everyone pays $20. (iv) It is regressive; it takes a larger percentage of a low-income individual's income to pay the tax.

c. (i) The base is the total amount of gasoline sold in Ontario; the state collects 7.5% of the cost of each gallon of gasoline sold. (ii) It is based on the benefits principle; it's another source of revenue to fund motor vehicle services and maintain the roads. (iii) It is a proportional tax; taxpayers pay the same proportion of the cost of each gallon of gasoline they buy. (iv) It is a regressive tax in that gasoline purchases represent a larger proportion of low-income individuals' earnings, and therefore the tax will represent a larger proportion of their income as well.

d. (i) The base is total income in Ontario; the structure is that individuals earning less than or equal to $750 pay 1% of their income in taxes; individuals earning more than $750 but less than or equal to $2,250 pay 2%; individuals earning more than $2,250 but less than or equal to $3,750 pay 3%; individuals earning more than $3,750 but less than or equal to $5,250 pay 4%; individuals earning more than $5,250 but less than or equal to $7,000 pay 5%; and individuals earning more than $7,000 pay 6%. (ii) The tax is based on the ability-to-pay principle; the higher an individual's income the greater the percentage of income an individual pays in taxes. (iii) It is a proportional tax; individuals pay a percent of their income in taxes. (iv) It is a progressive tax; the higher an individual's income, the higher the proportion of his or her income paid in taxes.

3. a. The following table shows the taxes each family will pay and shows the marginal and average tax rates. The marginal tax rate is the rate at which the last dollar is taxed, while the average tax rate is the family's total tax bill divided by income. With the exception of families who pay no taxes, the marginal tax rate is always higher than the average tax rate.

Family	Income	Tax on income less than or equal to $10,000	Tax on income greater than $10,000 but less than $50,000	Tax on income greater than $50,000	Total tax bill	Marginal tax rate	Average tax rate
Johnson	$5,000	$0	$0	$0	$0	0%	0.0%
Klein	15,000	0	1,000	0	1,000	20	6.7
Lee	49,000	0	7,800	0	7,800	20	15.9
Martinez	51,000	0	8,000	400	8,400	40	16.5
Norton	80,000	0	8,000	12,000	20,000	40	25.0

b. The following table shows the effective incomes (earned income plus benefits) for five families earning less than $10,000 and how their incomes will change if they earn an additional $1,500. For the Olson and Quinn families, their effective incomes increase by $1,500 when they earn $1,500 more; their effective marginal tax rate is zero. However, when the Pierce, Ruiz, and Singh families earn $1,500 more, their effective incomes only rise by $500. By earning $1,500 in income, they lost $1,000 in benefits; the effective tax rate is 67% (= $1,000/$1,500). The Olson and Quinn families will be more likely to exploit an opportunity to earn $1,500 more because they will have $1,500 more to spend. However, the Pierce, Ruiz, and Singh families will only see their potential spending rise by $500 when working for $1,500; they are more likely than the Olson and Quinn families to ignore the opportunity for more earned income.

	Before an additional $1,500 in income			After an additional $1,500 in income			
Family	Income	Benefits	Effective income	Income	Benefits	Effective income	Effective marginal tax rate
Olson	$1,750	$3,000	$4,750	$3,250	$3,000	$6,250	0%
Pierce	3,200	3,000	6,200	4,700	2,000	6,700	67
Quinn	3,500	2,000	5,500	5,000	2,000	7,000	0
Ruiz	6,500	2,000	8,500	8,000	1,000	9,000	67
Singh	9,600	1,000	10,600	11,100	0	11,100	67

4. a. To look at the distribution of income in Loppland by quintiles, we first must order the households in terms of income; the following table shows the families ordered by income.

Household	Income
Denton	$500
Hong	7,000
Gomez	8,000
Brown	15,000
Ellis	22,500
Irwin	35,000
Abbott	45,000
Feingold	57,000
Cruz	80,000
Johnson	120,000

Since there are ten families, each quintile consists of two families. The following table shows the income going to each quintile (the sum of the incomes for the two families in the quintile) and what that income represents as a share of total income. There does seem to be income inequality in Loppland. The six families (60% of all families) earning the least income share only 23% of total income, while the four families (40% of all families) earning the highest income share 77% of total income.

Quintile	Income	Share of total income
1	$7,500	2%
2	23,000	6
3	57,500	15
4	102,000	26
5	200,000	51
Total Income	$390,000	100%

b. Income inequality may be less than it appears in Loppland because the incomes of families fluctuate over time. It may be that those at the bottom are having an unusually bad year, while those at the top are having an unusually good year. If we looked at average annual income over a long period of time, we would expect to see less inequality. Also, the distribution of income may reflect the age distribution of the population; perhaps the 60% of the population earning the least income are those who are either very young or very old.

5. a. Average tax rate = ($10,000/$40,000) = ¼.
Marginal tax rate = ($10,000/$15,000) = 2/3.
b. increases, increases, higher, decreased
c. less progressive

6. About 32% of the total tax revenues are from income taxes, 20% from sales taxes, 10% from corporate income taxes and property taxes, and 7.5% from payroll taxes. Income taxes are progressive; those with low-incomes receive tax-exemptions and those with higher incomes are taxed at an increased marginal rate. Sales taxes are regressive. Corporate taxes and property taxes are progressive, while payroll taxes are proportional. Federal and provincial taxes (with the exception of the sales tax) are generally progressive, while local municipal taxes are generally regressive.

7. The "low-income-cut-off" (LICO) determines the poverty line in Canada. About 17% people in Canada live below the poverty line. Aboriginals and visible minorities account for most of the poverty-stricken people in Canada. Single-parent families have the highest incidence of poverty. Children in these families live below the poverty line. Children account for 32% of total population; they account for 40% of the poor population. The likelihood of living in poverty is higher if one lacks education, if one lacks employment, if one is a single-parent, and if one is an Aboriginal or a member of a visible minority group.

The poverty rate tends to respond to economic cycles. The poverty rate reached a 20-year low during the economic boom of 1989. The over-all poverty rate has remained the same in Canada over the last 20 years, but there have been substantial changes in its composition. The poverty rate of the elderly has been declining, while the poverty rate for single-parent families and for children has been increasing in the recent past.

8. The majority of the people believe that the poor should pay less taxes and the rich should pay relatively more taxes and that the poor should get some social assistance. The debates raise the following questions: is our income tax system too progressive, are we giving too much social assistance, and are we promoting disincentives to work?

Income distribution in Canada shows considerable inequality. The poorest 20% of the families received 2% of the total market income. In recent years, income-inequality has increased. Income redistribution will reduce income inequality. A high degree of income inequality leads to more crimes, greater social disharmony, and less economic wellbeing. More income equity promotes social cohesion and trust, which have economic payoffs for efficiency and growth.

Those who argue against redistribution believe that the redistributing income is not a legitimate role of government and that its role should be restricted to dealing with issues of law and order. They argue that there is a considerable efficiency loss when we pursue equity goals with respect to taxes and transfers.

## chapter 22

Technology, Information Goods, and Network Externalities

Information goods and network externalities pose unique economic problems. We can deal with information goods the same way we have dealt with natural monopoly in Chapter 14 and artificially scarce goods in Chapter 20. But free-rider or free-copying problems t may deter producers from producing any information goods. Patent laws and temporary monopoly rights will counter the problem of excessive uses of information at zero prices (by consumers), and they will allow monopolists to retrieve their fixed costs and gain some profits. We also discuss the network externalities and see how network size, critical mass, and tipping are related to network externalities. We also look at the role of competition policy in Canada.

How Well Do You Understand the Chapter?

Fill in the blanks using the terms below to complete the following statements. Terms may be used more than once. If you find yourself having difficulties, please refer back to the appropriate section in the text.

below	free	missed	software
benefit	gain	network externalities	standard
Betamax	government	network externality	technology
brand-name	greater	operating systems	temporary
Competition Policy	high	overturned	threshold network size
conditional	ideas	patent(s)	tip
copyrights	increase	positive feedback	tipping
costs(s)	increasing	property rights	top row
creators	inefficiency	QWERTY	traditional downtown
critical mass	information	rapidly	value
decrease	lose	regardless	value information
discouraging	low	reverse engineering	zero
erode	lower	sales network	
few	many	set standards	
first mover	Microsoft	size	

1. Information goods are products whose _____ comes not from their physical characteristics but from the _____ they embody. Examples of _____ goods include computer software, recorded music, and pharmaceuticals. Information goods have been gaining _____ importance and they are creating new challenges in a market economy. The fixed costs associated with producing information goods are very _____, similar to those facing natural monopolies, but the marginal cost (MC) is very _____ or zero. Since the MC is low, the efficient price is also low.

2. The problem of _____ regarding information goods comes about in a unique way. The monopoly output occurs where the monopolist's marginal _____ equals its marginal revenue (MR) and the monopoly price is a positive price at the profit-maximizing monopoly output. But from the viewpoint of consumers, the efficient market price (P) is where P = MC = zero. Since the copying of the information good costs nothing, consumers will download the good and use it up to a point where the price (P) is _____. If the consumer were able to obtain the good for free (where price is _____), the consumer would _____ a consumer surplus, and the producer surplus would fall by much less than the change in consumer surplus. However, if the firm expects that many consumers will only want the good for _____ or at a low price, it will not produce the good at all. Both producers and consumers _____ if the good is not produced. Economists generally agree that a(n) _____ monopoly may be necessary to assure that information goods are produced.

3. For firms to produce information goods, they must be assured that they will have some kind of _____ to the information that the goods embody. Patents and _____ are two ways that the government gives property rights to the creators of knowledge. _____ give inventors the sole right to make, use, or sell their inventions for a period of time, usually between 16 and 20 years. Copyrights give the _____ of literary or artistic works a similar monopoly but for a longer period. It is sometimes difficult to distinguish whether a(n) _____ good is an invention or a literary work; software, for example, has elements of both. Both patents and copyrights grant _____ property rights that are hopefully long enough to assure the good is produced but short enough that the _____ in the market does not persist indefinitely. The system is not perfect, however, and may lead to some _____ opportunities.

4. In some cases, innovations are hard to _____. The innovation may not be a discrete, patentable invention as much as a combination of existing _____. Wal-Mart is an example of an innovator without anything to _____. Wal-Mart became the nation's number-one retailer partly by building large stores away from the _____ and using information technology to manage inventories efficiently, which gave it a(n) _____ advantage over its competitors. Even with a patent or copyright, it may be possible for competitors to copy the innovation using _____ (taking a patented product apart to see how it is made and then developing something similar to avoid violating the patent).

5. When an innovation cannot be patented or is subject to reverse engineering, there are still advantages to being the _____ in an industry. The firm's head start may give it a technological advantage or it may help it establish _____ recognition. An example of a successful first mover without any patent or copyright protection is Amazon.com; its success is based on advantages of _____ and name recognition. These advantages may give the firm a(n) _____ monopoly. However, such monopoly positions tend to _____ over time, as others duplicate the innovation and even innovate further to make the original good obsolete.

6. A good is subject to a(n) _____ when the good's value to an individual is greater when a large number of other people also use that good. Examples of network externalities include many communications goods, such as telegraphs, telephones, fax machines, and e-mail accounts. The marginal _____ of these goods to any one individual depends on the number of others using it. Transportation services also generate _____; a flight between two airports becomes more valuable if one or both of the airports is a hub with connections to other places. The Windows operating system is a case of an indirect _____. Although you can use a computer for many things that do not directly depend on other people using the same operating system (word processing, spreadsheet calculations, and generating e-mail), it is helpful to do those tasks in such a way as to make them usable on other computers. Also, Windows is so widely used that most _____ is written to run on that system.

7. Strong network externalities are associated with _____ in which success or failure is self-reinforcing. If _____ people buy the good, others are also likely to buy it. However, if _____ people buy the good, others will be less likely to buy it. Goods with network externalities often need to reach some level of _____ before the industry can take off. We can distinguish between unconditional and _____ buyers of a good with network externalities. The unconditional buyer will buy the good _____ of how many others buy the good, but the conditional buyer will only buy the good if enough other people have it.

8. The smallest number of current members of the network that leads a conditional buyer to join the network of users is called the _____. The threshold network size may differ for different _____ buyers, but as long as the threshold network size is similar for many such buyers, the analysis does not change. Once the number of unconditional users reaches a(n) _____, a number large enough to exceed the threshold network size for conditional buyers, the market begins to grow _____.

9. Improvements in technology may lead to both a(n) _____ in the number of unconditional buyers and a(n) _____ in the threshold network size for conditional buyers. In this way, improvements in _____ may lead to a new critical mass. Conditional buyers are willing to purchase the good because the number of unconditional buyers is _____ than the threshold size.

10. _____ occurs when positive feedback due to network externalities causes consumers to switch to one of two competing goods or technologies. Often, a small initial advantage of one good over another good may _____ consumers in favour of a good or technology. An example of tipping occurred when VHS overtook _____ as the dominant form of videocassette recorders.

11. Network externalities lead firms to emphasize building their _____ even if it is at the expense of short-term profits (you need to lose money to make money). It is important for the good or industry to reach _____. This explains why you sometimes see new high-tech products sell at a price _____ their production costs.

12. Although information goods present new challenges for government policy makers, the government can still use _____ and set standards to increase efficiency in markets with information goods.

13. Monopolies occur in industries with high fixed costs but low marginal costs, which is the case for information goods, and are necessary to assure that potential producers will recoup the high fixed _____ of production. Competition policies do not forbid monopolies. Rather, they constraint "monopolization," or take actions designed to create a monopoly or reduce competition. Governments can also increase efficiency when they _____ for an industry that induce competing goods to operate as a single network. A(n) _____ is a set of rules for operation that induces competing goods to operate as a single network. In some cases, industries have set the standards without any _____ intervention; companies agreed on the standard for digital video discs without any government action. However, it is important that the standard chosen is the one that leads to _____ costs or superior quality. When an industry gets stuck using an inferior standard, we say that it suffers from the _____ problem. The QWERTY problem refers to the _____ on a standard computer keyboard; it was chosen because it prevented keys on a mechanical typewriter from jamming, but it is not clear that it is the best layout for a computer keyboard.

14. The most important recent case of monopoly involved antitrust charges against

_____. The U.S. government claimed that Microsoft had used its

position in _____ to give its products an advantage over competitors

in other markets. The government argued that unnecessary monopolies were being

created and Microsoft was _____ innovation. The original ruling

found Microsoft in violation of antitrust regulation and ordered it split into an

operating-system company and a company selling the firm's other products.

However, on appeal this judgment was _____. The government and

Microsoft agreed to a settlement in which the company agreed to provide other

companies with the _____ to develop products that would interact

seamlessly with Microsoft's software, removing Microsoft's special advantage.

Learning Tips

TIP #1: Firms selling information goods are similar to natural monopolies in that they face high fixed costs of production but low marginal costs.

A natural monopolist faces decreasing average total costs over the relevant range of output due to high fixed costs of production; as output increases, average total costs fall. In Figure 22.1 we see a natural monopolist: its demand curve intersects the average total cost curve while the average total cost curve is declining. Since the average total cost curve is declining, we know that marginal cost is less than average total cost. (In Figure 22.1, marginal costs are constant.) A natural monopolist would produce at a price of P_M and equilibrium output would equal Q_M; it would earn a profit equal to the rectangle with diagonal lines. If this market were perfectly competitive, the equilibrium price and quantity in the market would be P_C and Q_C; the perfectly competitive solution is efficient because that is where price equals marginal cost. The excess burden, or deadweight loss, associated with the monopoly is the shaded triangle in Figure 22.1.

Figure 22.1

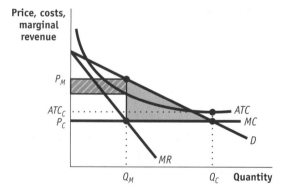

Figure 22.2 is very similar to Figure 22.1 but it shows the market for an information good. The producer of the information good will set a price of P_I and sell a quantity equal to Q_I. The firm will earn a profit equal to the rectangle with diagonal lines, and the shaded triangle shows the loss of total surplus (deadweight loss) associated with production at Q_I units of output. The efficient price is P_C, where the producer would sell Q_C units of output; however, the firm will not choose to produce Q_C units of output at a price of P_C because it would be earning a loss. If a potential producer of an information good believed that it would have to sell the good at a price of P_C, it would anticipate a loss and choose not to produce the good. Given the opportunity for other producers to copy the innovation or technology, producers of information goods must have secure property rights or they will not undertake the high fixed costs necessary to bring the good to market.

Figure 22.2

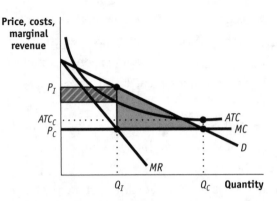

TIP #2: Technological innovations can help producers of goods with network externalities to reach critical mass.

When a good has network externalities, some buyers may be reluctant to purchase the good until they're assured that the market is large enough to make it worth their while. The book explains how network externalities played a role in the explosion of fax machines and e-mail. Let's consider the market for a superior new computer operating system, Doors, to replace Microsoft's Windows. There would be some unconditional buyers of the system, serious computer users looking for the advantages associated with this new system. Potentially there could be many conditional buyers who are also eager for a better system but who are reluctant to change until they are sure that there will be enough support and software for Doors. It may be that the potential market for Doors is for 10 million copies. There are 1 million unconditional buyers, but the conditional buyers have a threshold network size of 4 million users. With this number of unconditional buyers and threshold network size, the network fails to reach its critical mass and will not take off. However, if there are some innovations that attract more unconditional buyers and lower the threshold size for the conditional buyers, it may be that the number of unconditional buyers will exceed the threshold size for enough conditional buyers and that critical mass will be achieved, and the market will take off.

Multiple-Choice Questions

1. An information good is one
   a. that provides information.
   b. that requires information to use.
   c. whose value comes from the information it contains.
   d. both a and b.

2. An information good is similar to a good produced by a natural monopolist in that
   a. both have high fixed costs of production.
   b. both have low marginal costs of production.
   c. the efficient price equals marginal cost.
   d. all of the above.

3. Which of the following goods provides the best example of an information good?
   a. a map of the world
   b. a new video game
   c. a piece of cake from an award-winning recipe
   d. an economics textbook

4. The average total cost curve for an information good
   a. declines over the relative range of output.
   b. falls only at low levels of output and rises thereafter.
   c. always lies above the demand curve.
   d. reflects high average variable costs of production.

5. If a potential producer of an information good faces the demand and cost curves shown in the following figure and believes that the price of the information good will equal the marginal cost of producing it, the producer

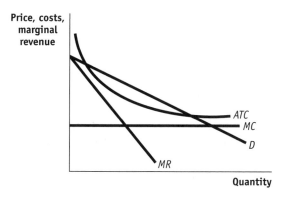

   a. will not produce the good.
   b. will break even.
   c. will earn a monopoly profit.
   d. will earn a loss but continue to produce.

Answer the next three questions based on the following figure. The figure shows the demand and marginal revenue curves for a new software package. The total fixed costs of production are $1 million per year and the marginal cost of production is zero.

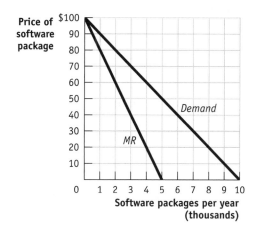

6. If a software company is considering producing this new software package and can be assured of a temporary monopoly position, it will charge a price of _____ for _____ thousand packages of the software.
   a. $90; 1
   b. $70; 3
   c. $50; 5
   d. $0; 10

7. For how long should the software company have a monopoly on this software in order to recoup its fixed costs?
   a. 2 years
   b. 4 years
   c. 10 years
   d. 20 years

8. Total surplus will be maximized when the price equals _____ and quantity equals _____ thousand software packages.
   a. $90; 1
   b. $70; 3
   c. $50; 5
   d. $0; 10

9. Economists generally agree that
   a. the government should intervene to be sure that producers of information goods do not have a monopoly in the market.
   b. monopolies are detrimental to society and should be avoided at all costs.
   c. the government should guarantee temporary property rights to producers of information goods.
   d. the government should guarantee permanent property rights to producers of information goods.

10. A copyright
   a. lasts for 16 to 20 years.
   b. lasts for the life of the creator.
   c. is given to creators of literary or artistic works.
   d. grants the creator a sole right to make, use, or sell the invention for a temporary period of time.

11. A first mover refers to
   a. the firm that can sell (move) the good the fastest.
   b. the firm that introduces the good or innovation first.
   c. the firm that introduces a good and then sells the rights to the good for a profit.
   d. none of the above.

12. Reverse engineering
   a. may make it possible for competitors to "copy" a patented product.
   b. may destroy a firm's monopoly on an information good.
   c. occurs when a firm figures out how an information good works and how it is made.
   d. is all of the above.

13. If a good's value is related to how many people use the good, we say the good is subject to
   a. commonalities.
   b. network externalities.
   c. joint profits.
   d. peer pressure.

14. Which of the following is an example of a good with network externalities?
   a. fax machines
   b. cell phones
   c. airplane routes
   d. All of the above.

15. A new good is subject to network externalities. There are 10,000 unconditional buyers and 200,000 conditional buyers. If the threshold network size is 20,000 users,
   a. the good will take off.
   b. technological innovations are needed for the good to take off.
   d. critical mass is 200,000 buyers.
   d. both a and c.

16. With regard to information goods, tipping occurs when
   a. a firm leaks information that it will be introducing a new information good.
   b. one firm offers another firm money for the details on its innovation or invention.
   c. one firm leaks detrimental information about another to the press.
   d. positive feedback due to network externalities causes consumers to switch to one of two competing goods or technologies.

17. Goods subject to network externalities
   a. will always sell for the profit-maximizing price.
   b. will never earn a profit.
   c. may initially emphasize sales, even at the expense of profits.
   d. are always sold on the Internet.

18. Antitrust policies outlaw
   a. monopolies.
   b. monopolization.
   c. actions designed to restrict competition.
   d. both b and c.

19. Industry standards
   a. are problems associated with information goods.
   b. help create a single network among competing goods.
   c. require government intervention.
   d. always result in the adoption of a superior standard.

20. The government brought an antitrust suit against Microsoft because
   a. it had a monopoly on the Windows operating system.
   b. it had a monopoly in word-processing and spreadsheet software.
   c. it was beginning to produce computer hardware.
   d. it was using its monopoly position in operating systems to give its other products an advantage over competitors.

21. The marginal cost of information goods is
   a. large.
   b. positive.
   c. negative.
   d. zero.

22. The total fixed cost of information goods is
   a. large.
   b. positive and it affects the optimal output decisions.
   c. negative.
   d. zero.

23. The efficient price of information good is
   a. large.
   b. positive and it affects the optimal output decisions.
   c. negative.
   d. zero.

24. If an efficient price is in operation in a market for a given information good, the producer of the information good will produce a
   a. large amount.
   b. positive amount.
   c. negative amount.
   d. zero amount.

25. Which of the following statements is **false?**
   a. Tipping occurs when positive feedback due to network externalities causes consumers to switch to one of the competing technologies.
   b. More buyers mean less negative externalities.
   c. Transportation services generate network externalities.
   d. Patents and copyrights are needed to ensure sustenance of information goods.

Problems and Exercises

Read each question carefully and then write your answers in the space provided or on a separate sheet of paper.

1. The following figure shows the demand, marginal revenue, marginal cost, and average total cost curves facing a potential producer of an information good.

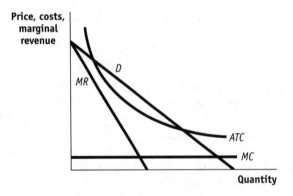

a. What price and output will the producer of the information good choose if he or she wants to maximize profit? How much profit will the producer earn? What are the advantages and disadvantages to society of this price and output? Show your answers on the preceding figure.

b. If the government offered the firm a patent on its good if it would produce at the efficient price (where price equals marginal cost), would the firm agree? Why or why not? How much would the firm produce? How much profit would the producer earn? What are the advantages and disadvantages to society of this price and output? Show your answers on the following figure.

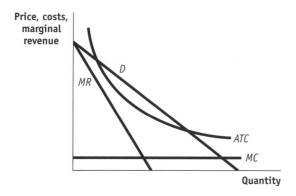

c. If the government offered the firm a patent on its good if it would produce at the break-even price (where price equals average total cost), would the firm agree? Why or why not? How much output would the firm produce? How much profit would the producer earn? What are the advantages and disadvantages to society of this price and output? Show your answers on the following figure.

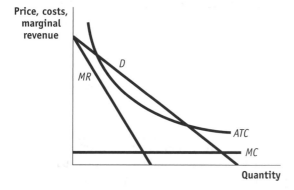

2. A pharmaceutical company is considering research that would lead to the development of a drug that would cure the common cold. It anticipates years of costly research but believes the process could still be profitable if they are protected from competition for long enough after the drug comes to market to earn back all its total costs plus a 25% return. It anticipates that its fixed costs will equal $16 million, that its marginal cost of production will be virtually zero, and that its demand and marginal revenue curves per year will be as shown in the following figure.

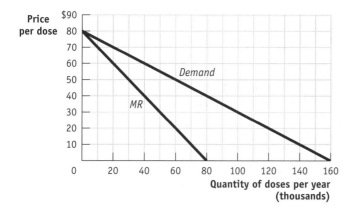

a. If the government grants a patent to the pharmaceutical company, how many years (ignoring the time value of money) will it take the firm to earn back its fixed costs plus 25%? Show the deadweight loss to society in the preceding figure.

b. If the government grants the usual patent for this drug, will the protection time be too long, too short, or just right?

c. What will happen in the market after the patent expires?

d. Is there an advantage to being the first producer of a drug to cure the common cold?

3. Suppose two competing companies are building their sales networks to reach critical mass. What will be the effects if the larger company decides to sustain bigger losses than the other smaller company?

*4. Consider an information good with the following inverse demand function:

$P = 40 - Q$, where P is the dollar price per unit of output (Q).

The monopolist's marginal revenue (MR) is

$MR = 40 - 2Q$.

The monopolist's marginal cost (MC) is zero.

The monopolist's total fixed cost is $200.

a. If the monopoly is given the property rights (and enforced by law), what will be the monopoly price, output, consumer surplus, and producer surplus?

b. What will be the efficient price and quantity? What will be the consumer surplus at the efficient quantity?

c. If the market allows uses of information goods at the efficient price, what will be the output produced by the monopolist? What will be the net losses of consumer surplus and producer surplus when Q is zero as compared to a situation where Q is the monopoly equilibrium Q?

Answers to How Well Do You Understand the Chapter

1. value, information, information, increasing, high, low

2. inefficiency, cost, zero, zero, gain, free, lose, temporary

3. property rights, copyrights, patents, creators, information, temporary, inefficiency, missed

4. patent, ideas, patent, traditional downtown, cost, reverse engineering

5. first mover, brand-name, size, temporary, erode

6. network externality, cost, network externalities, network externality, software

7. positive feedback, many, few, critical mass, conditional, regardless

8. threshold network size, conditional, critical mass, rapidly

9. increase, decrease, technology, greater

10. tipping, tip, Betamax

11. sales network, critical mass, below

12. competition policy

13. costs, set standards, standard, government, lower, QWERTY, top rows

14. Microsoft, operating systems, discouraging, overturned, technology

Answers to Multiple-Choice Questions

1. An information good is one whose value comes from the information it contains. Information goods are increasingly important in the U.S. economy. **Answer: C.**

2. Goods produced by a natural monopolist are similar to information goods in that they both have high fixed costs of production and low marginal costs of production. For all goods, the efficient price equals the marginal cost of producing that good. **Answer: D.**

3. It can be hard to distinguish information goods from conventional goods. A map of the world and an economics textbook provide information to their owners, and a piece of cake made from an award-winning recipe also contains the information from the recipe. However, the best example is the new video game. It fits our definition of a good with high fixed costs and low marginal costs of production. **Answer: B.**

4. Since information goods have high fixed costs of production and low, if any, marginal costs (low variable costs), the average total cost curve reflects average fixed costs, and average fixed costs decline over the relative range of output. **Answer: A.**

5. Given the figure, if a potential producer must sell output at a price equal to marginal cost, average total costs will exceed the price and the firm will earn a loss. The producer will not produce the good. **Answer: A.**

6. The software company will produce where marginal revenue equals marginal cost and set price off the demand curve. The firm will produce 5,000 software packages and charge a price of $50 per package. **Answer: C.**

7. The firm will earn $250,000 per year under its temporary monopoly; it will take 4 years for it to recoup its fixed costs. **Answer: B.**

8. Total surplus is maximized when price equals marginal cost, and that occurs when price equals zero and quantity equals 10,000 packages of software. **Answer: D.**

9. Economists generally agree that without a temporary property right to assure potential producers of being able to recoup their fixed costs, some information goods will not be produced. However, to minimize the deadweight loss to society of the monopoly, the property right should be temporary. **Answer: C.**

10. A copyright gives a temporary monopoly to creators of literary or artistic works that lasts for their lifetime plus at least 70 years. **Answer: C.**

11. A first mover is the firm that first introduces the good or innovation. First movers often can establish brand-name recognition that may give a firm some monopoly power. **Answer: B.**

12. Reverse engineering is when a competitor figures out how an information good works and how it is made. In this way they may make minor adjustments to the process to avoid patent violations and participate in the market, destroying their rival's monopoly. **Answer: D.**

13. When the value of a good to an individual is greater when a large number of other people also use that good, we say that the good is subject to network externalities. **Answer: B.**

14. Fax machines, cell phones, and airplane routes are all examples of goods with network externalities. Fax machines and cell phones only have value when they have other fax machines and cell phones to interact with. Airplane routes increase in value when they link up with other airplane routes. **Answer: D.**

15. If a good is subject to network externalities and there are 10,000 unconditional buyers, 200,000 conditional buyers, and the threshold network size is 20,000 users, the good is not ready to take off but may if technological innovations either increase the number of unconditional buyers or decrease the threshold network size. **Answer: B.**

16. Tipping occurs when a small initial advantage for one of two competing goods or technologies proves self-reinforcing and positive feedback eventually forces one competitor out of the market. **Answer: D.**

17. Goods subject to network externalities will often try to reach threshold network size by emphasizing sales, even at the expense of profits, when introduced. **Answer: C.**

18. Antitrust policies do not outlaw monopolies but activities that create a monopoly (monopolization). Any activity that reduces competition is prohibited by antitrust regulation. **Answer: D.**

19. Industry standards are rules for operating that induce competing goods to operate as a single network. They do not always require government intervention. **Answer: B.**

20. It was the government's belief that Microsoft was using its monopoly position in operating systems to give its products an advantage over competitors in other markets that drew antitrust scrutiny. **Answer: D.**

21. The marginal cost of information good is zero. **Answer: D.**

22. The total cost of information goods is large and it does not affect the profit-maximizing output. **Answer: A.**

23. Since the efficient price rule is $P = MC$ and since MC is zero, the efficient price (P) is zero. **Answer: D.**

24. The producer will produce nothing at the efficient price, because there will be negative profits. **Answer: D.**

25. More buyers mean more network externalities. **Answer: B.**

Answers to Problems and Exercises

1. a. The firm will maximize profit by producing at the quantity where marginal revenue equals marginal cost. It will produce at Q_A units of output and charge a price of P_A. Total profit will equal the rectangle with the diagonal lines. The disadvantage to society is the deadweight loss, which can be measured as the shaded triangle below. The advantage to society of the firm's monopoly is that the good is produced: the firm earns a profit and buyers earn some consumer surplus. If the firm is forced to produce where price equals marginal cost (where there is no deadweight loss), the potential producer would not produce at all.

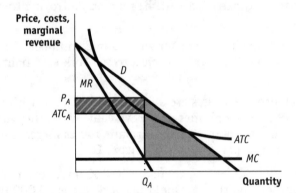

b. If the government offered a patent on the good if the firm would produce at the efficient price, the firm would not agree. In the following graph, we can see that at the efficient price, P_B, the firm would expect that profit would be negative, as shown by the shaded rectangle, and the firm would choose to not produce the good at all. There is only a disadvantage to society; the good would not be produced.

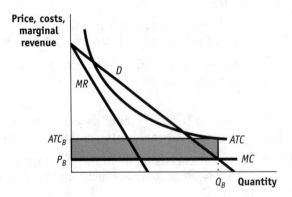

c. If the government offered a patent on the good for the firm to produce at the break-even price, the advantage to society is that the firm would agree to produce the good and the deadweight loss from the monopoly would be minimized. The firm would produce Q_C units of output and charge a price of P_C (which equals ATC_C). The firm would break even, the good would be produced, and the deadweight loss would be minimized (shown as the shaded triangle below).

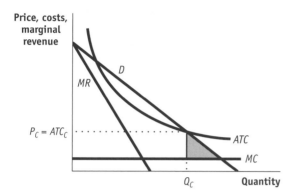

2. a. If the firm has a patent on the drug, it is assured of a monopoly position in the market. The firm will produce the level of output at which marginal revenue equals marginal cost, 80,000 doses, and will charge $40 per dose. It will earn annual revenue of $3.2 million. Given that the fixed costs of production are $16 million and the firm wants a 25% return on their fixed costs (an additional $4 million), it will take 6.25 years for the firm to earn the $20 million. The shaded triangle in the following figure shows the deadweight loss of the patent.

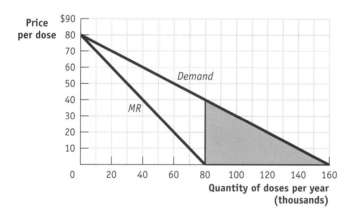

b. The usual patent lasts between 16 and 20 years. This will give the firm more protection than necessary. They only require 6.25 years to earn back their fixed costs plus 25%.

c. When the patent expires, the price of the good will fall to near zero and 160 thousand doses will be bought and sold.

d. There may be a first-mover advantage to being the firm that brings the drug to market that cures the common cold. With careful marketing, the firm may be able to establish a temporary monopoly position without a patent.

3. If the larger company can sustain initial losses, the buyers will tip in favour of the larger company and the larger company will be able to reach critical mass and enjoy a monopoly.

4. a. The monopolist follows the rule of $MC = MR$. Since MC is zero, we can solve
$Q = 20$ [from $MR = 40 - 2Q = 0$].
$P = \$20$.
Revenue = $400.
Profit = $400 − total fixed costs = $200.
Consumer surplus = $200.

b. The efficient price rule is $P = MC$.
With zero MC, we can write $0 = 40 - Q$ and solve Q as 40.
The consumer surplus is $= 1/2(\$40)(\$40) = \$800$.

c. The monopoly output (Q) will be zero. The loss of consumer surplus will be $200 and the loss of profit will be $200.